Doing Busin..
Kazakhstan

Doing Business in
Kazakhstan

Consultant Editors:
Nadine Kettaneh and Marat Terterov

In association with

KOGAN
PAGE

Publishers' note
Every possible effort has been made to ensure that the information contained in this handbook is accurate at the time of going to press and neither the publishers nor any of the authors can accept responsibility for any errors or omissions, however caused. No responsibility for loss or damage occasioned to any person acting, or refraining from action, as a result of the material in this publication can be accepted by the editor, the publisher or any of the authors.

First published in 2000

Kogan Page Limited
120 Pentonville Road
London N1 9JN

Web site: www.kogan-page.co.uk

© Kogan Page Limited, and contributors, 2000

British Library Cataloguing in Publication Data

ISBN 0 7494 3168 7

Typeset by Saxon Graphics Ltd, Derby
Printed and bound in Great Britain by Bell & Bain Ltd, Glasgow

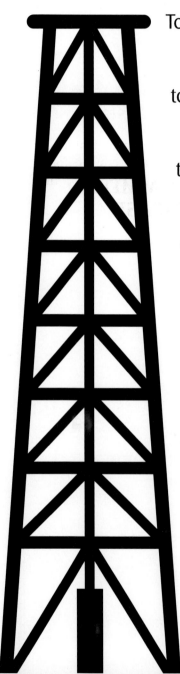

To get

to a solution

that lies

deep

inside

you need

special

tools

Acknowledgements

We would like to thank the Commercial Section of the British Embassy in Kazakhstan and the Commercial Section of the US Embassy in Kazakhstan for their assistance with this publication.

This publication is sponsored by the European Union's Tacis Programme, which provides grant finance for know-how to foster the development of market economies and democratic societies in the New Independent States and in Mongolia.

Contents

List of Contributors   xv
Foreword *Kanat Saudabayev*   xxi
Foreword *Charles Bland*   xxiii
Map 1: Kazakhstan and its neighbours   xxiv
Map 2: Infrastructure of Kazakhstan   xxv

Part 1: The Business Context

1.1   The Political Environment   3
Douglas Townsend, ITIC

1.2   Economic Overview, Priorities and Reform   11
HSBC Bank Kazakhstan

1.3   The Role of the National Bank   19
The National Bank of Kazakhstan

1.4   The Investment Climate   25
European Bank for Reconstruction and Development (EBRD)

1.5   Foreign Trade   35
Alica Henson

1.6   The Legal Framework   39
CMS Cameron McKenna

1.7   Privatisation   45
Alica Henson

1.8   Privatisation and the Legal Environment for Reform   49
Prof Yury G Basin and Dr Olga I Chentsova, AEQUITAS

1.9   The Banking System   55
HSBC Bank Kazakhstan

1.10 Capital Markets   59
Grigori A Marchenko, President, Deutsche Bank Securities (Kazakhstan)

1.11 The First Time Visitor   63
ABN AMRO

Part 2: Market Potential

Natural Resources

2.1   Natural Resources   69
      The Kazakhstan Investment Promotion Centre
2.2   Metallurgy   75
      The Kazakhstan Investment Promotion Centre
2.3   Overview of the Petroleum Industry   81
      Ernst & Young
2.4   Oil and Gas: Dynamics and Logistics   89
      Russell W. Lambert, Managing Partner
      PricewaterhouseCoopers
2.5   Oil and Gas: Industry Legislation   95
      James E Hogan, Aigoul Kenjebayeva and Donald K
      Blackwell, Salans Hertzfeld & Heilbronn
2.6   Oil and Gas: Taxation   105
      Arthur Andersen
2.7   Oil and Gas: Pipeline Transport   123
      The Kazakhstan Investment Promotion Centre

Industry Sectors

2.8   Agriculture   129
      The Kazakhstan Investment Promotion Centre
2.9   The Chemical and Petrochemical Industry   139
      The Kazakhstan Investment Promotion Centre
2.10 Construction   145
      The Kazakhstan Investment Promotion Centre
2.11 The Electric Power Industry   151
      The Kazakhstan Investment Promotion Centre
2.12 The Environment   157
      Heide Leighty and Sonia Heaven, BG International
      Chair of Environmental Technology, KazGACA
2.13 Imports and Exports   163
      Shelly Fitch and Globalink
2.14 Insurance   167
      Marsh
2.15 The Machine Engineering Industry   173
      The Kazakhstan Investment Promotion Centre
2.16 Telecommunications: The Market   177
      Roger MacNair, Business Intelligence, BT British
      Telecom/A&M

2.17 Telecommunications: Product Services   183
     Curt Hopkins, Nursat and Jeff Andrusevich, MCIWorldCom
2.18 Transport Networks   189
     The Kazakhstan Investment Promotion Centre

Part 3: Business Development

3.1 Progress in the Business Climate   207
     Douglas Townsend, Mia Nybrant and Kathryn Wells, ITIC
3.2 Investment Strategy   211
     Mark Campbell and Yelena Titova, KPMG Almaty
3.3 The Foreign Investment Regime   215
     *James E Hogan, Aigoul Kenjebayeva and Donald
     K Blackwell, Salans Hertzfeld & Heilbronn*
3.4 Structuring Transactions   221
     *Zaid S Sethi, Director of Tax and Local Services,
     PricewaterhouseCoopers*
3.5 Financing with the European Bank for Reconstruction and   227
     Development (EBRD)
     European Bank for Reconstruction and Development (EBRD)
3.6 Venture Capital   235
     Marat Terterov

Part 4: Building an Organisation

4.1 Incorporating a Company   245
     *Russell W Lambert, Managing Partner,
     PricewaterhouseCoopers*
4.2 Agency Distribution and Franchise Agreements   251
     *Zhaniya B Ussen, Assistance LLC in Almaty and
     Alastair Moody, Ledingham Chalmers in Edinburgh*
4.3 Accounting and Audit   259
     Ernst & Young
4.4 Taxation: An Overview   263
     Ernst & Young
4.5 Information on the Conventions for the Avoidance of Double
     Taxation as of 1 September 1999   275
     *Russell W Lambert, Managing Partner,
     PricewaterhouseCoopers*
4.6 Intellectual Property   277
     *Zhaniya B Ussen, Assistance LLC in Almaty and
     Alastair Moody, Ledingham Chalmers in Edinburgh*

4.7 Property Holdings 293
  CMS Cameron McKenna
4.8 Employment Law 299
  Russell W Lambert, Managing Partner,
  PricewaterhouseCoopers
4.9 Dispute Resolution 307
  CMS Cameron McKenna

Part 5: Case Studies

5.1 The Almaty Poultry Farm (Bertra) 315
  Marat Terterov
5.2 BG International: Our Experience in Kazakhstan 321
  BG International
5.3 De Vries Alexander Financial Services 323
  Ben Carter, De Vries Alexander
5.4 Fitzpatrick International Ltd 327
  Marat Terterov
5.5 FoodMaster 331
  Erlan Sagadieôv, General Director, FoodMaster
5.6 Gallaher Plc 335
  Marat Terterov
5.7 Globalink: Our Experience in Kazakhstan 339
  Siddique Khan, Globalink
5.8 Godbeer Construction Group Ltd 343
  Marat Terterov
5.9 Scot Holland Estates 347
  Roger Holland, Scot Holland Estates and Marat Terterov
5.10 The Tsessna Corporation 351
  Marat Terterov
5.11 The Usk Kamenogorsk Poultry Farm 355
  Marat Terterov

Appendices

Appendix 1: Investor Opportunities 361
Appendix 2: Visitors' Information 369
Appendix 3: Regions of Kazakhstan 381
Appendix 4: Business Organisations and Associations 391
Appendix 5: Sources of Further Information 413
Appendix 6: Contributor Contact Details 435

Index of Advertisers 441

Isn't it nice to be greeted by
a familiar face
WHEREVER YOU GO?

HSBC ◆
YOUR WORLD OF FINANCIAL SERVICES

In Almaty you will find us at HSBC Bank Kazakhstan
Address: Dostyk 43, Tel.: 8 (3272) 58 13 33; Fax: 8 (3272) 50 15 01

List of Contributors

ABN AMRO Bank Kazakhstan was the first international bank to start operations within the Republic of Kazakhstan in 1994. Currently the fourth largest bank, it is considered one of the soundest banking operations in Kazakhstan. In May 2000 the bank will open its branch in Atyrau City on the Caspian Sea coast, which is well known for its oil and gas deposits.

The **Aequitas** Law Firm was founded in Almaty in January 1993 by a group of legal scholars and practitioners with broad experience in state foreign trade firms, academic institutions, arbitral bodies and the customs agency of Kazakhstan. The firm is an independent private entity, engaged exclusively in providing a wide range of legal services to foreign and Kazakhstani clients. For a number of years Aequitas has been involved in several of the most important ventures and other projects in Kazakhstan, particularly those in oil and gas, mining, securities offerings and privatisation, as well as arbitration and litigation matters.

Since 1993, **Arthur Andersen** has provided a wide range of professional services to both foreign investors and local private and state enterprises in Kazakhstan. Market offerings include assurance, business consulting, corporate finance, outsourcing and tax services. The Almaty office currently employs over 80 professionals, including ten expatriate partners and managers who have acquired extensive experience working with clients in a wide range of industries key to Kazakhstan.

BG International first came to Kazakhstan at the very beginning of the 1990s to evaluate business options in the country. In Kazakhstan BG now has a 40-year Production Sharing Agreement (PSA) relating to Karachaganak, the major oil field in western Kazakhstan producing gas and condensate. It has equity in, and capacity rights to export, liquids from Kazakhstan through the Caspian Pipeline Consortium (CPC), which is currently under construction. BG also has an interest in a PSA covering exploration areas in the northern Caspian Sea.

At the time of writing, **Mark Campbell** was a Senior Tax Manager with KPMG Almaty. Mark spent in excess of four years in the former Soviet Republics of Azerbaijan and Kazakhstan and, as a result, gained wide experience of issues faced by new and existing investors into CIS states.

Mark has since (April 2000) relocated to KPMG Croatia in Zagreb where his skills are now being put to use principally in Croatia but also in some of the other former Yugoslav states.

De Vries Alexander specialises in the provision of offshore financial advice to expatriates residing in Russia, Central Asia and Eastern Europe. With its expatriate team living on station alongside its clients, the company provides independent and impartial financial advice, structured through the solutions and techniques of a large number of household name institutions, which are located in regulated world-class tax-efficient jurisdictions.

Ben Carter is the Chairman of De Vries Alexander, and is based at the company's main CIS office in Moscow. He founded the company after some years spent in the offshore financial services in Dubai and Azerbaijan. After being educated at Queens' College, Cambridge, he was Office Manager with a trading division at Thyssen Garfield Ltd and in 1996 joined the offshore financial services industry as a Consultant with PIC, in Dubai. He is proud to have been the first-ever resident IFA in Kazakhstan.

Eagle Kazakhstan Fund (formerly GIMV Kazakhstan Post Privatisation Fund) is a venture capital fund that focuses on small and medium sized enterprises and was created with €30m of funding from the European Bank for Reconstruction and Development. The Fund is managed by Eagle Venture Partners, which is a consortium of investment companies that include GIMV, Corpeq, Rabobank, Ewic-West and Sigefi. GIMV has also committed to invest up to €3m alongside the Fund, thus bringing the Fund's total capital to €33m. The Fund is furthermore supported by a technical assistance grant of €20m from the European Union's Tacis Programme.

Ernst & Young was the first professional services organisation to establish a presence in Central Asia when it opened an office in Almaty in 1992. In addition to Almaty, EY has also opened offices in the new Kazakhstani capital, Astana. These two offices serve our clients in Central Asia's emerging markets: Kazakhstan, Kyrgyzstan, and Uzbekistan. In Kazakhstan, as in Russia and the Caspian Region, we are the pre-eminent provider of audit, tax, corporate finance and business advisory services to the energy sector.

The **European Bank for Reconstruction and Development (EBRD)** was established in 1991 in response to major changes in the political and economic climate in central and eastern Europe. Inaugurated less than two years after the fall of the Berlin Wall, the Bank was created to support the development of market economies in the region following the widespread collapse of communist regimes. Based in London, the EBRD is an international institution with 60 members (58 countries, the European Community and the European Investment Bank). It has offices in all 26 EBRD countries of operations in the region. The Country Director for Kazakhstan, Michael Davey, is based at the Bank's Almaty Office.

Shelly Fitch has been working in the international transportation business for 13 years, and in Kazakhstan for more than three years. She is co-chair of the Customs Working Group of the American Chamber of Commerce in Kazakhstan.

David Griston has advised lenders, borrowers, sponsors and state agencies on projects, project financings and privatisations throughout Central Asia and the Russian Federation since 1994. In the Republic of Kazakhstan, he recently completed a multi-million dollar power sector financing and several structured financings in the telecommunications market. At the time of writing, David was an Associate with CMS Cameron McKenna, but has since joined Allen & Overy in London.

Alica Henson brings several years' experience with countries of the former Soviet Union, having worked mostly in Ukraine, but also in Tajikistan, Russia and Belarus. She further developed her knowledge of economic and political issues in the region, in particular Kazakhstan and Uzbekistan, as an East Europe and CIS analyst-editor with a UK consulting firm, which produces analyses of emerging market regions. Alica is currently working on a local government reform project in Ukraine.

Roger Holland is a 42-year old entrepreneur with a background in finance and marketing. He successfully developed several ventures in Eastern Europe before entering the prospective growing CIS market in late-1994. Since then, Scot Holland Estates has become a leading real estate service provider to many large foreign investors in Kazakhstan. Services include development consultancy, finance sourcing, valuation, project and property management, in addition to the regular rental and purchase/sales activities. The company also organises an 'Ideal Home Exhibition' every April, and is this year launching *Property* – a new magazine in Russian for the local market.

HSBC Bank Kazakhstan is a 100 per cent subsidiary of the HSBC Group and opened for business in Almaty in January 1999. The bank offers a wide range of banking services to personal and corporate clients, both resident and non-resident. These include current, savings and deposit accounts, electronic banking, trade finance, personal and business loans, foreign exchange, securities trading and custody.

The **Kazakhstan Investment Promotion Centre** is a central executive body that is distinct from government and exercises the functions of state management and control in the area of State support for direct investments in the Republic of Kazakhstan.

Its basic tasks are developing and implementing strategy with respect to investment policy, improving the investment climate in Kazakhstan, stimulating direct investment into Kazakhstan, promoting and providing information about investment opportunities, representing the legal rights and interests of foreign investors, and encouraging co-operation between national and international investors. It has been granted wide-ranging powers and functions to help it in the achievement of these objectives.

Siddique Khan is the founder and Managing Director of Globalink. Established in Almaty in 1993 and employing ten people, Globalink has since expanded and now has 11 offices in Central Asia and the Caucasian Republics, employing over 200 people. With services ranging from removal and relocation to freight forwarding, Globalink's speciality lies in project logistics for oil and gas mining. Globalink has two subsidiary companies: Global Intermodal and Globalsped. Global Intermodal specialises in multimodal transportation in both Western Europe and to and from Eastern Europe, including the former Soviet Republics, while Globalsped specialises in transportation to and from Eastern Europe and Central Asia.

Ledingham Chalmers established an office in Baku, Azerbaijan in 1995 and has been advising clients on a variety of projects in Azerbaijan and the wider Caspian Region.

Alastair Moody is a corporate solicitor based in the Edinburgh office of Ledingham Chalmers and has been involved in projects in Kazakhstan and elsewhere within the region.

Roger MacNair graduated from Oxford University with a Masters Degree in Modern History and Economics. Previously responsible for Business and Market Intelligence relating to satellite communications in BT's Aeronautical and Maritime Division — a key element of which has been developing a good understanding of the potential business opportunities in the Caspian Basin region — Roger has since moved on to perform a similar function for the Internet and Web Hosting Division of the company.

At present **the National Bank of Kazakhstan** implements all functions of a central bank: financing Second Tier Banks in order to maintain liquidity, monetary and foreign exchange regulation, banking and insurance supervision, payment systems etc. Since the implementation of Kazakhstan's own national currency, the tenge, the role of the National Bank in monetary regulation has increased.

Nursat is an emerging telecommunications operator in Kazakhstan, started by Lucent Technologies as a part of a US government demilitarisation programme in the former Soviet Union. It is facilities-based, leading the market as a corporate network solutions provider, competitive local exchange carrier and internet service provider.

The **PricewaterhouseCoopers** office in Almaty is headed by Russell W Lambert, Managing Director, and has a total staff of 120 people who are resident in Almaty and experienced in the complexities and challenges that make Kazakhstan a unique business environment for most foreign companies. The staff includes expatriate and national experts in machinery and equipment valuations, audit and business advisory services, corporate finance and tax and legal services. The office also benefits from the global resources that the world-wide firm has available, which means that it is possible to source experts within the firm that can solve virtually any problematic business situation that a client may have.

Erlan Sagadiev has been the General Director for FoodMaster since 1994 and is one of the original founders. He has a Master's Degree in Agricultural Economics from the University of Minnesota and an undergraduate degree in Political Economics from the Kazakh State University.

Salans Hertzfeld & Heilbronn (SHH) is a multi-national law firm of over 300 lawyers with offices in Paris, New York, London, Moscow, St Petersburg, Warsaw, Kyiv, Almaty and Baku. It represents clients from all over the world in a broad range of cross-border transactions and disputes. At the same time, each office provides a full spectrum of in-depth legal services for local law matters. The combination of international capability and domestic expertise enables SHH to provide comprehensive services matching the needs of global and local clients alike, while the diverse backgrounds, professional experience, qualifications and linguistic capabilities of its lawyers enhance its ability to handle international and local matters.

Marat Terterov has developed substantial experience working with the ex-Soviet Central Asian states as both a consultant in business development issues and as a scholar empirical-researcher, having published several articles on the region. Since coming to England from Australia on a scholarship from the British Foreign Office in 1995, Marat has worked on a consultancy basis for a number of organisations, including the Department of Trade and Industry Central Asia Section. He currently lives in Oxford and is working on his doctoral thesis at St Antony's College, Oxford University.

Yelena Titova now works for Halliburton in Kazakhstan, where her skills are now employed on the client's as opposed to the consultant's side of business and tax management in Kazakhstan.

Douglas Townsend is Senior Advisor at ITIC London, as well as Director of the UK business consultancy, TEMAS Ltd, which specialises in trade and investment with the emerging markets of the former eastern bloc. He is also an associate of the Centre for Euro-Asian Studies at the University of Reading (UK) and a former Australian Ambassador of Kazakhstan (1995–1997), Hungary (1988–1992), Switzerland, Côte d'Ivoire and Senegal (1985–1988) and Australian Investment Commissioner Europe (1992–1995).

Zhaniya B Ussen is a Kazakhstani, Russian and New York attorney. Specialising in international law at the Moscow State University School of Law, she graduated with a Diploma in 1992, followed by a Master of Laws with Honours as a Freedom Support Act Scholar from the Northwestern University School of Law, Chicago in 1995. Prior to going to the USA for legal studies, she worked as a lawyer and consular assistant with the US Embassy in Almaty and worked as in-house counsel for a consulting company in Moscow. Following her graduation from the Northwestern University School of Law, she was admitted to the New Bar and became the first Kazakhstani lawyer to achieve this distinction. She is now a Partner and Director of Foreign Investments Practice with Assistance LLC which is the oldest private law firm in Kazakhstan

Foreword

Having become an independent state in 1991, the Republic of Kazakhstan chose the path of developing democracy, creating a civil society and a free market economy.

The Strategy of 'Kazakhstan 2030' document by President Nazarbayev states that one of the most important priorities for the country is the provision of sustainable economic development while actively attracting foreign investment.

Due to the creation of a favourable investment climate backed by the huge potential of the oil, gas and mining industries, as well as the potential in infrastructure development and other areas, Kazakhstan has, in recent years, achieved considerable success in implementing these objectives.

This is supported by the fact that by the first half of 1999, Kazakhstan had received about US$8.5 billion in direct foreign investment since 1993, a large tranche of this coming from Great Britain.

Having overcome the negative consequences of the Asian and Russian financial crises, Kazakhstan achieved some GDP growth in 1999 and intends to strengthen these positive trends in economic development.

We are pleased that the United Kingdom is one of Kazakhstan's most important foreign partners, being its third largest investor and second largest European trading partner. We are confident that our mutually beneficial co-operative relationship will strengthen and develop in the new millennium.

I hope that this publication will be a valuable guide for people who wish to link their business fortunes with Kazakhstan, a country confidently building its own future.

Kanat Saudabayev
Head of Prime Minister's Chancellery of Kazakhstan
Co-Chair, Kazakh–British Trade and Industry Council
Kazakhstan's Ambassador to the United Kingdom (1996–1999)

Foreword

As Co-Chairman of the Kazakhstan—British Trade and Industry Council I am delighted to share with my colleague, Mr Saudabayev, the task of introducing this book. The Kazakhstan—British Trade and Industry Council is dedicated to working with the government of Kazakhstan to improve conditions for British companies in the market.

Since Kazakhstan achieved independence in 1991 the business environment has developed quickly; there is a bright future there for business, and for partnership, between the two countries in the development of trade. However, companies have found Kazakhstan a difficult market to approach: I hope that this book, which aims to provide practical advice on the business environment in Kazakhstan for both investors and traders, will address some of the issues that have most frequently affected them.

There are good grounds for optimism about trade and investment in Kazakhstan. The oil and gas industries continue to develop, the pipeline from Kazakhstan to Novorossisk is well on the way to completion and there are signs of recovery in Russia's economy. This is a good time for this book to appear. It is a rich source of information of the business environment in Kazakhstan and I am sure it will contribute to the promotion of trade there.

Charles Bland
British Co-Chairman, Kazakhstan—British Trade and Industry
Council

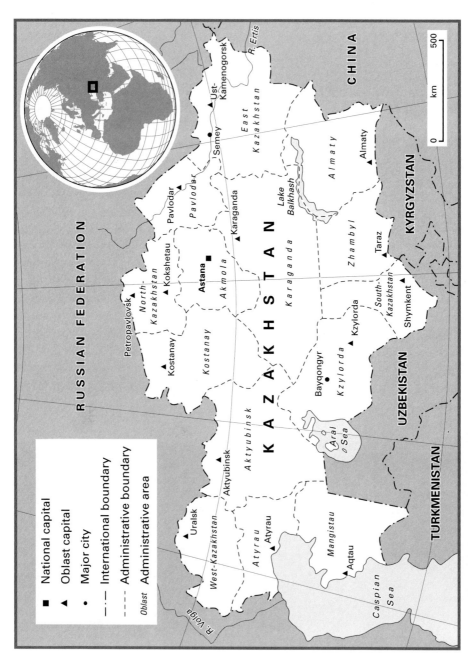

Map 1: Kazakhstan and its neighbours

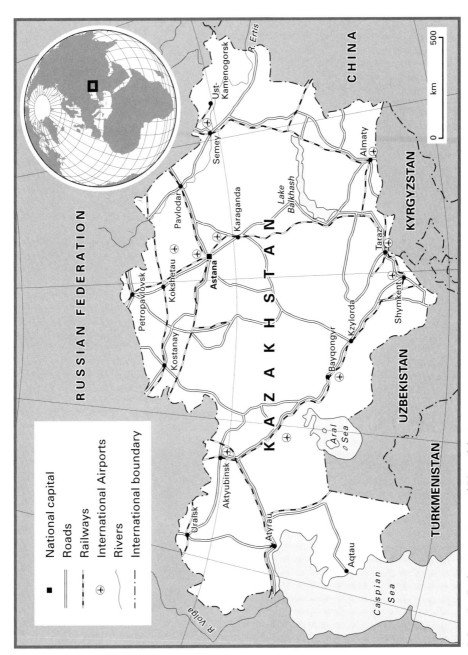

Map 2: Infrastructure of Kazakhstan

Part 1

The Business Context

1.1

The Political Environment

Douglas Townsend, ITIC

Introduction

Kazakhstan, a landlocked and rugged country roughly the size of western Europe, has a dispersed population of 15.8 million, increasingly urbanised in a handful of cities. The official capital Astana, in the rather bleak north, and the business capital Almaty, in the more agreeable south-east, are critical economic development centres. Other conurbations are generally related to projects for the exploitation of natural resources.

Governing such a vast country with remote resource-rich provinces is not a straightforward matter. At its simplest, the interests of central, regional and local governments and the interaction of their respective responsibilities for economic development need to be harmonised. Kazakhstan has a range of climatic regimes although the climate overall could be characterised as extreme continental with occasional Mediterranean influences, essentially in the south. Supply of energy and water, not necessarily on commercial terms, is critical public policy priority for social stability and economic development.

Kazakhstan's neighbours are Russia, China, Kyrgyzstan, Uzbekistan and Turkmenistan as well as Caspian Sea littoral states Azerbaijan and Iran. Countries of interest to Kazakhstan from a business point of view include the USA, Ukraine, Turkey, India, Pakistan, Japan, Korea and those in the European Union (EU). Countries of concern – for different reasons – include Tajikistan, Afghanistan and the Caucasian states. In such volatile surroundings Kazakhstan seeks to avoid making regional enemies and to balance relations with its powerful immediate neighbours; however it also seeks to diversify relations and integrate fully into the international community, thereby involving more powerful if more distant states directly in its destiny.

Foreign languages are still not widely spoken in Kazakhstan. Russian remains the 'lingua franca' and an official language. Promotion of Kazakh, the state language, proceeds steadily, however, and its popular usage nationwide increases, notwithstanding some reluctance on the part of the myriad other minority ethnic groups in Kazakhstan. Maintenance of ethnic harmony is a domestic and foreign policy imperative for Kazakhstan, a country of one hundred nationalities that neighbours the powerful home-lands of important minority groups such as the Russians and that has its own substantial diaspora in China. Despite the sustained efforts of the Kazakhstani leadership to elevate multiculturalism as a pillar of its nation-building and as a centrepiece of interstate relations, substantial skilled emigration by Slavs and Germans has nonetheless steadily accompanied independence. Many members of minority ethnic groups have reacted in this practical way both to unfavourable economic circumstances and to suspicions of hegemonism among the majority ethnic group.

Religion is not a dominant influence in public life, partly reflecting Kazakhstan's modern history of atheistic communism. Kazakhstan, constitutionally a secular state, is multi-confessional, the major faiths of Sunni Islam and Orthodox Christianity coexisting with many other familiar world religions and some less familiar spiritual movements. Fundamentalist Islamic and Christian movements share minority posi-tions in the society. Foreign support for religion is widespread.

Kazakhstan's major attractions for business include its natural resources base, market infrastructure development opportunities, education levels and the elite's overall commitment to economic reform. Major impediments to business include bureaucracy, political and cultural elements of the business environment, the legal system, the tax/fiscal regime and the market infrastructure. Removal of these impediments and access to the attractions are broadly but not completely achievable through government action in a country where the state continues to play a major role both as entrepreneur and as regulator. That major role can also provide opportunity for official rent-seeking. Blandishments to that effect need to be resisted, if only in narrow self-interest: it is in Kazakhstan an offence to give as well as to receive.

The Kazakhstani elite is widely travelled and generally keen to do business, the younger members particularly on terms familiar to west-erners. Sometimes, however, the manner in which business is conducted can fall short of genuine partnership. This failure can reflect a number of factors – for example, inadequate management, the local negotiating tradition of playing both sides off against the middle, an unfamiliarity with essential western business concepts such as investment project appraisal and the time value of money, as well as a determination to avoid being 'ripped off' by foreign 'carpetbaggers' through (often locally aided) 'scams' often involving abuse of transfer pricing provisions.

The elite's consensus in favour of foreign investment and global trade relations prevails but globalisation is not generally popular and economic nationalism can surface at the operating level, reflected in sentiments that foreigners get preference and that privatisation means 'selling-off the family silver'. Nor is the 'playing-field' level for domestic business since an industry policy of 'picking winners' offers opportunity for favouritism and in practice often discriminates against small and medium-sized enterprises (SMEs), which still lack an effective voice in policy development. These and other domestic political factors underlie the continuing review of earlier privatisation contracts whose policy thrust is an upward re-evaluation of the former state assets then transferred and a higher return to the exchequer.

Polity

The Presidency

According to its Constitution, Kazakhstan is a presidential, unitary and secular republic. The President, popularly elected for seven years and eligible for re-election for an unlimited number of terms (but only two consecutively), has enormous executive powers. These include direction on issues of national security, making key appointments (such as Prime Minister; Procurator General; chairpersons of the National Bank and National Securities Commission, National Security Committee and State Investigation Committee, Civil Service Commission and Anti-Corruption Agency; and governors of the 14 provinces plus the cities of Astana and Almaty), appointing members of the Constitutional Council and the Judiciary, ruling by decree in widely defined circumstances and generally overseeing the work of government.

To assist in the discharge of these functions the President maintains his own significant administration and 'kitchen cabinet', key members of which can have an *éminence grise* role in government superior to that of the Prime Minister and the Cabinet.

Government

Government does not necessarily benefit from the duality mentioned above. Previous cabinets have, however, not been noted for their dynamism and expectations are not high for the latest government, not withstanding the major reform agenda it faces. Continued reductions in the number of bureaucrats in recent years have not been matched by reductions in the number of government ministries, committees or agencies, hence the high overall number of parties formally involved in business development and regulation. There are understandable domestic political reasons for maintaining a deep patronage pool. This provides scope for the regular 'churning' of the members of the administration, a practice that has come to characterise government in Kazakhstan. However, adverse practical consequences include a lack of continuity in official contacts and a mismatch of priority function with commensurate staffing. For example, the central office of the State Tax Committee has proportionately fewer staff than virtually any other national tax jurisdiction, though it suffers from the inevitable failings in the tax system that form by far the main burden of business complaints. The central administration itself finds coordination elusive with, for example, business being subjected to regulation generally in a consecutive rather than concurrent manner. And centre/region coordination is often ragged. Moreover, a professional civil service based on common training and standards exists only on the drawing-board – connection still rules selection.

Parliament

Parliament comprises two bodies. The upper chamber, the Senate, is composed of 7 members that are appointed by the President and the remainder are indirectly elected – 2 from each of the 14 regions and 2 each from Astana and Almaty – by the local assemblies of those areas for a term of 6 years. The lower chamber, the Majilis, is made up of 67 deputies directly elected from single-member constituencies of roughly equal voting size plus 10 deputies elected nationally by proportional representation from party lists, for a term of 5 years.

Dynamics

President Nazarbayev has ruled energetically since independence and manoeuvred the Kazakhstan polity adroitly in the direction of a stronger executive and more centralised control, at the expense of proponents of parliamentarism and decentralisation as well as political rivals seeking to establish viable bases of opposition. Although Kazakhstan has established its sovereign state position in the world community and by and large hoed to the path of the market economy, it is not altogether clear that all the population identifies with the type of state that Kazakhstan is becoming. There are real issues of eventual political succession and the regime's legitimacy, law-and-order, economic policy, socio-economic inequalities and regional instability, elements that figured strongly in the 1999 presidential and legislative elections campaigns.

On 10 January 1999 President Nazarbayev was overwhelmingly elected – against only minor, eligible opposition from the Communist Party and Independents – for a further term until 2006. According to the Constitution, he is eligible for re-election in 2006 although not immediately again in 2013. If the President should fail to see out a term, the Constitution provides that for the remainder of that term the powers of the President would be exercised by the Chairperson of the Senate; failing him, by the Chairperson of the Majilis; failing him, by the Prime Minister, each of whom would correspondingly give up his other powers.

It is too early to define the historical significance of the Nazarbayev presidency although it is hardly disputable that it has maintained stability and ethnic coexistence if not affection. If not yet a genuine democracy and viable civil society, there is in Kazakhstan a movement away from oligarchy. This stability has been critical for the development of business and the attraction of investment.

It could perhaps be helpful for understanding to see the President as the executive chairman of a 'coalition' of members of important family, regional and economic interests who rarely exit the system. For this and successor executive chairmen – a chairwoman is hard to visualise – there can be at one time only one sun in the sky. For those who exit the system voluntarily, treatment as a foreign body is likely. Although formally a unitary state with the provincial governors responsible to the President, and the provinces having only the most limited fiscal powers, Kazakhstan – with its vastness, great natural resources, clan divisions, ethnic mix and porous borders – is hardly immune from centrifugal forces. Containing these forces, through their inclusion in a broad coalition or by careful vigilance, is necessary for ensuring the writ of government runs nationally.

Business itself needs to be alert to local ambitions and prepared to spend time developing an understanding of the politics, if only because of the significant economic role sustained by government. Business needs to be aware more or less, and at any one time, of the following potentially involved official actors:

- The presidency, relevant specialists of the President's administration and members of his 'kitchen cabinet'.

- The Prime Minister and the key agencies under him, eg Investment, Competition, Economic Planning, Small Business, State Procurement.

- The relevant Deputy Prime Minister, the Finance Minister and Minister for State Revenue (and his agencies the Tax and Customs Committees, Tax Police).

- Other relevant central government ministers and their regulatory agencies, eg Labour, Industry-Energy-Trade, Natural Resources and Environmental Protection.

- Provincial and local governments.

- Parliament and its specialist committees (economy, ecology, law, social development) as well as the regional and local political assemblies.

Their interest could vest with that of business, for example with parliamentary deputies seeking business for their constituencies or otherwise exercising their important constitutional role in economic development.

The political economy

It may be unfair if understandable to compare the country's post-independence growth performance with its former status in integrated Soviet times. The structure of the economy, for example, in terms of available investment and marketable output immediately and irrevocably changed with independence, taking with it large slabs of economic activity and related employment while beggaring many regional centres. With the demise of the centrally planned economy went the welfare state. Reconstructing this inheritance is a Herculean task and it would not be quickly achieved; but it is critical that the prize inheritance of high education levels not be lost if Kazakhstan is to win the contemporary struggle to hold its place in the world development league.

The Astana leadership has been conscious of the economy's overdependence on the commodities' cycle and extractive industries and sensitive to criticism that it has neglected the country's own skills base. While investment in natural resources continues to be welcomed, the government has sought with incentives to stimulate interest in resources processing and related industries – food, TCF, machinery, agricultural support, pharmaceuticals, plastics and paints – with a view to serving local and regional markets.

Economic policy had been favourable to free trade partly as a means of avoiding supply problems arising out of the collapse of industry. Kazakhstan sought for a long time throughout 1997–98 to withstand pressure on the economy arising from the impact on its trading position and growth prospects of the Asian and Russian crises. The leadership finally responded to these crises in a somewhat dirigiste manner that among other things favoured import-substitution and protectionism. This 'hands-on' economic policy approach was accompanied by significant constitutional change in October 1998 that had the effect both of strengthening the presidency as an institution and advancing the position of the incumbent ahead of early elections in January 1999. By April 1999 markets had, however, asserted themselves and the currency went into free float, devaluing at once by one-third and by some 40 per cent to date. By the anniversary of the float in April 2000, the currency is expected to have more than halved.

Devaluation and the recovery in commodities' prices have contributed to optimism about a return to growth in 2000. The economy continues to be dependent on the commodities' cycle and the bulk of investment continues in the extractive industries, with implications both for regional development in the great majority of areas devoid of resources-related projects and for political relations with the resource-rich provinces. The performance of the main economic indicators reflects the commodities' cycle.

In 2000 the government envisages GDP (gross domestic product) growth of 1 per cent, a budget deficit of 3 per cent of GDP, inflation of 15 per cent and an average exchange rate of KZT157/$US1. Tax revenues are estimated to rise from 10 to 18 per cent of GDP, the achievement of which constitutes a major challenge for government and business. The stalled privatisation programme is planned to resume, with sale envisaged of state shares in major undertakings Kazakhoil, Kazakhtelecom, People's Bank, Kazakh Copper, Mangistau Oil & Gas, Aktobe Oil & Gas, Kazakh Zinc and Kazakhstan Aluminium. Implementation of privatisation plans overall could depend not only on the condition of state finances but also the local politics of state property management and the terms upon which the state shares would be offered to investors.

Critical to continued investment flows is support from the International Monetary Fund (IMF), which has urged the Astana leadership to consolidate the state's fiscal position, maintain a prudent monetary policy and sustain economic reform as the means of returning to growth. The IMF is cautious about the potential for inflation, concerned about comparatively large budget deficits and has urged tax reform to broaden the vase and improve the administration. It has welcomed the improved rules-based investment incentives programme, the World Bank-funded legal system reform project, the resumption of the privatisation programme and improved regulation of the financial sector. It has been less complimentary about protectionist trends in Kazakhstan's trade policies and practices which inhibit progress towards World Trade Organisation (WTO) accession.

The European Bank of Reconstruction and Development (EBRD), a major commercial project lender to Kazakhstan and principal partner in President Nazarbayev's Foreign Investors' Council (of major investors) established in 1998, has consistently urged the Astana leadership to level the 'playing-field' by providing a fairer industry policy for domestic business and an improved and more stable tax system for all business. The EBRD has also recommended greater access to the decision-making process for SMEs. While not the only forum for promoting business and naturally concentrating on big investor concerns, the Foreign Investors' Council is significant because of the 'hands-on' involvement of the President and the government and the opportunities therefore for directly pressing business concerns with the regulatory authorities.

Prospects

Times are currently tough in Kazakhstan and the region, with pressures rising on governments and putting a premium on sound leadership. For the medium term, economic prospects are encouraging, provided the reform thrust is sustained, the 'playing-field' is levelled to ensure competition and the tax system improved to stimulate investment. If this approach were sustained, in the longer term a more diversified and stronger economy would have emerged to underpin the critical regional role allotted Kazakhstan by its geopolitical location.

There is no shortage of major issues or major players with interests in Kazakhstan and the region. The fall-out from the Russian economic crisis strained intra-regional relations with 'beggar-thy-neighbour' and self-sufficiency policies and practices being exacerbated. Military insurgencies in neighbouring and regional countries, with their symbiosis of politics, arms and drugs, are likely to deflect scarce resources into defence and internal security. Heightened tensions are hindering progress in regional cooperation on water and energy. New associations of states also are developing in Transcaucasia and Central Asia, reflecting re-evaluations of the balance of political and economic advantage in inherited alliances. The policy 'gridlock' in Russia, created by its current domestic political struggles and Caucasus problems, has blocked progress on freer trade relations. Kazakhstan has managed to maintain harmonious relations with all regional and extra-regional powers, great and small, involved or interested in Central Asia. It is, however, no easy task to reconcile potentially conflicting differences over resources and territory as well as to navigate through the competition for influence in the region.

The search for security in all its forms – military, economic and social – thus informs the policies of the Astana leadership. Practical manifestations of this search include membership of the United Nations and the Bretton Woods system, NATO association, Commonwealth of Independent States (CIS) involvement, Central Asian borders' settlement treaties, OSCE participation, Islamic Conference and Islamic Development Bank connections, diversified economic relationships and agreements with the Organisation for Economic Co-operation and Development (OECD) countries and Asian Tigers, and the single-minded pursuit of Eurasian cooperation across the public policy spectrum. Business can play a fundamental part in assuaging security concerns. By encouraging competition, protecting economic gains and integrating Kazakhstan into the global economy, it can help to ease some of the anxiety which brakes progress from oligarchy to market democracy.

1.2

Economic Overview, Priorities and Reform

HSBC Bank Kazakhstan

Economic overview

For Kazakhstan,1998 was a difficult year. The collapse of the Russian economy not only damaged Kazakhstan internally but also diminished its influx of foreign investment. Comparatively high production costs and low world commodity prices depressed export revenues. Industrial production fell by 3.5 per cent in 1998, and was down by 3.3 per cent for the first three months of 1999. Fuel and metallurgy industries, which account for about 50 per cent of industrial output and are heavily export-oriented, were no longer able to compensate for falling world commodity prices by expanding volume. Most other industries have been suffering sharp declines in production for some years as a result of insufficient investments and structural reforms. All of these conditions led to a fall of domestic and foreign demand in 1998. By year-end, the real output in the economy had fallen by 2.5 per cent compared to a moderate increase of 1.7 per cent in 1997. In the first quarter of 1999, the Kazakhstan economy experienced a further decline in real GDP (gross domestic product) growth by 3.6 per cent compared to the same period in the previous year.

During the first years of independence the country faced a substantial decline in real annual GDP growth, from –0.8 per cent in 1991, year-to-year, to –25.4 per cent in 1994. By 1995, the real domestic product contracted to below half of its 1990 level. Signs of recovery were seen in late 1995 when the metal, gas, petroleum and chemical industries recorded increases in production output. In 1996, the real GDP growth rate rose to 0.5 per cent from –8.2 per cent in 1995, while inflation dropped to below 40 per cent from about 1,900 per cent in 1994.

Economic growth continued in 1997 with real GDP growing by 1.7 per cent during the year. However, the economy started to slow-down from the last quarter of 1997 due to a marked decline in the price of the country's leading exports, namely oil, metals and grain, which in turn, caused a significant decline in the country's export income and thus government revenue. From the last quarter of 1997, Asia's economic turmoil followed by Russia's financial crisis has affected the flow of foreign investment into Kazakhstan. Crisis expectations, based mainly on Russia's financial turmoil, prevailed among foreign investors. In August 1998 the government and the National Bank announced an economic programme the main objective of which was to minimise the negative influence of Asia's and Russia's financial crisis on the economy and further stabilisation of economic development. This helped to mitigate the adverse impact of external factors on the economy.

An extremely restrictive monetary policy trimmed annual inflation to 1.9 per cent in December 1998. For the first seven months of 1999, inflation was estimated at 12.9 per cent. This increase in consumer prices was mainly due to the introduction of a floating exchange rate regime in April 1999 and higher world commodity prices.

After several years of successful movement towards economic stabilisation, in the second half of 1998 Kazakhstan's economy faced significant difficulties. The model of export-oriented macroeconomic development followed by Kazakhstan in previous years caused the vulnerability of its economy to external price shocks. Prices of Kazakhstan's leading exports – oil, metals and grains – had all dropped markedly since the summer of 1997, resulting in a significant decline in government revenues. In 1998 the drop in the world price of crude oil and metals resulted in a fall in price for Kazakhstan's major exports by about 20 per cent. A fall in price was partially compensated by an increase of export volumes. But still the foreign trade turnover declined by 10 per cent in 1998 compared to the previous year. This was mainly due to lower levels of the country's exports, which shrank by 16.1 per cent. In the first quarter of 1999 the foreign trade turnover fell by 23.3 per cent compared to the corresponding period of the previous year and again mainly as a result of the substantial contraction of exports by 33.6 per cent while imports remained almost unchanged (decreasing by 0.7 per cent). The main reasons for this were the contraction of industrial production and low prices for the country's basic exports on the world market. Fuel and oil products, which made up almost 39 per cent of total exports in 1998, saw further decline in early 1999 in both the export value (40 per cent) and the export share (8 per cent). Exports of other primary resources fell too. Thus, ferrous metal exports decreased by 15 per cent compared to the end of 1998 and copper supplies, by approximately 40 per cent.

The structural reorientation of Kazakhstan's foreign trade to non-CIS (Commonwealth of Independent States) countries continued in 1999; in the first three months their share of foreign trade turnover rose from 52.3 per cent to 56 per cent. Foreign trade with the CIS decreased by 24.8 per cent and trade with Russia fell by 19 per cent. However, Russia remains one of the main trading partners of Kazakhstan absorbing about a third of the country's exports.

The South East Asian financial crisis initiated a general reassessment of investment risk into emerging markets. The potential risk of a development strategy based on exports of primary resources and foreign capital inflow materialised into real losses. The financial crisis in August 1998 in neighbouring Russia created a second wave of pressure on Kazakhstan's economy. After dramatic rouble depreciation, cheap Russian goods flooded onto the Kazakhstan market. To protect its own producers, the government imposed tariff barriers for some goods imported from Russia, Kyrgyzstan and Uzbekistan. But this was not as effective as was expected. Unregulated imports from Russia comprise about 60 per cent of total imports, which make it difficult to implement any control over trade operations.

Until recently the managed floating exchange rate regime pursued by the National Bank of Kazakhstan because of the falling price of oil and metals led to a decline in Kazakstan's exports and official reserves becoming exhausted. Kazakhstan's raw materials and metals became non-competitive on the world market. In the long term, the devaluation should be beneficial by bringing down the overvalued tenge, thereby facilitating the rise of export volumes and eliminating the need for trade barriers for cheaper CIS imports imposed early in1999. Moreover, the major effect of changes in the exchange rate regime will be the easing of pressure on the official reserves that shrank by an estimated US$500 million to US$1.6 billion in 1998, highlighting the country's balance of payments problems.

The deficit in Kazakhstan's current account has been widening since 1995, reaching about US$1 billion in 1998. In the past the growing current account deficit has largely been financed by the foreign direct investment (FDI) inflows. By the end of 1997, FDI totalled US$5.4 billion, the largest portion of which (49 per cent) was in the oil and gas sectors, followed by metallurgy (25 per cent). Following the general reassessment of investor risk on emerging markets, further inflow of capital in Kazakhstan can no longer be assumed. Until recently, growth continued only in the oil and gas sectors.

Budget reform

Kazakhstan has been suffering a budget deficit since the early 1990s when the deficit amounted to 7.2 per cent of GDP. A dramatic fall in government revenue occurred as a consequence of the cessation of subsidies from the centralised Soviet Union budget following its dissolution and because of the significant decline in the production sector caused by the destruction of economic relationships among the former Soviet Republics.

In 1994, when production declined significantly, total government budget revenue amounted to 23 per cent of GDP, while tax revenue fell from 24 per cent to 16 per cent of GDP compared to the previous year. State expenditure varied from 56 to 58 per cent of GDP. Furthermore, a significant volume of investment was financed by the government (approximately one-fifth of total expenditure), which placed a burden on current expenditure. The inability of state authorities to finance the payment of wages and pensions in the government arrears resulted in a sharp decline of domestic demand and overall standard of living. The final result was a deterioration in the financial sector of the economy. In addition, the absence of a monitoring system for taxpayers contributed to a low level of tax discipline and the flourishing of a 'shadow economy'.

The implementation of the Tax Code in July 1995 marked a turning-point for reforms in the tax administration. The new tax legislation offered a host of advantages. The list of various types of tax stipulated by the newly enacted code was characterised by the uniform nature of tax rates and their segregation into national and local (municipal) taxes and levies. In 1998, amendments to the tax legislation were introduced in order to improve tax administration and remove differences between certain articles. To improve the administration of government financial resources, the government budget and non-budget funds were consolidated into a single financial statement beginning January 1999.

However, Kazakhstan's tax revenue is still extremely low by world standards – only 12.6 per cent of GDP in 1998. Government efforts in the past two years to increase collections through strengthening tax policy have been largely unsuccessful. The problem of low tax collection is common to the CIS and can be attributed to the large-scale shadow economy and administrative difficulties in tax collection.

In 1998 the government began working towards improving tax administration. The installation of computer systems for tax and customs services is aimed at improved monitoring of tax collection from big enterprises. But still, Kazakhstan's tax authorities may initiate even more tax inspections of domestic and foreign companies, as pressure on the budget increases.

Privatisation, capital markets and pension reform

In 1996 Kazakhstan introduced a long-term strategy to develop a financial market for the country. It included privatisation, the development of capital markets and pension reform.

Privatisation

Privatisation in Kazakhstan is a major component of economic reform and of the transition to a market economy. A notable reform measure has been the government programmes for the privatisation of state enterprises, which were aimed at creating a private sector and generating revenues for the budget.

The first programme was the Privatisation Programme of 1991–92, whereby enterprises were transformed into joint-stock companies, and their preferred and common shares were offered to their employees. This programme resulted in the privatisation of about 12 per cent of state enterprises.

In March 1993 the government introduced the second programme (planned to end late 1995), under which privatisation was directed at small and medium-sized enterprises (SMEs). This resulted in substantial FDI of US$7.5 billion in 1993, especially in the oil and gas industries (40 per cent).

The main target of the third stage of privatisation (1996–98) was the sale of export-oriented companies on a case-by-case basis. The 'blue-chip' programme is part of the third stage; under a decree issued in December 1996, 56 enterprises were deemed to be 'blue-chip'. Stakes varying from 1 to 5 per cent in the country's major companies were sold through voucher and cash auctions during 1995 and 1996.

Privatisation continued at a rapid pace in 1997. Kazakhstan's currency reserves were greatly increased by the privatisation of the electrical power and oil companies and proceeds from privatisation amounted to 21 per cent of total budget revenue. Despite the unfavourable situation in the international capital markets and the subsequent delay of Kazakhstan's 'blue-chip' programme, the government received US$548 million from privatisation in 1998. It planned to raise US$413 million in 1999; by early 1999 it had already received US$200 million through the oil sector alone.

Capital markets

In general, with the exception of the government securities market, the capital markets in Kazakhstan are still underdeveloped. Current activity on the Kazakhstan Stock Exchange (KASE) is very low, mainly as a result of an insufficient range of corporate securities. This low level of activity has coincided with a decline in the level of interest in emerging markets on the part of international investors. Low demand, both domestic and international, for the shares of Kazakhstan's enterprises was the reason that the 'blue-chip' privatisation programme was delayed. Now 'blue-chip' companies comprise only four entities: one copper producer, two oil firms, and an integrated magnesium and titanium producer.

In March 1997 Parliament adopted several amendments to the securities legislation and this was followed by several regulations issued by the National Securities Commission. A new company law, adopted in July 1998, was designed to simplify the issuing of corporate bonds and to introduce the notion of convertible bonds. It also included a requirement for shares of public companies to be kept with a central registrar, connected to a central depository; this was to further simplify the system and cut overall transaction costs.

Pension reform

Kazakhstan has been preparing a complete overhaul of its pension system. In the existing 'pay as you go' system, contributors pay in and pensioners receive payment at the same time. Due to changing demographic conditions and to the continuing budget deficit, the state pension system is now unable to service the pension payments. The envisaged reform aims at replacing the existing state pension system with a private system. During a transitory period of the next 40 years, the pension gap will be funded from the budget. Individuals may choose between the two funds to allocate their contributions.

In the past, pension contributions were tailored via the state-owned pension fund, which was part of the state budget. Now employees can choose between the state-owned pension fund and 13 private accumulative pension funds. Private pension funds are established in the form of closed joint-stock companies and now account for at least 23 per cent of total pension contributions. Contributions to the state-owned pension fund comprise the other 77 per cent, but this balance is likely to shift as the population gains confidence in private pension funds. For instance, in the second half of 1998 average monthly contributions collected by private pension funds increased 2.7 times compared to the first six months.

A new pension system was needed not only to improve the situation with respect to pension payments but also to facilitate the development of the country's securities market, where pension funds would become major institutional investors in corporate stocks and bonds and government securities. In 1998, Kazakhstan's pension funds accumulated some KZT23.5 billion (US$282 million), of which KZT1.8 billion (7.7 per cent) was in the form of investment revenues transferred to individual pension accounts. Thus, the private pension funds are becoming active participants in the domestic capital markets. Another potentially important group of investors is asset management companies (AMCs). The activities of AMCs are licensed, regulated and supervised by the National Security Commission. These companies could invest at least 50 per cent of their assets in government securities and up to 30 per cent in high-quality corporate securities.

Economic outlook

Despite recent regional economic turmoil, Kazakhstan has maintained relative economic stability and held the interest of international financial institutions and major investors.

The market perception is that although the macroeconomic situation worsened in 1999, there were some positive signs for growth by the end of the year due to higher oil prices and an improving overall economic situation in the region. GDP is now not likely to drop sharply. Gradual depreciation of the tenge with moderate fluctuations was expected, and the annual inflation rate is unlikely to have exceeded 18–20 per cent.

The devaluation of the tenge should help to restore growth and narrow the trade deficit over time and moderate improvement of the current account is expected. At the same time, the weaker tenge might decrease the confidence in the national currency, which would lead to further dollarisation of the economy.

Kazakhstan is expected to continue pursuing strict monetary and fiscal policies that aim to maintain a low inflationary environment and to increase tax collection in order to meet higher expenditure by the government. However, a complicated tax code and a rising tax burden could create new cases of tax evasion and further broaden the 'shadow economy'.

The situation in Kazakhstan's financial markets is considerably different from that in Russia: domestic debt is much lower with foreign investors holding less than 5 per cent of government securities. In Russia, before August 1998, foreign investors held more than 30 per cent of securities issued by the Russian government. Official reserves fully cover the money supply in the country and offer import cover of around three months. Despite the recent tenge devaluation, Kazakhstan unlike Russia shows no signs of default in the servicing of its foreign obligations.

Further development of Kazakhstan's economy depends on both internal and external factors. Large-scale restructuring of tax legislation is needed to create more favourable conditions for domestic production. Tax reform should be aimed at decreasing the tax burden while increasing the volume of revenue collection. Political and considerable economic stability are expected to prevent an outflow of foreign investments. The recovery in world commodity prices will facilitate the government's ability to increase its revenue and improve the overall economic environment in Kazakhstan.

1.3

The Role of the National Bank

The National Bank of Kazakhstan

Kazakhstan has experienced extensive economic transformation since the introduction of a national currency, the tenge, in mid-November 1993. The government's structural reforms have achieved significant results in the key areas of financial stabilisation, privatisation and price liberalisation.

The banking system

The banking system in Kazakhstan is subject to laws and regulations that are similar to other examples of international regulations and legislation.
The banking system consists of two tiers:

1. The National Bank of Kazakhstan
2. Commercial or second tier banks (STBs).

The major functions of the National Bank of Kazakhstan are as follows:

- to implement monetary policy;

- to supervise the activities of commercial banks, insurance companies and non-banking financial organisations;

- to manage gold and foreign exchange reserves;

- to organise payments' systems.

The Bank is expected to maintain the tenge in a free floating exchange rate regime. At present the rate of the national currency is determined by market forces – supply and demand – though the Bank will not allow sharp fluctuations of the rate that exceed rational expectations.

Strict monetary policy will be applied only to curb inflation within reasonable limits. Broad money will be set according to the real needs and possibilities of the economy. Under the conditions of a free floating exchange rate, the main instrument of the Bank's influence upon monetary aggregates will be open market operations. Changes to official interest rates will be implemented by the Bank while taking into consideration inflation and the status of financial markets and with the purpose of influencing market expectations.

The Bank's activities will be directed towards further strengthening and consolidation of the banking system, encouraging capital growth and the increase of banks' capitalisation ratios, diminishing banking risks, which in turn is hoped to stimulate deposits, generating investment and extending credit by banks for domestic production of goods and services.

On 5 April, 1999 the government and the National Bank of Kazakhstan carried out the transition to a free floating exchange rate regime for the national currency – the tenge. The Bank then implemented measures to decrease the state's share in banking capital and introduced stricter regulations for the increase of capitalisation ratios, and for the opening, licensing and internal control of banks. The implementation of these policies has allowed the Bank to mitigate the negative influence of the world financial, and especially Russian, crises upon Kazakhstan's financial markets and economy and to transit smoothly to the new exchange regime. The monitoring system of monetary funds, including currency and deposit flows, in the banking system was broadened, thus allowing the Bank to react quickly and control the situation in the banking sector during the crises.

This major structural reform means not only that the banking system, is more efficient but also that real opportunities for investment now exist. For example, there are major tax advantages to be had because of the reforms (income on interest on middle- and long-term investment loans and on turnover realized in financial services is tax free). In order for Kazakhstani banks to attain international service standards, increase their competitiveness, and improve the financial stability of the banking system as a whole, the National Bank of Kazakhstan is ensuring the transition of the banking system to international standards. Individual Kazakhstani banks will then be required to achieve international standards independently. Non-compliant banks will be liquidated or reorganized.

Monetary policy

The National Bank of Kazakhstan has held a strict monetary policy since 1995. At that time, this was a measure necessary to bring down the high inflation rate and to ensure the stability of the national currency. At present, holding a strict monetary policy is justified by the efforts of the Bank to alleviate the negative impact of the world and the Russian financial crises upon financial markets and upon the economy of Kazakhstan.

Targets of monetary policy

The National Bank of Kazakhstan determines and implements the state's monetary policy, the main objective of which is to ensure the stability of the national currency, its purchasing power and rate of exchange relative to leading foreign currencies.

Major instruments of monetary policy

The major instruments of monetary policy are as follows:

- Remuneration (interest) rates on loans granted by the Bank to other banks.

- Regulation of reserve requirements on deposit with the Bank, including possible terms, volumes and types of reserves (reserve requirements) differentiation.

- Open market operations on buying and selling government securities.

- Loans to banks.

Remuneration (interest) rates on loans granted by the National Bank of Kazakhstan
The National Bank of Kazakhstan sets the official refinance rate and other remuneration (interest) rates. The official refinance rate is fixed according to the money market, to levels of supply and demand on loans, to the inflation rate and to expectations for inflation. Market remuneration (interest) rates are influenced by the Bank within the framework of a coherent monetary policy.

Reserve requirements
In order to regulate the volume of loans granted by banks, to decrease banks' liabilities for non-payment risks, and to protect both depositors' and shareholders' interests, the National Bank of Kazakhstan uses the mechanism of reserve requirements. The norm for reserve requirements is calculated as a percentage of total liabilities minus obligations to banks. A change in the reserve requirement norm cannot be introduced any earlier than a month from the day of the decision to institute a change being taken. The Bank will return assets it is reserving within a week in the case of a bank ceasing its activities.

Open market operations
Open market operations consist of buying and selling government securities in order to regulate money supply. Limits for open market operations are approved by the Bank's Board of Directors.

Loans to banks

The procedures, conditions, types, terms, and limits of loans made by crediting banks are determined by the Bank. The Bank regulates lending banks' total volume of credits in accordance with its monetary policy, and as the creditor of last instance, it may provide banks with loans denominated in national and foreign currency, covered and non-covered, according to procedures and terms adopted by its Board of Directors

The transition to the tenge free floating exchange rate regime

The significant devaluation of the national currencies of Kazakhstan's trading partners, particularly of the Russian rouble, resulted in a similarly significant appreciation of the tenge against those currencies. Consequently, this led to a marked decrease in the competitiveness of Kazakhstani goods, to a decrease in gold and foreign currency reserves, to a fall in the country's GDP and to an increase in its trade account deficit. The practical impossibility of maintaining economic growth in the country while having an open external trade regime and an overvalued national currency was thus demonstrated.

As a result, the government and the Bank decided to adopt a free floating exchange rate as the most appropriate means of integrating Kazakhstan into the world economy and international financial and commodity markets.

Kazakhstan carried out the transition to the free floating exchange rate regime under favourable conditions, created by recent economic policy. Namely, the reform of the banking system, a new basis for entrepreneurship, a favourable investment climate in the country and a new basis for tackling the problems of the social protection system.

Project financing

Learning from the past, looking to the future

Shortage of finance from internal sources led to the necessity of finding external sources of financing, primarily through loans from international financial organisations. Project financing is being implemented in Kazakhstan by organisations such as the World Bank (IBRD), the International Monetary Fund (IMF), the European Bank for Reconstruction and Development (EBRD), the Islamic Development Bank (IDB) and the Asian Development Bank (ADB).

Within the context of official development assistance, Kazakhstan was granted loans by the IBRD, the ADB, the EBRD, the IDB, Japanese financial organisations (Eximbank of Japan and the Fund of International Economic Cooperation), and other commercial banks and governments.

In 1998 more than 15 of the largest Kazakhstani banks participated in implementing loans from, among others, the IBRD, the EBRD and the ADB. The loans were extended within the framework of banks' institutional development programmes on twinning agreements and financed projects for small and medium-sized enterprises, agricultural development programmes and other projects.

The activities of the National Bank of Kazakhstan, in its role as the central bank, are of great importance in promoting cooperation with leading international financial organisations, in attracting loans for the continuing reform of the economy and the financial sector, and in receiving technical assistance.

The Investment Climate

*European Bank for Reconstruction and Development (EBRD)**

Introduction

Kazakhstan, with vast oil and gas reserves both onshore and beneath the Caspian Sea, aims to be one of the top ten exporters within a decade. The country is also rich in minerals, including iron, lead, copper and uranium. As in most transition economies, the services sector has grown considerably since the beginning of reforms. Trade, housing, communications and financial services represent good opportunities for foreign investors. Particularly noteworthy is the strong push to establish financial service institutions. The government has made determined and thus far successful efforts to attract foreign direct investment (FDI), with incentives for priority sectors and ongoing dialogue with investors. It has placed a high priority on the establishment of a legal and commercial environment that is attractive to foreign investment.

Economic background

Since 1994 Kazakhstan has embarked on a comprehensive stabilisation and reform programme, which has brought benefits in the form of high FDI, relative macroeconomic stability, early access (among the Commonwealth of Independent States – CIS) to the international capital market, and – until the Russian crisis of August 1998 – some first signs of output recovery. In the second half of 1998 the economy of Kazakhstan was buffeted by the fall-out from the Russian financial crisis of August. The main effects were decreasing demand for Kazakhstan's natural resources and deteriorating trade. The government was decisive in addressing the situation, particularly in introducing fiscal austerity measures and redou-

* Information correct as of October 1999.

bling efforts to attract foreign investment. Kazakhstan's short-term economic prospects were significantly affected by the Russian crisis. Output was stunted in 1998 and early 1999, due to the dependence of exports on the Russian market – in excess of 30 per cent – and the contractionary effects of macroeconomic adjustment in response to low oil prices. The government was quick to respond with fiscal tightening and an acceleration of privatisation.

Expectations of continued economic growth were disappointed in 1998, as year-end estimates recorded a decline of –2.5 per cent. This was contrary to the growth record Kazakhstan had established, achieving 2 per cent growth in 1997. In the first half of 1998, both gross domestic product (GDP) and production had continued to grow positively, but the trend was reversed sharply by the knock-on effects of the crisis. Recent government estimates put third-quarter 1999 growth at marginally positive rates, after declines of 3.7 per cent and 3.3 per cent in the first and second quarter. Devaluation and the oil price recovery are helping to relieve the tensions from the Russian crisis.

Growth prospects in the medium-term may also be affected if foreign investor confidence in emerging markets remains low and the slump in world commodity prices leads foreign investors to scale down their exposure to emerging markets. The government has consequently taken action to reassure investors of its commitment to macroeconomic stability and ongoing structural reform.

Foreign direct investment

Foreign direct investment (FDI) totalled US$1.132 billion in 1998, which was on a par with 1996–97. The government had set a target of US$1.2–1.5 billion in FDI for 1999. The inflow of FDI in 1998 was less than targeted, largely due to the depressed values of the 'blue chip' companies scheduled for privatisation, which caused the government to postpone planned public offerings of stakes in these companies. In cumulative per capita terms, Kazakhstan has recorded the second highest FDI inflow in the CIS, exceeding US$300 over 1989–98, second only to Azerbaijan. Investment flows have increased steadily, reaching a cumulative total of US$7.06 billion by mid-1998.

Thus far, most foreign investment has been directed towards the natural resource sector, led by oil, gas and non-ferrous metals. According to National Bank of Kazakhstan (NBK) statistics, by December 1998 US$3.76 billion had been invested in the country's oil and gas sector, which represented 47.5 per cent of total foreign investment since 1993, with non-ferrous metals accounting for approximately 24.1 per cent in the same period. This trend is likely to continue if the present transportation and pipeline bottlenecks can be alleviated.

The US is the biggest source of FDI into Kazakhstan. According to NBK data, by the end of December 1998, US investments totalled over US$2 billion, followed by South Korea (US$1.46 billion) and the UK (US$1.03 billion). Other major sources include Turkey, Canada and Belgium.

Reasons to invest in Kazakhstan

- Ongoing economic reforms have resulted in macroeconomic stability.

- Structural reforms progressing with an acceleration of the privatisation programme.

- Vast natural resources: among the world's largest oil and gas deposits; world-ranking deposits of chrome, zinc, manganese, copper, lead, uranium, silver and gold.

- Open foreign investment climate evidenced by the presence of major foreign investors and continuing FDI flow.

- Widespread opportunities for privatisation or greenfield investment in:
  - grain storage and distribution, fertiliser production and distribution;
  - chemicals and pharmaceuticals;
  - manufacturing;
  - power generation and distribution;
  - telecommunications, water treatment and other infrastructure.

- No restriction on capital repatriation, with tax and other FDI incentives.

- European Union (EU) Partnership and Co-operation Agreement, including most-favoured nation trade agreement; negotiations progressing for World Trade Organisation (WTO) membership.

Investment opportunities by sector

Oil and gas

Due to investor efforts, oil and gas production is climbing back towards levels last seen in 1991. Current annual production is roughly 26 million tonnes of oil and 8 billion cubic metres of natural gas. The huge hard currency earning potential of the oil and gas sector is gaining even more importance due to budgetary pressures.

Kazakhstan produced 25.9 million tonnes of crude oil in 1998. After Russia, it is the second largest oil producer in the CIS, and has the potential to become one of the world's ten largest producers by 2006.

Kazakhstan produces over half a million barrels of oil per day, almost half of which comes from three large onshore fields – Tengiz, Uzen and Karachaganak. The oil and gas industry is the most rapidly developing sector, and foreign firms are engaged in widespread exploration and development. The country's known oil reserves total 15.5 billion barrels (2.2 billion tons), but potential reserves could be far greater, particularly those beneath the Caspian Sea.

Kazakhstan also has large reserves of natural gas, mostly located in the Karachaganak field on the northern border, which is an extension of Russia's Orenberg field. Estimates for total gas reserves vary from 53 to 83 trillion cubic feet.

Privatisation in the oil and gas industry has proved to be effective in improving the efficiency and financing of production and in introducing new management and marketing techniques. Kazakhstan's active reform process and the presence of a consortium led by Chevron Corporation (Chevron) have paved the way for other large investments in the oil and gas sector. A large amount of investment is flowing into the industry's upstream oil sector, for which speedy development is a government priority. Another priority is the required export infrastructure. The downstream oil sector is also attracting investment.

Oil transportation

Kazakhstan's efforts to develop its oil industry have been hampered by a lack of adequate outlets to world markets. Currently, the country's oil and gas production is transported by pipeline, rail, road and sea. To accommodate the increased volume of oil and gas extraction, Kazakhstan needs to secure commercially and politically viable routes for oil and gas export pipelines to hard-currency markets. The domestic oil market remains small, as is the demand for Kazakhstani oil in neighbouring countries. However, the proposed Caspian Pipeline Consortium project will give a huge boost to production. Kazakhstan is also considering other transport options including a pipeline link across the Caspian into Azerbaijan's main export routes.

Oil refining industry

Kazakhstan has three main oil refineries: Pavlodar, Atyrau (on the Caspian Sea) and Shymkent. Since independence, these oil refineries have suffered a significant decline in output. Consequently, the immediate problem facing the country's refiners is underutilisation; however, looking to the medium-term, the government has been pursuing foreign investment to modernise these plants.

Mining and metallurgy

Metallurgy plays a very important role in the Kazakhstani economy and, together with metals, constitutes approximately 30 per cent of the country's exports. Significant efforts have been made to revitalise this sector through privatisation tenders and the issuing of management contracts. Controlling stakes in all major metals companies have been sold to strategic investors. These deals have resulted in joint venture-type structures, with the government left in control of large stakes. This resulted in large-scale investments during 1995–97, with modernisation of technology and of the production process in these companies. Restructuring programmes produced widespread cost-cutting and growth in output, with non-ferrous and ferrous sectors recording growth of 24 per cent and 15 per cent respectively in 1997. Ferrous metals production was negatively affected by the Russian crisis in 1998, falling by 13 per cent but this is expected to be a temporary blip only, while non-ferrous metals grew by over 10 per cent in 1998.

Manufacturing

Kazakhstan had developed an active industrial base under Soviet rule, including light manufacturing and processing facilities. Light industries were particularly hard hit by the interruption of supply routes and the disappearance of markets caused by the breakup of the Soviet Union. Rising costs, poor capital stocks and an inability to compete with foreign goods have all exacerbated the problems. Consequently, there exists an urgent need for capital in these sectors to be combined with a developed skill base and traditional industrial facilities, especially in the north of the country. The government is encouraging value-adding production that can be achieved locally and through domestic processing. In cotton, food processing or light manufacturing, foreign participation is actively being sought to upgrade existing technologies and to boost the competitiveness of Kazakhstan's products.

Agriculture

Agriculture is an important sector to the economy, contributing over 8 per cent to GDP. However, it faces acute problems derived principally from the legacy of the command economy, the breakup of the former Soviet Union and the interruption of the old input and output distribution system. Kazakhstan's total agricultural area has been steadily shrinking because of the need to remove marginal land from production and due to a severe drop in fertiliser usage over the past six years. Further restructuring in this sector is likely to provide the basis for future recovery and, with investment, wheat could again become an important foreign exchange earner. Food processing, the development of storage capacities and trading activities are areas where rapid progress is feasible. In addition, the government has identified more than 400 projects for potential foreign investment.

Infrastructure

Telecommunications

With only 12 lines per 100 inhabitants, Kazakhstan's telephone system remains underdeveloped and is in need of repair and modernisation. The European Bank for Reconstruction and Development (EBRD) is negotiating a financing package for Kazaktelecom (KTC), which was due to be put in place by the end of 1999.

Energy

Kazakhstan imports about 30 per cent of its domestic electricity needs, although it is also a minor exporter. About 80 per cent of domestic power is generated by 54 mostly coal-fired thermo-electric power plants, which are concentrated in the north of the country. Most of the power stations are obsolete and need to be upgraded or replaced.

The Kazakhstan government has been proactive in efforts to reform the electrical energy sector, including major privatisations. All the major power generation stations have been privatised. In 1999 the government planned to privatise local distribution systems. At present about 85 per cent of Kazakhstan's power generation system is in private hands, with western companies playing a major role in privatising the country's electric utilities. Between 1996 and 1997, more than half of Kazakhstan's generating capacity was sold to western investors. While existing power plants will continue to rely on Russian made parts for their Soviet-era equipment, the market for western equipment is likely to grow as existing facilities are renovated and new plants are built.

Transport

Because of its geographical position Kazakhstan is dependent upon its neighbours' transport links to get its goods to world markets. In general terms, Kazakhstan relies upon ageing and poorly maintained railways, which have 13,600 km of track including 5,500 of double track; some 4,000 km of track are electrified. Prior to independence, spare parts and rolling stock were mostly imported from Russia and Ukraine; however, these are now in short supply.

The Caspian Sea port of Aktau is Kazakhstan's shipping gateway. The US$74 million renovation and modernisation of the port began in 1997 with the help of a US$54 million 15-year loan from the EBRD. The Kazakhstan government has provided US$20 million for the project. In 1998, the port handled 80 per cent more cargo than the previous year, including a significant amount of oil. As a result of the modernisation programme the port will have an annual capacity of more than 7.5 million tonnes of oil and 1 million tonnes of dry freight.

Tourism

The tourist industry is in its infancy, contributing just 1 per cent to GDP. Kazakhstan is well endowed with natural scenic beauty and has seven national parks. The government has identified four major projects for which it is seeking foreign investment. These include the construction of a four-star tourist hotel in Taraz and the development of a health and ski resort at Chimbulak.

Financial sector

Although the financial system is at an early stage of development, significant progress has been made in establishing the legal framework for a stable banking sector. In an ongoing process, it has been strengthened through consolidation, privatisation and foreign entry. Strict central bank supervision and a comprehensive banking sector reform programme aimed to achieve international standards across the sector by 2000. Current reform also focuses on the securities market, development of the stock exchange and the new pension funds.

Banking sector

Kazakhstan has a two-tier banking system, the foundations of which were established in August 1995 when the Law 'On Banks and Banking Activities' was adopted. On the top tier is the central bank – the National Bank of Kazakhstan (NBK). All other banks belong to the second tier.

Banking sector reform

Since 1995, the NBK has been conducting a reform programme designed to create a low-risk environment for banking operations, and dealing with problem loans and insolvent banks. A timetable was established to phase-in enforcement of the new regulations over a period of five years. Banks were required to submit restructuring plans in exchange for a period of regulatory forbearance. The reform programme also introduced a minimum capital adequacy requirement for banks, set at KZT1 billion (approximately US$12.7 million). The minimum requirement is the same for all banks operating in Kazakhstan, including banks with foreign participation. By the end of 1998, 30 banks (in the 'fast track' group) had met this requirement, as well as all the international prudential standards, and another 30 were expected to meet them by the end of 1999. Another indicator of the healthy condition of the banking sector is progress in reducing non-performing loans and in loan loss provisioning.

By December 1998 the number of banks had fallen to 72, following takeovers, bankruptcies, and the withdrawal of licences from banks with insufficient capital. Of the 72 banks, five were state-owned, one was an interstate bank, and 25 were banks with foreign participation (including subsidiaries of non-resident banks). Under the NBK's strict supervision, the number of banks is still falling and, according to NBK forecasts, was due to come down to about 55–60 by the end of 1999.

Foreign investment in the banking sector

Twenty-five banks with foreign ownership comprise almost a quarter of banking sector assets. At present, there is a 25 per cent restriction on the aggregate share of foreign capital in the banking sector, but this is likely to be removed in the near future, leading to an increase in foreign participation and much greater competition.

Non-bank financial institutions

Development of an equity market made progress in 1997 when the government created the necessary infrastructure to bring issuers and investors together. The Laws 'On Securities Market', 'On Registration of Transactions with Securities' and 'On Investment Funds' were passed in March 1997, and provide a legal framework for securities transactions, stock markets, investment banks, registries, custodian services and investment companies which conform to international standards.

A major impetus to the development of non-bank financial institutions was expected to come from the 'blue chip' privatisation programme, whereby residual state shares in privatised companies would be sold on the domestic stock market. This programme has been delayed by the current depressed market conditions, and several brokerage houses set up to benefit from the expected upturn of secondary market trading have closed. It was envisaged that public offerings of state shares in predominantly smaller companies would accelerate in 1999, while 'blue chip' privatisation would begin to be implemented towards the end of that year.

CONCLUSION

A number of serious challenges face Kazakhstan over the coming years as it continues to make progress towards a market economy. As already indicated, the country has much untapped potential, where long-term projects are likely to lead to positive results as the country continues to accelerate its rate of change.

1.5

Foreign Trade

Alica Henson

Introduction

During the Soviet era, Kazakhstan exported its goods to the rest of the Soviet Union and generally ran a negative trade balance. In 1989–90, Kazakhstan is estimated to have exported about 30 per cent of its 'net material product' (the standard Soviet-era measure of output). However, under the command economy system, this trade deficit was covered by subsidies provided by the central government.

With independence in 1991, Kazakhstan lost these subsidies and has since been forced to rely more heavily on increasing export revenue and reducing the trade deficit. In support of this, the government has undertaken a programme of trade liberalisation. Export quotas and export and import licences have for the most part been abolished. In addition, the government banned barter trade in 1996. This was complemented by efforts to diversify Kazakh export destinations and trade links, particularly with non-CIS (Commonwealth of Independent States) countries. In general, Kazakhstan has taken steps to promote an environment more conducive to trade, and in many areas the government has significantly reduced the level of state interference, with most state monopolies and state trading practices abolished. These measures have been undertaken in order to develop profitable relations with foreign markets, which in turn will benefit the transition of domestic markets, particularly the non-energy sector industries.

Kazakhstan relies mainly on its exports of raw materials. Its principal exports include:

- oil products, such as diesel fuel and mazut (heavy oil), and gas;
- metals, such as copper, zinc, magnesium;
- ferrous ores and coal;
- cotton and wheat.

In 1997, exports of fuel and oil products comprised about 33 per cent of total exports by value; ferrous metals 15 per cent, copper and copper products 11 per cent and wheat 8 per cent. Kazakhstan's main imports include machinery (16.4 per cent in 1997) and refined fuel and oil products (14.3 per cent).

Trade with Russia

Russia has long been Kazakhstan's main trading partner. Trade turnover with Russia amounted to US$4.25 billion in 1997. However, trade with Russia, particularly after the Russian financial crisis and rouble devaluation of August 1998, has declined considerably, as Kazakh goods became more expensive in Russia. In addition, the Kazakh market was flooded by inexpensive Russian goods, with which domestic producers were unable to compete. In response, Astana imposed a temporary ban (which was extended following the tenge devaluation) on Russian consumer goods, including mostly food products. In April 1999 economic conditions led to the government allowing the tenge to float freely. Since then, the currency has lost over 30 per cent of its value. However, the move was welcomed by international financial institutions such as the IMF, and has helped to increase export levels – and hence revenue – as Kazakh goods became more competitively priced.

Only a few years ago, Russia accounted for around 50 per cent of total Kazakh exports; in 1998 this figure had fallen to 34 per cent. Together with other CIS countries, Kazakhstan is trying to reduce its dependence on Russia, mainly to avoid the adverse effects of declining Russian economic performance, and is looking to develop more direct trade links with other CIS countries and, more importantly, with non-CIS countries.

CIS trade relations

In 1998, 43 per cent of Kazakh exports went to CIS countries. Shuttle trade accounted for 40 per cent of imports into Kazakhstan in 1997. Following the Russian financial crisis in 1998, some restrictions were put in place against neighbouring Kyrgyzstan and Uzbekistan in early 1999. However, the restrictions against Kyrgyzstan were later rescinded.

In addition to its membership of the CIS, which has been working to establish a mutually advantageous trade policy, Kazakhstan forms part of a customs union that includes Russia, Belarus, Kyrgyzstan and Tajikistan. Together with Tajikistan, Kyrgyzstan and Uzbekistan, Kazakhstan is also a member of the Central Asian Economic Community, which aims to create a regional grouping similar to the European Union (EU). However, the goal of establishing a single free-trade zone has not yet been realised.

Russia and Ukraine remain Kazakhstan's main trading partners within the CIS. In the first half of the year 2000, 33 per cent of Kazakh exports were sent to CIS countries; 20.1 per cent of exports went to Russia and 3.1 per cent went to Ukraine. Over the same period, over 50 per cent of imports to Kazakhstan came from CIS countries. Overall, the trend appears to be declining trade with CIS countries, particularly Russia.

External Trade Links

In 1998, the trade balance with non-CIS countries was positive, while the balance with its CIS trading partners was negative. The foreign trade balance amounted to US$12.4 billion. Since 1991 Kazakhstan has signed more than 45 bilateral and multilateral foreign trade agreements with over 40 countries. The government has initiated links with various trade organisations:

- Kazakhstan is a member of the TRACECA (Transport Corridor Europe–Caucasus–Central Asia) and INOGATE (Interstate Oil and Gas Transport to Europe) groups.

- Kazakhstan is currently undergoing accession negotiations with the World Trade Organisation (WTO). It currently holds observer status and expectations are high that membership will be extended by the end of 2000. Membership of the customs union between Russia, Belarus, Kyrgyzstan and Tajikistan continues. Although membership of the customs union may delay Kazakhstan's accession to the WTO, the members have decided to coordinate their tariff structure in line with WTO requirements as much as possible.

- In 1995, the EU–Kazakhstan Partnership and Co-operation Agreement was signed. This agreement came into effect on 1 July, 1999. The Co-operation Council, the agreement's principle vehicle, held its first meeting in late July 1999. The Council determined that in 1999 and 2000, relations would focus mainly on promoting the development of a business environment in Kazakhstan, in anticipation of accession to the WTO. In addition, the Council will promote the further development of TRACECA and INOGATE.

- Kazakhstan is a member of the 'Shanghai Five', which includes Russia, China, Kyrgyzstan and Uzbekistan. The group was established in 1994 and met most recently in August 1999 to discuss developing economic and security ties in the region.

Table 1.5.1   EU trade with Kazakhstan (1998)

Country	Exports from Kazakhstan (% of total Kazakh exports)	Imports to Kazakhstan (% of total Kazakh imports)
UK	9	5
Italy	9	2
Switzerland	6	2
Germany	5	9
The Netherlands	5	2

In addition to broadening its trade links with EU countries, Kazakhstan is also trying to increase trade volumes with China and South Asia. Reminiscent of the old Silk Route that ran from China through Kazakhstan and south to Lebanon and Syria, Kazakhstan is now exporting goods, mainly raw materials, back to Asia. In 1998, 7 per cent of Kazakh exports were sent to China. The total trade volume with China amounted to US$375 million in the first five months of 1999, double the level of the same period in 1998. Exports to South East Asia are growing; Thailand and Malaysia being the two most significant trading partners. Overall, Kazakhstan's main trading partners outside the CIS include the Netherlands, China, Switzerland, Germany and the UK.

1.6

The Legal Framework

CMS Cameron McKenna

Introduction

Although the Republic of Kazakhstan became an independent state in 1991, parts of the Soviet-era body of law still remain in place today. On independence, the pre-existing legal framework was formally adopted to the extent that it did not conflict with later-adopted legislation. This was clearly necessary in order to prevent a legislative vacuum being created on the first day of independence. Unfortunately, the process of adopting replacement legislation is slow and very often the old law will still be the applicable governing enactment for a particular issue (for example, administrative derelictions are principally regulated by the Administrative code, adopted in 1984).

One of the principal policy objectives of the government is to make the country attractive to investors. In order to achieve this, significant legislative reforms have been made in the last few years. In 1998 two new corporate laws were adopted together with legislation dealing with banking, corporate finance and the taking and perfecting of security. In the summer of 1999, a new Special Part to the Civil Code was adopted together with the Civil Procedure Code. These developments build upon a host of other legislative enactments dealing with such diverse subjects as banks and banking, the regulations of companies, mortgages and their registration, pension funds, securities and many more. Recently, the European Bank for Reconstruction and Development (EBRD) has announced projects for the development of railways and telecommunications laws.

The Constitution

The current Constitution was adopted by referendum on 30 August 1995, replacing the earlier 1993 version. As the central strut of the legislative framework, the Constitution has supremacy over all other domestic legislation and subordinate regulations.

The Constitution separates the powers of the legislature (Parliament), the executive (Government) and the judiciary (the Supreme Court, the Oblast courts, the Almaty City Court/Military courts and the District courts).

The Parliament is a bicameral institution consisting of the Majilis (lower house) and the Senate (upper house). Members of the Majilis are elected by the general population while members of the Senate are elected by the local legislative bodies (the Maslikhat) and by the President. The President is also elected by the general population and is the head of state. The members of the government are appointed directly by the President. The Supreme Court is the principal judicial authority in Kazakhstan and its members, nominated by the President on the recommendation of the Supreme Judicial Council, are elected by the Senate.

Unfortunately, the separation of powers is not well defined and critics often allege that the executive (and, in particular, the President) has far too great an influence on the legislative process. For example, the power of Parliament as the supreme legislature is fettered by the power the President holds to veto proposed legislation. Moreover, in certain circumstances (such as in 1995 when Parliament had been dissolved), the President may enact legislation directly through decree. Domestic legislation is also enacted by the government and by specific ministries and state committees, as well as by regional and local authorities.

The Civil Code

Kazakhstan is a civil law country and, as such, its laws appear in codified form. The principal enactment dealing with civil law relations is the Civil Code, the General Part of which was enacted on 27 December 1994 (and which has been amended on numerous occasions), while the Special Part was adopted on 1 July 1999. The law adapting the Civil Code provides that the Civil Code overrides all other forms of domestic legislation other than the Constitution itself.

The Civil Code enshrines the following fundamental principles of civil law: freedom of contract, protection of property, equal treatment before the law, preservation of rights and absence of arbitrary state interference.

Although individual fields of commercial activity are covered by specific legislation, the Civil Code has an impact on almost all commercial transactions. The Civil Code (General Part) is wide-ranging in scope and contains three main sections:

Section 1 deals with civil rights, the status of individuals and legal entities, the form of corporate organisations, commercial transactions, powers of attorney and limitation periods.

Section 2 covers property rights and, in particular, the acquisition, cessation and protection of such rights.

Section 3 contains the general law of contract (form, privity, rights and obligations).

Similarly, the Special Part of the Civil Code is divided into sections:

Section 1 deals with specific types of agreements, including sale and purchase, subcontracting, rental and loans, and contains provisions on insurance and bank deposits.

Section 2 covers intellectual property and the rights attaching thereto.

Section 3 relates to rights of inheritance.

Section 4 contains provisions dealing with private international law and the proper law of contract.

Other codes

Subordinate to the Civil Code are the Labour Code, the Civil Procedure Code, the Administrative Code, the Customs Code and the Criminal Code. In conjunction with the Civil Code, these codes govern relations in the specific area captioned. Unfortunately, the Labour Code (adopted in 1972) and the Administrative Code (adopted in 1984) are outdated and incompatible with present-day reality. It is anticipated that both Codes will be scheduled by Parliament for replacement in the next year. Note that the main body of tax law is often referred to as the 'Tax Code' but it does not have the legal status of a code.

Foreign investment legislation

In addition to being governed by general domestic legislation, foreign investment relations in Kazakhstan are also specifically governed by the Foreign Investment Law (27 December 1994) (as amended) and the Law on State Support for Direct Investment (28 February 1997).

The Foreign Investment Law defines the basic framework for the attraction and regulation of foreign investments. In order to qualify as a foreign investor under this law, it must be shown that the investor is a foreign legal entity or individual, a foreign state or multilateral institution or, in certain circumstances, a Kazakhstani citizen, permanently resident outside the country. In addition, an enterprise with foreign participation (where at least 35 per cent of the equity or at least US$1 million of the equity holding is foreign-owned) will also qualify. It seems that a

Kazakhstani branch or representative office of a foreign company does not qualify as a foreign investor but this has not prevented many large investments in the country being made by means of a branch.

Of significant interest to qualifying foreign investors are the guarantees that the Foreign Investment Law provides – equal treatment, a ten-year grandfathering period and freedom from nationalisation/expropriation. The Law also provides specific rights – to transfer profits, income and interest received from activities conducted in Kazakhstan (subject to any withholdings), to open and maintain both foreign and local currency accounts, to choose a foreign law to govern a contract and an international body to settle any contract disputes. It is important to bear in mind, however, that the guarantees and rights provided by the Foreign Investment Law are subject to public policy restraints. Thus, where an industry in which a foreign investor has made an investment is nationalised for reasons of 'paramount public interest', the foreign investor will not be able to prevent such nationalisation but instead will be entitled to receive immediate and adequate compensation. Similarly, where legislation is subsequently amended/revoked on grounds of national security, the ten-year 'grandfathering' or stabilisation period will not apply but the foreign investor will be entitled to receive compensation for any loss suffered as a result of such change. A foreign investor intending to do business in Kazakhstan should seek detailed advice on the provisions of this Law prior to structuring any investment.

The Law on State Support for Direct Investments further enhances the benefits available to particular foreign investors (as well as local investors). Again, for qualifying investments made in certain priority sectors, various privileges are available. For example, these may include state grants, tax exemptions for a period of five years, income tax exemptions for a period of five years from its moment of achieving the first taxable income but not more than eight years from the date of the relevant investment contract, land and property, and full or partial customs duties exemption for goods and materials required for the investment project. It also provides further legislative guarantees for preferred investors. Among the most important of these are: no price controls to be imposed on the products of the investment and no monopolies to be created by the government in the industry in which the investment project operates.

The Investment Agency is established by this law as the single state entity with responsibility for implementing the support system and dealing directly (and entering into contracts) with prospective qualifying investors. As well as attracting investors to the country, this agency has the power to coordinate the actions of other state bodies (including ministries) to work in a consistent and smooth manner to facilitate the making of the investment. Thus, the licensing procedure (where applicable) should be substantially simplified for the foreign investor.

Although the Investment Agency has a great deal of authority under the legislation and a fair degree of discretion in exercising its powers, criticism is often made of the application (and processing) procedure, which is perceived as being overbureaucratic and time-consuming and a fundamental deterrent to its use by foreign investors.

Practical advice

Before firming-up any investment proposal, it is recommended that the foreign investor meet with officials of certain government bodies to make them aware of the broad terms of the contemplated investment. In Kazakhstan, a good relationship with the government, or at least those bodies with whom a foreign investor will come into contact, is very important. Following the recent official transfer of the capital from Almaty to Astana, most government bodies have relocated there. Meetings should be scheduled with, among others, the relevant ministry (for example, the Ministry of Energy, Industry and Trade) and the Tax Department of the Ministry of Finance. Other potentially important bodies include the Customs Committee, the National Bank of Kazakhstan, the National Securities Commission and the Anti-Monopoly Committee. Such meetings may be especially useful where the intended investment is in a regulated industry or will require a licence.

Other laws

The above are only a few examples of the many laws that a foreign investor will need to take into consideration when doing business in Kazakhstan. A list of other significant legislation would include the Law on Limited and Additional Liability Partnerships, the Law on Joint-Stock Companies, the Law on Licensing, the Law on Development of Competition and Limitation of Monopolistic Activity, the Law on Bankruptcy, the Decree Concerning Privatisation, the Laws Concerning Pledges of Movable Property and Mortgages of Immovable Property, the Labour Law, the Code on Subsoil and Subsoil Use, the Customs Code, the Law on Currency Regulations and the Tax Code. Many of these are discussed elsewhere in this book.

Treaties and international conventions

Shortly after independence, the Republic of Kazakhstan applied for membership and subsequently became a member of many important international bodies that help to regulate the community of nations. The Republic is a member of the United Nations, the International Monetary Fund, the World Bank, the International Finance Corporation, the European Bank for Reconstruction and Development, UNESCO and several other international institutions.

The Republic of Kazakhstan has also entered into a number of bilateral treaties with foreign countries, including treaties for the elimination of double taxation, and investment treaties. Double taxation or income tax treaties had been signed with various countries including the UK, the USA, Italy, the Netherlands and Canada. The fostering of international relations is supported by Kazakhstan's official representation in over 30 countries and by the more than 50 embassies and international organisations with a presence there.

Kazakhstan has played an active role in the establishment and development of the Commonwealth of Independent States (CIS) but the diversity of interests of the former members of the Soviet Union has meant that the CIS to date can boast few definite achievements. However, Kazakhstan and various members of the CIS have worked to harmonise some of their laws and to develop bilateral or multilateral treaties for the reduction of customs duties or for the coordination or reduction of value added tax.

Conclusion

The legal system in the Republic of Kazakhstan is becoming more attuned to the requirements of foreign investors and seeks to provide stability, open up competition and promote the operation of a market-economy. Numerous problems remain, however, the most serious being inconsistencies between different laws, legislative gaps and inadequate or poor drafting of much legislation, and a tendency for implementing regulations that are overly bureaucratic and out of tune with the needs of industry. Despite this, it is clear that the government remains committed to the original policy objectives set for itself and the process of legislative reform should continue for the foreseeable future, enhancing the attraction of the country as a place for foreign investors to do business.

1.7

Privatisation

Alica Henson

Introduction

Privatisation has proceeded relatively rapidly over the past several years,
assisted by the Law on Deregulation and Privatisation which was passed
in 1991, and other legislation governing the transfer of state assets to
private ownership. Recognising the necessity of garnering support
among the population, the government undertook a significant education
campaign to inform the public about the need for and benefits of privatisation for the future economic prospects of the country. Not only would
privatisation reduce the burden on the state budget, but it would also
provide a wider, more competitively priced range of goods and services
for the public, provide wider employment opportunities in privately
owned businesses, and increase budget revenue and investment in the
country's infrastructure.

Privatisation history

The privatisation of small enterprises was considered complete in 1997,
although small firms continued to be sold through cash auction and mass
(voucher) privatisation. By mid-1998, 13,000 small enterprises had been
transferred into private ownership. Agricultural privatisation has also
proceeded relatively smoothly, with 80 per cent of farmland transferred
to private hands under long-term leases and 90 per cent of farms privatised. In 1995, a law was passed permitting private land ownership,
although several restrictions prohibiting the ownership of certain types of
land still exist.

Mass privatisation was launched in 1993, and ended at the beginning of
1996. It enabled each citizen to purchase shares of enterprises, or to
invest them in privatisation investment funds. Generally, 10 per cent of an
enterprise's shares was transferred to the employees, about 51 per cent
were transferred to privatisation funds and 39 per cent were sold via cash

auction to domestic and foreign investors. Overall, 1,700 enterprises were privatised by mid-1998 using this method, and 170 privatisation funds were created to manage shareholdings in enterprises. However, the privatisation funds are for the most part now defunct, or the enterprises they managed went bankrupt.

Case-by-case privatisation was launched in 1996. The enterprises earmarked for privatisation using this method were often natural monopolies that traditionally employed over 5,000 employees each. The sale agreements have usually included commitments to invest capital in the enterprise.

Between 1995 and September 1998, 2,100 large enterprises were sold through cash auction. In addition, stakes in 80 large enterprises were sold to foreign investors on a case-by-case basis. In early 1997, restructuring was undertaken in the railways, telecommunications, power, heat and airlines sectors, in preparation for their privatisation. While energy privatisation has been attractive to foreign investors, power distribution and telecommunications have also attracted the interest of buyers. Thus far, all of Kazakhstan's major power stations have been sold off, mostly to foreign investors, and 5 of the 15 local distribution systems had been earmarked for privatisation in 1999. A 40 per cent stake in the state telecoms monopoly Kazakhtelekom has already been sold, in addition to other public utilities. In March 1998, TuranAlem Bank was privatised by the National Bank of Kazakhstan for US$72 million. Zhilstroibank and Kazagroprombank were also sold in 1999. In the first of a three-stage privatisation plan, Halyk Savings Bank sold a 20 per cent stake to depositors.

In total, over 75 per cent of all state-owned enterprises have been privatised. Nevertheless, in a number of these enterprises the state retains a majority shareholding. The European Bank for Reconstruction and Development (EBRD) estimated the private sector share of total GDP (gross domestic product) at 55 per cent in 1997; up from 40 per cent in 1996 and 25 per cent in 1995. At the end of 1998, 330 large enterprises, the output of which together accounted for an estimated 35 per cent of GDP, remained under state ownership.

Privatisation prospects

In 1998 Kazakhstan raised almost KZT50 billion in privatisation revenue, in excess of its KZT45 billion target. Most of this revenue came from the sale of 14.3 per cent of the Offshore Kazakhstan International Operating Company (OKIOC), the Caspian Sea offshore joint venture, for US$500 million. A 90 per cent stake in the Eastern Kazakhstan Copper and Chemical Plant was also sold for US$6.3 million.

In 1999 the government had initially hoped to raise KZT49 billion, including KZT30 billion from its 'blue chip' privatisation programme. However, as a result of lower export revenue and fall-out from the Russian financial crisis of August 1998, the government amended its budget targets, reducing spending in several areas, as well as raising its privatisation revenue target to KZT64 billion.

Also in 1999, the US company Mobil Corporation bought a 25 per cent stake in the TengizChevroil oil field for around US$200 million. Other owners of the Tengiz field include Chevron, which owns 45 per cent, a joint venture between Russia's Lukoil and US firm Arco (5 per cent), and the state (25 per cent). However, recent statements indicate that the government plans to sell a further stake of up to 12.5 per cent, valued at between US$1.2 billion and US$1.6 billion.

A 20 per cent stake in the country's largest bank, Halyk Savings Bank, was due to be sold by the end of 1999 through tender to strategic or portfolio investors. The bank also plans to issue 20 per cent of its existing equity capital to raise its capital fund. The government hopes that the privatisation will be complete by 2001. Eximbank is currently being prepared for privatisation.

'Blue chip' privatisation

Raw materials are found in abundance in Kazakhstan, with its copper, lead, zinc and iron deposits accounting for an estimated 10, 19, 13 and 10 per cent, respectively, of world reserves. The government expects that plants that mine or process these raw materials will provide an attractive opportunity for investors. The government's 'blue chip' programme foresaw the sale by the end of 1999 of:

- a 15 per cent stake in state telecommunications monopoly Kazakhtelekom (a further 30 per cent stake may be sold by commercial bank Kazkommertsbank);

- a 25.2 per cent stake in oil producer Aktobemunaigaz, and a 30 per cent stake in Mangistaumunaigaz for an estimated US$56 million

- a 25.2 per cent stake in the Ust-Kamenogorsk titanium and magnesium plant for an estimated US$13 million, 27.65 per cent of Kazzinc, and 35 per cent of the Kazakhmys copper extraction and processing plant.

Initial plans to sell many of these stakes on the Kazakhstan stock exchange have been amended and instead strategic investors will be targeted. However, stakes in several other companies have been and will continue to be sold on the stock exchange by the Department of State Property and Privatisation, including agricultural enterprises, industrial enterprises and hotels.

1.8

Privatisation and the Legal Environment for Reform

Professor Yury G Basin and Dr Olga I Chentsova, AEQUITAS

Introduction

Privatisation in Kazakhstan has been carried out on a three-stage basis and has been implemented following a variety of methods.

It is possible to identify two major stages in the privatisation process: (1) privatisation between 1991 and 1998, and (2) the Privatisation Programme for 1999–2000. This latter programme was outlined in the Programme for Privatisation and Increasing Effectiveness of State Property Management for the Years 1999–2000, as approved by Resolution No 683 of the Government of the Republic of Kazakhstan, dated 1 June 1999.

From 1991 to 1998 a programme of privatisation, including small- and large-scale privatisation, privatisation of individual projects and separate sectors, was implemented. A large part of state-owned production assets was privatised and private property became the basis of the market economy.

The Privatisation Programme for 1999–2000 stipulates specific features of privatisation for:

- state shareholdings in 'blue chip' companies;

- large facilities to be privatised;

- state shareholdings in 'the second echelon' enterprises;

- state shareholdings in joint-stock companies and state shares in business partnerships that have already been transferred into trust management;

- privatisation of social facilities.

Privatisation as an economic process was accompanied by the adoption of many normative acts including laws, presidential decrees and edicts, government resolutions, departmental regulative acts, and special acts outlining specific features for the privatisation of various individual facilities. As the Programme of Privatisation for 1999–2000 suggests, many new legal regulations are expected to appear soon in the sphere of privatisation.

The first stage of privatisation

The first acts regulating privatisation in Kazakhstan were a Resolution of the Supreme Council, On Major Trends of Denationalisation and Privatisation of State Property in the Kazakh SSR, dated 16 February 1991, and the Law on Denationalisation and Privatisation, dated 22 June 1991 and effective until 23 December 1995.

The legal definition of 'denationalisation', as outlined in the Law of 22 June 1991, was vague enough to also include purely structural changes in the system of state management of the economy, thus enabling the state to retain its monopoly in the operation of production assets. The Law was clearer in its definition of privatisation as being the transfer of state assets to ownership by individuals and by non-state legal entities. But the Law also reduced the scope of privatisation to include mainly the lease of enterprises to labour collectives with the subsequent purchase and buy-out of the state enterprise's assets by members of the labour collective.

Decree No 549 by the President of the Republic of Kazakhstan, dated 13 September 1991, approved the Programme of Denationalisation and Privatisation of Property in the Kazakh SSR for 1991–1992 (first stage). The Decree stipulated on the one hand the *compulsory* privatisation of certain enterprises, and on the other hand the *possibility* of privatising some enterprises at the initiative of labour collectives, thus granting many privileges to labour collectives. State-owned facilities not subject to privatisation in the first stage were also listed.

Three methods were used for the first stage of the denationalisation and privatisation process: auction, tender and corporatisation. The method was to be chosen by the labour collective, which had substantial advantages over other buyers. The programme of privatisation for the first stage outlined specific features for the privatisation of state property in various spheres of the national economy, including 'small-scale' and 'large-scale' privatisation. For example, the Programme stipulated that the privatisation of state-owned housing was to be on the basis of a 'coupon' mechanism and that privatisation coupons were to be allotted to all citizens who contributed to the development of the economy. Participation of foreign citizens and foreign legal entities in the privatisation process was restricted.

Many legal features of the first stage of privatisation proved to be untenable, and were subsequently repealed.

The second stage of privatisation

The second stage of privatisation began with the adoption of Decree No 1135, On National Programme of Denationalisation and Privatisation in the Republic of Kazakhstan for the Years 1993–1995 (second stage), dated 5 March 1993.

In accordance with the classification of the facilities to be privatised into small, medium and large enterprises, the second stage accounted for:

- the privatisation of large and unique property complexes on a project-by-project basis;

- the mass privatisation of medium-sized enterprises;

- the small-scale privatisation of small trade, utility, catering and servicing enterprises.

Along with privatisation coupons for the purchase of housing, privatisation investment coupons were introduced.

Much attention was paid to the corporatisation of state sector enterprises, which meant their reorganisation into 100 per cent state-owned joint-stock companies, the shares of which were subsequently transferred wholly or partially to legal entities and the public (including members of the labour collective) on a paid or free basis.

In the second stage of privatisation, the state abandoned the method of privatisation that had allowed for the transfer of state enterprises into the ownership of, or the leasing to, labour collectives.

Great attention was paid in the second stage to holding companies; these were to be established as closed-type joint-stock companies, ensuring effective regulation of basic sectors of the national economy.

The second stage also provided for the privatisation of very large and unique facilities and enterprises on a project-by-project basis by way of:

- selling to an investor according to pre-agreed conditions;

- selling through auctions or tenders;

- open selling of shares;

- executing a management agreement. This method of privatisation was excluded from the programme on 12 May 1995; from that moment on, the management agreement became a tool to be used when privatisation of a certain facility was considered to be unfeasible or premature.

Privatisation by auction was by open competitive bidding, where a buyer was not required to meet any specific conditions concerning the facility to be privatised, and where the title was transferred to the buyer who offered the highest price.

In a tender sale, a buyer had to meet certain requirements in respect of the facility to be privatised; requirements could include maintaining the function of the enterprise, retaining a number of jobs, financing social facilities, etc. Both commercial and investment tenders were provided for in the second stage. Commercial tenders were held through open bidding, and the buyer was the bidder who offered the highest price while complying with tender requirements. In an investment tender, state enterprises (or shares in enterprises reorganised as joint-stock companies) were sold to the buyer who put forward the best investment programme within the tender requirements.

Open sale of shares meant that these were sold to legal entities and the public on the securities market.

The second stage of the Privatisation Programme included a special section regulating the participation of foreign legal entities and physical persons in the privatisation process.

The 1995 Presidential Decree on privatisation

On 23 December 1995, The Presidential Decree On Privatisation was adopted. The Decree jettisoned previously used methods of transferring privatised assets into the ownership of the working collective, and various types of denationalisation. Privatisation was now redefined as the sale of state property only to physical persons, non-state-owned legal entities and foreign legal entities.

Facilities to be privatised included both physical state property (state enterprises and institutions as a whole, including property holdings) and state-owned shares in the charter funds of business partnerships and joint-stock companies.

The Decree also outlined the main principles of privatisation, such as openness, competitiveness and succession. Direct sale was permitted only if attempts to sell the property at auction had failed. Privatisation on a project-by-project basis was specifically provided for, again on a competitive basis.

The Decree allowed for preliminary privatisation stages by way of corporatisation of state enterprises, their lease or trust management through the selection of lessees or trustee managers, and the selling of shares through tender.

Hundreds of state enterprises were privatised on the basis of this Decree. This gave rise to many disputes concerning the violation of both the privatisation procedures and of the terms and conditions of the agreement under which the winner of a privatisation tender became owner of the privatised facility. Violations of the privatisation procedures mostly included non-compliance with tender requirements through lack of actual competition between buyers, non-conducting of the tender, and so on. Privatisation agreements were violated by both the authorised state agencies (incorrect evaluation of liabilities of the entities sold, delays in their transfer, etc) and by the buyers of the privatised facilities (breach of investment conditions, non-repayment of the entities' debts, non-attainment of contractual production figures, etc).

All this often led to conflict between foreign investors that had purchased large state enterprises through privatisation and authorised state agencies representing the Republic of Kazakhstan.

Finally, the Foreign Investment Law dated 27 December 1994 was amended (16 July 1997) to eliminate any restrictions on the participation of foreign investors in the privatisation process.

The third stage of privatisation (1999–2000)

The Privatisation Programme for 1999–2000 (third stage) makes clear that although current privatisation legislation played a positive role in the privatisation process, it nevertheless needed to be reviewed. The Programme therefore dwells upon improving the legal basis for privatisation and the management of state property. It also stresses the need to regulate the relations (such as investment relations) that were created as a result of privatisation and the transfer of state property into trust management (concession).

The Programme provides for post-privatisation monitoring of investment obligations. It notes that in the period 1995–98, many facilities were privatised through investment tenders. While the state budget received considerably less money than it was due from these sales, new owners were burdened with long-term obligations. Many investment obligations were not clearly defined in legal terms, with investments not being differentiated as the fixed or working capital of entities.

During 1999, audits of the implementation of investment and other obligations by investors who purchased privatisation facilities through investment tenders, were to be performed and were to include an economic analysis of the effectiveness of these entities (facilities). Based on the audit results, negotiations with investors would be conducted to prepare additional agreements in order to revise the original contracts.

One of the most urgent goals for the government during 1999–2000 was the ultimate settling of problems and disputes arising as a result of privatisation made in previous years. A number of entities and facilities were not privatised in full compliance with legislative requirements, including non-compliance with the principle of succession of the buyer (or seller) with respect to obligations to creditors. As a result, the number of demands and claims by legal entities and physical persons against the government is increasing, including claims by creditors of privatised enterprises and institutions.

Another problem involves the completion of coupon privatisation. Many investment privatisation funds were not able to convene general meetings of shareholders, and some funds need to solve management and asset management issues. In 1999 the government was expected to draft and submit to Parliament corresponding draft laws allowing the complete reorganisation of the investment privatisation funds into open joint-stock companies, the consolidation of their assets and the putting in place of qualified management.

Conclusion

The privatisation process is currently in a state of flux, as was highlighted by two statements in articles published in different editions of the same newpaper during 1999. The first, which appeared in *Panorama* on 2 July, stated: 'Privatisation is past its peak and has become so in an atmosphere of imperfect laws and improvident procedures of state property sales. The government's privatisation plans for the foreseeable future are rather organisational, and it is to revise fundamentally the existing privatisation legislation as well as adjust the mechanism for management of the remaining assets.' However, an article in the 10 September edition noted that privatisation was actively progressing and, in particular, 'denationalisation of the Narodny Bank and Kazaktelecom is moving along quite quickly due to the sale of a portion of the state's shareholding in these companies. The issue of privatising the state's shareholdings in the six largest oil and mining companies that have foreign participation is under discussion.'

Whether privatisation is 'past its peak' or is 'actively progressing', one thing is for sure: it will not go away.

1.9

The Banking System

HSBC Bank Kazakhstan

Introduction

After the Soviet mono-banking system that existed in Kazakhstan before independence was disbanded, a new system comprising the National Bank (the central bank) and five large state banks was introduced. In the dislocation that accompanied the break-up of the Soviet Union, more than 200 new banks were licensed between 1991 and 1993. Most of these were initially owned by state enterprises, but with the privatisation of these enterprises, the banks were also privatised. Since April 1993, Kazakhstan's banking system has been formally arranged as a two-tier system, with the National Bank of Kazakhstan (NBK) as its first tier. All other commercial banks are by definition second-tier banks.

Banking regulations

The banking industry in Kazakhstan is regulated by the Law on the National Bank and by the Law on Banks and Banking Activity, which were adopted in 1993.

In 1996 the NBK imposed new banking regulations which were designed to stabilise the banking sector and provide favourable conditions for the development of the financial market as a whole. To achieve this, the authorities introduced strict capital adequacy and liquidity norms. Consequently, more than half of the 200 banks operating in 1995 have been closed or have merged with other banks. Further consolidation was expected, and this may finally result in only 55–60 banks being in business by the end of 2000.

The strict division between commercial and investment banks was eased in 1997. The most significant restrictions imposed by the banking regulations concern:

- the upper limit of foreign banking capital (the aggregate registered charter fund of banks with foreign participation may not exceed 50 per cent of the aggregate registered charter fund of all banks in Kazakhstan);
- the origin of foreign investment in banking capital (money laundering issue);
- the qualification requirements of top executives in commercial banks and financial institutions;
- the standard BIS (Bank for International Settlements) prudential regulations;
- the limitations to investing in non-banking institutions;
- securities trading.

The NBK has introduced new capital adequacy requirements according to the BIS standard of 8–12 per cent risk-adjusted limits with a minimum capital of KZT1 billion (US$7.6 million). According to this, commercial banks are divided into two groups: the first group was to meet international standards by the end of 1998, while the second group was to achieve this by the end of 2000. In addition to capital adequacy, banks are required to maintain certain standards regarding asset quality, portfolio diversification, management qualification, accounting standards and protection of information.

All banking activities, including accepting of deposits, maintenance of correspondent accounts, cash operations, money transfers, foreign currency operations and lending are subject to licensing. Only the NBK has the right to grant licences for banking activity.

Local payments

The retail payments between banks in Kazakhstan are channelled through Interbank Payment Centre (IPC), an electronic network linking all second-tier banks. This network accounts for most of the daily interbank transfers. While IPC is a separate legal entity, it is supervised and controlled by the NBK.

There is no cheque clearing system in Kazakhstan. Cheque books issued by commercial banks are used by corporate customers only for cash withdrawal.

For international transfers Kazakhstan's banks use SWIFT (Society for Worldwide Interbank Financial Transmission) and their network of correspondent accounts.

The National Bank of Kazakhstan

According to the Law on the National Bank of the Republic of Kazakhstan the NBK bears the entire responsibility for the operation of the monetary system, and represents Kazakhstan's interests in its relations with central banks and the financial institutions of foreign countries. The NBK is a state-owned bank and an independent legal entity, capitalised at KZT20 billion. The NBK regulates banking activity in Kazakhstan, issues licences for banking operations and prudential requirements which are binding on all second-tier banks.

In 1998 the NBK pursued a rigid monetary policy. The money supply was regulated by means of refunding rates, reserve requirements and open market operations. For the financial market 1998 was a difficult year, characterised by high devaluation expectations caused by the financial crisis in neighbouring Russia. Excessive demand for US dollars put an upward pressure on the market interest rate. However, the NBK managed to preserve stability on the financial market and provide relative stability for the national currency.

In April 1999, the NBK and the government adopted a free floating exchange rate regime as the policy most likely to enhance foreign trade and protect its official reserves. The NBK will continue to follow a strict monetary policy aiming for low inflation and currency stability. Marginal monetary aggregates will be used as the main control tool.

Banks

As of 1 July, 1999, 71 banks were operating in Kazakhstan. Of these, 23 have some form of foreign participation, including HSBC, Citibank, Société Genérale and ABN AMRO Bank. The value of the commercial banks' assets was estimated at KZT247.8 billion (US$1.88 billion) as at June 1999. At the same time the total equity capital of second-tier banks amounted to KZT72.8 billion (US$552 million).

Among local banks, three dominate: Halyk Savings Bank of Kazakhstan, Kazkommertsbank and BankTuranAlem. As at 30 June 1999, these represented about 58 per cent of all banking assets in the country.

Halyk Savings Bank of Kazakhstan (Halyk) is the successor to Sberbank (Savings Bank) of the Soviet Union. The Government of Kazakhstan owns 80.04 per cent of the bank's shares. Halyk has the largest market presence and the advantage of a large retail deposit base, and it holds 67 per cent of individual retail deposits and 30 per cent of corporate deposits throughout its network of some 181 branches around Kazakhstan. Halyk is the second largest bank in Kazakhstan measured in terms of assets, and has plans to make an offering of minority 'blue-chip' sales.

Kazkommertsbank (KKB) is the largest in terms of assets and the leading private commercial bank in Kazakhstan. With its headquarters in Almaty, KKB has 15 branches throughout the country. In July 1997 KKB became the first company in Kazakhstan to make an international share offering by issuing 28 per cent of its share capital in the form of American depository shares. This raised US$50 million and effectively doubled its capital. KKB is also involved in different programmes with the European Bank for Reconstruction and Development (EBRD) and the Asian Development Bank (ADB) whereby the bank receives long-term financing for specific types of projects. The International Finance Corporation has provided KKB with a US$10 million seven-year loan and has undertaken to arrange a US$20 million syndicated loan in the future.

BankTuranAlem (BTA) was formed in order to reorganise and restructure the business operations of Turanbank (industrial construction) and Alem Bank (attraction of foreign investments under government guarantees). The bank is among the largest in Kazakhstan in retail banking operations. In July 1999 BTA received a short-term loan from a syndicate of nine international banks, including ING Barings and American Express, to finance a US$13.5 million cotton export project. The International Finance Corporation (IFC) is expected to provide an additional US$15 million over a seven-year period and simultaneously to purchase a US$5 million option to participate in the bank's equity.

The banking system and foreign capital

Foreign banks in Kazakhstan may operate representative offices, subsidiaries and joint ventures. Banks with foreign participation are defined as banks in which a third or more of the shares are owned or managed by a non-resident entity. A foreign bank must maintain a representative office in Kazakhstan for one year before being entitled to open an operating subsidiary.

The liberalisation of Kazakhstan's economy has resulted in an increase in the number of foreign banks. As at 1 January 1999, the share of foreign capital in the cumulative registered authorised capital of banks amounted to 28.9 per cent.

At the time of writing, four international banks offer banking services in Kazakhstan. In 1998 two foreign banks, Société Générale and Citibank, established 100 per cent-owned subsidiaries in Almaty. ABN AMRO Bank Kazakhstan, in which the ABN AMRO Group holds 51 per cent, has operated since 1994. In early 1999 HSBC established a 100 per cent-owned subsidiary bank in Almaty.

1.10

Capital Markets

Grigori A Marchenko, President, Deutsche Bank Securities (Kazakhstan)

It is essential to remember that in Kazakhstan the development of capital markets is important not only in itself but also as an integral part of a three-pronged strategy developed in 1996 and consisting of capital markets' development, pension system reform and completion of privatisation. Privatisation was to be carried out through sales by tender to strategic investors and complemented by sales of significant minority state-owned stakes through the stock market.

The main objectives of this strategy were:

- to augment privatisation transparency by first tendering off majority blocks of shares to strategic investors and then gradually selling off remaining government-owned shares through the stock exchange ('blue chip privatisation');

- to maximise fiscal revenues from privatisation and to use a major part of these to cover the solidarity pension system deficit that had been created by a transfer of a share of mandatory contributions to the accumulative pension system;

- to personalise pension savings and to provide a strong link between personal pension contributions and personal pension benefits;

- to create a new class of national institutional investors, represented by private pension funds and pension asset management companies, that will invest pension savings and provide for a greater stability of local capital markets;

- to develop a life insurance market and, in the first instance, an introduction of annuity products, which provide for the best option of after-retirement support;

- to create a legal, institutional and technical infrastructure to support viable capital markets; to create solvent demand for paper by attracting foreign and domestic investors and to provide a primary supply of paper through sales of government-owned shares;

- to attract sizeable funds of foreign direct investment (FDI) from both strategic investors and portfolio investors, who would invest in the equities and debt instruments of local companies through capital markets;

- to improve the transparency of financial statements and the quality of disclosure by local companies by converting their accounts to new Kazakh accounting standards, which are IAS compatible, conducting audits with one of the 'big five' companies and going through proper listing procedures;

- to issue novel financial instruments, ie corporate and municipal bonds, mortgage-backed securities, etc that will allow investor portfolio diversification and the mobilisation of financial resources to new segments of the financial system;

- to lengthen the yield curve (increasing issue maturities) and deepen the government securities market.

Private pension funds, through their asset managers, would be significant and increasingly important institutional investors in capital markets, including corporate stock and bond and government securities markets and in municipal and mortgage-backed bond markets, if and when they develop. At the same time, privatisation revenues both from tender sales and through IPOs would be used to cover a deficit in the old solidarity or pay-as-you-go (PAYG) system. The deficit developed as a result of switching to a three-pillar pension system starting 1 January 1998 with part of the mandatory contributions being channelled to funded or accumulative pension funds. Using privatisation proceeds to pay pension benefits makes sense on several counts; for instance, it could provide more support for reforms as well as bring a feeling of social justice. Also, privatisation revenues could be viewed as being a windfall, or extraordinary gains for the government, because of the switch from the old economic system to a market economy, and expenses to support the pension benefits payments could be viewed as extraordinary expenses because of this transition. So a government of the day could just balance extraordinary gains and benefits through consecutive budgets. However, privatisation revenues are only a medium-term solution and eventually oil and gas revenues should play an increasing role in funding the PAYG system or the first pillar.

The stock market

After three pieces of securities legislation were adopted by Parliament in March 1997, and were followed by several new regulations outlined by the National Securities Commission (NSC), the legal and regulatory infrastructure was almost complete but for a new company law. This last piece of legislation was only introduced to Parliament in April 1998 and adopted in July 1998, though its draft, developed with the assistance of United States Agency for International Development (USAID)-sponsored lawyers, was ready in July 1997. The new company law is important as it introduced a whole range of shareholder protection features that, although fairly common in Anglo-Saxon jurisdictions, were rarely used in CIS (Commonwealth of Independent States) countries. These features include the fiduciary responsibilities of board members, cumulative voting, a limit to asset transfers without shareholders' consent, etc. The new law could also be instrumental in starting a corporate bonds market, as it simplifies their issue and introduces a notion of convertible bonds. Another important feature was the introduction of a private placement tier for qualified investors.

The technical infrastructure of the stock market is arguably the best in the CIS as it includes a Kazakhstan stock exchange (KSE) with appropriate listing requirements, a central depository owned by banks and brokers, and a number of independent registrars licensed by the NSC. Furthermore, shares are handled in a dematerialised form, broker-dealers and custodians can act as nominee owners for their clients and the settlements system as a whole fulfils the Group of 30 recommendations, including T+3 settlement, DVP (delivery versus payment) principle, etc. The new law also includes the requirement that shares of public companies should be kept with a central registrar connected with the central depository, which would even further simplify the system and cut overall transaction costs.

There are several broker-dealer companies present on the market that are very eager to trade either on behalf of clients or for the benefit of their own business. Since the end of 1996, broker activities have become exclusive and a brokerage can no longer be involved in other business. Capital requirements have also been increased twice already and in order to have a first category licence, which enables a broker to act as a nominee owner for clients, a company must now have at least US$250,000 or equivalent in own capital. The NSC regulates brokers.

The demand for shares exists – there were several investment funds established offshore for Central Asia, with overall capitalisation of over US$400 million and with Kazakhstan as the major country; these are still not fully invested in. Compared with other regions, the Asian flu epidemic of autumn 1998 had little effect on demand as money is locked in these funds for a fixed period and the country's leverage in general is very low. There are also local banks that have expressed an interest in buying equity though they are allowed to invest only in shares of listed companies and only to a certain limit. Another source of demand is private clients and, provided that there are proper asset management services offered, there is an interesting possibility of raising money from these in the medium term.

Given that an adequate infrastructure is in place and that there is a demand, it is basically only because of a lack of tradable securities on the market that the volume of trading has not picked up. There are presently only six companies listed 'A' on the KSE and this is inadequate, especially given that almost none of these companies' stock is traded locally. KKB (Kazkommertsbank) and Kaztelecom stocks are mostly traded abroad through their ADR/GDR programmes, and other companies, mostly owned by strategic investors, offer a minimal amount of free float.

The securities market

As for fixed income measures, the government securities market is by far the most developed. It has been in existence since April 1994, when the first auction for three-month T-bills was conducted. The market developed steadily until the end of 1998, when it was affected by the Russian crisis. The Ministry of Finance (MoF) preferred not to accept higher yields, which market participants were demanding and, as a result the outstanding amount of paper contracted significantly. In the middle of 1998 there were about US$420 million–worth of tenge-denominated 3-, 6- and12-month paper, a small amount of 2-year bonds and about US$450 million-worth of 10-year bonds, which had been converted from a direct debt of the MoF to a direct debt of the National Bank of Kazakhstan (NBK) and were barely traded. By the end of the year the outstanding amount of short-term paper had contracted to US$350 million.

A further blow was delivered after the devaluation of the tenge in April 1998, when population deposits in banks and pension fund holdings were protected but other investors were not. Also, devaluation of the tenge coupled with the Russian crisis has resulted in the government securities market contracting considerably in US dollar terms. Overall, tenge-dominated measures are not very popular because of the persistent fear of further devaluation.

There was a first issue of municipal bonds at the end of July 1999, when Mangistau province successfully placed KZT400 Mio on the market. Several other provinces were interested in doing the same but declined to do so after the introduction of amendments to the Tax Code, under which it appeared that this type of paper would lose its tax-free status. Future prospects in this area are unclear.

As for corporate bonds, current tax legislation hardly allows for their development.

The First Time Visitor

ABN AMRO

Planning

Welcome to Kazakhstan. If you are reading this you are probably packing your bags and wondering what else you might need to take with you to make your business trip a success. The FSU Republic, CIS Independent Republic, or Stan or any other politically correct name you might have heard in reference to Kazakhstan, is an interesting and potentially rich place to visit for business.

Funds

- **Cash** Crisp new US dollar bills (only those printed after 1990); if you have brought used bills, don't worry, but you might have to pay a commission when changing to local currency. Be sure to declare every single penny when arriving in the country or you will have to pay a fine. *No more* than US$3,000 in cash is allowed – any more will be subject to an extra tax.

- **Traveller's cheques** Not many places accept them, so you will be cashing them in a local bank. Be ready to pay a slightly higher commission than you are used to paying in other parts of the world.

- **Wire transfer** You can wire money (maximum US$3,000, as per local regulations) for your benefit to one of the international banks, by giving your name and passport number. Again, be ready to pay a commission when withdrawing these funds in US dollars; however, you will save on the security.

- **Entry visa** Be sure to have an entry visa before arriving in Almaty, as the visa regulations have changed and it is now no longer easy to get one upon arrival. You will require a letter of invitation from a company in Kazakhstan, to which and you will be required to forward your passport details. It will then assist you by sending the invitation letter to the Kazakh embassy in the country where you will be collecting your visa.

On arrival

- **Transportation** If you have not made any arrangements for an airport pick up and do not see a transfer bus to one of the two five-star hotels, get ready to pay. Taxi drivers will try to pick up your bags (assist) and will shout Taxi really loud. Stay calm, avoid any hassle and ask the last driver you see to drive you to the hotel where you have made reservations. Hopefully, you will have arranged for an interpreter or a local partner to meet you at the hotel the next day. If need be, either of the five star hotels can organise an interpreter for you.

- **Accommodation** There are now several hotels to choose from including the Hyatt Regency Rahat Palace Hotel (five-star), the Regent Ankara Hotel (five-star), the Astana Hotel (three-star) and the Ambassador Hotel (three-star).

- **Ovir** If you are staying for more than three days, you are required to register with the Ovir office; this can be organised through the hotels. If you do not register you may have trouble when leaving the country.

Working

Let's say you have done your homework as far as the business you want to conduct in Kazakhstan and you now need to open a bank account to be able to operate there.

Opening a private account

To open a private account you must have the following:

- A local tax ID. This does not mean that you will have to pay local taxes, but for statistical purposes you will need to register. A tax ID number will be given to you without any difficulty if you are planning to stay in the country for more than six months. You will have to take this certificate with you to the bank to open an account.

- A copy of your passport.

- Bank documents, which will be provided when you visit a bank.

Opening a corporate account

To open a corporate account you must have the following:

- Your company's Article of Association, translated into Russian and notarised in your country and in Kazakhstan.

- A Registration Certificate from the Judiciary Ministry. Yes, you must register your company in Kazakhstan before you can do anything. For a large fee, one of the top five international legal/audit firms will help. For a smaller fee and just as good service, you could use a local company. For a relatively small fee or for a free service, one of the non-profit-making organisations can guide you through the local bureaucracy.

- A tax ID, which can be obtained from your neighbourhood tax authority.

- Bank documents.

Living

Now you are ready to live and work in Kazakhstan.

A first word of advice. Save all the paper receipts and documents that you might think are insignificant today – they will be your lifesavers tomorrow.

Appreciate the local customs and traditions; try to learn some local key words or phrases. Don't say no to a drink, but also know your limit, as the vodka is strong. Be ready to try some exotic foods – the national dish is horsemeat! Many deals are done after office hours and in the local pubs.

Now good luck and prosperity in Kazakhstan!

Part 2

Market Potential

Natural Resources

The Kazakhstan Investment Promotion Centre

Introduction

Kazakhstan has a colossal amount of natural and geographic promise. It is one of the few states in the world to boast substantial deposits of both minerals and raw materials, 99 elements having been recognised in its subsoil.

The raw materials base of the Republic is emphasised by the large number of gas- and oil-fields and by the large variety of mineral resources. At the present time, 493 fields are known and these contain 1,225 kinds of minerals. In terms of the reserves of uranium, chromium, lead and zinc, the Republic is ranked second in the world; in terms of manganese, it is ranked third, and in terms of copper it is ranked fifth. It is one of the leading ten countries of the world for reserves of coal, iron and gold; and it ranks twelfth, thirteenth and seventeenth, respectively, for reserves of gas, oil and aluminium.

In terms of material wealth Kazakhstan ranks first among the CIS (Commonwealth of Independent States) countries in reserves of chromic ores and lead (equal to 97 per cent and 38 per cent of all CIS reserves), second in oil, silver, copper, manganese, zinc, nickel and raw phosphor, and third in gas, coal, gold and tin.

The gross value of explored (categories $A+B+C_1$) and provisionally estimated (category C_2) material wealth of Kazakhstan in subsoil, amounts to over US$2 trillion. Their mineable value is US$1.1 trillion. The total product of both the mineral and natural resources of the Republic accounts for 57.6 per cent of Kazakhstan's total industrial product, including 20.2 per cent in respect of the oil and gas, 8.6 per cent for ferrous metallurgy and 11.6 per cent for non-ferrous metallurgy.

Geographical Distribution

The distribution of natural resources in Kazakhstan is shown in Table 2.1.1.

Table 2.1.1 Distribution of natural resources in Kazakhstan

Territory	Fields
Kazakh Small Knolls	Copper, lead, zinc, rare metals, coal, iron
Rudny Altai	Copper, lead, zinc, silver, gold, tin, rare metals
Turgaiski Depression	Iron ore, bauxites, brown coal, oil
Ambenskoye Plateau and the Mugodzhars	Chromates, copper, asbestos
Caspian Lowland and Mangyshlak	Oil, gas, mineral salts
Karatau Ridge	Phosphates, lead, zinc, and vanadium ores

Kazakhstan's output of minerals and raw materials greatly exceeds its domestic needs. Therefore, it exports up to 90 per cent of its metallic bismuth, spongy titanium, argyle, refined copper, manganese ores and concentrates; up to 80 per cent of its oil, metallic lead and zinc; and more than 50 per cent of its gas, coal, iron ore, and chromium.

Fuel and Energy Resources

Oil and gas

In terms of the amount and variety of its fuel and energy resources, Kazakhstan is ranked first in the whole of Asia.

The subsoil of the Republic contains 5 per cent of worldwide-proven (prospected) oil reserves and 2 per cent of gas reserves. Considerable reserves of oil and gas are situated within the basins of the Caspian and North Caucasian–Mangyshlak oil-and-gas-bearing provinces. In absolute figures, recoverable reserves (categories $A+B+C_1+C_2$) of oil total 3 billion tons, recoverable reserves of gas total 2 trillion cubic metres.

The outlook for oil-and-gas sector development is determined by the availability of essential undiscovered resources (categories A_1, B_2, C_3) in continental settling ponds. These are evaluated at 4.9 billion tons for oil and 5.9 trillion cubic metres for gas. The Caspian Sea, whose anticipated resources are appraised at a minimum of 10 billion tons of oil, provides the greatest potential for the sector.

Reserves of mineable categories of oil have been discovered in six oblasts of Kazakhstan; they are estimated to contain 94 per cent of national recoverable reserves of residual oil. A majority of the fields are located in four western oblasts (Atyrau, Aktyubinsk, Western Kazakhstan and Mangistau). All fields with more than 100 million tons of recoverable reserves of oil and 98 per cent of developed fields are located in these oblasts.

As for the rest of the country, industrial aggregations of oil have been detected in the Karaganda oblast (Kumkol field) and in the Kyzyl-Orda oblast. The overall reserves of oil in these oblasts equal 144.9 million tons.

In the Zhambyl and Southern Kazakhstan oblasts six shallow fields of hydrocarbon gas with considerable nitrogen and helium content have been explored.

Coal

Kazakhstan has considerable explored reserves of coal, equal to 31.8 billion tons (3 per cent of world reserves). Most of the reserves (67 per cent) are anthracites and hard coal. The prognostic resources are evaluated at 89.8 billion tons.

Many coalfields are situated within the Karaganda, Kostanai, Akmola, Pavlodar and Eastern Kazakhstan oblasts. The Karaganda basin (area 3,000 sq km) is by area and reserves inferior to the Donetsk, Kuznetsk and Pechora basins, though the presence of metallurgical coals confers great economic value upon it.

The potential recoverable value of both the fuel and energy fields is US$685.6 billion for coal and US$222.5 billion for oil. If Kazakhstan were to mine 140–150 million tons of coal per year, it would have enough commercial reserves to last 135 years (with 197 years of actual mining). The value of annually extracted coal averages US$3.341 billion. With today's rate of oil recovery standing at 19.6 million tonnes per annum, the lifetime of recoverable oil reserves is 113 years, providing an annual extraction value of US$1.96 billion. At current levels of mineral mining and processing, the value of annual recoverable reserves, for basic kinds of minerals, is assessed at US$7.7 billion.

Uranium

Kazakhstan boasts 15 per cent of world reserves of uranium and the prognostic resources are estimated to equal 600,000 tons. By official experts' estimations, the proven reserves are 469,700 tons, including 456,000 tons where the cost of mining is less than US$80 per kg. The majority of the reserves can be explored by applying advanced procedures of in-situ leaching. To date, 53 fields have been explored in all and 13 of these account for 82 per cent of Kazakhstan's national reserves.

Metal Minerals

All types of metals are present in Kazakhstan and over 60 elements are mined from the ores of metal minerals found there.

The total potential recoverable value of noble, non-ferrous and ferrous metals to be worked over the next 15–20 years is appraised at US$245.7 billion, or US$2.4 billion per year. Operating expenditures are evaluated at US$160–180 billion, and the potential bulk profit is rated at US$50–67 billion – provided that the mining sector attracts sufficient investment.

Kazakhstan has a powerful raw materials base for its ferrous metallurgy. In terms of quantity and quality, it can fully cater for both today's and the future's need of industry.

The country's known reserves of iron ores are 9.1 billion tons (4 per cent of world reserves), 40 per cent of which are easily dressable or require no dressing. Estimated resources of iron ores are evaluated at 15.4 billion tonnes. The average content of iron in the ores is 38.9 per cent.

To date, 29 fields have been explored. Commercial deposits of ferrous and manganese ores are found in Kostanai, Zhezkazgan, Karaganda and Shymkent oblasts. The majority (75 per cent) of the reserves are situated in four unique fields: the Aiatski iron-ore basin, the Lisakovskoye field, the Kacharskoye field and the Sokolovskoye field.

The Republic possesses 426 million tons of known reserves of manganese ores (8 per cent of world reserves), but undiscovered reserves are estimated at 519 million tons. The average content of manganese in the ores is 20.5 per cent. Nevertheless, an overwhelming 93 per cent of the reserves is considered to be competitive.

These reserves of manganese ores are massed in nine fields, the largest being the Zapadny Karazhal field embodying 67 per cent of national reserves.

Kazakhstan has a large base of chromium ores. Known reserves are 319 million tons (21 per cent of world reserves), but undiscovered reserves are estimated at 761 million tons. The quality of the ores is very high, the average content of Cr_2O_3 being 50.3 per cent. More than 60 per cent of the reserves are embodied in the Almaz-Zhemchuzhina field, which is unique in terms of its scale.

Despite the fact that a majority of the reserves can only be realised by underground quarrying, practically all reserves are competitive, and the outlook for development of these resources is very positive.

Kazakhstan also has considerable reserves of non-ferrous metals: copper, lead, zinc and aluminium.

Copper reserves equal 6 per cent of world reserves. There are 83 explored industrial deposits in the country, among which copper-porphyritics dominate (39 per cent of reserves). There are also substantial fields of cuprous sandstones (30 per cent of reserves) and copper sulphide (13 per cent of reserves). The largest copper fields are the Zhezkazgan, the Aktogai and the Aidarly. They contain 47 per cent of national reserves. The average content of copper in these fields is 0.68 per cent.

The prospects for the non-ferrous sector are governed by the presence of large undiscovered reserves of copper, which exceed the discovered ones by several-fold.

The current raw materials base of the lead–zinc industry of Kazakhstan is represented by considerable discovered lead and zinc, reserves accounting, respectively, for 12 and 14 per cent of world reserves.

The majority of the reserves of lead (78 per cent) and zinc (86 per cent) are combined in a group of complex deposits. The largest fields are Zhairemskoye and Shalkiya, which overall account for 28 per cent of the Republic's lead reserves and 33 per cent of its zinc reserves.

The average content of metals in the ores is rather low: 1.39 per cent for lead, 3.28 per cent for zinc.

The outlook for the lead–zinc raw materials base depends on the search for and exploration of new competitive fields within areas that have already been favourably appraised.

The explored reserves of bauxites – the basic aluminium mineral in Kazakhstan – are significant. However, they have a low content of alum earth (34.8 per cent) since they are substantially high-carbonate ores.

Kazakhstan also has large explored reserves of gold, the majority of which (69 per cent) are found in 127 bedrock gold-ore fields. Two of these fields Vasilkovskoye and Bakyrchik, store almost one-third of all national gold reserves, making them unique in terms of scope. Forty extraction plants account for 30 per cent of the reserves.

The average content of gold in gold ores mined in the Republic averages approximately 6 grammes per ton and by this index, Kazakhstan is inferior to only a few countries. However, only 41 per cent of the ores are easily dressable. Also, in some of the fields, gold is an associated component and the average content is only 0.12 grammes per ton.

Outlook

Private sector investment in mineral extraction is constantly rising. In 1992, 99 per cent of explorations were funded from the public purse and only 1 per cent by private investment. By contrast, in the period 1996–98 the share of public funding has been reduced to 2 per cent, and the share of private investment has grown to 96 per cent (including 85 per cent from foreign investors).

Against this background the level of foreign investment in the national mining sector has also grown. In 1998, total investment in this sector was US$3,674 million , of which 77 per cent was foreign investment.

Thus, investors in Kazakhstan are still attracted by the high quality of Kazakhstan's mineral resources, the most important of which is oil, then coal, copper, iron, lead, zinc, and gold. Half of the known reserves of iron ore and copper, 37 per cent of bauxites, 20 per cent of lead and zinc, 12 per cent of gold, 11 per cent of gas, 4 per cent of oil and manganese are ready for exploration.

Considerable investment is required in many multimetal deposits (Obruchevskoye, Strezhanskoye, Novo-Leninogorskoye), as well as in copper fields (Aktogai, Aidarly, Karachiginskoye, 50 Let Oktyabrya, Priorskoye), tin fields (Syrymbet), balsas (Kumdykol), bauxite fields (Tuansorskoye), uranium fields (Suluchekinskoye), gold fields (Gagarinskoye, Sarytas, Igilik, Betbastau, Zhosabai), silver fields (Pavlovskoye), and rare-earth metals fields (Akhmetkino, Verkhneye Kairakty).

2.2

Metallurgy

The Kazakhstan Investment Promotion Centre

Non-ferrous metallurgy

In the Republic of Kazakhstan, 50 elements of the Mendeleev table are produced from extracted ores and the final products comprise metals, alloys and chemical products including refined copper and lead, zinc, titanium, magnesium, rare metals, rare-earth elements and their compounds, rolled copper and lead.

The main branches of the non-ferrous metallurgy sector in Kazakhstan are copper, lead and zinc and, more recently, aluminium, titanium and magnesium. Each of these branches is of interstate importance and is represented by opencast mines, pit mines and ore processing plants, which sometimes are combined under the ownership of different groups of enterprises. This organisational form of non-ferrous metals production in Kazakhstan is related to the low content of pure metal – from 1 per cent up to 5–6 per cent, and scattered metals – even less than 1 per cent. Therefore ores of non-ferrous metals undergo repeated dressing and only then are concentrates with high metal contents produced. Usually ore contains some useful components, each derived separately through different operations, depending on the complex processing of the raw materials.

Kazchrome JSC, Aluminium Kazakhstan JSC, the Shymkent lead plant, Balkhashmys JSC, and the Kazakhmys corporation are the industry leaders. The products of these companies have frequently been accepted as the standard at the London non-ferrous metals exchange.

In the non-ferrous metallurgy sector it is vital to ensure the development of a raw material base, to deepen processing, to diversify the nomenclature of products, to continue realisation of the 'Gold of Kazakhstan' programme and to keep and expand Kazakhstan's position in the world market.

The main development directions of the non-ferrous metallurgy industry include the:

- development of a steady market (both domestic and international);
- restoration of the raw material base of the country, which has rich internal resources;
- creation of a system of enterprises involving independent manufacturers and the organisation of independent business operations;
- maintenance of a reliable power supply – essential for such power-intensive industries;
- maintenance of a rational ratio between raw materials and manufactured products;
- development of measures to prevent environmental pollution.

Copper production

Kazakhstan possesses significant deposits of copper; it is the third ranked country in the world, according to the size of its proven reserves. There are reserves of ore for approximately 30–40 years, allowing an increase in the metal output in the near future of up to 400,000 tons annually. In 1990 about 38.5 million tons of copper ore were extracted; in 1997, 31.4 million tons and in 1998, 31 million tons. This decrease was related largely to the transition of the country to a market economy, as well as to the use of obsolete equipment that could not be used to full capacity. The largest volume (462,000 tons) of copper was produced in 1988. The manufacture of refined copper in 1997 totalled 301,000 tons, and in 1998 325,000 tons. The financial, economic and property crisis within the markets of Asia has negatively affected the industrial output of Kazakhstan, including copper production.

During 1997 and at the beginning of 1998 Kazakhstan produced 2.2 per cent of the total world demand for copper among the main (50) manufacturing countries. Copper occupies almost 10 per cent of the value and 47 per cent of the total sales volume of Kazakhstan's non-ferrous metal exports.

Copper-mining is mostly based in two regions: North Pribalhashye and Betpakdala. There are two big mining and smelting combines in these regions. In addition, there are some copper-containing polymetal deposits and metallurgical plants in Rudnyi Altai. Large copper deposits such as in Zhezkazgan and Kounrad have been exploited for many years. The copper industry of the Republic mainly produces blister copper, whereas the integrated facilities at Zhezkazgan and Balkhash produce cathode and refined copper. Almost 100 per cent of all refined copper is processed into bronze, brass and copper-nickel products.

The Kazakhmys Corporation, now managed by the South Korean company Samsung, is one of the largest producers of copper and metallurgy within Kazakhstan and the Commonwealth of Independent States (CIS). In 1997 Kazakhmys produced 99.7 per cent of Kazakhstan's total volume of refined copper. In 1998 about 324,500 tons of refined and 336,000 tons of blister copper was manufactured; that is, respectively, 7.8 per cent and 8.3 per cent more than in 1997. The joint-stock company Zhezkazgantsvetmet, the main facility of Balkhashmys JSC and others are included in the corporation's structure.

Apart from Kazakhmys the other largest copper producers in the country include the Zhezkentskii ore dressing and East Kazakhstan copper-chemical combines.

Lead and zinc production

The lead and zinc or polymetal industry is based in the east and south of Kazakhstan. The oldest centre of this industry, Leninogorsk, and the newest, Ust-Kamenogorsk, are in Altai. They use lead and zinc concentrates from local dressing factories. In the country's southern regions the Shymkent lead plant operates using ores from the Karatau deposits. The important centres of the polymetal industry are Tekely in the mountains of Dzhungarskii and Alatau and Zhairem in central Kazakhstan.

The extraction of lead and zinc ores is carried out by ten organisations: Leninogorskii, Irtyshskii, Achisaiskii polymetal mining combines; Zhezkentskii, Zhairemskii, Karagailinskii, Akchatauskii ore mining combine, the Zyryanovsk lead processing combine, the Tekely lead and zinc dressing combine and the East Kazakhstan copper-chemical combine.

Concentrates are processed at the Shymkent lead plant, Ust-Kamenogorsk lead and zinc combine, and Zyryanovsk lead combine.

Bauxite-mining and the aluminium industry

Currently there is no complete cycle for the production of aluminium. There are two bauxite-mining enterprises – Turgaiskoye and Krasnooktyabrskoye in Kostanai oblast. The Pavlodar aluminium factory produces alumina from bauxite and ships it to Russia and non-CIS countries for processing into aluminium.

Gold-mining industry

Gold-mining enterprises that are purely concerned with the extraction of gold deposits in Kazakhstan provide about 65 per cent of the total gold output. The remaining share is produced by enterprises from the lead and copper industries, as an associated product.

In the first half of 1998, 8,866 kg of refined gold were produced, equivalent to only 92 per cent of the 1997 output. The reduction was caused by

a combination of the high production costs for gold and poor
management. Dependence on existing exploration facilities while a feasibility report was being prepared on deposits in Suzdalskoye, Mizekskoye
and other areas, contributed to the reduction in gold production and
created a shortage of ore base for both gold-mining enterprises and enterprises producing polymetal concentrates. This, coupled with a lack of
investment in the processing industry, means that the majority of
companies are facing the possibility of a production shutdown.

Table 2.2.1 Main indicators of performance in the non-ferrous metallurgy
sector*

Indicators	*1994*	*1995*	*1996*	*1997*	*1998*
1. Number of enterprises	48	61	66	98	
2. Output (US$ million)	482.7	895.4	999.3	1,312.4	1,084.0
3. Volume index of output as percentage of previous year	77.2	103.8	103.6	13.8	110.6
4. Production of selected metal products					
Baryte concentrates (000s tons)	90	83	94	31	9
Alumina (000s tons)	822	1,025	1,084	1,094	1,085
Extraction of copper ore (000s tons)	25,276	21,592	22,026	31,382	31,043
Copper concentrates (000s tons)	725	686	764	1,188	1,264
Molybdenum concentrate (tons)	18	156	44	81	100
Lead (000s tons)	138	89	67	82	92
Zinc (000s tons)	173	169	170	189	242
Metallic cadmium (tons)	1,097	794	567	745	1,463
Refined gold (kg)	10,444	10,921	10,300	9,659	8,866
Refined silver (000s kg)	408	371	414	390	536
Bauxite (000s tons)	2,584	3,319	3,346	3,416	3,437
Refined copper (000s tons)	279	256	267	301	325

*   At the National Bank's rate on 1 February 1999 (85 tenge/US$)

Ferrous metallurgy

Ferrous metallurgy is a rather young branch of heavy industry in
Kazakhstan. It is represented by enterprises involved in both complete
and partial production cycles. The main products of this sector are cast
iron, steel products and ferro-alloys.

The largest enterprise in the ferrous metallurgy sector of the Republic is
the Karaganda metallurgical combine in Temirtau. It combines two
factories – a complete production cycle using delivered concentrates from
Kostanai oblast, and a partial production cycle using scrap metals. The
combine manufacturers cast iron, steel pipes, rails and thin-sheet iron.

An important branch of Kazakhstan's ferrous metallurgy industry is the production and dressing of iron ores at the Sokolovsko-Sarbaiskii, Lisakovskii and Kacharskii mining and dressing combines in Kostanai oblast.

Ferro-alloy factories in Aktyubinsk and Ermak are involved in the production of quality ferrous metallurgy products. The first of these uses chromium from Chromtau and produces ferro-chromium, the second uses imported quartz from the Urals and manufactures ferro-silicon.

The main objectives of the ferrous metallurgy sector are the:

- maintenance of ore production capacities;

- development of new capacity and the reduction in production delays.

The ferrous metallurgy sector accounted for 5.1 per cent of the total volume of Kazakhstan's 1998 industrial output.

Table 2.2.2 Main indicators of performance in the ferrous metallurgy sector*

Indicators	1994	1995	1996	1997	1998
1. Number of enterprises	37	47	43	53	
2. Output (US$ million)	477	1,055	908	1,139	482
3. Volume index of output as percentage of previous year	71	112	83	125	87
4. Production of selected products					
Steel (000s tons)	2,969	3,027	3,217	3,880	3,122
Extraction of iron ore (000s tons)	10,521	14,902	12,975	13,133	
Rolled ferrous metals (000s tons)	2,357	2,153	2,288	3,030	2,557
Cast iron (000s tons)	2,435	2,530	2,536	3,089	25,942
Sheet and tinplate with coating (000s tons)	125	222	126	126	115
Ferro-alloys (000s tons)	650	809	607	843	

* At the National Bank's rate on 1 February 1999 (85 tenge/US$)

2.3

Overview of the Petroleum Industry

Ernst & Young

A brief history

For foreign investors, the upstream oil and gas industry is the most significant part of the economy of Kazakhstan. It accounts for the largest part of an estimated US$12 billion of foreign investment in the country. Current oil production is in the region of 500,000 barrels per day.

At independence in 1992, Kazakhstan already had a developed upstream oil and gas sector. However, independence exacerbated a number of serious challenges to this sector of the economy through, for example, a shortage of funds and technology to develop the existing hydrocarbons, to transport them to market and to identify new deposits. Even prior to the collapse of the USSR, the government of the Kazakh Soviet Socialist Republic had been seeking out western investors to help overcome these challenges, seeing hydrocarbons as the key to the development of its economy.

The first large deal to be completed after independence was the purchase of a 50 per cent interest in the Tengiz oil field by Chevron in April 1993. Not all negotiations were so speedy. Although British Gas and Agip have participated in the Karachaganak field since 1992, it was only in late 1997 that the Karachaganak consortium (by then including Texaco and LukOil) finally concluded a production-sharing agreement (PSA) with the Republic.

Potentially, the most significant transaction to be concluded by the government is the PSA covering the most promising parts of the north Caspian. While this was signed in November 1997, a consortium of western oil companies had been exploring offshore since 1994. The fruits of this extensive seismic data acquisition programme include the identification of the Kashagan East structure, estimated to be three times the size of Tengiz, which itself is one of the largest hydrocarbon fields in the world. At the time of writing, the consortium had recently started drilling its first well on Kashagan East. The result of this will have a major impact on the petroleum industry in Kazakhstan. The discovery of a large oil field would give a tremendous boost to Kazakhstan's economy, which has recently been flagging under the pressure of lower oil prices, economic uncertainty brought on by the crisis in Russia and in the Far East, some disappointing exploration results in the region and by the continuing delay in resolving the issue of new export routes.

In addition to these three major projects many other oil and gas companies are active in the upstream sector in Kazakhstan. These have predominantly been the large US and European companies, though there has been some interest from independents and from Chinese, Russian, Japanese and Indonesian investors.

The status of the Caspian Sea

A large proportion of Kazakhstan's anticipated hydrocarbon reserves lie under the Caspian Sea; the legal status of the Sea is therefore a key issue facing the oil and gas industry.

A 1921 treaty between Persia (now Iran) and the newly created USSR split the Caspian between both countries, but the breakup of the Soviet Union in 1991 created new states and uncertainty over the division. The potential for dispute is, of course, significantly increased by competition for any hydrocarbons that may lie under the seabed.

Today, five countries border on the Caspian Sea. Three of these, Kazakhstan, Russia and Azerbaijan, have (or hope to have) significant offshore hydrocarbon reserves. The other two, Iran and Turkmenistan do not (though Turkmenistan has laid claim to fields also claimed by Azerbaijan).

There is not yet a consensus regarding the treatment of the Caspian, although Russia and Kazakhstan signed an agreement embodying their common approach to its division in July 1998. Under this, they agreed that the seabed should be divided between the Caspian states while the surface should be under joint jurisdiction of all the Caspian countries. Iran, on the other hand, proposes the joint use of Caspian resources with a 'fair' share for all the Caspian states. Turkmenistan appears to support Iran's position, while Azerbaijan has stated that it wishes to see control of the surface divided in the same way as the seabed.

So far the disagreements over the Caspian have not significantly disrupted offshore activities in the area where Kazakhstan claims jurisdiction over the seabed. The discovery of large hydrocarbon deposits in the Kashagan East structure may have a destabilising impact on this position, however.

Oil pipelines

Because of the small market for oil and oil products in the region, long-distance transportation remains one of the key challenges facing the petroleum industry in Kazakhstan.

The existing pipeline network in the region was put in place as part of the integrated USSR oil industry. It served the needs of the planned economy but has proved a major obstacle to the development of an independently functioning oil and gas sector in Kazakhstan that looks for customers outside the Commonwealth of Independent States (CIS).

Currently, the oil fields of western Kazakhstan are linked into the Russian pipeline network via Atyrau and Samara. Russia's Transneft has imposed a limit on export of Kazakhstan crude via the existing route. As a result, the Tengiz field exports a large proportion of its production by rail and by tanker across the Caspian to link to the Azerbaijan export route to the Black Sea. Further east, fields in the Aktobe area are linked by pipeline to Russian refineries, while the refineries of eastern Kazakhstan (Pavlodar and Shymkent), have no link to western Kazakhstan's oil fields.

The major route to markets outside the CIS is the pipeline from western Kazakhstan to Samara. From there oil is transported to Novorossisk on the Black Sea. The capacity of the existing pipeline on this route is potentially a limit on Kazakhstan's production but the route's capacity will be considerably expanded by the completion of the Caspian Pipeline Consortium (CPC) route from Tengiz to Novorossisk. The partners in CPC include Russia, Kazakhoil and a number of oil companies. The construction work on this pipeline commenced in 1999; first shipment is planned in 2001.

The Novorossisk route poses two problems:

1. It perpetuates Kazakhstan's dependence on Russia, whose territory the pipeline crosses. Moreover the pipeline traverses the politically unstable regions of Chechnya and Dagestan.
2. Tankers loaded at Novorossisk must negotiate the narrow straits linking the Black Sea and the Mediterranean. This imposes a limit on the size of vessels and raises environmental concerns for Turkey.

The Republic has a clear interest in multiple export routes to avoid continued dependence on Russia or simply replacing dependence on Russia with a similar reliance on one of its neighbours. There are thus several other options under consideration:

- A link across the Caspian from Kazakhstan and/or Turkmenistan to the current and planned Azeri export routes which reach the Black Sea via Georgia. This does not avoid the Black Sea, and raises questions over the availability of capacity in the Azeri system. A future Azeri export route through Turkey to the Mediterranean at Ceyhan may make this more attractive, but the cost of such a pipeline will be significant. It will also cross areas of Turkey that are politically unstable.

- A pipeline to the Persian Gulf via Iran, or simply to the refineries of northern Iran with a swap for Iranian crude at terminals on the Gulf shore. Though one of the least expensive to construct, the status of relations between the USA and Iran have rendered this route impractical for US companies to support. In the longer term, an economic revival in the Far East may mean that this route finds sufficient backing to go ahead without US support.

- A pipeline via Afghanistan to Pakistan. This route continues to look impractical because of the political instability in Afghanistan.

- A pipeline from western Kazakhstan to western China. Because of its enormous length this project seems the most expensive option by some way. Although in July 1999 the governments of China and Kazakhstan agreed to support the project and to push for completion by 2005, less than a month later the Chinese National Petroleum Company announced that it would not proceed with the project because of the cost.

- In August 1999 the Russian pipeline monopoly Transneft announced the construction of a new pipeline capable of linking western Kazakhstan with the Gulf of Finland. It is intended that this will be ready by 2001. As this route will also be used by Russian producers, the available capacity may be low.

In addition, KazTransOil, the state-owned oil pipeline company, is understood to be considering a number of options to improve the distribution of crude within Kazakhstan to ensure the more industrial and populous east has access to oil produced in western Kazakhstan in addition to Siberian crude.

Refining and marketing

Kazakhstan has three oil refineries, located at Atyrau in the west, Shymkent in the south and Pavlodar in the north-east.

Because of the existing pipeline network, the Atryau Oil Refinery (AOR) in western Kazakhstan is the only one able to process crude from the prolific oil fields in that area. AOR, controlled by KazakhOil, suffers from a lack of recent investment, however, and is unable to process more than half of its design capacity of 450,000 tons per month. Plans for an extensive modification are being considered and interest has been expressed by

Japanese companies. The forecast cost of several hundred million US dollars suggests that the future of the refinery remains in the balance, pending the outcome of the Kashagan East well in the north Caspian.

The Shymkent Refinery was originally intended to use Siberian crude to provide the southern Kazakhstan area with gasoline and other products. The refinery was privatised in 1996. The current owners are a mixture of foreign and domestic investors. The only field in Kazakhstan to which it is linked by pipeline is the Kumkol field in the Aral Sea region; this is now the principal source of crude to the refinery. The difficult relationship between the operators of Kumkol, Hurricane Hydrocarbons of Canada, and ShNOS, the operator of the refinery, has been a regular subject of press coverage, and the possibility of a merger between these two companies has been widely discussed.

The Pavlodar Refinery is owned by the Republic and managed by CCL Oil Ltd of the US. The refinery processes crude from fields in Russia. Its annual capacity is 7.5 million tonnes of crude, though it is now operating at a significantly lower level. Product is sold in north and east Kazakhstan, where competition from illegally imported and cheaper Russian fuel has a significant impact on the refinery's market share.

Marketing of petroleum products within Kazakhstan is dominated by domestic firms. Western oil companies (Texaco, Chevron and Mobil) have established retail sites in major cities, but do not yet command a significant share of the market.

Gas

Kazakhstan has in the region of 1.8 Tcm (trillions of cubic metres) of gas reserves, 40 per cent of which is in the giant Karachaganak field in north-west Kazakhstan. The original Soviet plan was that the gas from Karachaganak would be processed in Orenburg – now in the Russian Federation – and pumped into the Soviet gas pipeline network. Following the collapse of the USSR, negotiations have been under way with Gazprom to make this plan a reality but little progress has apparently been made and the field continues to produce at significantly less than full potential.

Though significant amounts of gas are produced elsewhere in the country, particularly in the west (and flared or exported to Russia), there is a lack of transport pipelines linking the east to the west. This means that Kazakhstan continues to import the bulk of the gas it needs for domestic and industrial use in the more populous east from Turkmenistan, Uzbekistan and Russia.

The domestic and industrial market for gas mainly comprises small consumers. Collection difficulties and the country's economic problems are major inhibitors to new investment in the gas distribution infrastructure.

The role of the state

Since independence, Kazakhstan has introduced a significant amount of legislation governing foreign investment in general and the petroleum industry in particular. Subsequent chapters of this book will cover the legal and taxation aspects of petroleum operations in Kazakhstan in detail.

Legislation refers to companies engaged in hydrocarbon exploration and production activities as *subsurface users*.

The Agency of the Republic of Kazakhstan for Investment (ARKI – previously designated the State Committee on Investments) has primary responsibility for negotiating new contracts with subsurface users. In addition, new contracts undergo a specialist tax review by a department of the Ministry of Finance before they are concluded.

The legal framework

Kazakhstan's legislation establishes that the state owns mineral resources in the ground. Minerals, once extracted under the terms of an appropriate licence and contract, become the property of the subsurface user.

The two most important pieces of legislation governing subsurface use are the Subsurface Code and the Petroleum Code. The former deals with the granting of rights to use the subsurface while the latter deals in more detail with the rights and obligations of subsurface users.

One of the most important aspects of the legal framework is the availability of stabilisation. Both the Subsurface and the Petroleum Codes entitle subsurface users to protection from subsequent changes in laws that would worsen their position. Such stabilisation is also available under the Foreign Investment Law and, specifically for tax purposes, the Tax Law.

Taxation

The current Tax Law was introduced in July 1995 and has specific rules for upstream oil and gas activities. Two bases for taxing hydrocarbon are envisaged. The first is production sharing, based on well-established international models. The alternative is a contract without any allocation of production to the state, but that includes a potentially higher tax burden. In both cases the tax regime is specified in detail in the contract and normally closely based on the Tax Law as it stood on the date the contract came into effect. The legislative framework limits the availability of tax concessions, though it may be possible to negotiate favourable tax rules in practice, particularly in the case of large projects. There is normally a specific provision giving some measure of stability to the tax rules written into the subsurface user's contract.

Tax law changes frequently in Kazakhstan: as of August 1999 there have been no less than 29 sets of amendments since the current Tax Law was enacted. For this reason the operation of the tax stability clauses means that there is great variation in the tax rules applying to subsurface users' contracts. For foreign companies this significantly complicates the process of investing in existing hydrocarbon projects.

The role of KazakhOil

KazakhOil National Oil and Gas Company (KazakhOil) was formed in March 1997 in order to act as a vehicle for the Republic's interests in oil and gas projects in Kazakhstan. It now plays a central role in the country's petroleum industry. Previously, responsibility for the Republic's hydro-carbon resources was split between the Ministry of Oil and Gas and Kazakhstanmunaigaz. The establishment of KazakhOil was designed to streamline the process of privatisation and assist in securing foreign partners for future oil and gas deals. KazakhOil represents Kazakhstan's interests in major domestic projects including the North Caspian Consortium, the Uzen and Tengiz fields and the CPC pipeline project. It also holds the Republic's stake in the Atyrau Oil Refinery. KazakhOil subsidiaries produce a significant proportion of the total oil production of Kazakhstan.

In November 1998 the government announced that KazakhOil would have a guaranteed 25 per cent interest in new oil and gas projects, appearing to guarantee it a critical role in the future of the oil and gas industry in the Republic. In late 1998 the 14.3 per cent stake in the North Caspian Consortium held by KazakhOil on behalf of the Republic was sold to Phillips of the US and the Japanese oil company Inpex.

2.4

Oil and Gas: Dynamics and Logistics

Russell W. Lambert, Managing Partner,
PricewaterhouseCoopers

Although Kazakhstan has a diverse economy, it is the petroleum industry that has attracted most attention from foreign investors. Currently, the petroleum industry comprises only a part of Kazakhstan's economy but, with its enormous potential reserves, this sector holds the largest and most immediate prospect for generating hard currency earnings from exports.

Introduction

During the Communist period, decisions affecting every aspect of Kazakhstan's economy were made in Moscow. As a result, development within the Republic was often stimulated by the needs of other parts of the USSR. This is exemplified by the presence of oil refineries, metals smelters and processing plants in Kazakhstan that were designed to process materials from Russia.

Historically, several problems have been identified in the Kazakhstan hydrocarbon infrastructure, primarily involving its technical capabilities. As a result, Kazakhstan's oil industry depends heavily on other CIS (Commonwealth of Independent States) republics, and particularly Russia, for its operational capabilities, including the ability to maintain and provide spare parts for the production facilities and pipelines.

Recent years have considerably reduced the impact of these problems through the increased interest by western companies in Caspian resources. Although this interest waned in the latter part of 1998 because of the Russian crisis and fluctuating level of worldwide oil prices, most large western oil companies consider their investment in Kazakhstan as long term and have not significantly decreased their initial investment projections.

Indeed, as the recent ripple effect on Kazakhstan's economy will attest, Russia will continue to exert influence on oil development and expansion activities in the Republic for years to come because of Kazakhstan's landlocked position and its continued reliance on Russia for a variety of natural resources and consumer goods. The other Central Asian republics also depend largely on Russia for energy supplies and will, no doubt, closely monitor the future direction of the Kazakhstan oil industry as an indication of their options for the early part of this century. If the Kazakhstan government can facilitate new pipeline development or major refurbishment of the existing system, and if western companies continue to fund investment in Kazakhstan to increase shareholder value, the country may become one of the most attractive in the world for foreign investment and technological assistance in the oil industry.

Industry overview

Kazakhstan is one of the most promising (and problematic) of the world's petroleum provinces that remain to be developed. However, it is land-locked. For its oil to reach international markets on a regular basis, this oil must be piped either through Russia to the Black Sea or, through Iran to the Persian Gulf, or through the Caucasus to reach Turkey. Other routes have been considered through Uzbekistan and Afghanistan or through China to Pakistan and the Indian Ocean, but all of these have two common characteristics: they are expensive and time-consuming.

Following this is the question of political stability in Kazakhstan or, more precisely, of legal stability. While President Nazarbayev firmly controls the political process in Kazakhstan, there is still much public debate over how resources should be developed and what price should be exacted for them by the government.

KazakhOil – the national oil and gas company

KazakhOil's primary function is to represent the state's interest in organ-isations engaged in hydrocarbon exploration, production, transportation and refining, as well as in production-sharing agreements (PSAs). KazakhOil also participates in tenders for hydrocarbon exploration and production contracts on behalf of the government and handles the marketing and sale of hydrocarbons on behalf of the state. Probably the largest task that KazakhOil faces is to govern the redevelopment and restructuring of the oil and gas industry in Kazakhstan.

Oil prices

Average export prices from Kazakhstan to countries outside the CIS do not tend to differ significantly from the world crude oil market. However, average domestic prices in Kazakhstan are below the world market.

Average export prices to CIS countries lie in between the domestic price and the export price but, since autumn 1998, have become more consistent with Kazakhstan domestic prices.

Oil and gas transportation

The current export pipeline capacity of Kazakhstan is limited; the majority of pipelines pass through the Russian Federation. The Kazakhstan government and producers are, however, seeking alternative routes in an attempt to increase capacity and to reduce the dependency on export through Russia.

The existing domestic oil and gas pipelines deliver Kazakhstan crude to one of the three Kazakhstan refineries or the southern Russian refineries. They also deliver natural gas from Uzbekistan to cosmopolitan centres.

KazTransOil owns the domestic pipeline system and is 100 per cent owned by KazakhOil. Transportation through Kazakhstan for Kazakhstan oil producers is provided by this entity and is overseen by the Kazakhstan Ministry of Energy, Industry, and Trade. Quotas for access to the Russian pipelines are adjusted quarterly, based on the amount of oil produced. Oil quality is also controlled. Producers frequently experience problems due to limited access to and reliability of the pipelines.

A small percentage of oil is also transported by rail, road and water (by barge).

Pipeline tariffs

Tariffs for transportation of hydrocarbons in Kazakhstan are set by KazTransOil, and approved by joint resolution of the Government Committee for Regulation of Natural Monopolies and Development of Competition, and the Ministry of Energy, Industry and Trade. Tariff rates in Kazakhstan for oil and gas transportation mainly depend upon three factors: logistics costs, tariffs for power energy, and the interest rate on bank credits. Significant changes in any of these factors may cause tariff rates to be amended.

During 1998, tariff rates in Kazakhstan rose, on average, slightly for pipeline transportation. Since then, however, various factors, including the Russian crisis and the declining price of oil, having come to the fore, the Ministry of Energy has stated that it has no intention to increase tariffs in the near future.

Refineries

There are three refineries in Kazakhstan: the Shymkent refinery in the south, primarily servicing the Kumkol field; the Atyrau refinery in the north-west, servicing the Tengiz and other western fields; and Pavlodar in the north-east, handling mostly Russian crude. These refineries operate below capacity, with available capacity limited due to outdated technology and lack of capital for maintenance. Total production of the three Kazakhstan refineries amounted to 8.4 million tons in 1998, down almost 10 per cent from 1997.

Domestic petroleum usage

Despite reform policies implemented since the dissolution of the Soviet Union, the Kazakhstan economy continues to contract. The difficult economic conditions over the past few years have resulted in reduced domestic demand for many goods and services, including crude oil and refined products.

Kazakhstan was affected by the Asian crisis and decreased investment from that region. Interestingly, however, the impact of the Russian crisis was not as severe as expected, although the full effect may not yet be realised.

Petroleum sector regulations

The Subsurface Users Law and the Law Concerning Petroleum Operations are the main documents setting out fundamentals for petroleum exploration and production in Kazakhstan. The basis for any operation related to subsurface use is a subsurface use contract, concluded between a subsurface user and the state, generally represented by the appropriate state body. Although there are no restrictions with regard to the type of subsurface use contract, production-sharing agreements and hydrocarbon contracts are more common.

Chapter 21 of the current Tax Code sets out specific provisions concerning the taxation of subsurface users.

Licensing requirements

Operations related to subsurface use are subject to licensing. Obtaining a licence is a precondition for negotiating with the government provisions of the future subsurface use contract.

Environment

Under the Soviet system there was extensive environmental degradation and pollution in Kazakhstan. Soviet plans to develop the country's vast resources led to the adoption of ecologically unsound and wasteful processes for their extraction. As a result, Kazakhstan suffers from significant air and water pollution.

On the whole, Kazakhstan has a fairly strong environmental movement, which has been successful in encouraging the government to adopt legislation to protect the environment. It is expected that environmental issues will become an increasingly important consideration in the economy's development.

SHH

SALANS HERTZFELD & HEILBRONN

Our Almaty office focuses on energy and natural resources, industrial and infrastructure projects, and financings, providing a full range of legal services for foreign investors and financial institutions.

For further information please contact :

ALMATY
AIGOUL KENJEBAYEVA
TEL: 7 3272 582 380
FAX: 7 3272 582 381

LONDON
ROBERT STARR
TEL: 44 20 7509 6000
FAX: 44 20 7726 6191

NEW YORK
GLEN KOLLEENY
TEL: 1 212 632 5500
FAX: 1 212 632 5555

PARIS
JAMES HOGAN
TEL: 33 1 42 68 48 00
FAX: 33 1 42 68 15 45 / 46

www.salans.com

LONDON PARIS NEW YORK WARSAW MOSCOW ST. PETERSBURG KYIV ALMATY BAKU

Oil and Gas: Industry Legislation

James E Hogan, Aigoul Kenjebayeva and Donald K Blackwell, Salans Hertzfeld & Heilbronn

Introduction

The principal pieces of legislation governing petroleum operations in the Republic of Kazakhstan are the Petroleum Law[1] and the Subsoil Code.[2] Both the Petroleum Law and Subsoil Code were amended in the late summer of 1999, in a manner significantly changing the regime for granting rights for the use of the subsoil in conducting oil and gas operations.

The Subsoil Code and Petroleum Law

The Subsoil Code, which relates both to hydrocarbons and to other subsoil resources, is the principal legislation applicable to the granting of subsoil rights in the Republic of Kazakhstan. It establishes that the subsoil, including minerals in their underground state, are state property, while minerals that are brought to the surface belong to the subsoil user, unless otherwise provided by the applicable contract.

Subsoil use rights

Pursuant to the Subsoil Code, the government maintains the primary role in defining the overall rules and procedures by which subsoil rights are granted and exercised. The government-appointed 'competent body', currently the Agency of the Republic of Kazakhstan on Investments, is responsible for negotiations with the subsoil user over the terms of the subsoil rights to be granted and for the conclusion of a contract setting forth those terms. Local government bodies are responsible for issues connected with the granting of surface rights to subsoil users, as well as for ensuring compliance with ecological requirements. They are also charged with granting subsoil use rights with respect to 'minerals of widespread general use', such as sand, clay and gravel.

The contracting process

Subsoil use rights were formerly granted on the basis of both a licence and contract. Following the new amendments the licensing scheme has been abolished and, henceforth, subsoil use rights will become effective upon the conclusion of a contract with the competent body. Existing licences will continue in effect according to their terms. The Subsoil Code concentrates upon the contracting and subsoil rights aspects of a hydrocarbon project, while the Petroleum Law emphasises the specific rights and obligations of subsoil users in the conduct of petroleum operations.

The process begins with the establishment by the government of an annual list of subsoil blocks to be submitted for open or closed investment tenders. Parties that wish to participate in the tender process may submit an application to the competent body. The terms for conducting open tenders are then published, and those of closed tenders communicated to potential participants. The application is considered by a commission of experts appointed by the government after payment of a tender deposit. The participants are given an opportunity to purchase geological data on the available blocks. The winner of the tender is selected on the basis of a number of criteria. These include the time period for the commencement of exploration and the intensity of exploration, the anticipated amounts of production and payments to the budget, the amount of investment, and the nature of the financing and capital investment programmes.

Oil and gas contracts may be awarded for exploration and/or production, for production sharing, and for the construction of underground facilities. The exploration contract is granted for a period of up to six years, with the possibility of up to two extensions of two years each, subject to fulfilment of the conditions of the work programme and the performance of other obligations. In the event of a discovery, the subsoil user has the right to an extension of the contract for a period necessary for appraisal of commercial potential. In the event of a commercial discovery, the holder of exploration rights has an exclusive right to negotiate a production contract with the government.

A production contract may be granted for a period of up to 25 years (40 years in the case of large deposits). The term may be extended on the basis of an application submitted no later than 12 months prior to the expiry date. An extension of a production contract is possible with the agreement of the competent body.

The Petroleum Law provides that the terms of subsoil use, including the minimum work programme, are defined in the contract by agreement of the parties. The work programme is obligatory and may only be changed by agreement with the competent body upon a showing that fulfilment of the obligations is unreasonable under the circumstances. The competent body may also insist upon changes needed to ensure compliance with good oil field practices or to avoid detrimental consequences to public health or the environment. All petroleum operations carried out in Kazakhstan are to be governed by the laws of Kazakhstan.

The competent body's approach to negotiations over each project is guided for the most part by the economics of the respective project. Accordingly, negotiations over the economic terms to apply are based upon an economic model of the project, which is prepared on the basis of input from the two sides.

The approval process

The subsoil use contract is subject to the mandatory approval of a number of governmental bodies, including the tax authorities. In addition, the competent body may, at its discretion, require an expert review prior to signing. All contracts must be registered with the competent body, which in turn issues a certificate of registration. Under the previous Law, the contract took effect upon registration. The language of the current Law, as amended, is unclear, but it appears to make the contract effective from the date of its signing.

Apart from the subsoil use contract pertaining to a given hydrocarbon project, and the specific conditions stated therein, certain additional documents must be prepared prior to the commencement of petroleum operations. These include project reports and field development plans, containing a detailed work programme completed in the prescribed form. In addition, the subsoil user must procure a state expert study on appraisal of the reserves in the relevant deposit. The subsoil user is to submit all pertinent documentation for the purpose of the required state ecological study.

Stabilisation

Both the Subsoil Code and the Petroleum Law contain stabilisation clauses stating that changes and amendments to legislation which worsen the position of the subsoil user are not applicable to contracts issued and executed before such changes and amendments. The guarantee does not extend to legislation in the areas of national defence or security or ecological safety and public health. In addition, new, related amendments to the Law on Licensing,[3] provide that all contracts issued under the prior legislative scheme remain in effect, and all matters of revocation, suspension and termination are expressly governed by the previous Law.

In addition to the Subsoil Code and the Petroleum Law, both the Tax Code[4] and the Foreign Investment Law[5] set forth their own stabilisation provisions with respect to subsoil users. The applicable provision of the Tax Code, however, is permissive in that it applies only to cases where the parties mutually consent to contract amendments. In this respect it differs from the true stabilisation provisions cited in other legislation.

The proper interaction between stabilisation provisions of the Petroleum Law, the Subsoil Code and the Foreign Investment Law, on the one hand, and those set forth in the Tax Code, on the other, is of critical concern. Kazakhstan legislation, unfortunately, offers little guidance as to the priority in the application of the differing rules that might be applied to the issue.

Rights and obligations of subsoil users

Pursuant to the Petroleum Law, the subsoil user has various stipulated rights, which include the following:

- to conduct petroleum operations on an exclusive basis (if so provided in the contract);

- to erect in the contract territory the necessary production and social facilities for the normal course of work;

- to dispose of its share of production freely, both within and outside Kazakhstan;

- to conduct on a priority basis negotiations for the extension of the contract period, as well as to waive its rights and terminate its activity in accordance with the contract.

Among the obligations of the subsoil user are the following:

- to use the most effective methods and technology for the conduct of petroleum operations, based on world standards;

- to use the contract territory solely for the purposes specified in the contract;

- to conduct such operations strictly in accordance with applicable law and to observe requirements for protection of the environment and the subsoil and for worker safety;

- to give preference to Kazakhstan personnel, as well as to engage Kazakhstan service providers and to use locally produced equipment, materials and finished products where they conform to standards and requirements;

- to observe tax obligations;

- to participate in the development of local infrastructure;

- to preserve the environment and objects of historical significance;

- to restore portions of the contract territory that were damaged as a result of petroleum operations.

The Petroleum Law provides for the mandatory application of the generally applicable currency, tax and customs legislation to the conduct of petroleum operations. This fact has virtually excluded the possibility of obtaining tax or customs duties exemptions under a contract, since both the Tax Code and the Customs Code[6] preclude such a possibility, except where such laws are specifically amended to provide for the exemption.

An additional matter of note to subsoil users is that the state has a right to requisition production from a subsoil user under certain extraordinary circumstances. In such a case, the subsoil user is entitled to receive compensation in freely convertible currency 'at world market prices in effect on the date of the requisition'. Moreover, the Republic of Kazakhstan at all times has a statutory right of first refusal to purchase production from the foreign subsoil user at world market prices.

Revocation, suspension or termination of rights

Of principal concern to the foreign investor in the hydrocarbon sector is the risk of suspension or revocation of the subsoil use rights pertaining to its project. Both the Subsoil Code and the Petroleum Law contain specific grounds on which the Kazakhstan government may unilaterally revoke, suspend or terminate subsoil use rights.

It should be emphasised that the government has not been reluctant to exercise its authority to suspend or revoke subsoil use rights in the past, both in connection with the projects of small independent companies, as well as those of prominent international petroleum companies. For this reason, extreme care should be taken by subsoil users to ensure strict compliance with the terms of a contract, particularly where minimum work obligations and investment requirements are specified.

Transfer of subsoil use rights

The Subsoil Code provides for the possibility of a transfer of a subsoil use right, but only with the permission of the competent body. Such permission must be obtained in each specific case; the granting of a general right of transfer is prohibited.

Pursuant to the Subsoil Code a subsoil right may be pledged, in which case the financing received in exchange for the pledge must be used exclusively for the subsoil use objectives set forth in the contract. However, due to the recent changes to the Law, no permission from the competent body is now necessary. It should be noted that international arbitration of disputes concerning the conclusion and performance of the contract is expressly permitted by the Petroleum Law.

The national oil company

In conjunction with a reorganisation of the Kazakhstan government in March 1997, a national oil and gas company, KazakhOil, was created. The functions of KazakhOil include:

- participation in the development of strategy on the use of production rates and further increases in resources of petroleum;

- representation of state interests in contracts with contractors conducting petroleum operations by means of mandatory share participation in contracts;

- participation in the organisation of tenders for petroleum operations;

- preparation and realisation of new projects connected with petroleum operations.

In addition, the obligations of the competent body with respect to monitoring and control over the observance of subsoil use contracts are to be conducted jointly with the state body on the use and protection of the subsoil and the national company.

Tax legislation

The Tax Code, which officially entered into force on 1 July 1995, has been amended several times. In addition to the taxes of general application, the Tax Code includes a specific section governing the taxation of subsoil users. It is provided that the tax regime to apply to subsoil users shall be defined in the subsoil use contract concluded between the subsoil user and the competent body, in the manner established under Kazakhstan legislation. However, in all cases the tax regime established by such a contract must comply with tax legislation of general application that is in effect on the date of conclusion of the contract.

The Tax Code sets out two specific models that may apply for the purposes of the tax regime under a subsoil use contract. The first simply envisages the payment by the subsoil user of all taxes of general application under Kazakhstan legislation. The second concerns the transfer of a defined share of the production of the subsoil user pursuant to a production-sharing agreement (PSA), together with the mandatory payment of the income tax on legal entities, and an extended list of other taxes.

The Tax Code provides that the value added tax applies to *all* goods, work and services, including goods, work and services imported into the territory of Kazakhstan. The Tax Code also lists special taxes and payments that apply to subsoil users, which include: (i) bonuses: signature, commercial discovery and production; (ii) a royalty; and (iii) excess profits tax. While three types of bonuses are mentioned, the question of which bonuses will apply, as well as the final amounts of the bonuses, in a given project is a matter for negotiation with the competent body on the basis of project economics.

With respect to the payment of a royalty, which is mandatory under the legislation, the Tax Code provides that it is payable in monetary form, but may temporarily be paid in kind, on the basis of an additional agreement of the parties. The Tax Code does not set forth applicable rates of royalty.

All bonuses, as well as the royalty, are deductible for the purpose of determining taxable income and excess profits tax. Loss carry forwards are permitted for subsoil users only for a maximum period of seven years. The Tax Code also expressly provides that income received from an assignment of rights under a contract is taxable in the manner provided therein.

The Tax Code also provides that all subsoil users, with the exception of those conducting activities under a PSA, are obliged to pay excess profits tax, which is assessable in all cases where the subsoil user's internal rate of return is in excess of 20 per cent. The applicable rates of excess profits tax range from 4 per cent of net profit for an internal rate of return between 20 and 24 per cent to a maximum rate of 30 per cent of net profit, where the subsoil user has an internal rate of return in excess of 30 per cent.

The Tax Code sets forth a general provision that prohibits the granting of special benefits, such as the locking in of profits tax rates in effect on the date of conclusion of the subsoil use agreement.[7]

Accordingly, any such benefits will prove to be invalid, unless they were included in a special amendment to the Tax Code itself.

Other issues

Export of production

One of the major difficulties facing foreign investors in the petroleum sector is the limited possibility for the export of hydrocarbons from Kazakhstan to foreign markets, given the country's landlocked location and inadequate pipeline infrastructure, as well as the obvious geopolitical factors. Export quotas for the transportation of oil from the existing pipelines are based on a general quota for Kazakhstan established on an annual basis by agreement with the Russian Federation.

Environmental claims

Throughout the CIS (Commonwealth of Independent States), where infrastructure is often outdated and in poor condition, and where attention to environmental protection and work safety traditionally has been inadequate, the risk of third party claims in connection with a project in Kazakhstan is a significant concern. For this reason the conduct of a thorough environmental audit before the commencement of a project is important, in order to protect the foreign investor, or its investment vehicle, from subsequent environmental claims for which it was not responsible.

The conduct of a mandatory state environmental study is a prerequisite to obtaining subsoil use rights. However, such a study will not necessarily protect a subsoil user from subsequent environmental liability.

Finally, where a subsoil user conducts offshore petroleum operations, a strict liability standard applies. The subsoil user is responsible for all damage to life and the environment, and safety, irrespective of fault.

Notes

[1] Edict of the President of Kazakhstan, having the force of law, 'On Petroleum', dated 28 June 1995, as amended, (the 'Petroleum Law').

[2] Edict of the President of Kazakhstan, having the force of law, 'On the Subsoil and Subsoil Use', dated 27 January 1996, as amended (the 'Subsoil Code').

[3] Edict of the President of the Republic of Kazakhstan, having the force of law, 'On Licensing', No 2200, dated 17 April 1995.

[4] Edict of the President of the Republic of Kazakhstan, having the force of law, 'On Taxes and Other Obligatory Payments to the Budget', dated 24 April 1995, as amended (the 'Tax Code'), Article 94–3.

[5] Law of the Republic of Kazakhstan, 'On Foreign Investment', dated 27 December 1994, as amended (the 'Foreign Investment Law').

[6] Edict of the President of the Republic of Kazakhstan, having the force of law, 'On Customs in the Republic of Kazakhstan', dated 20 July 1995 (the 'Customs Code'), Article 148.

[7] Tax Code, Article 2.4.

SALANS HERTZFELD & HEILBRONN

Salans Hertzfeld & Heilbronn is a full service international law practice with offices in Paris, New York, London, Warsaw, Moscow, St. Petersburg, Kyiv, Almaty and Baku. For more than three decades partners in the firm have been pioneers providing legal advice in the CIS and Eastern Europe. Today, a team of over 90 of our lawyers is specifically dedicated to advising clients in the region.

In Kazakhstan, Salans has been active in counselling companies, financial institutions and government entities in the legal aspects of investment, trade and finance since 1990. We officially opened the Almaty office in 1994.

Our Almaty office strives to combine detailed knowledge of Kazakh law and practice with the firms unparalleled experience elsewhere in the CIS in similar legal specializations and industries. As a result, the Almaty office works closely with lawyers in other offices of the firm on a client-by-client basis in order to deliver tailored legal services that take advantage of the expertise of all members of the firm. The office currently consists of ten lawyers plus support staff. In addition to the resident partner of our office, partners in Paris, London and Moscow support the office on a daily basis. All of the lawyers involved in our Kazakhstan practice are fluent in English and Russian, and several speak Kazakh as well.

With lawyers qualified to act on the whole spectrum of legal issues in Kazakhstan, the particular specialties of our Almaty office are:

- energy and natural resources
- foreign investment
- corporate finance and project finance
- privatization
- securities, and
- telecommunications.

Our most senior Almaty-based lawyers have extensive experience in government negotiations at the highest level.

Salans' long history of involvement in the region, the dedication of our talented, multilingual attorneys, coupled with the priority we accord our practice in the CIS and Eastern Europe, enable us to provide expert legal advice to foreign and domestic clients in Kazakhstan.

For further information about our experience and capabilities in Kazakhstan, please contact:

Aigoul Kenjebayeva
Salans Hertzfeld & Heilbronn
Ulitsa Gogolya, 86
480091 Almaty
Kazakhstan
Tel: **7.3272.582.380**
Fax: **7.3272.582.381**
Email   **akenjebayeva@salans.com**

Full details are also available on our website: **www.salans.com**

2.6

Oil and Gas: Taxation

Arthur Andersen

Subsurface use legislation

'Subsurface user' is the term used in Kazakhstani legislation to describe a
company that extracts natural resources, including oil, gas, precious
metals, precious minerals, underground water and common minerals.
Most legislation stipulating special taxes and payments does not apply to
companies extracting 'commonly occurring useful minerals', such as
sand, clay rubble, etc that are used in their natural condition or after
insignificant processing to satisfy local business needs.

Subsurface users must all individually conclude a contract with the
government of the Republic of Kazakhstan. There are two types of
contract: a production-sharing agreement (PSA) – referred to in tax
legislation as a Model 2 Contract; and a contract which does not
envision production-sharing – referred to as a Model 1 Contract. From
a tax perspective, PSAs differ from regular contracts in that PSAs
generally exempt the petroleum producer from excise tax, excess profit
tax, land tax and vehicle tax. However, under PSAs, the government
essentially becomes a carried partner of the subsurface user and a
significant portion of the output of the field is given to the government
after the payment of costs out of produced petroleum (or metals and
minerals).

Three major laws in Kazakhstan govern the economic terms established in a subsurface use contract. They are the Subsurface Use Law,[1] the
Petroleum Law,[2] and the Tax Code.[3] In the discussion that follows, we
focus mainly on the tax provisions, although certain principles, such as
economic stability, general contract terms, and licensing procedures, are
elaborated in the Subsurface Use Law and Petroleum Law.

Subsurface use contracts and their structures

Stability of the tax regime

Ordinarily, the economic terms of a subsurface use contract entered into between a subsurface user and the authorised body of the Republic of Kazakhstan will remain valid for the entire term of the contract. This includes the tax terms, which means that the Tax Code applicable to any subsurface user is the Tax Code that was in effect on a specific date referenced in the subsurface use contract (ordinarily the signing date of the subsurface use contract).

Most subsurface use contracts signed after 1 January 1996 (and any still to be negotiated) must undergo an obligatory tax expert evaluation, and must follow the Tax Code in effect on the date of signing of the contract. Subsurface use contracts signed prior to 1 January 1996, or those that implement agreements entered into prior to 1 January 1996, are not required to incorporate tax legislation effective on the date of signing of the subsurface use contract. The obligatory tax expert evaluation has traditionally been performed by a branch of the Ministry of Finance or by the Ministry of Revenue.

Ring fencing

A subsurface user comprising organisations and physical persons that conduct business under a single contract are deemed for taxation purposes to be a single taxpayer obliged to pay taxes and levies as established in the contract. Operationally, a number of methods have been used to address this requirement when multiple legal entities are partners in developing a contract area. In practice, this means that the tax base is calculated in aggregate for the companies but actual taxes may in fact be paid individually.

Subsurface users which carry on business under more than one subsurface use contract may not deduct costs incurred under one contract from revenues earned in respect of another. Each contract must be treated as a separate taxpayer for tax calculation purposes.

Establishing tax terms applicable to a subsurface user

Current legislation establishes that only subsurface use contracts may establish provisions concerning the payment of taxes and levies relating to operations on licences in the Republic of Kazakhstan. Separate agreements with the government may not do so.

General structure of a subsurface use contract

The usual provisions contained in a contract for subsurface use are as follows:

- preamble;
- definitions;
- purpose of the contract;
- validity term of the contract;
- contracted territory;
- title of ownership to property and information;
- the right of the state to acquisition and requisition of economic minerals;
- common rights and obligations of the parties;
- work programme;
- period for exploration;
- commercial discovery;
- period for extraction;
- accounting and reporting;
- measuring the minerals extracted;
- performance of subcontractual works;
- funding;
- taxes and payments;
- accounting procedures;
- insurance;
- liquidation and liquidation fund;
- protection of subsoil and environment;
- safety of population and staff;
- liabilities of parties for violation of contract provisions;
- *force majeure*;
- confidentiality;
- transfer of rights and obligations;
- applicable law;

- procedure for resolving disputes;
- guaranties for contract stability;
- terms for termination and suspension of the contract;
- language of the contract.

A contract for subsurface use will normally establish all taxes applicable to the subsurface user over the term of the contract, either directly or by way of reference to the Tax Code, in effect on the date of signing the contract.

Applicable taxes, duties, investor's bonuses, and royalties

Taxes and other obligatory payments applicable to a company exploring for, producing and selling oil and gas are as follows:

- bonuses (subscription,* commercial discovery,* production);
- the share of the product to the Republic of Kazakhstan as stipulated in a PSA;
- royalties (rates will normally be set between 1 and 20 per cent based on project economics);*
- corporate income tax (30 per cent);*
- value added tax (20 per cent);*
- customs duties (rates depend on specific item being imported);*
- excise tax (currently the excise tax on domestically produced crude oil is zero; various rates apply to domestically produced and imported petroleum products that may be needed for the exploration and production of minerals);*
- excess profit tax (rates vary from 4 per cent to 30 per cent of net profit depending on internal rate of return of contract area);*
- branch profit tax/dividend withholding tax (15 per cent unless reduced by double tax treaty);*
- personal income tax (rates vary from 5 to 30 per cent of income. The 30 per cent rate is applied to all income above approximately US$4,815);*
- tax on issue of securities (initial emission – 0.1 per cent, additional emission – 0.5 per cent of the shares' value);
- land tax;*
- property tax;*

- tax on vehicles;[*]
- fee for auction sales;
- payments for the use of water;
- payments for the use of forests (if applicable);
- payments to the Environment Protection Fund;
- social charges for local and foreign employees.

([*]For a more detailed discussion, see 'Tax terms applicable to subsurface use contracts' below.)

Negotiation of subsurface use contracts

A contract for subsurface use will be negotiated between the party wishing to explore for and produce oil and the appropriate arm of the government. Historically a subsurface user was required to bid successfully on a licence first and then negotiate a contract with the State Investment Committee. A number of organisations, including the Ministry of Finance and the Environmental Department, would have their input before the contract was signed. The terms of the contract were normally negotiated so that, based on anticipated future conditions, the subsurface user has an internal rate of return between 12 per cent and 20 per cent on the concession in question. (Recent amendments to the Subsurface Use Law changed this procedure so that a licence need not be first acquired before a contract is negotiated (the subsurface use contract, once negotiated, would establish the right to explore for and produce petroleum).

Within the IRR (Internal Rate of Return) constraints discussed above, the subsurface user and government can opt to negotiate either a PSA (Model 2) or non-PSA (Model 1) contract. A non-PSA contract will include all taxes and levies enumerated in 'Applicable taxes, duties, investor's bonuses, and royalties' above. A PSA contract, on the other hand, envisions the subsurface user taking the government as a carried partner in the contract area.

This means that the subsurface user is expected to pay all initial exploration and development costs for the contract area and subsequently recover the costs of carrying the government's interest in the contract area from the government's share of oil revenues.

A PSA contract will ordinarily not include the following taxes that are applicable to a Model 1 Contract:

- excise tax, except for the excise tax on crude oil;
- excess profit tax;

- land tax;

- property tax;

- vehicle tax;

- tax on issue of securities;

- fee on auction sale.

(NB: These last two taxes are in general not applicable to a subsurface user and therefore may be placed outside the scope of a contract for subsurface use.)

In the past, a number of different options could be negotiated that would determine the tax and other payments applicable to a specific contract; any contracts prospectively negotiated will be based on either a PSA or non-PSA contract.

The participation percentage of the government under a PSA contract will vary widely depending on how the contract is negotiated – it may be as little as 20 per cent and as much as 80 per cent – and may vary depending on production from the contract area.

All contracts to be signed between negotiating parties must undergo an obligatory tax expert evaluation (discussed under 'Stability of the tax regime' above) in accordance with the procedure defined by the Government of the Republic of Kazakhstan. This provision also applies to amendments and additions introduced into pre-existing contracts.

The agreed-upon tax regime must be included in the final text of the contract.

Tax terms applicable to subsurface use contracts

The taxes and levies listed below will normally be applied to the activities of a subsurface user under both PSA and non-PSA contracts.

As previously discussed, a Model 1 Contract envisages paying all taxes and levies established above (see 'Applicable taxes, duties, investor's bonuses, and royalties'), while a Model 2 Contract is a production sharing agreement. The law establishes that the ultimate burden of payments to the government should be equal under both. In reality, the payment burden will differ if the economics of a project are more or less favourable than those originally anticipated when the project was negotiated. In general, a production sharing agreement may give a more positive result for a field that exceeds initial expectations, while a non-PSA contract may provide a more favourable result for a field that does not.

Bonuses
Bonuses are fixed payments of subsurface users and they are paid in cash in accordance with the procedure stipulated in the subsurface use contract.

Subsurface users are expected to make two types of bonuses as established by the subsurface use contract:

- subscription bonus
- commercial discovery

In the past, many contracts established production bonuses that were payable when certain production levels were reached. These are no longer included in contracts negotiated after 1 July 1998, as the production bonuses are essentially no different from royalties, and were deleted by legislative changes.

Subscription bonus   The subscription bonus is a single fixed payment by a subsurface user for the right to carry out subsurface use, paid when a contract is signed in accordance with the following procedure established by legislation:

- Initial amounts of subscription bonuses are defined by the Government of the Republic of Kazakhstan, or by the competent body, or pursuant to the terms for conducting a tender.

- The final amount of the subscription bonus will be stipulated in the contract in relation to the economic value of the fields (terrain) that are handed over for subsurface use.

- The time of payment of the subscription bonus is determined in the subsurface use contract, or based on agreements between the parties (subsurface user and government), but no later than 30 days after the contract is signed.

- The subscription bonus will generally be from US$500,000 to US$2 million, depending on the size of the field, expected economics, etc. For exceedingly large and profitable fields the subscription bonus may be in hundreds of millions of dollars.

- In certain cases, in lieu of a subscription bonus a subsurface use contract may establish fixed expenditures on seismic work and exploration. However, if the company fails to spend the agreed amounts, then it is obliged to pay the difference between the fixed expenditures and actual expenses plus a penalty.

Commercial discovery bonus   The commercial discovery bonus is a fixed payment that is paid by subsurface users when a commercial discovery is made in the contract territory.

Under contracts for the exploration of fields of useful minerals that do not envisage subsequent production of those minerals, the commercial discovery bonus is not required.

The procedure established by legislation for calculation of the amount and deadline for the payment of commercial discovery bonus is as follows:

- The amount of any commercial discovery bonus will be established in the contract.

- Normally, a commercial discovery bonus is set at a rate of no less that 0.05 per cent of the approved (estimated) extractable deposits. In practice, the size of the bonus for an average field can be anywhere from US$500,000 per 1 million tonnes of production. For extremely large and profitable projects it can be as large as US$250 million.

- The commercial discovery bonus is due 30 days after the commencement of extraction of the oil or other minerals.

Royalties

General provisions concerning royalties   A separate royalty regime applies to each type of useful mineral produced in the contract area (ie in a field producing both natural gas and oil, each may have a different royalty rate).

Form of royalty payment   Royalties are normally expected to be paid in cash unless the contract establishes payment in kind. Cash royalty payments will usually be calculated by multiplying the production by a discounted benchmark price.

Setting royalties on hydrocarbons   Royalties are calculated on the value of the produced output of hydrocarbons. This value is calculated on the basis of the average selling price of the hydrocarbons in the reporting period, without indirect taxes, reduced by the actual transportation expenses to the place of sale.

In contracts for the production of hydrocarbons, royalties will be established on a sliding scale as a certain percentage, in relation to production outputs. Royalties are calculated on a cumulative basis over the life of the contract.

Royalty rates are set based on the risk of the project and complexity of exploration and production, assuming an estimated internal rate of return (IRR) range of between 12 and 20 per cent. In some cases the government may accept an IRR of greater than 20 per cent when setting royalty rates. This will depend on a number of factors, risk and complexity being foremost.

Table 2.6.1 represents a rough rule of thumb for royalty rates, based on the expected volumes of extracted hydrocarbons. Higher royalty rates may be set if there are other positive economic factors.

Table 2.6.1 Royalty rates, based on expected volumes of extracted hydrocarbons

Value of produced hydrocarbons on the contract territory (million tonnes)	Royalty rates for the contract %
To 0.5	1–5
0.5–2	3–8
2–20	6–10
20–40	8–12
40–130	10–20
130 and more	17 and up

Royalty payment procedure   Royalties must generally be calculated and paid monthly. Royalty calculations must be submitted before the tenth day of the month following the reporting month, and must be paid by the fifteenth day of the month following the reporting month.

Land tax
Land tax varies from US$0.01 to US$526.3 per hectare depending on land quality and purpose.

Tax on vehicles
Most vehicles are subject to tax according to established rates. Tax on vehicles is paid annually and computed as a percentage of the minimum monthly computation index. The monthly computation index currently equals 715 tenge or US$5.2. The tax ranges from US$25 to US$750 per year depending on the size of engine.

Corporate income tax
The corporate income tax rate is 30 per cent of taxable income.

Deductions   The following deductions are allowed in computing corporate income tax:

- All expenses associated with generating revenue.

- Statutory payments (ie payments to the government of amounts other than taxes).

- Interest expense.

- Reserves for site remediation and clean up. (The terms for site remediation are established in the subsurface use contract. Whereas in the past oil and gas companies were required to make contributions to a special reserve fund for site remediation and clean up, amendments to the Tax Code have changed the procedure. According to current legislation, subsurface users are now only required to reserve a certain amount of their capital for site remediation.)

- Expenditures on geological exploration and on operations conducive to extraction of natural resources. (The definition of geological studies, exploration and operations conducive to the production of useful minerals include the following: appraisal, creation of infrastructure, general and administrative expenses, and costs associated with the payment of the subscription bonus and commercial discovery bonus.

  These costs may be deducted after the commencement of production of useful minerals as though they are group 2 assets (25 per cent declining balance basis). This provision also applies to expenditures on intangible assets incurred by a taxpayer while acquiring the right to geological exploration, development, or extraction of natural resources.

  Subsurface users who wish to use state gathered geological data, may have to reimburse the state for expenses incurred by the state in conducting geological exploration. These expenses are also deductible.)

- Taxes paid, except for the taxes already excluded prior to determining aggregate annual income, income tax paid in the territory of the Republic of Kazakhstan and in any other states, and the tax on excess profit.

- Fines and penalties, except for those for late or deficient payments of taxes and obligatory payments to the government.

- Charitable contributions to the state social spheres-orphanages, handicapped organisations, and others. Only a portion of the amount donated can be deducted and the tax legislation dictates how much that will be.

- Expenditures actually incurred by a subsurface user in training Kazakhstan personnel and in the development of the social sphere of rural areas, within amounts stipulated in the subsurface use contracts.

- Losses pertaining to subsurface use contracts may be carried forward for up to seven years.

- Royalties may be deducted.

Depreciation A breakdown of depreciation rates is shown in Table 2.6.2.

Table 2.6.2 Depreciation rates of fixed assets

Group (sub-group) No.	Description of Fixed Assets	Maximum Depreciation Rate (%)
I.	*Buildings, structures*	
1.	Buildings, structures	8
II.	*Structures*	
1.	Oil and gas wells	20
2.	Oil and gas storage facilities	10
3.	Navigable water channels	10
4.	Bridges	7
5.	Dams, dam-like structures	7
6.	River and marine warf structures	7
7.	Railway tracks of enterprises	8
8.	Shore-enforcement embankment facilities	7
9.	Reservoirs, cisterns, tanks and other facilities	8
10.	Intra-business and inter-business irrigation network	7
11.	Close-circuit collector and drainage network	7
12.	Runways and landing strips, paths and parking areas of aircraft	8
13.	Park and zoo facilities	8
14.	Sports and recreation facilities	10
15.	Green houses and glass houses	10
16.	Other facilities	7
III.	*Conveyor facilities*	
1.	Devices and distribution electric grids and communication lines	10
2.	Internal gas pipelines and pipelines	8
3.	Running water, sewerage and thermal energy networks	7
4.	Other	7
IV	*Power generating machines and equipment*	
1.	Heating equipment and related technical equipment	15
2.	Turbine equipment and gas turbine installations	15
3.	Electric engines and diesel generators	10
4.	Integrated facilities	8
5.	Other power machinery and equipment (except for mobile transport)	7

Group (sub-group) No.	Description of Fixed Assets	Maximum Depreciation Rate (%)
V.	Functional machinery and equipment by type of operation (aside from mobile transport)	
1.	Machinery and equipment of chemical industry	20
2.	Machinery and equipment of chemical industry	20
3.	Machinery and equipment of the petroleum-processing and petrochemical industries	20
4.	Machinery and equipment for petroleum and gas production	15
5.	Machinery and equipment of the mining industry, including quarry self-dumping trucks with weight lifting capacity in excess of 40 tonnes	25
6.	Electronic industry equipment	20
7.	Machinery and equipment for manufacture of building materials	20
8.	Machinery and equipment for wood-processing and pulp industry	20
9.	Machinery and equipment for printing industry	15
10.	Machinery and equipment of light industry	20
11.	Equipment of food industry, fish meat and milk industry	20
12.	Machinery and equipment for retail trade and public catering	15
13.	Equipment for manufacture of transport facilities, machinery and mechanisms	20
14.	Agricultural tractors, machinery and equipment	20
15.	Machinery and equipment for casting equipment for abrasive and diamond production	20
16.	Digital electronic relay and data communication equipment, equipment of digital systems, transmission, digital analytical communications items	25
17.	Satellite, cellular, radio telephone, paging and trunking communications	15

Group (sub-group) No.	Description of Fixed Assets	Maximum Depreciation Rate (%)
18.	Analogue relay equipment for transmitting systems	10
19.	Specialized equipment of cinema studios, equipment for medical and micro-biological industry	8
20.	Machinery and equipment for other industries	10
VI.	*Other machinery and equipment (except for mobile transport)*	
1.	Industrial tractors	20
2.	Metal cutting equipment	15
3.	Compressor machinery and equipment	15
4.	Forging equipment and presses	15
5.	Pumps	20
6.	Lifting and transport, loading and unloading machinery and equipment, machinery and equipment for earth-moving, open-pit and road-construction operations	15
7.	Machinery and equipment for stilt-driving operations, crushing and milling, sorting, concentration equipment	20
8.	Machinery and equipment for underwater technological operations	20
9.	Machinery and equipment for electric welding and cutting	10
10.	All types of tanks for technological processes	8
11.	Other machinery and equipment	10
VII.	*Mobile transport*	
1.	Railway rolling stock	15
2.	Marine, river fleet, fleet of fishery industry	10
3.	Rolling stock of automobile transport, business transport (except for passenger cars and taxis)	10
4.	Passenger cars and taxis	7
5.	Main pipelines	15
6.	Public transport	10
7.	Aviation transport	15
8.	Other transport facilities	7

Group (sub-group) No.	Description of Fixed Assets	Maximum Depreciation Rate (%)
VIII.	Computers, peripheral devices and equipment for data processing	
1.	Computers	30
2.	Peripheral devices and equipment for data processing	20
IX.	Fixed assets not included into other groups	
1.	International plantations	8
2.	Intangible assets	15
3.	Office furniture	10
4.	Tools, productive and auxiliary items and accessories	8
5.	Copying equipment	15
6.	Analytical and regulating instruments and devices, laboratory equipment	10

Value added tax

Oil sold in the territory of Kazakhstan is subject to 20 per cent value added tax (VAT). Export of crude oil is subject to zero rated VAT; however, exports to other CIS (Commonwealth of Independent States) countries, except for Kyrgyzstan, Moldova and Azerbaijan, are not considered exports and are subject to 20 per cent VAT.

Imports of goods and equipment are subject to 20 per cent import VAT, except for the import of certain foodstuffs. The government has also established a list of certain goods and equipment that may be imported pursuant to a special procedure that effectively results in no import VAT being paid. Some oil and gas equipment is included on this list.

Customs duties

Article 149.15 of the Customs Code provides that goods imported under subsurface use contracts to be used for 'petroleum operations' are exempt from customs duties, except for a customs clearance fee of 0.2 per cent of the goods' customs value.

For goods which are not imported for the needs of subsurface users, customs duties will normally apply at rates ranging from 5 to 30 per cent. The import of most oil and gas equipment will be subject to customs duties between 5 and 10 per cent. Equipment imported for exploration activities will often be exempt from customs duties.

The customs legislation provides for a temporary import regime that in general exempts goods and equipment from customs duties, import VAT and excise taxes, in the event these goods and equipment will be re-exported.

Excise tax/road use tax on petroleum product production or importation
Previously, crude oil was subject to excise tax at the moment of sale or at the moment of transfer to a processing facility. Domestically produced crude oil is currently exempt from excise tax.

Table 2.6.3 shows rates of excise tax and road use tax that apply to domestically produced and imported petroleum and petroleum products.

Table 2.6.3 Excise tax and road use tax rates for domestically produced and imported petroleum and petroleum products

Product	Excise tax per ton			
	Domestically produced		Imported	
	Euros	US$	Euros	US$
Petrol	64	68	133	141
Diesel fuel	6	6.3	88	93
Crude oil, including condensed gas	0	0	15	16

Property tax
Property tax is calculated as 1 per cent of the value of depreciable assets other than vehicles and land. The value of assets is determined by the tax legislation.

Personal income tax
The following rules are applicable

- Individual income tax is a progressive tax that ranges from 5 per cent on income of up to US$916 to 30 per cent for income in excess of approximately US$3,971.

- Individuals working in Kazakhstan for more than 183 days in any consecutive 12-month period are deemed to be residents of Kazakhstan and are taxed on their worldwide income.

- Individuals staying in Kazakhstan for more than 30 but less than 183 days in any consecutive 12-month period are liable for taxes on their Kazakhstan source income.

- Individuals working in Kazakhstan for less than 30 days in a 12-month period and earning less than US$2,648 are not subject to Kazakhstan income tax.

However, if an individual is a resident of a country with which Kazakhstan has signed a double tax treaty, tie-breaker provisions may be applied and an individual may be subject only to tax on his Kazakh source income or not taxed at all in Kazakhstan.

Under domestic legislation, the employer must make payments of certain social taxes and payments for its local and foreign employees. The responsibility for payments of social taxes rests with the employer. The total amount of social taxes is 32.5 per cent of each local employee's gross salary. Different rates apply to foreign employees.

Excess profit tax

Subsurface users who do not operate under a production sharing contract or under contracts are subject to excess profit tax in accordance with the procedure below and at the rates shown in Table 2.6.4. (NB: Older PSA-type contracts may also incorporate provisions similar to the excess profit tax.)

The tax base and the procedure for the calculation of excess profit tax

Excess profit tax is levied on subsurface users that receive an internal rate of return in excess of 20 per cent in a tax year. All profits of the subsurface user in that year, not merely the 'excess', will be subject to excess profit tax.

Table 2.6.4 Excess profit tax rates

Internal rate of return (IRR) (%)	Rates of excess profit tax (% of net)
Less or equal to 20	0
More than 20 but less or equal to 22	4
More than 22 but less or equal to 24	8
More than 24 but less or equal to 26	12
More than 26 but less or equal to 28	18
More than 28 but less or equal to 30	24
More than 30	30

Procedure for calculating IRR for the purposes of calculation of excess profit tax

The IRR calculation is based on annual cash flows adjusted for inflation in compliance with procedures established by the Ministry of Finance of the Republic of Kazakhstan.

The annual cash flow of a subsurface user is determined as the difference between annual gross revenue and expenses attributable to the particular contract.

The amount of annual gross revenue for a contract is determined according to the tax legislation of the Republic of Kazakhstan.

Expenses incurred by a subsurface user in the reporting year on a contract include:

- capital expenses;
- expenses deducted according to the tax legislation, except for depreciation and interest payments;
- income taxes and taxes on dividends for the reporting year, as well as excess profit tax assessed for the year preceding the reporting year.

However, certain contracts may provide for a different methodology of IRR calculation.

Adjustments for inflation of annual cash flows are made from the second year after operations are launched.

Branch profits tax

In addition to corporate income tax, the permanent establishment of a foreign legal entity is subject to a branch profits tax of 15 per cent, levied on net income after corporate income tax.

Double tax treaties may reduce the amount of branch profits tax to as little as 5 per cent. However, subsurface use contracts concluded after a double tax treaty has been signed usually take into account the reduced branch profits tax rate in arriving at the estimated internal rate of return of the parties. A contract may also contain clauses prohibiting a subsurface user from taking advantage of a double tax treaty signed after the contract has been negotiated.

Notes

1. Edict of the President of the Republic of Kazakhstan, having the force of Law, 'Concerning the Subsurface and its Utilisation' of 27 January 1996.
2. Edict No 2350 of the President of the Republic of Kazakhstan, having the force of Law, 'Concerning Petroleum' of 28 June 1995.
3. Edict No 2235 of the President of the Republic of Kazakhstan, having the force of Law, 'Concerning Taxes and Other Obligatory Payments to the Budget' of 24 April 1995.

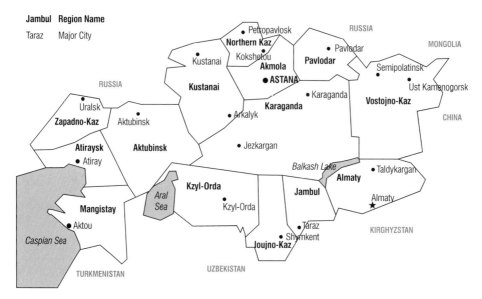

Figure 2.6.1 Kazakhstan – Its regions and major cities

Oil and Gas: Pipeline Transport

The Kazakhstan Investment Promotion Centre

Oil pipelines

Background

In Kazakhstan there are more than 6,000 km of main oil pipelines, 1,000 km of subsidiary oil pipelines and 3,400 km of main water ducts.

When opening up oil fields in Kazakhstan with the involvement of foreign investors, a paramount priority is the building of export pipelines. These are necessary to provide an outlet for Kazakhstan's oil into international markets, to reduce transportation costs to a competitive price and to enhance the reliability of the transport system.

Currently, Kazakhstan exports most of its oil via the Atyrau–Samara pipeline. Based on the estimation of crude oil production volume between the period 2000 and 2005, the throughput capacity of the oil transport system will be insufficient. This situation will deteriorate further over the period 2010–15, when the production levels are expected to reach 100–140 million tons.

The Ministry of Power, Industry and Trade has identified the projected priority export routes for oil pipelines in the following order:

1. Atyrau–Samara;
2. Tengiz–Novorossiysk (Caspian Pipeline Consortium);
3. Trans-Caspian;
4. Kazakhstan–China;
5. Kazakhstan–Iran;
6. Trans-Asian.

Atyrau–Samara

The possibilities for oil exports along the Atyrau–Samara pipeline are restricted by its throughput capacity and by the quota set by Russia. This is a constraining factor for the growth of both crude oil production and export supplies. To increase the throughput capacity from 10 to 15 million tons per year, a series of technical measures in Kazakhstan and Russia must be taken at a total cost of US$22 million. The Russian institute, GIPROTRUBOPROVOD, is currently preparing a feasibility report for the project.

Tengiz–Novorossiysk (Caspian Pipeline Consortium)

The Caspian Pipeline Consortium's (CPC's) oil export pipeline project is the short-term priority westward. This project ensures an independent outlet for Kazakhstan's oil exports to Novorossiysk on the Black Sea and opens up good opportunities for the attraction of foreign investments in the oil-and-gas sector of the national economy. The necessary CTC Agreements of the project participants have already been signed and project operations initiated. The commissioning of the pipeline is scheduled to take place in 2000.

The CPC pipeline route to the Black Sea has only one negative factor – a possible limitation, by Turkey, on the passage of oil tankers via the Bosphorus due to the possible ecological threat that they pose. (Estimates related to this project are shown in Table 2.7.1.)

Trans-Caspian

Planned to follow a route through the Black Sea to Turkey, the Trans-Caspian oil pipeline project is considered to be a priority.

The pipeline will stretch from western Kazakhstan to an outlet on the Mediterranean (the Turkish port of Ceihan) via the Caspian Sea. The territory of Azerbaijan, Georgia and Turkey create risks for the project related to the complicated mountainous terrain and water barriers and the need to cross zones where conflict is taking place. (Estimates relating to this project are shown in Table 2.7.1.)

Kazakhstan-China

From 2004 on, as a result of the development of the fields in the Kazakhstan section of the Caspian shelf, the volume of crude oil production will increase. The export oil pipeline of the CPC alone cannot resolve the problem related to the efficient transportation of oil from this hydrocarbon-rich region. Preliminary engineering and economic calculations have shown that transportation eastward to China is a promising and economically favourable project. The Kazakhstan–China oil pipeline project can, simultaneously, meet Kazakhstan's national security interests and provide an outlet to a large market with a growing demand for oil.

The pipeline will pass over the territory of Kazakhstan, and China will guarantee the project funding. The downside of the project is that the People's Republic of China can potentially control the price paid for the oil. (Estimates relating to this project are shown in Table 2.7.1.)

Kazakhstan–Iran

The Kazakhstan–Iran pipeline provides another possible export route to the south. However severe competition from OPEC countries can bring about a reduction in the price paid for oil from the Persian Gulf. Consequently, a reduced load on the pipeline may occur at some time in the future due to the low profitability of oil sales in that market. No terms for investment mobilisation for this project have yet been defined. (Estimates related to this project are shown in Table 2.7.1.)

Trans-Asian

The Trans-Asian pipeline via Kazakhstan, Turkmenistan, Afghanistan and Pakistan to an outlet in the Arabian Sea is highly risky in a political sense, due to the fact that it passes over the territory of Afghanistan. Currently, consideration is being given to the basic question of how the funding will be organised for the project. (Estimates related to this project are shown in Table 2.7.1.)

Table 2.7.1 Estimates related to proposed oil pipeline projects in Kazakhstan

Project	Cost (US$ million)	Length (Km)	Diameter (mm)	Capacity million tons/year
Tengiz-Novorossiysk	2,700	1,500	1,000	50
Trans-Caspian	4,000	2,536	800–1,067	50
Kazakhstan–China	2,650	2,900	500–1,000	40
Kazakhstan–Iran	2,700	2,511	800	25
Trans-Asian	4,300	1,500	1,020	50

Provision of the following conditions is necessary when engaging financial market resources to fund the proposed projects:

- a good financial reputation of the enterprises involved;
- provision of the indispensable minimum load of the oil pipeline;
- conformity of transportation rates to international standards as well as some indication of their predictability and competitiveness.

The basic purpose of the strategic plan for Kazakhstan's oil pipeline system development is to create a multi-vector system of export oil pipelines.

Gas-transport system

For the time being, gas is supplied to 8 of the 14 oblasts of the Republic – Western Kazakhstan, Atyrau, Mangistau, Aktyubinsk, Kostanai, Almaty, Zhambyl and Southern Kazakhstan. About 60 per cent of this gas is spent on energy needs.

The 'Contract of Concession of Interior and International Gas-Transport Systems and Business Activities' was concluded between the Kazakhstan government and the Belgian company Tractebel on 14 June 1997. Under the terms of this contract, the assets of the gas-transport system of Kazakhgaz JSC, Alaugaz JSC, Batystransgaz JSC and its affiliated joint-stock companies: Uralsktransgaz, Aktautransgaz, Zhaiktransgaz, Aktobetransgaz, Kazenergoremont, Gaztelecom, and Kazintergaz were leased to Tractebel for a period of 15 years.

Responsibility for restructuring the debts of these joint-stock companies, ie the repayment of debts, the return of accounts receivable and the settlement of the mutual accounts between creditors and debtors was assigned to Aktsept-Profil Ltd. This was undertaken according to the 'Contract for the Right of Control, Use and Management of State-Owned Stockholding of Batystransgaz JSC and State-Owned Stockholdings of Affiliated Joint-Stock Companies of Uralstransgaz, Aktautransgaz, Zhaiktransgaz, Aktobetransgaz, Kazenergoremont, Gaztelecom, Kazintergaz, Alaugaz JSC, Assets and Liabilities of Kazgaz SHC and the State-Owned Enterprise of Kostanaitransgaz'.

Following the enactment by the Kazakhstan government of the Law 'On Measures to Create a State-Owned Gas-Supply Network in the Southern Regions of the Country', the functions of selling gas to consumers were assigned to Energotsentr-ES-Kazakhstan. This is a state-owned company that has received assets previously held under state ownership, ie the high, medium and low-pressure gas conduits and relevant structures in them were handed over to joint-stock companies for gas facilities in the Southern Kazakhstan, Zhambyl, Atyrau, Almaty, Mangistau, and Kostanai oblasts.

State regulation of the gas-transport rates along local gas conduits was maintained during 1998.

Gas conduits

Despite the huge extractable reserves of gas (more than 2 trillion cubic metres), Kazakhstan imports more than 75 per cent of its needs, ie about

8 billion cubic metres of gas per year, from Russia, Uzbekistan and Turkmenistan. This situation arises due to the deficiency of the gas-processing facilities in the Karachaganak gas field and the geographic remoteness of gas-producing regions from the consuming centres. The building and commissioning of new gas mains will solve the problem of supplying gas to those regions in need of natural gas. The Ministry of Power, Industry and Trade has identified the gas transportation projects shown in Table 2.7.2 as priorities:

Table 2.7.2 Priority gas transportation projects

Projected gas conduits	Cost (US$ million)*	Length (km)	Diameter (mm)	MM of KG
1. Aksai-Akmola	1,093	1,777	1,000	12.7
Aksai-Krasniy Oktyabr (VECO-Engineers)	626	475	1,000	4.7/12.7
Krasniy Oktyabr-Kostanai (OKEAN and ENRON)	355.1	543	1,000	10.7
Kostanai–Kokshetau	263	461	1,000	10.7
Kokshetau–Akmola	128	293	1,000	10.7
2. Chelkar–Shymkent	575	1,111	1,000	5
3. Bukhara gas-bearing region of Almaty (circumvention of Kirghizia)	28.5	152	1,000	Up to 5
4. Bukhara gas-bearing region of Almaty	30	20	1,000	Up to 5

* At the National Bank's conversion rate on 1 February 1999 (KZT85/US$1)

2.8

Agriculture

The Kazakhstan Investment Promotion Centre

Introduction

Kazakhstan is a major producer of marketable grain, meat and wool; thus the agricultural sector is one of the key elements of the economy. Farmland occupies more than 220 million hectares (74 per cent of the country's total area), of which 185.7 million hectares (68 per cent of all farmland) is pasture and 13–14 million hectares is used for growing grain. Individuals, collective farms and organisations utilise 81 per cent of all farmland and 98 per cent of all pastures.

Agricultural sector reform

Based upon the successful experience of several other countries, Kazakhstan has embarked upon a strategy of restructuring (through the establishment of new corporate entities and privatisation) that will help to create a strong, privately owned agricultural sector. Thus the Farming Law provides the following rights:

- private ownership of property (land, real estate);
- free separation of land and property from collective farming in order to establish private farms;
- protection from the illegal expropriation of property;
- freedom of choice concerning the type of agricultural activity followed and production operations;
- equal access to markets, materials, information and finance.

Measures undertaken under the strategy include the following:

- A number of state agricultural and processing companies have undergone restructuring, including meat processing, dairy and sugar plants.

- Firms involved with logistics machinery, spare parts, mineral fertilisers, plant protection agents and servicing, and other companies have been privatised.

- Various agricultural market logistics schemes are being developed. (With the help of European Union (EU) experts, farm credit funds have been established in the provinces of Akmola, Almaty and South Kazakhstan.)

- Special procedures have been established to pass agricultural company management into private management and to attract international investment. (In 1998, according to the Ministry of Agriculture, 253 firms were passed into private management or sold to investors. In this context, 943 loan agreements were arranged.)

So far, the strategy has been very successful: private ownership is now the dominant form of organisation in the sector. In 1998 there were 70,000 farms, of which 99.6 per cent were in the private sector. Some 61,000 farms were transferred to the private sector on the basis of long-term tenure. This involved 27.2 million hectares of land, 4,300 farming cooperatives, over 4,000 partnerships and 505 joint-stock companies and other entities. Also in 1998 large farms accounted for 73.5 per cent of land, small farms 18.6 per cent; state-owned farms 4.0 per cent; and individuals 0.2 per cent.

Land regulations

The country's parliament recently ratified amendments to the Law 'On Land' and reform in this context will happen in two stages.

The first will involve the adoption of the Law 'On Land'. Private ownership of unoccupied farming land or state reserve land will be introduced. This will cover arable land, or land identified as being available for sale to local residents only. The second will complete the process of land privatisation.

The land law of the Republic of Kazakhstan already allows for title to be transferred in a number of ways, with the right to inherit ownership, or to sell, grant, lease, pledge and transfer rights to joint-stock companies, associations and cooperatives (including those with foreign participation).

In order to attract foreign capital, the period of land lease available to foreign investors has been extended to 99 years.

In late 1998, according to state statistical data, more than 2.3 million people were landowners. More than 1.9 million transactions in the abatement, lease, sale and purchase of land use rights were arranged and 93 per cent of all private farms received their land ownership confirmation documents. Banks issued loans amounting to more than KZT700 million in the form of land mortgages.

Interstate co-operation

Central Asian states support the creation of an agricultural product consortium to regulate mutually beneficial agricultural product operations. A water resource consortium has already been established and the countries of Central Asia plan to continue their efforts to establish a common agricultural market within the Commonwealth of Independent States (CIS).

Market infrastructure

A new market infrastructure is being developed in accordance with the agricultural plan adopted by the President.

The country's new land regulations are designed to assist in the development of a market infrastructure. A total of 167 wholesale markets, 22 commodity exchanges and 13 credit associations are already functioning and associations of commodity producers and other service organisations have also been established.

There are currently 34 grain-producing companies – members of the Grain Union of Kazakhstan. This is a non-governmental organisation (NGO), acting on a voluntary basis to combine efforts and to coordinate grain market activity. The primary objectives of the Grain Union include developing the concept of a grain market and introducing a standard grain contract practice, an independent arbitration system, common rules for grain operations and an agricultural securities market.

The Grain Union represents the interests of Kazakhstan at the International Grain Council in London, and is about to join the GAFTA association, whose members represent the world's largest grain producers. In 1998 members of the Grain Union sowed more than 2 million hectares of arable land.

Kazakhstan's volume of gross agricultural output in 1998 totalled KZT246.6 billion at current prices, with animal farming (57 per cent) and plant growing (43 per cent) being the dominant contributors.

Food processing

The agriculture processing industry has also made some progress. In 1998 the production of sugar increased, in comparison with 1997, by 50 per cent. Over the same period, yoghurts and other dairy products and carbonated beverages increased by 40 per cent, brewery and meat products by 20 per cent, fruit and nut processing by 9.8 per cent, dairy products and cream by 8.1 per cent, pasta products and mayonnaise by 2.7 per cent, vegetable oils by 2.1 per cent and grain flour by 1.4 per cent.

To support the domestic population's current needs, the agricultural sector must provide 3 million tons of grain, 1.2 million tons of vegetables, 1.2 million tons of potatoes, 4.6 million tons of milk, 1 million tons of meat, 330,000 tons of sugar, 132,000 tons of vegetable oil and 3.3 billion eggs. (See Table 2.8.1.)

Table 2.8.1 Internal demand of food resources (net of exports)

Food resources	Volume (million tons)
Grain	12.0–12.5
Potatoes	1.9–2.0
Vegetables and fruit	1.4–1.5
Sugar	0.4–0.34
Vegetable oil	0.17–0.2
Meat	1.0–1.2
Milk	5.5–6.0
Eggs	3.9–4.0*
Fish	0.2–0.2

* Billions of eggs

Low efficiency, low productivity of cattle and production losses remain the basic reasons for the increasing costs of all basic kinds of agricultural production. The increase in costs are largely caused by a constant increase in the price of agricultural engineering services, fuel and lubricants, construction materials and spare parts supplied by industry to rural areas.

In 1999 the government was due to spend KZT13.1 billion on agriculture support, 32 per cent more than in 1998.

Characteristics of agricultural production

The territory of Kazakhstan includes forest-steppe, steppe, half-deserted and deserted zones. The natural climatic conditions determine the low natural efficiency of agricultural arable lands that require significant volumes of investment.

These investments should be distributed among the following nine agricultural production zones:

1. *The grain–animal farming zone* occupies large territories of dry temperate steppe and covers 64 agricultural districts of the country.

   This zone covers 32.8 million hectares of agricultural arable land, including 14 million hectares occupied by grain fields (42.7 per cent), with a per capita distribution of 51 hectares of arable land. This is the country's highest indicator. Soils are black and dark chestnut, the annual precipitation level totals nearly 300 mm. Annually, the total positive temperature indicator (ie the sum of temperatures) above 10°C is 2,250°C.

   The large areas of arable land provide cost-effective opportunities for private grain-producing industry and animal farm development. Conditions in this zone are favourable for the production of large amounts of high-quality grain as well as meat and dairy farming.

2. *The animal–grain-farming zone* is situated in dry steppe on dark-chestnut and chestnut soils. The annual precipitation level totals 250 mm. Annually, the total positive temperature indicator above 10°C is 2,690°C.

   This zone covers 58 agricultural districts.

   It is the largest zone and its agricultural land totals 56 million hectares, including 8.8 million hectares of arable land. Animal farming is the major activity as grain farming is less effective in this zone.

3. *The fine-fleeced sheep-breeding zone* covers semi-deserted areas. Soils are light chestnut and brown. Annually, the total positive temperature indicator above 10°C ranges from 2,800°C to 3,500°C. The zone covers 20 agricultural districts.

   The total area of agricultural land equals 30.8 million hectares, including 7.1 per cent of arable land. Pastures cover more than 85 per cent. Sheep and cattle breeding are the major livestock activities.

4. *The meat–tallow sheep-breeding* zone occupies central Kazakhstan's semi-deserted and deserted areas.

   Soils are light chestnut and brown, the annual precipitation average totals 200 mm in the north and 100 mm in the south, and the annual total temperatures over 10°C range from 3,200°C to 3,900°C.

   This zone covers 12 agricultural districts.

   The area of agricultural land totals 38.3 million hectares, and includes 2.7 million hectares of arable land (4.4 per cent) and 36 million hectares of pasture.

5. *The Karakul sheep-breeding zone* covers the deserted areas with brown and grey-brown soils. The average annual precipitation fluctuates from 150 mm in the north to 100 mm in the east.

   This zone covers 13 districts.

   The agricultural land totals 31.5 million hectares, including 0.8 million hectares (2.5 per cent) of arable land and 30.3 million hectares of pasture.

   This animal farming zone specialises in the production of sheepskin (karakul).

6. *The animal and fruit-growing zone with industrial crops zone* is located at the foothills and between mountain valleys to the east and

east-west of Kazakhstan. The average annual precipitation fluctuates from 200 to 350 mm, and the total positive temperature indicator above 10°C is between 2,100°C and 3,800°C.

This zone covers 29 districts and 15.4 million hectares of agricultural land including 2.3 million hectares of arable land (14.9 per cent).

This is the main zone of intensively ploughed irrigation land (41 per cent of the country's total amount). Valuable industrial crops are produced here (sugar beet, tobacco). Pastures cover 12 million hectares and are used for sheep and cattle breeding.

7. *The rice zone* includes the downstream areas of the Sirdarija river. Soils are grey-brown and the precipitation totals nearly 120mm a year, the total positive temperature indicator above 10°C is 3,800°C.

The rice growing areas cover all districts of the Kzyl-Orda oblast (excluding Aralsk). The area of agricultural land equals 11.6 million hectares, including plough land, and 0.2 million hectares of pasture (96 per cent).

The rice production in the area may be combined with sheep and cattle breeding.

8. *The cotton zone* covers the middle part of the Sirdarija river. Soils are grey-brown, the annual precipitation totals 220 mm, and the total positive temperature indicator above 10°C is 4,440°C.

The zone covers the following districts of the East Kazakhstan Oblast: Ordabasynsky, Zhetisaysky, Kelessky, Kirovsky, Mahtaaralsky, Sairamsky and Turkenstansky.

The area of agricultural land totals 2.2 million hectares, including more than 0.2 million hectares of pasture.

This zone also provides favourable conditions for fruit farming.

9. *The suburban (vegetable–milk) zone* is located close to the urban centres in densely populated areas. The climate conditions of this zone are different because it covers different districts of the country – although homogeneous economic conditions result in identical production methods to provide urban residents with vegetables, milk products and berries. This zone occupies 3.6 million hectares of agricultural land, 0.7 million hectares of pasture and 150,000 hectares of irrigated land. The zone's economic presence is small because production is management intensive and labour-consuming.

Plant growing

Non-irrigated agriculture is practised in north, north-eastern and central Kazakhstan – areas characterised by high precipitation levels. This area covers 34 million hectares – 12 per cent of the total land area of Kazakhstan. The growth in non-irrigated areas in these regions was caused by the development of virgin and disused lands. According to research data, 12 million hectares of ploughed land in Kazakhstan require erosion protection and over 5 million hectares are washed away areas.

The productive soil layer (humus) loss over the last 25–30 years has totalled 20–25 per cent.

According to quality analysis, 4.7 per cent of the soil has a high level of humus (23.9 per cent), 46.5 per cent has a low level (2–4 per cent) and 24.9 per cent a very low level (below 2 per cent).

Irrigated agriculture is developed mainly in southern and south-eastern regions and is determined by low precipitation levels and hot climate conditions. The total irrigated land area is 2 million hectares.

The application of new water-saving methods in soil irrigation and the reconstruction of land used for rice and other forms of crop growing is very costly and demands substantial investment.

A reduction in the use of fertilisers has occurred in Kazakhstan due to their high cost. To increase consumption will require investment in the mineral fertiliser production industry and the introduction of cost-reducing technologies. This would improve the market competitiveness of Kazakhstan producers against their Russian and Uzbek counterparts.

Grain crops

Kazakhstan is one of the world's largest grain producers and exporters. Soil and climate provide ideal conditions for growing wheat, barley, rice, corn, millet and buckwheat.

The main grain crop is a high-class wheat with a high protein content.

The average annual grain output in the period 1992–98 equalled 15–16 million tons. The average annual export of grain crops for the period of 1995–98 was 3 to 3.4 million tons, with major customers including the CIS countries of Russia, Uzbekistan, Tajikistan, Azerbaijan, Belarus, Georgia, Kyrgyzstan, Turkmenistan and Ukraine. Nowadays there is a growing tendency to export Kazakhstan grain to other international markets. The list of Kazakhstan grain importers now includes Austria, Afghanistan, the UK, Venezuela, Latvia, Lithuania, Estonia, Poland, Turkey, Switzerland, The Netherlands, Saudi Arabia, Iran, China, Korea and Mongolia.

In 1998, 11.4 million hectares were harvested totalling 84 per cent of the grain area, and 2.1 million hectares (16 per cent) were written-off due to severe drought in western and northern regions of the Republic. According to the Ministry of Agriculture, 12.5 million hectares will be sown with grain crops and legumes in 1999.

On the basis of the last three years' grain statistics, the National Statistic Agency estimates an 8.7 million ton grain harvest in 1999, exceeding 1998's harvest by 2.3 million tons (36 per cent).

Industrial crops

The main industrial crops grown in Kazakhstan include beetroot, cotton and oil crops.

In 1998 the beetroot output increased by 80 per cent. This was due to an extension of the growing area, resulting in an increase in the harvest output growth from 11.6 to 14.3 tons per hectare. The beetroot harvesting area in 1998 was equal to 15,800 hectares and the total output was 224,900 tons.

Cotton is the most important industrial crop grown on the irrigated soils of southern Kazakhstan. The harvesting area last year was 114,400 hectares and the total output equalled 161,600 tons.

The oil crops grown in Kazakhstan include, among others, sunflower (the most widespread crop), flax, soybean and mustard. In 1998 the harvested area was 198,400 hectares and the total yield equalled 83,300 tons. Compared with 1997 the total yield increased by 29,000 tons (53 per cent).

Table 2.8.2 shows annual production figures for all categories of basic crops produced in Kazakhstan during the period 1993–98.

Table 2.8.2 Annual production of basic crops (all categories), 1993–98

Crop	1993 (000s tons)	1994 (000s tons)	1995 (000s tons)	1996 (000s tons)	1997 (000s tons)	1998 (000s tons)
Grain crops	21,631	16,454	9,506	11,237	12,309	6,415.8
Wheat	11,586	9,052	6,490	7,678	8,895	4,733.3
Corn	355	234	136	122	111	188.7
Millet	231	130	39	30	64	19.7
Buckwheat	130	84	53	29	18	11.9
Rice	403	283	184	226	255	236.1
Industrial crops						
Row-cotton	200	208	223	183	198	161.6
Sugar beet	843	433	371	341	128	224.9
Sunflower seeds	86	97	99	64	54	83.3
Other						
Potatoes	2,296	2,040	1,720	1,656	1,472	1,260.5
Vegetables	808	781	780	778	880	1,070.6
Fruit, berries	125	137	166	154	103	54.7

Animal farming

Animal farming is an integral part of Kazakhstan's agriculture. It supplies the food needs of the population and provides light industry with raw materials.

Animal farming output fell in the 1990s due to the low productivity of flocks and herds. There was also a rapid reduction due to hay shortages and financial problems in the industry, and because of low numbers of cattle and poultry kept. (For example, as of 1 January 1999, agricultural firms stocked only 748,000 tons of hay, ie 44 per cent of the 1998 level.)

Nevertheless, it is generally recognised that animal farming in Kazakhstan is improving.

Table 2.8.3 Animal husbandry development 1997–1998

	1997 (000s tons)	1998 (000s tons)	1998 (as percentage of 1997)
Cattle and poultry for slaughter	1345.8	1206.0	90
Agricultural enterprises	323.0	163.1	50
Population	947.5	972.9	103
Farmers	75.3	70.0	93
Total milk yield	3287.1	3354.5	102
Cow milk yield			
Agricultural enterprises	427.9	262.2	61
Population	2712.1	2942.0	108
Farmers	147.0	150.3	102

As Table 2.8.3 shows, in 1998 there was an increase in animal husbandry development as compared with the previous year: meat output (cattle and poultry) was reduced to 1.2 million tons (a drop, but not as much as previous years); and milk yield increased to 3.3 million tons. There was also an increase in egg production – to 1.4 million tons – and in wool production – to 24,300 tons – (not shown in Table 2.8.3).

The data shows a slow reduction of livestock numbers in recent years and a significant growth of poultry.

Nowadays cooperative farms and joint-stock companies, as well as individual farmers, provide the bulk of animal farming products; the growth in cattle productivity was determined by an increase in market demand and with the implementation of specially designed development programmes, individual or family farms will provide future growth in animal farming production.

Table 2.8.4 Number of livestock and poultry (000 heads)

Name	1993	1994	1995	1996	1997	1998
Cattle	9,376.3	9,346.6	8,072.9	5,410.4	4,307	3,999.5
Cows	3,687.2	3,396.7	3,045	2,535.5	2,109.6	1,956.0
Pigs	2,445.2	1,982.7	1,622.7	1,037.5	881.5	859.9
Sheep and goats	34,208.1	25,132.1	19,583.9	13,741.9	10,384.3	9,598.9
Horses	1,776.6	1,636	1,556.9	1,311.6	1,082.7	964.9
Poultry	49,591.9	32,715.9	20,809.9	15,312.8	15,858.2	16,919.5

2.9

The Chemical and Petrochemical Industry

The Kazakhstan Investment Promotion Centre

Introduction

The Republic of Kazakhstan possesses a huge wealth of natural resources for producing chemical and petrochemical products. It has rich reservoirs of potash and other salts, borates, compounds of bromine, sulphates, phosphorites, diversified raw materials for the paint and varnish industry, and enormous reserves of oil and gas. There are unlimited possibilities for producing a whole range of products associated with petrochemical processing (especially those made of ethylene, polypropylene, rubber), synthetic detergents and soap, feed microbiological protein, man-made fibres and threads, and synthetic resins and plastics.

Kazakhstan has 221 plants in the chemical and petrochemical industry (including the pharmaceutical industry). They manufacture man-made fibres and threads, chromic compounds, calcium carbide, plastic, a wide assortment of general mechanical rubber goods, and other products. There is also a large industry concerned with mineral fertilisers and synthetic detergents and with the processing of phosphate ore and yellow phosphorus. The industry accounted for 2.2 per cent Of Kazakhstan's Industrial output in 1997.

In 1998 the production of yellow phosphorus, phosphorous flour, mineral fertilisers and tripoliphosphate of sodium decreased, when compared to production levels in 1990. The production of 11 different export products ceased completely, resulting in the closure of 11 large plants. Others continue to work below capacity. The number of employees in the sector has also decreased.

Today, Kazakhstan imports chemical commodities worth more than US$500 million per year including among others caustic, chlorine, plant-protection chemicals, plastic, and household chemical goods.

Table 2.9.1 Main indicators of the performance of the chemical and petrochemical industry (including the pharmaceutical industry)

Year	No of enterprises	Output (US$ million)*	Volume index of output as percentage of previous year
1994	192	150.16	58.9
1995	225	287.15	103.6
1996	166	300.36	73
1997	221	208.02	70.1
1998**	474	148.39	63.0

*   At the National Bank's rate on 1 February 1999 (KZT85/US$1)
** Performance indicators of the chemical industry.

The main reasons for the substantial slump in production within this sector and its current instability are:

- a downturn in the demand for mineral fertilisers;

- the high energy intensity of the phosphor industry and the way it is affected by the instability of electricity and gas supplies;

- the failure, because of its imperfect structure, to attract strategic investors and controlling corporations. As a result, corporations failed to meet their forecast commitments thereby destabilising the operation of the larger export-oriented chemical industries.

To overcome this situation, the Kazakhstan government is providing comprehensive support to the petrochemical sector. The railroad tariffs for carriage inside Kazakhstan for plants in this sector have been reduced, loans have been issued, attempts have been made to attract investors, and plants have been transferred to foreign companies in an effort to improve their commercial viability.

Aktyubinskiy Zavod Khromovykh Soyedineniy JSC (Aktyubinsk Plant of Chemical Compounds), controlled by the Special Chemical Incorporation, has maintained its production of chromic salts. The plant has restored its circulating assets and has brought its capacity up to that for which it was designed. It has also paid off all its debts and obligatory budgetary charges. In 1998 Texuna Chemicals Inc, a Hong Kong-based corporation, began operating in Kazakhstan. It has control of four Kazakhstan plants – Tarazfosfor JSC, Zavod Mineralnyh Udobreniy JSC, Fosforit JSC and Promtrans JSC, and is committed to investing a total of US$260 million. In 1999 an offer was accepted from the English corporation UIG to provide direct investment in Karagandarezinotehnika to optimise and restore the production of high-quality general mechanical and rubber goods.

Foreign companies investing in this sector are generally attracted by the combination of available natural resources for producing chemical and petrochemical commodities and the Republic's sound legislative base.

The chemical complex

In 1998 the chemical industry's manufactured products amounted to US$1,484 million at wholesale prices. The output index was 63 per cent in 1997. In 1998, unlike in 1997, growth was observed in the production of metacarbonic acid (by 500 per cent), styrene polymers in primary forms, sodium bichromate, etching acid and sulphuric acid in monohydrate, detergents (by 20 per cent), calcium carbide (by 15.4 per cent) and chromic anhydride (by 7.3 per cent).

Most of the companies that operate in the national chemical industry use local mining and chemical resources. For example, Karatau JSC carries out its operations within the fields of the phosphorite-bearing basin of Karatau, where the largest deposits in the Commonwealth of Independent States (CIS) are massed. The highest density of phosphorus five-monoxide is a hallmark of these ores. Karatau JSC is the sole ore base in the Asian region of the CIS, being a self-contained production complex specialising in mining, initial ore dressing and supplying further phosphor processing plants in Kazakhstan, Uzbekistan, Turkmenistan and Russia. The conversion of the Karatau preparation plant into a chemical-floatation facility for the dressing of ore will produce an annual yield up to 600,000 tons of high-quality phosphorite concentrate with a 30 per cent content of P_2O_5.

Large plants in Kazakhstan that are associated with phosphorite processing, as well as with the production of different chemical products, are Khimprom JSC, Nodfos JSC, Fosfor JSC, Inderbor JSC and the Alginskiy chemical plants.

Pavlodar Khimprom JSC produces chlorine in vials for motor oils, floatation agents for cleaning non-ferrous metal ores, mineral salt precipitation inhibitors, anti-freezing compounds, hydrochloric acid, and so on. Currently, the plant operates on imported raw materials. Khimprom JSC uses Kazakhstan raw materials (yellow phosphorus – Taraz, Shymkent) and can manufacture 5,000 MTA of five-sulphurous phosphorus.

Nodfos JSC is involved in the production of agglomerates, yellow phosphorus, thermal phosphoric acid and sodium tripoliphosphate. Its established capacity for yellow phosphorus production is 230,000 MTA and for thermal phosphoric acid 120,000 tons. The plant is equipped with domestic and foreign process apparatus.

Union Chemical Ltd (Khimprom OJSC) in Taraz City specialises in yellow phosphorus, phosphoric acid, feed components for animal industries, and mineral fertilisers.

Fosfor JSC is involved in the production of yellow phosphorus (capacity – 170,000 MTA), thermal phosphoric acid (369,000 tons), sodium tripoliphosphate (320,000 tons), synthetic detergents (60,000 tons) and reactive phosphorus salts (18,200 tons). At present, the factory stands idle because it has no circulating assets. In 1998 it filed for bankruptcy and liquidation. The circulating capital needed to start up and to fund the plant's production capacity amounts to US$22–25 million. The availability of raw supplies (phosphoric ore) and the liquidity of phosphor commodities in the world market are the two main factors that predetermine the prospects for the phosphor industry. The state is currently doing everything in its power to stabilise the situation within the sector.

Aktyubinsk Plant is involved in the production of chromic compounds using chromium ores from the Don field. The plant has been controlled by the Special Chemical Incorporation since 1996. Regular investments have been made to restore its necessary circulating assets, to bring production capacities up to potential, and to repay all debts and obligatory payments. The total amount of investment is US$24.7 million. The plant is designed to produce 121,000 tons of chromium salts. About 90 per cent of chromic compounds are exported to CIS and non-CIS countries.

Table 2.9.2 Production of major commodities of the chemical and petrochemical industry in 1998 (000s tons)

Commodities	1998
1. Styrene polymer in primary forms	3,075
2. Sulphuric acid in monohydrate	605
3. Sodium bichromate	54.5
4. Calcium carbide	33.1
5. Chromic anhydride and hardener	26.1
6. Phosphoric fertilisers (mineral or chemical)	13.9
7. Yellow phosphorus	12.9
8. Nitrogenous fertilisers (mineral or chemical)	8.8

The main strategic purpose of developing the chemical and petrochemical industries is to form a complex of facilities producing new commodities based on the comprehensive processing of raw materials to:

- saturate the national market;

- reinforce export potential by producing high-tech and competitive commodities;

- lower the national economy's dependency on foreign imports.

The outlook for this sector is connected to the integration of the refining of western Kazakhstan petroleum and to the establishment of new facilities using phosphorite fields.

It is intended to create conditions for the growth of sectoral production using primary coke, chemical, petrochemical and mineral resources, by modernising and reconstructing operating plants and by commissioning new facilities for propylene production.

The petrochemical complex

The petrochemical sector in Kazakhstan has recently undergone reform. A number of refineries produce petrochemical products and make finished products such as thermoplastics and elastomers.

At present, organic synthetic industries utilise basic raw materials such as natural and associated gases, gas and pool hydrocarbons from oil refining, cracked and pyrolytic decomposed petroleum, solid paraffin hydrocarbons, heavy petroleum residue, coke oven gas and coking gum.

Current petrochemical facilities in Kazakhstan include Aktauskiy Polymer JSC (AKPO), Polipropilen JSC in Atyrau City, Karagandarezinotehnika JSC, Shymkentshina JSC, and others. These plants are able to produce various sorts of petrochemicals though they require additional investment to solve some of the problems they face. Mutually advantageous co-operation with foreign associates in the petrochemical sphere is one of the major business trends. Petrochemical plants, refreshed by foreign capital and know-how, will be able to manufacture high-demand products for both domestic and world markets.

The industry for synthetic resins and plastics is represented by AKPO JSC and Polipropilen JSC. AKPO JSC is the largest chemical complex producing polystyrene plastics in the CIS. At the moment, the capacity for producing impact-resistant and general-purpose polystyrene is 55,000 tons per year, and the capacity for foaming up to 25,000 tons per year. The company is currently bankrupt, however, due to its inability to rehabilitate its precarious financial and economic standing. Polipropilen JSC makes polypropylene as well as hay-binding twine and polypropylene bags. Raw materials are imported from Russia and the Ukraine. The plant is designed to produce 30,000 tons of polypropylene, 2,300 tons of hay-binding twine and 6 million bags but was working at only 52.6 per cent capacity in 1996. In 1996, the plant filed for bankruptcy because it was short of raw materials for polypropylene production in Kazakhstan. In 1998 there were talks with Marubeni, a Japanese corporation, regarding the restoration of the factory. Marubeni was attracted by the condition of the factory and the proximity of a power source (Atyrau Heat Electropower Station). Also, during the reconstruction of the Atyrau refinery, the possibility of setting up a propylene production facility became apparent.

Also vital to the Republic are the tyre and mechanical rubber industries. These industries include two production facilities (Karagandarezinotehnika JSC and Shymkentshina JSC) that are equipped with up-to-date technologies. Karagandarezinotehnika JSC filed for bankruptcy in 1998: reinstatement of the plant requires US$3.3 million. Currently, production equipment facilities remain undisturbed and can be operated once they can be supplied with raw materials and energy. Proposals, put forward by a British corporation (UIG), which consist of a step-by-step buyout of the plant and the injection of new direct investment are currently being considered. UIG have also agreed to purchase the treatment facilities and the mazut storehouse. Shymkentshina JSC is the only specialised plant in Central Asia manufacturing tyres for trucks, passenger cars and farming machinery. The factory has the capacity to produce 3 million tyres and 5 million inner tubes for cars, per year. In terms of its technology, Shymkentshina JSC is the most advanced plant among the 17 tyre factories that exist in former USSR countries.

One of the major problems facing Kazakhstan's petrochemical industry is the lack of a complex that provides the technology for interconnecting petrochemical production to utilise available hydrocarbon resources and supply the developing consumer market both within Kazakhstan and abroad.

2.10

Construction

The Kazakhstan Investment Promotion Centre

Introduction

The construction and construction materials industry in Kazakhstan traditionally occupies an important place among all sectors of the economy. It is represented by cement factories, numerous factories producing building materials and construction companies. As of 1 January 1999, 7,170 legal entities operated in the construction industry; including 193 state-owned and 6,875 private firms.

The construction industry provides a favourable investment climate for foreign investors. There are 153 joint ventures with foreign firms and 102 enterprises with 100 per cent foreign capital, operating as affiliates. Most of the main industrial enterprises in this sector have been transferred into foreign management. The Karaganda cement factory was transferred to Central Asia Cement (Malaysia) and Shymkentcement JSC's transfer into the management of French companies is under consideration.

Almost all industrial enterprises and organisations in the construction industry have been privatised in accordance with the state privatisation programme.

The construction sector

The country's general economic situation has affected the construction industry. The effect is indicated by a reduction in the construction sector's share of gross domestic product (GDP), from 12 per cent in 1990 to 4.2 per cent in 1997. The construction materials industry's share of GDP also fell from 5.6 per cent to 2.2 per cent. At the same time, however, investments in the construction industry are likely to bring about a fast turnaround in this situation.

Foreign investment has been attracted to construction projects in Astana and in some key sectors of industry (petrochemicals, metallurgy, mining), however the volume of foreign investment in developments within the construction materials industry was insignificant.

In 1997–98 Kazakhstan received a soft loan of DM7.3 million from the Federal Republic of Germany. However, an additional grace loan of DM37 million for the realisation of projects in the construction materials industry (for example, Maralan JSC, the Ust-Kamenogorsk cement factory JSC, Mantra JSC), is expected to be provided in the near future.

The Construction Committee under the Ministry of Energy, Industry and Trade of the Republic of Kazakhstan is one of the major state bodies responsible for implementing a policy of stimulating foreign investment in the construction industry. The Committee negotiates with the representatives of international organisations and submits project proposals to the Intergovernmental Committee on Trade and Economic Co-operation.

Capital construction

In 1998 the volume of investments in capital construction by large and medium-sized enterprises totalled US$2,035.3 million. In comparable prices this is 39 per cent more than in 1997. Investments in fixed assets totalled US$941.2 million. About 36 per cent of the fixed assets were invested in manufacturing industry enterprises, 19 per cent in mining and 16 per cent in housing construction. About 41 per cent of the investments were committed to housing construction and renovation.

The mining and processing industry, as well as the transportation and communications industries, were priority investment sectors throughout the entire year. They attracted 42, 14, and 12 per cent of the total volume of investments, respectively, for the creation and reproduction of fixed capital in these sectors. Foreign investment was 38, 26 and 22 per cent, respectively. The volume of investment attracted for the construction of education and agriculture facilities was insignificant.

Non-financial corporations provided significant investment in the construction industry – in 1998 their investments in capital construction totalled approximately US$1,823.5 million (90 per cent of the country's volume). Financial corporations and official bodies invested only an insignificant share – US$43.5 million (2 per cent) and US$108.2 million (5 per cent), while private householders invested US$51.8 million (3 per cent).

Most state and local budgets were directed towards the construction and reconstruction of state enterprises (97 per cent). An insignificant share of these investments (3 per cent) was distributed among private enterprises and organisations involved in the construction of housing foundations, air transportation, oil and gas production, steam and water supply facilities, the chemical and automobile industries, and stock-breeding. The share of local governmental budgets within the total volume of capital construction investment, considered regionally, is highest in the Kzyl-Orda (26 per cent), South Kazakhstan (19 per cent) and Kostanai (13 per cent) oblasts.

The share of construction investment financed by the state budget was highest in the North Kazakhstan oblast (44 per cent of the total regional investment volume) and in Astana (50 per cent).

The share of foreign investment in fixed capital was highest in western Kazakhstan (77 per cent), and in the Mangistau (central Kazakhstan – 66 per cent), East Kazakhstan (57 per cent), Almaty (56 per cent) and Aktubinsk (western Kazakhstan – 48 per cent) oblasts.

Table 2.10.1 Major indicators of capital construction in the Republic of Kazakhstan

Indicators	1994	1995	1996	1997	1998
Current rate fixed asset investments (US$ millions)*	386.8	1,249.7	1,371.8	1,351.1	944.8
Investments in fixed capital at actual current rates (US$ millions)*	952.3	1,748.1	1,399.8	1,644.6	2,038.8
Including: Housing construction and renovation services at actual current rates (US$ millions)*	421.5	728.2	605.6	644.2	836.8
Construction industry output share in GDP (%)	9.6	6.5	4.4	4.2	
Volume of contract operations at actual current prices (US$ millions)*	573.7	951.5	772.7	762.2	627.5
Housing construction (000 sq m of the total area)	2,322	1,663	1,407	1,344	1,079
Number of construction firms (year end)	7,056	3,820	3,399	3,019	1,207

* At the National Bank's rate on 1 February 1999 (KZT85/US$1)

Housing construction

During 1998, 1,084,200 sq m of housing facilities for all kinds of property were constructed (85 per cent of the 1997 level).

Construction materials industry

The resolution of the Government of the Republic of Kazakhstan 'On the Structural Reorganisation of the Industrial Base of Construction in 1996–2000' was adopted in 1996 with the purpose of providing state support to the development of the construction materials industry. The resolution is designed to attract US$1,250 million in foreign investment. A list of construction materials investment projects, including those involving advanced foreign technologies and investment, has been developed and submitted to the Agency on Investments and the Strategic Planning Agency.

The development priority for the construction materials sector is to establish import-substituting construction-materials production facilities, based on modern technologies and equipment. Currently the industry manufactures such products as prefabricated ferro-concrete structures and units, wall materials, soft roofing materials, linoleum, ceramic plates and tiles, cement, bricks, lime, mineral isolation materials, concrete, asbestos-cement sheets and pipes.

Strategic objectives for the construction industry

Strategic objectives for the development of the construction sector include the establishment of a high-grade market for housing and public utility services, design and contraction services, and the modernisation and technical re-equipment of industrial facilities.

The realisation of these strategic objectives will involve:

- the implementation of financial and investment policies to ensure favourable conditions in the investment environment;

- the improvement of pricing policies in construction;

- the improvement of architectural and urban development control;

- the reform of design and research service organisations;

- interstate co-operation in the field of construction.

Stages of reforms

The first stage of reform, 1997–2000, includes overcoming the recession in construction, the establishment of preconditions for a growth in investment activity and the expansion of sources of financing. In 1999 construction materials industry output should have totalled US$267.4 million, while the investment to be attracted into the industry was planned to total US$558.4 million. The planned 1999 production financing by the state budget was to total US$0.92 million. Capital investment for the realisation of the programme (Structural Reorganisation of Construction Industrial Facilities) was to reach US$244.5 million.

The second stage of reform, 2001–10, will include the revitalisation of manufacturing, the realisation of particular investment projects concerned with the modernisation of existing facilities in the housing construction sector and the development of a design service market.

The third stage of reform, 2011–30, will include the industry's structural reorganisation in accordance with international standards and the resolution of current housing construction problems.

Table 2.10.2 shows the basic parameters for the construction industry's long-term strategy.

Table 2.10.2 Basic parameters for the construction industry's long-term development strategy

Indicators	2000	2010	2020	2030
Construction materials industry				
Volume of output at the current comparable wholesale rates of 1997 (US$ millions)*	183.2	287.8	468.8	793.1
Capital construction				
Investments at the expense of all sources of financing (US$ millions)*	351.8	1,678	2,534.2	3,426.8
Including: Investment in housing construction and purchasing (US$ millions)*	234.5	1,519.3	2,331.3	2,649.1
Capital investment in housing construction at the expense of the state budget (US$ millions)*	6.3	5.1	4.2	0.6
Design services at the expense of the state budget (US$ millions)*	1.14	1.36	1.42	1.24
Scientific and technical development at the expense of the state budget (US$ millions)*	0.87	1	0.71	0.47
Foreign investments (US$ millions)*	109	151.2	196.6	422.5

* At the National Bank's rate on 1 February 1999 (KZT85/US$1)

Regulations and procedures

Individuals or legal entities (including foreign contractors and companies) must secure a proper construction licence to carry out architectural or construction services in Kazakhstan. The resolution 'On Types of Architectural and Municipal Construction Services, Requiring Licensing' lists 5 categories (and over 40 sub-categories) of construction activities requiring licensing. The activities subject to licensing range from the creation of architectural plans and blueprints, to the construction, repair and renovation of facilities.

The relevant licence must be obtained from the Construction Committee. General construction licences are not available. However, an individual or company may apply for and obtain a licence that covers one or a number of activities.

Legal entities looking to carry out construction activities in Kazakhstan for the first time will be issued a licence for a term of one year. This licence may be renewed.

2.11

The Electric Power Industry

The Kazakhstan Investment Promotion Centre

Introduction

The electric power industry is a major element of the fuel and energy infrastructure of Kazakhstan. The country owns an advanced network of power plants and grids. Thermal electric plants produce the dominant share of electricity and hydroelectric plants produce the remainder. The established national power industry capacity totals 18,200 MW.

The structure of electric power output falls into the following energy source categories: coal-powered plants (70.3 per cent of the total), gas-fuel oil-powered plants (17 per cent), hydroelectric plants (12 per cent), nuclear power plants (0.7 per cent). The vast territory of Kazakhstan has determined the development and size of its electric systems. The total length of all grids is 460,000 km (see Table 2.11.1).

Power generation

Table 2.11.1 Total length of power grids of all voltage in one-chain calculation

Voltage (kW)	1.150	500	220	110	35	6–10	0.4
Length (000 km)	1.4	5.5	20.2	44.5	62.1	204.0	122.1

The highest power industry output results were recorded in 1990 – an electric power output of 85.3 billion kWh and consumption of 104.7 billion kWh. The power deficit of 18.4 billion kWh was covered by the importation of electric power from other states. Northern Kazakhstan, operating within the common energy system (CES) of Russia, was able to operate at peak capacity using power from Siberian hydroelectric stations, and southern Kazakhstan operating within the unified energy systems (UES) of Central Asia, was powered by hydroelectric power plants in Kyrgyzstan and Tajikistan. After the USSR collapsed, Kazakhstan

CES operated independently, for political and economic reasons, and did not fully meet consumer requirements in terms of the reliability and the quality of energy supply.

Table 2.11.2 The balance of electric power in Kazakhstan from 1993 to 1998 (in billions of kWh)

Indicators	1993	1994	1995	1996	1997	1998
Electric power consumption	89.15	79.43	74.38	66.16	57.12	53.03
Electric power production	77.44	66.40	66.98	59.31	52.17	49.22
Deficit		-11.70	-13.03	-7.40	-6.85	-4.95	-3.81

The generation of electric power in Kazakhstan slowed at a faster rate during this period than the contraction of demand. In 1993 domestic production totalled 77.44 billion kWh, while Kazakhstan needed 89.15 billion kWh of electric power – a deficit of 11.71 billion kWh (see Table 2.11.2). New generating units put into operation between 1993 and 1998 included the 110 MW turbine power unit in the Karaganda thermal power plant 3, the 100 MW gas turbine unit installed by Akturbo JSC and the 117 MW hydroelectric power generation unit in the Shulbinskaya hydro-electric station.

However, the sharp reduction in demand for electric power and the permanent deficit of fiscal assets prevented the effective repair, maintenance and technological improvement of obsolete power stations. Thus the production of electric power fell from 52.17 billion kWh in 1997 to 49.22 billion kWh in 1998 (see Table 2.11.2).

Structural changes in the consumption of various power sources have also occurred. Due to the considerable increase in oil and gas tariffs, many consumers switched to fuel oil (mazut), which was previously utilised as a reserve fuel. A certain interest also occurred in the utilisation of associated gas.

Restructuring the industry

Between 1996 and 1997 the Kazakhstan government actively implemented a programme of de-monopolisation and privatisation of the power industry. Certain guarantees for operators of power stations, liberalisation from excessive state regulations, investments in modernisation, technical re-equipment and reconstruction of generating sources and the realisation of a power-saving policy are some of the positive results obtained as a result of the privatisation of the power industry.

The restructuring of the electric power sector has resulted in 80 per cent of energy sources being privatised or transferred to the management of the national power grid. It has also resulted in the creation and organisation of a competitive market for electric power and the determination of a future programme of development for the electric power market.

In 1996 the power sector of Kazakhstan attracted US$126.1 million in direct foreign investments, in 1997, US$128.3 million, and in the first half of 1998, US$125.8 million. Modernisation of the gas-fired turbine power plant GTS-144, to provide a reliable and independent electric power supply for the exploration and production sites of the Tengizshevroil Company, has been completed. The power station operates using associated gas from oil sites. To facilitate future development of oil production, the company is designing a new gas-turbine power station with a 480 MW capacity using the associated gas from oil sites, which has traditionally been burned off.

Also in 1996 the Silk Road Group, a division of AES, acquired one of the largest coal-fired stations – the Ekibastuzskaya TEZ-1 (currently AES-ST Ekibastuz), the Ust'-Kamenogorskaya and Shulbinskaya hydroelectric stations were passed to new management in a 20-year concession and 4 thermal power stations (Semipalatinskaya, Sogrinskaya, Leninogorskaya and Ust'-Kamenogorskaya) halted power production. In early 1998 the total amount of investments in the Ekibastuzskaya Power Plant-1 totalled US$45.37 million.

Ispat-Karmet JSC took over the running of the thermal power plant Karagandinskaya TEZ-2 and this currently ensures a stable power supply for the Karaganda-based metallurgical group. The volume of investment provided to develop the Karagandinskaya TEZ-2 during the period 1997–2000 amounted to US$36.5 million.

The Kazakhmys corporation, created by Zhezkazgantsvetmet JSC, currently includes the Zhezkazganskaya and Balkhashskaya thermal power stations, the Karagandinskaya GRES-2 as well as the copper-smelting and coal-mining companies. By the beginning of 1998, their investment in the development of thermal power stations stood at US$30 million.

Kaztzink JSC includes the Tekely power complex as well as the Karaterinskaya and Bukhtarminskaya hydroelectric stations, seven mines, three concentrating mills, two zinc plants, one lead plant, a mechanical repairs plant and a shop for precious metals refining. The Swiss-based company Glencore International AG currently owns a controlling stake in Kaztzink JSC.

Co-operation with Central Asian countries and Russia

The project agreement to coordinate the operation of Central Asia's state power systems was designed by the Council of Central Asia's UES with the participation of five country representatives: Kazakhstan, Uzbekistan, Kyrgyzstan, Turkmenistan and Tajikistan. The most important clauses in this agreement include:

- the principle of self-balancing the electrical capacity and energy of each power system in Central Asia's UES, in accordance with the contract;

- the possibility of creating a regional power pool in Central Asia for the formation of a common market in electric power and capacity;

- the coordinated adoption and non-use of customs duties, taxes and other duties on the current and future transition of electric power, supplied via the interstate grids, as well as for services relating to the frequency of regulation.

Accident-prevention automation units have been reconstructed to conduct parallel operations for the Central Asia–Kazakhstan transit. A new 500 kW reactor at the Agadyr substation is about to begin operations in order to provide a more stable passage for the north–south transit.

A protocol on co-operation in relation to the electric power industry, between the Republic of Kazakhstan and the Russian Federation has been signed. The major areas of co-operation cover the production, transfer and distribution of power, the creation of conditions for the restoration of a unified power system operation and the organisation of wholesale and retail markets of electric power.

Investment opportunities

Major goals for the electric power industry include:

- restoration of the electric power output of working power stations up to projected capacity, rehabilitation and reconstruction of power stations and maintenance of their capacity through effective equipment modernisation;

- improving the north–south 1,150–500 kW electric transfer system to replace electric power imported from other countries in Central Asia;

- the development of electric power sources in southern and western Kazakhstan, utilising associated gas;

- the gathering of market research on the power requirements of different countries for the purpose of developing electric power exports.

The construction of new power generation facilities (the Mainakskaya hydroelectric station GRES, Kerbulakskaya GRES, the Dzhungar Gate Wind Power Generation Complex, and the gas-turbine power station in western Kazakhstan) are proposed as part of the development strategy for the electric power complex. The search for potential investors for the realisation of the civil-engineering designs of these power stations is continuing. Currently, the appropriate documents for investment tenders relating to the construction of the western Kazakhstan power station and the privatisation of Akmolinskaya thermal electric stations 1 and 2 are being prepared.

Network facilities, including the export direction grids will be developed to satisfy the domestic and international markets. The following investment projects are considered to be essential for the fulfilment of this task:

Transmission grid north–south of Kazakhstan (1,416 km)

Agadyr-U-KGRES-500 kW (390 km)

Ekibastuz-Topar-1,150 kW (357 km)
Topar-Agadyr-500 kW (157 km)

U-KGRES-Zhambyl-500 kW (512 km)

2.12

The Environment

Heide Leighty and Sonia Heaven, BG International, Chair of Environmental Technology, KazGACA

Introduction

Kazakhstan is extremely rich in natural resources and served chiefly as a repository of raw materials for the Soviet Union. The exploitation of those natural resources to feed the rapid industrialisation of the Soviet Union has left a legacy of catastrophic environmental degradation that the Kazakhstan government is now trying to address with a comprehensive plan of action.

Kazakhstan covers a vast territory of 2.7 million sq km in the centre of Eurasia. A range of climate zones from dry subtropics and hot deserts to high mountainous tundra and glaciers covers this immense area. A nomadic steppe culture occupied the area until resettlement at the order of Soviet central planners. The sparsely occupied area held extensive wealth, in terms of both land and mineral resources.

The wealth of mineral resources led to the rapid development of the mining industry. Grasslands were converted to grazing lands for livestock and crop cultivation. The empty landscape provided huge territories for military bases and weapons-testing grounds, including nuclear weapons.

When the USSR collapsed, Kazakhstan, along with other former Soviet republics, was left with environmental degradation and ongoing pollution problems including soil contamination and loss, water pollution, radiation poisoning and reductions in biological diversity. Human health has been greatly affected. In order to make the transition to a market economy, Kazakhstan has had to find a way to address these environmental problems while still taking advantage of its natural resources.

National environmental action plan

Lack of financial resources has emphasised the importance of focusing on the most pressing problems and identifying priorities at both the national and regional level. The National Environmental Action Plan for Sustainable Development (NEAP) in the Republic of Kazakhstan was prepared under Government Resolution No 137 of 3 February 1997 'On Approval of the Schedule for RK Environmental Safety Conception Implementation'. The National Environment Centre for Sustainable Development (NEC) was created under the Ministry of Natural Resources and Environmental Protection to coordinate the activities of the ministries, departments, local agencies and public organisations in preparing and implementing the NEAP.

With the co-operation of the World Bank, the United Nations Development Programme (UNDP), the European Union (EU) Technical Assistance for the Commonwealth of Independent States (TACIS) programme and other international organisations, the Kazakhstan government has gone through a process of analysing the situation, identifying priority environmental problems in the country and preparing and implementing action plans (projects) to tackle the priority problems.

A priority list of 33 projects was prepared and presented at an international technical donor conference in June 1998. The NEC is now coordinating involvement in project implementation, as well as negotiating with potential donors.

It is in the project implementation phase that there is considerable potential for foreign involvement, especially in engineering and consultancy. A great deal of expertise will be required to address the daunting environmental conditions in Kazakhstan. The following sections list a number of priority projects, divided by sector. (From NEC, Kokshetau, Kazakhstan.)

Conservation of water resources

- Development and implementation of interstate measures targeted at balance preservation of transboundary water courses ecosystems.

- Rehabilitation of the water-protecting zone of the Syrdarya river.

- Study of methods and approval of actions aimed at reducing the negative impact of highly toxic mercury pollution: namely, in the sediments of the Nura river (the Karaganda region); in the ground water (the city of Pavlodar).

- Improving water resource management in the Balkhash-Alakol river basin (pilot project).

- Reduction in drinking water consumption and losses in municipal sector (demonstration project for Almaty as a case study).

- Construction and rehabilitation of sewage treatment facilities in Kzylorda and Shymkent (pilot project).

- Preventing kerosene-containing underground water leaching into the Irtysh river (Pavlodar oblast).
- Preventing water sources pollution with filtration and waste water from mining and industrial waste dumps of the Northern industrial unit (East Kazakhstan oblast).

Oil and gas pollution reduction

- Conservation of flooded oil deposit wells and exploratory wells to conserve biological diversity of the northern Caspian.
- Organisation of northern Caspian ecosystem environmental monitoring and pollution prevention system.
- Clean-up oil pollution from past activities of oil fields in Zhyloy district, Atyrau oblast (pilot project).
- Utilisation of associated gases in Prorva and Kumkol oil deposits (pilot projects).

Solid waste reduction

- Industrial waste minimisation, including prevention; establishing cleaner production centres (four pilot projects).
- Mitigation of the negative impact of toxic arsenic-containing and radioactive waste on health and environment in the Pavlodar and East Kazakhstan oblasts (pilot projects).
- Improvement of the system of collection, utilisation and storage of municipal solid waste (MSW) in the cities of Pavlodar, Shymkent, Almaty (pilot projects).
- Improving collection, utilisation and storage system for organic waste, including livestock complex waste.

Rehabilitation of urban air basins

- Development and implementation of measures on reduction of air pollution with lead dust in city of Ust-Kamenogorsk.
- Development and implementation of measures on reduction of air pollution with industrial emissions of non-ferrous metallurgy enterprises in the Pavlodar oblast.
- Development and implementation of measures on reduction of air pollution with radioactive dust of 'Koshkarata' tailing dump in Aktau city.

- Mitigation of the negative impact of road transportation in Almaty on environment and population health.

- Mitigation of the negative impact of road transportation in the city of Shymkent on environment and population health.

Reduction in emissions, including GHGs, in the energy sector

- Introduction of wind rotor electric power stations to generate power for group consumers and for the distribution network as illustrated by wind power resources assimilation in Jungar Gate, Almaty oblast.

- Introduction of wind rotor electric stations of small capacity for individual consumers.

- Introduction into the national energy balance of hydroelectric power resources of small rivers and construction of a pilot microhydro-electric power station to reduce air pollution with traditional energy sources.

- Development of environmentally sustainable housing construction on the basis of utilisation of renewable sources of energy.

- Reduction in energy consumption in the municipal sector for the mitigation of anthropogenic impacts of energy sources on the environment.

- Involvement in the energy balance of Kazakhstan's thermal water energy and in demanding a reduction in the use of ecologically hazardous sources of heat and electric power.

- Facilitation of methane production in the mines of the Karagandy coal basin for use in coal-fired or combined fuel-fired boilers.

- Development of solar energy engineering in order to mitigate air pollution produced by energy enterprises.

- Use of solar energy in the heat supply systems in objects of various purposes in cities and populated areas of Kazakhstan.

Conservation of arable land and pastures

- Inventory registration of environmentally degraded low-productive lands and their transformation.

- Improvement of rational pasture use system; creation of sown pasture to prevent desertification process in Kzylorda, south Kazakhstan and Almaty oblasts.

- Establishing centre for soil degradation problems in Akmola oblast.

- Development and implementation of measures on improving arable land fertility (pilot projects in South Kazakhstan, Kzylorda, North Kazakhstan, Akmola oblasts).

Conservation of landscape and biological diversity

- Extension of forest areas for restoration and conservation of biodiversity and biocenosis.

- Improving anti-fire surveillance system in coniferous forests (East Kazakhstan oblast).

- Development of the system of especially protected natural territories and ecotourism based on the above.

- Organisation of environmental and resources monitoring of forests.

Supporting institutional projects

- Establishment of a system for management of priority projects.

- Strengthening public awareness and participation in NEAP/SD project implementation.

- Formation of environmental education system in educational institutions, taking into account the RK environmental protection priorities and strategies.

- Improvement of mechanism for the accomplishment of environmental conventions with the example of the intersectoral framework project of 'The Carbon Initiative of Kazakhstan.'

- Establishment of an international centre for investigation of the impact of the Semipalatinsk nuclear testing site on health and the natural environment.

- Development of the mechanism and improvement of the interaction between the RK NEAP/SD, and development of similar plans of the countries of Central Asia and central and eastern Europe, and international organisations.

Because of the economic situation, implementation of these projects is largely dependent on donor funding. Funding for certain areas covered by the NEAP has already been provided by the European Union (EU) through its TACIS programme, the Japanese government, the Global Environment Fund (GEF), UNDP, USAid and other organisations, while other projects are in the pipeline. Typically, the projects are open to participation by consultants or consortia, and are advertised in international journals in accordance with the requirements of the funding agencies. To date the work is mainly at the stage of developing terms of reference and carrying out feasibility studies. A joint World Bank/UK government Know-How Fund mission has considered the question of water supply to the new capital Astana, for example, and the implications of mercury pollution in the River Nura on the available options. The Japanese government has funded studies on air pollution in Pavlodar oblast and on solid waste management in Kazakhstan. There are also a number of larger international initiatives such as the Caspian Environmental Programme, which involves all five Caspian states and includes elements funded by the GEF, the EU's TACIS programme, UNDP and USAid. In Kazakhstan the project includes the establishment of specialist centres for biodiversity and water level fluctuation, and subprojects in the field of education and training.

Conclusion

In summary, Kazakhstan's environmental problems have a direct bearing on its present, its future and on the potential for doing business in the country. The current legacy of degradation and pollution has a huge impact on the health of the population, and on the productivity of industries such as agriculture and fisheries. If the country's industries are to be modernised, foreign investment is essential – but foreign investors will not be prepared to take on unlimited or unknown liabilities for pollution and environmental damage. There is thus a need for environmental assessment, and for training to transfer the skills to carry out this work within the country. There is also potential for a huge range of environmental projects, as described above. Which of these projects are implemented and which opportunities materialise depends entirely on the future growth and development of the economy.

2.13

Imports and Exports

Shelly Fitch and Globalink

Importing and exporting

The import–export market in Kazakhstan is characterised by rapid and sometimes radical change. Over the past three years, Kazakhstan has moved from the position of being a net exporter to that of a net importer.

Kazakhstan is currently experiencing an industrial decline, which became particularly evident in 1998 when overall export revenues totalled US$194 million, a drop of almost 20 per cent over 1997 revenues. Exports continued to decline in early 1999. This is due in part to the fact that oil, metals and chemicals, which account for two-thirds of Kazakhstan's exports and are the main contributors to Kazakhstan's economy, were affected by a general decline in world prices of about 25 per cent over 1997 price levels.

In April 1999 the tenge was allowed to float 'freely'. It was hoped that this would make Kazakhstani exports more attractive in world markets. Despite a devaluation of the tenge by about 30 per cent since then, positive results have yet to be felt by Kazakhstani industry.

Although imports into Kazakhstan continue to grow, the growth rate has slowed significantly. In 1997 overall imports were valued at US$940 million – an increase in growth of 37 per cent over 1996 levels. In 1998 overall imports were valued at US$1.05 billion, exceeding 1997 levels by only 12 per cent. Imports run the gamut from foodstuffs and medical equipment to building materials and electronics. More than 60 per cent of Kazakhstan's imports continue to be provided by non-CIS (Commonwealth of Independent States) countries.

In January 1999 Russia, Kazakhstan's largest single trading partner, was prohibited from exporting subsidised, and therefore cheap, foodstuffs to Kazakhstan in order to protect unsubsidised local industry. At the same time, Uzbekistan and Kyrgyzstan were subjected to 200 per cent duties on selected exports to Kazakhstan. Although most of these barriers have since been lifted, Kazakhstan is still viewed by the International Monetary Fund (IMF) and other international organisations as being too eager in its protectionism of the agricultural and industrial sectors, as evidenced by steadily increasing tariff levels and the proliferation of specific and mixed tariffs.

Licensing continues to be required for the import and export of a variety of strategic, excise and medical goods. The local Kazakhstani importer or exporter is responsible for fulfilling licensing requirements.

Customs

In a positive step towards achieving world service standards, Kazakhstan began licensing freight forwarders/customs house brokers in 1999.

Despite the difficulty in obtaining up-to-date information on constantly changing customs rules and regulations, Kazakhstani customs house brokers and freight forwarders are, as a rule, extremely effective in dealing with the mostly confusing and daunting system. Overwhelming bureaucracy, arbitrary demands for excessive amounts of documentation and a lack of answerability on the part of customs officials continue to characterise dealings with Kazakhstani customs.

Radical restructuring was imposed on Kazakhstani customs in 1998 and 1999, following the move in 1997 of the government to the new capital, Astana. The customs department now falls under the aegis of the relatively new Ministry of State Revenues. In an effort to cut costs and streamline services, customs' huge personnel base has been reduced significantly and efforts are being made to purge it of corrupt and incompetent officials. It is openly admitted that graft and corruption continue to be one of customs' greatest challenges.

During the summer of 1999 a new Chairman of Customs was appointed to replace the controversial former chief, who left to pursue a career in politics.

Since 1997, customs procedures have been partially computerised as part of an ongoing programme intended to bring services in Kazakhstan up to internationally accepted levels.

The customs department continues to work towards the implementation of more user-friendly procedures, such as the pre-arrival declaration procedure. Under this procedure, the importer is able to clear cargo through customs, up to the point of physical inspection, before the arrival of the shipment. Customs is also considering increasing the amount of time (currently three hours from time of arrival) during which a shipment must be cleared before it can be sent to a customs temporary storage warehouse.

NB: Due to the ever-changing nature of customs procedures in general, importers and exporters are encouraged to contact customs agents and juridical and 'big five' accounting firms operating in Kazakhstan.

Customs clearance

Customs clearance procedures in Kazakhstan have improved incrementally over the past eight years, most notably since 1998. At the very outset, it was at times extremely difficult to deal with customs authorities and to clear shipments. Kazakhstan's system, inherited from the Soviet era, was essentially incompatible with those of the rest of the world. Inconsistencies in procedure, in how duties were applied, in who was exempt and who was not, etc, could lead to a shipment being tied up in a customs warehouse for weeks or months, while incurring cumulative fines and penalties. This was largely the result of there being no consistently defined procedures in place, and in retrospect, this was entirely understandable.

In 1998, however, reforms in the customs clearing process brought higher standards. Only registered and licensed customs brokers, for instance, could now clear shipments. Brokers were also required to have third-party liability cover and other requirements were instituted; these changes contributed to eliminating many of the rotten apples that were previously surviving on arcane loopholes in the system. Recent changes to the customs code have eliminated value added tax (VAT) being charged on customs declarations, further simplifying the process.

It is important to remember that Kazakhstan is an almost entirely landlocked republic and is surrounded by countries that are for the most part much worse off economically. This makes it an ideal market for illegal goods, which customs must try as best as possible to prevent from flooding over the long and largely unprotected borders. With limited resources this can be a difficult, if not impossible, job, and it is therefore crucial to be aware of this if one hopes to relate productively with customs officials and understand their mindset. A recent crackdown on corruption by Kazakhstan's government and the recent installation as customs chief of a former KGB official have resulted in the shifting of personnel from region to region. It is ultimately better to think of customs authorities as allies rather than enemies. Kazakhstan – like many other former Soviet countries – has received some bad press when it comes to customs clearance, but looking at the region, it could be considered a very positive example.

Customs clearance is a complex issue, but it is one that has recently become simpler in Kazakhstan. Bottlenecks can occur anywhere along the long paths that freight travels, and it is surprising to note that most frequently, the delays occur elsewhere.

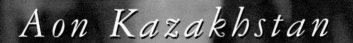

2.14

Insurance

Marsh

Introduction

Any company investing in a developing market faces risks that must be analysed and quantified. The ultimate decision on whether you proceed with an investment is determined by an evaluation of whether the potential commercial gains exceed the risks faced. As part of this equation, companies rely on insurance to transfer some of these risks and thus reduce some of their financial exposure. But this of course implies the existence of a stable insurance market, capable of meeting its financial obligations in a professional manner.

At the time when Kazakhstan became an independent state, insurance was virtually unknown as a financial tool. Since that time there has been a rapid evolution with insurance laws having been developed and companies established to meet the needs of private individuals and investors alike.

Insurance laws and regulations

The key piece of legislation for the Kazakhstan insurance market is the Decree on Insurance of 11 October 1995, as modified in 1999, that sets out the framework within which the insurance market operates.

This legislation sets out a number of key rules for the conduct of insurance:

- Supervision of the market is undertaken by The National Bank of Kazakhstan.

- All insurers must obtain a general licence and licences for each type of policy they issue. This process is managed by The National Bank.

- A separate company is required to transact life insurance business.

- All risks on the territory of Kazakhstan that are insured must have an insurance policy issued by a registered insurance company.

- The minimum capital requirement for an insurer is 40,000 times the minimum monthly wage (approximately US$250,000). It is anticipated that this will be increased as the National Bank seeks to increase the strength and stability of the local insurers.

- No single insurer is allowed to retain financial risk of more than 10 per cent of its combined share capital and premium reserves on a single policy.

- A minimum of 5 per cent must be retained in Kazakhstan on any one single risk.

- Foreign shareholders can establish Kazakhstani insurance subsidiaries that are 100 per cent foreign-owned, but only a maximum of 25 per cent of the total market capitalisation can be owned by foreign entities.

- Insurance brokers are required to obtain a licence from the National Bank.

The development of the insurance market

The legal and regulatory framework described above has permitted the development of free competition in the insurance market. An insurance buyer has the right to select:

- its insurance broker;

- the scope of insurance it wishes to purchase;

- its Kazakhstani insurer;

- all re-insurers.

This environment has resulted in the rapid growth of both the number of insurers and their capitalisation (see Table 2.14.1).

Table 2.14.1 Number of insurers and their capitalisation, 1995–98

	1995	1996	1997	1998
Number of insurers	53	56	65	70
Registered capital (US$ millions)	6.73	11.9	20.21	24.70

Source: The National Bank of Kazakhstan

By the end of 1998 insurers had combined investments of US$66.8 million invested as shown in Figure 2.14.1.

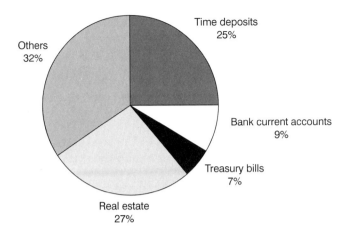

Figure 2.14.1 Investments by insurers in 1998

Source: The National Bank of Kazakhstan

The volume of insurance business has also expanded rapidly (see Figure 2.14.2).

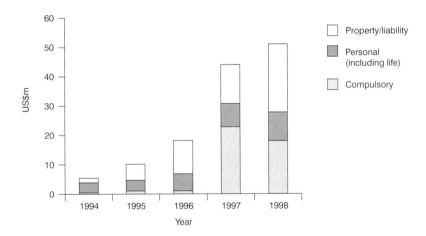

Figure 2.14.2 Insurance premiums

Source: The National Bank of Kazakhstan

Within this pattern there are a number of key trends to highlight:

- Motor liability became the largest single class of insurance after it became compulsory in 1997.

- Personal insurance has grown steadily as consumers recognise the need and benefits of insurance. However, life insurance has remained a small percentage of this market with only three licensed insurers registered by September 1999.

- Commercial insurance represented by property and liability is widely available and is increasingly being purchased. This class has experienced rapid growth. The largest single buyers in this market tend to be companies with foreign shareholders or companies involved in international trading.

Compulsory insurance

Certain classes of insurance have been made compulsory. These include:

- motor liability, where cover is provided for a limit of approximately US$3,500 under the compulsory arrangements. Rates are based on a set tariff, but the buyer can choose its insurer;

- agricultural risks;

- passenger liability for operators of transport systems;

- employee injury, where the Law on Safety at Work creates a liability on employers of more than ten times the annual salary of an employee, plus dependants' benefits, in the event of death during the course of employment;

- ecological damage for certain defined hazardous activities.

In practice, the only class of compulsory insurance that is actively enforced is motor liability. During 1997 and 1998 this form of insurance represented 96 per cent of all premiums received for compulsory insurance. It is anticipated that changes will be introduced for other classes of risk, which will result in modifications to the existing laws and greater enforcement. For example, there is currently no definition of the exact scope of insurance required to meet the liabilities defined in employee injury legislation. As a consequence, most companies have not purchased this type of insurance.

Claims

The loss ratios of the insurance market have generally been favourable. However, there is a marked difference in the loss ratios between different sectors of insurance.

Table 2.14.2 Claims paid as a percentage of premium received

| | | Percentage | | |
Class of insurance	1995	1996	1997	1998
Compulsory	1.0	1.6	9.3	31.4
Personal (including life)	44.6	37.3	48.9	48.3
Property/liability	20.7	5.9	8.1	19.0

Source: The National Bank of Kazakhstan

Compulsory insurance is predominantly motor liability insurance. The compulsory scheme has tariff premiums and is now widely purchased by motorists. As the public becomes more aware of this insurance, claims are also increasing.

The most profitable classes of insurance have been property and liability cover. However, it should always be remembered that many parts of Kazakhstan have a high risk of earthquakes. While there have been no claims for this risk in the recent past, it is inevitable that sooner or later claims will be made.

Reinsurance

Like many developing insurance markets, the capacity of local insurers to retain significant risks is limited. Consequently there is a dependency on international reinsurance to support the Kazakhstani market for larger projects.

At the early stages in the development of the market most reinsurance was arranged on an optional basis. As local insurers have increased their skill and experience, treaty reinsurance has developed as a means of reinsuring many classes of risk. This trend is expected to continue in the future. An additional benefit of reinsurance is that it increases the knowledge of local insurance staff and results in the development of sound international insurance procedures.

Training

The need for training staff working in the Kazakhstani insurance sector is widely recognised. The principal difficulties faced relate to the cost and language differences experienced when training is provided by western insurance specialists. Some funding for this task has been provided by international aid agencies. However, there is considerable scope and opportunity for further training in the future.

Why investors' insurance should be purchased in Kazakhstan

The question frequently arises as to why an investor should purchase insurance cover via an insurer registered in Kazakhstan. Sometimes it is claimed that international arrangements are cheaper, better, or more financially secure. Some of these arguments may be valid, but this does not mean that such an approach is the ideal solution or legally correct. Quite simply the laws of Kazakhstan, like most of the countries of the world, require all entities to insure their risks with an insurer who is registered in the country. Examples exist of companies that have not followed this approach and that have encountered difficulties at a later stage. Some of the problems include:

- encountering difficulties with government departments. Non compliance is illegal and can be treated accordingly;

- having several years premium disallowed as a business expense;

- fines for incorrect compilation of accounts;

- having claims settlements treated as income to the business and subject to tax;

- difficulties with audits from bodies such as the Ministry of Ecology;

- adverse publicity where the investor purchased illegal non-admitted liability cover.

Clearly a balance needs to be found whereby companies fully comply with the law but, for larger risks, ensure that there is adequate reinsurance in force. In this respect, all companies should seek professional advice from a source that is qualified and sufficiently experienced in working for investors in Kazakhstan.

Expected future developments

As insurance continues to mature as a concept, a number of developments are anticipated in the future. While it is difficult to be precise, the following is considered likely:

- The National Bank as the Insurance Regulator will continue to regulate the market and actively use some of its new powers, introduced in the 1999 legislation.

- The capital requirements for establishing an insurer will increase. A minimum capital base of US$1 million has been considered in the past.

- Consolidation is likely to occur with fewer larger insurers active in the market.

- Regulations for insurance and reinsurance brokers will be developed and enforced.

- Clearer rules for transacting reinsurance business will be introduced.

- Certain additional classes of insurance will become compulsory. The first type of risk to be reviewed is likely to be employee injury cover where clear rules of insurance are likely to be developed and enforced.

- While making some insurance compulsory will result in growth in the premiums paid to insurers, the ultimate success of insurers in Kazakhstan will be linked to the general economic success of the country.

2.15

The Machine Engineering Industry

The Kazakhstan Investment Promotion Centre

Kazakhstan's mechanical engineering sector is currently represented by 2,937 machine industry and metalwork plants. Tractor and farming machine industries are well represented in the Republic as, to a lesser degree, are the electrical, road building, and municipal engineering industries. Other priority branches of the sector, such as the air, chemical, and petroleum machine industries are under-represented. The import of rolling-mill machinery, mining machines and cutting machines has failed to improve the Republic's situation in this sector; however, efforts are currently being made to develop a motor industry within the Republic.

The fact that the machine-engineering complex possesses advanced machinery, such as mechanical flow, automatic transfer lines and automatic and auto-manual machinery is highly valuable for the industry's operative output. The level of equipment is particularly high in those engineering plants that operate at high production levels.

In the Republic, the manufacturing mechanical engineering complex is capable of meeting only 10 to 30 per cent of demand of the needs of certain industry sectors. The rest of the demand is met by the import of machinery and equipment from the CIS (Commonwealth of Independent States) and non-CIS countries. Different types of farm machines, trucks and passenger cars come from these countries. Many of the fixed assets of engineering plants are worn out and have become 40 to 60 per cent obsolete. As a result, many machines produced in Kazakhstan are uncompetitive in terms of design, engineering and price.

Kazakhstan's mechanical engineering complex and that of a majority of CIS countries can currently be characterised by reduced levels of production of high-tech commodities, a growth of energy and metal consumption and the low competitive strength of domestic products. Over the last few years in Kazakhstan the production of appliances and automated equipment has diminished by two- to three-fold.

According to the National Programme of Privatisation and Deregulation, the engineering plants' state-owned stockholdings are to be sold within the framework of mass and individual privatisation.

The basic sources of finance are the facilities of the plants themselves, their customers and new investors. State support through the Economic Conversion Fund is minimal and therefore has not had a significant impact on increasing production. Nevertheless, there is huge potential for development within the engineering complex and for enhancing Kazakhstan's progress and bringing it to the level of those countries that currently apply up-to-the-minute procedures and international standards.

In 1998 the machine industry's share of total industrial output was 3.6 per cent.

Table 2.15.1 Machine industry and metalworking basic indicators*

Indicators	1994	1995	1996	1997	1998
Number of plants	3,694	3,493	2,992	2,937	–
Output (US$ millions)	292	574	600	501	342
Production volume compared to previous year (%)	62.9	72.2	90.8	70.2	66.6

* At the National Bank's rate on 1 February 1999 (KZT 85/US$ 1)

For the time being, the trend towards lower production levels is persevering in the engineering sector. This reduction is caused by a series of intrinsic and extrinsic factors, namely:

- an increase in the cost of commodities and a rise in the price of power resources, raw materials, and transport services;

- the uncompetitiveness of Kazakhstan-manufactured machine products in the market;

- a reduction in the level of orders for the military-industrial complex;

- a general contraction of markets and the sluggish adoption of any new ways of doing business (privatisation, creation of joint-stock companies, etc).

The recent fall of the Russian rouble has resulted in an inflow of manufactured products into the Republic, at prices far cheaper than those charged by Kazakhstan's domestic producers. This has had a considerable adverse effect on the competitiveness of many plants in Kazakhstan.

Government incentives and investment opportunities

At present, the government is actively supporting domestic producers. A Small Business Development Fund has been created to provide credit to investment projects, a Financial Support Fund for Farming is to fund the manufacture of farming machines, quotas on imports have been imposed to protect domestic producers and enterprises have been granted tax concessions. Also, the restructuring, segmentation and diversification of production at many plants over the past five years has allowed producers to lower the cost price of their products and to find new consumers. These changes have had a positive effect on maintaining the business activity of many plants.

On the whole, the engineering complex of Kazakhstan has significant production potential. However, to fully realise this potential, it still requires financial and technical investment, scientific support and an improvement in market conditions.

As a result of the government's Action Programme for 1998–2000, a turnaround will be created in the engineering and metal-cutting sectors by encouraging inter-factory co-operation to produce both conventional and import-substituting products. Under the State Programme of Development and Conversion for the defence industry, the creation of high-tech product facilities will be promoted, future orders for repair shops will be provided and the export of a few kinds of machines and implements will be encouraged.

The short-term development priorities of the machine and metal-working industries are:

- an expansion of the spectrum and volume of production of spares and maintenance kits for the existing stock of mining equipment, farming machinery and transportation facilities;

- the production of certain types of machinery for the oil-and-gas, metallurgical, and steel industries using existing facilities;

- an expansion in the scope of the inter-factory co-operation to increase available capacities and to lower the imports of components;

- the creation of assembly facilities for machines of guaranteed demand based on the purchase of machine sets (lorries, combine harvesters, home appliances, etc) and the use of an increasing share of locally produced components.

The implementation of projects related to the exploration and transportation of oil and gas to the markets of the Mediterranean and the Black Sea, and also to China and Russia, makes it indispensable to develop the domestic machine industry so that it can produce articles for oil-and-gas plants. There are 36 plants in the Republic that can manufacture competitive machines (production trees, snaps, bolts, rebuilt machine tools for rotary-balanced jacks, pumps of different types, service rigs, and many others) for oil-and-gas plants. Currently, the government is promoting the development of domestic production facilities for machines and implements for oil-and-gas companies, as a means of participating in the implementation of oil-and-gas projects.

Further development of mining, chemical and petrochemical products will bring about a renewal of the machine-engineering complex. Currently these sectors desperately need retooling with up-to-date implements, machines and mechanisms.

According to a designed draft programme for the engineering complex, for the period 1999–2000, the following will be developed as soon as possible:

- the machine industry for the fuel, energy and agro-industrial complexes;

- the mining machine industry;

- production of facilities for railway rolling stock;

- the motor industry;

- the production of consumer goods.

The implementation of this programme will require the investment of additional funds using exterior sources of finance.

In the 1990s there was almost no inflow of foreign investment into the engineering sector. The placement of investments by potential investors was hindered by the substantial debts of the plants, by the salary debt, and by other commitments. Notwithstanding this lack of investment in existing facilities, many foreign firms are nevertheless successfully doing business in Kazakhstan. Joint ventures have been created with the Korean corporations Samsung, Daewoo and LG Electronics to manufacture videotape recorders, TV sets and refrigerators. Cryogenic tanks are also being produced jointly with Belorussian and Italian corporations.

At present, many plants in Kazakhstan still possess highly skilled specialists, unique machinery making reliable and excellent manufactured products, and ample production areas. Earlier lost business links with buyers and suppliers are now being restored. All these factors create a substantial platform for future investment in the machine industry sector.

Table 2.15.2 Machine industry output (no of pieces)

Item	1994	1995	1996	1997	1998
Press-forging machines	434	269	127	82	15
Cutting machines	429	57	114	42	8
Bulldozers	695	521	247	256	49
Centrifugal pumps	7,658	5,713	3,012	189	–
Tractors	1,988	1,803	2,465	1,922	404
Tractor mowing-machines	4995	2030	974	1127	–
TV sets	–	–	63,439	48,799	102,271
Washing machines	–	–	20,122	10,061	2,985

2.16

Telecommunications: The Market

Roger MacNair, Business Intelligence, BT British Telecom/A&M

Introduction

Modern telecommunications are in great demand worldwide. About 15 per cent of the world's population use 85 per cent of the world's telecommunications. In the developed world, the incredible growth in wireless services and data transfer has boosted economic growth. In the developing world, governments are becoming increasingly aware of the importance of modernising their telecommunications infrastructure, and thus providing an important ingredient in the quest for economic development and higher living standards for their citizens.

The telecommunications infrastructure in Central Asia is well behind that of the developed world, but has made significant progress from the days of the old command economy structure under the aegis of the Soviet Union. Governments in the region are aware that a coherent body of commercial law on telecommunications is essential to provide the confidence needed to attract the foreign investment for the establishment of a modern telecommunications system.

The telecommunications infrastructure

Kazakhstan enjoys some of the best telecommunications services within the Central Asia region. Its large territory at over 2.7 million sq km (the size of Western Europe), makes it the ninth largest country in the world, and because of its insufficient infrastructure, many investment opportunities remain. The Law on Foreign Investment of December 1994 and that on Direct Investment of February 1997 have helped stabilise the legal and commercial environment, and have helped create the right climate for foreign investment.

Obtaining a telecommunications licence issued by the Ministry of Communications is essential for conducting telecommunications activities such as:

- local, inter-city and international telephone services;
- data transfer;
- cellular and satellite services;
- television and radio;
- construction and assembly of telecommunications equipment.

Kazakhstan's telecommunications system comprises about 2.2 million lines: automatic connections to international networks, cellular networks, a diverse range of coaxial and fibre optic cables, microwave and satellite earth stations. There is, in addition, much obsolete equipment and technology inherited from the old Soviet telecommunications network. Telephone penetration is currently about 13 per cent of the population.

Kazakh Telecom

The law refers to Kazakh Telecom (KT) as the national operator of telecommunications. However, on 31 May 1997, the Government of the Republic of Kazakhstan under President Nursultan Nazarbaev signed an agreement to sell 40 per cent of the shares in KT to Daewoo, a South Korean firm that promised to invest US$1 billion in the development of Kazakhstan's telephone network. However, due to problems engendered by the Asian financial crisis in April 1998, Daewoo divested its holding, selling 75 per cent to Kazkommertsbank and the remaining 25 per cent to various banks and investment funds.

In essence, KT engages in commercial telecommunications activities on behalf of the state. The organisation has 48,000 employees, 14 regional offices and annual revenues approaching US$500 million. It has agreements with over 30 international operators and has invested over US$388 million in its network since 1993. This includes the installation of 43,000 km of cable, and the installation of a GSM cellular communications system based in Astana.

Furthermore, a Kazakh–Australian (Telstra) joint venture company called Satel has been providing international satellite communications since 1991. Two receiving stations having been built at Almaty and Astana. Last year, however, Satel failed to reregister its licence, and KT signed a contract with the Israeli firm Gilat Satellite Networks for the construction of a national satellite communications system.

Satellite communications

With its population of 15.7 million and its vast area Kazakhstan has one of the lowest population densities in the world at just 5.8 per sq km. Indeed, 45 per cent of the population are still classified as rural. The geography and demographics of Kazakhstan present something of a problem for telecommunications. PSTN and GSM networks, along with domestic and international private circuits have limited coverage. The means of communication that multinational corporations are comfortable using are not appropriate to local conditions over large parts of the country, yet the need for them to communicate is increasing exponentially, as the development of mineral, oil and gas resources continues apace. The ideal solution to these problems is satellite communications.

A range of satellite products is available. Inmarsat provides maritime and several land mobile services through a number of land earth station operators (LESO's) worldwide. These LESO's in turn sell both directly and through networks of agents and distributors. Inmarsat services have been evolving and improving in the face of competition from new satellite communications service providers such as Iridium.

The Inmarsat 'B' product is long-established, allowing digital voice, data, fax and telex communications at speeds up to 64 kb per second, from a suitcase-sized terminal weighing 22 kg or more. Inmarsat 'B' has been used all over the world for transferring files to and from corporate headquarters, sending video to newsrooms, supporting e-mail and giving access to the Internet, as well as enabling 'simple' voice communications.

In the last few years the mini-M product has emerged, giving voice communications with data and fax at 2.4 kb per second, from a terminal the size of a laptop computer and weighing just 2.4 kg. The introduction of mini-M technology has proved a huge step forward in terms of both portability and cost, making it much easier to carry satellite communications in the field and to establish bases in remote locations. Applications supported by this technology include file transfer, e-mail and Internet access.

The autumn of 1999 saw the launch of Inmarsat's Global Area Network, a service offering mini-M capability with 64 kb per second analogue and ISDN (Integrated Digital Services Network) compatible digital channels. Terminals weigh from 3.9 kg and, with the launch of the 64 kb per second Internet compatible service early in 2000, offer a remarkable raft of capabilities combined with genuine portability. Remote users will be able to connect to the corporate LAN (local-area network) as if they were at their desks, with full e-mail, Intranet, Extranet and Internet access. The ISDN capability allows the full range of ISDN applications, such as videoconferencing, data transfer, remote inspection, maintenance and telemedicine among others. The analogue channel supports modem speeds of up to 33 kb per second. This unique combination of high speed, versatility and portability is expected to have a major impact on the satellite communications market.

Inmarsat products may be taken into Kazakhstan without licences for up to one month. For longer periods, a licence costing US$1,000 per year is required (US$300 on renewal); import duties and value added tax (VAT) also apply.

VSAT services over networks such as those of Intelsat and Eutelsat are also available, at speeds of up to 8 Mb per second or more. With larger dishes, and a greater degree of complexity in their installation and commissioning, VSAT is more suitable for 'fixed' or long-term sites. VSAT can be provided with a diverse range of service and tariff options.

New satellite services such as the narrowband services offered/to be offered by Iridium, ICO, Globalstar, Thuraya, AceS and EAST could also be worth considering. Looking further into the future, the broadband services to be offered by Teledesic and Skybridge may offer a more acceptable alternative.

Several LESOs, such as British Telecom (BT) in the UK, offer the whole portfolio of Inmarsat services, plus Iridium and VSAT services. In BT's case, this offer is backed by a multilingual customer service unit that provides support 24 hours a day, 7 days a week, and a range of billing options. It is also possible to integrate these offerings with a company's domestic IT/communications network. Working with a LESO that has a full range of capabilities affords customers the option of custom-building a solution tailored to their specific needs.

Foreign investment in telecommunications

It is possible for foreign companies to hold a telecommunications licence in Kazakhstan. They will be required to sign an interconnect agreement with KT in order to secure connection to the national network. The agreement includes items relating to obligations of the parties, measurement of durations, routing, interconnection points, technical standards, charges, payments and escalation procedures. However, the great majority of foreign investors choose to work with a local partner in a joint venture registered as a company in Kazakhstan. This effectively creates a buffer between the foreign partner's 'home' operations and business in Kazakhstan, reducing the risk of claims on the parent company.

The Law on Direct Investment designates telecommunications as a 'priority sector' and consequently provides tax incentives for investors in that sector. Not surprisingly, therefore, given the regulatory framework, there are several local–foreign parent joint ventures. These largely relate to overlay network services, satellite communications, earth stations and microwave links. Licences are governed by the Presidential Edict 2200 On Licensing of April 1995 and by the Law on Communication of May 1999, which effectively granted KT the status of 'open public stock company'.

Notable foreign investors include some of the top multinational corporations. Siemens of Germany acting with KT successfully completed the Kazakhstan section of the Trans Asian European (TAE) fibre optic line linking Shanghai to Frankfurt. Nortel has an agreement with KT to install digital communications equipment. Alcatel is also involved with KT in a project to provide switching equipment to modernise the telephone network. Lucent Technologies is similarly involved in the installation of digital equipment. Cisco Systems is involved in the formation of a national data network with Kaznet, a subsidiary of KT. Kar-Tel, a joint venture with Turkey's Rumeli Group, operates under the trade name K-Mobile, and has been instrumental in introducing GSM phone services to the central Kazakhstan region. Other notable joint ventures with KT include: Becet International cellular services acting under the Altel trade mark, Arna, which provides telecommunications services to corporate clients; and Astel/Arna Sprint, which is assisting in the provision of a global data transfer system.

Kazakhstan is boldly making the transition from a command economy to a fully fledged market economy. A case-by-case privatisation programme has been in hand for the last five years. The fact that the government has been working closely with the International Monetary Fund (IMF), and within the terms of guidelines prescribed by it, has facilitated financial assistance from institutions such as the World Bank, the European Bank for Reconstruction and Development (EBRD) and the Asian Development Bank. The participation of such institutions has given multinational corporations the confidence to commit to ambitious foreign investment programmes. A competitive environment is being created and now provides an active market for communications services. These positive developments are being reinforced by the establishment of a solid body of commercial law and in particular by the passing of the Law on Communications.

2.17

Telecommunications: Product Services

Curt Hopkins, Nursat and Jeff Andrusevich,
MCIWorldCom

Background

Establishing trouble-free telecommunications in emerging markets is never easy and doing so in Kazakhstan is no exception. Kazakhstan, however, is working hard on improving its telecommunications infrastructure and services for consumers and businesses. As a result, the Kazakhstani telecommunications market is growing and services are improving as this new country enters the market economy. Since independence in 1991, investors have worked hard to introduce modern technologies into the telecommunications system, and their efforts are paying off.

However, a big challenge for telecommunications in Kazakhstan is the low density of population spread over a vast land mass. Saddled with an antiquated infrastructure inherited from the Soviet period, Kazakhstan has had a long way to go to 'catch up' with the modern world. Infrastructure has been poorly maintained for years, and the population is accustomed to a low quality and very low-cost service.

Kazakhstan has sought to develop the market in such a way that the telecommunications infrastructure will grow logically and so that competition can be fostered. This policy has been carried out primarily through mandating that the former state carrier, Kazakh Telecom (KT), must universally serve the entire population in Kazakhstan. To accomplish this, the government has regulated KT's local and domestic tariffs and allowed it to cross-subsidise these services through high international voice tariffs. At the same time, new entrants have been encouraged to invest in local infrastructure (though they must hand over all domestic and international traffic to KT) and in value added markets such as the Internet.

In order to enhance its position in the market, KT has focused on attracting outside debt and equity financing. First, KT received a 500 DM loan from the German agency KFW in order to finance the development of the Trans Asian European (TAE) fibre optic line through the south of Kazakhstan. In 1997 there was a tender for 40 per cent of KT's shares (the remaining 60 per cent was held by the government and management, at 50 per cent and 10 per cent respectively). Daewoo Telecom won the tender and assumed management of the company in May 1997. This, however, was short-lived as the Asian financial crisis caused Daewoo to withdraw its investment and to sell its shares to the locally owned Kazkommertsbank (30 per cent) and other Wall Street and European investment houses (10 per cent). The European Bank for Reconstruction and Development (EBRD) has recently announced that they will purchase an equity stake in KT taking 15 per cent from Kazkommertsbank and 15 per cent from the government. There has also been additional debt financing provided by the EBRD.

In the past year, Kazakhstan has seen the introduction of two GSM (Global System for Mobile Communications) companies to complement the existing analogue mobile operator. This comes in addition to a highly competitive Internet market that started in 1995 and has rapidly developed. Furthermore, KT has been making improvements to the city networks and to domestic voice and data trunks.

In spite of inheriting a semi-monopoly, KT has faced significant competition in Kazakhstan from competitive local access providers, Internet service providers, data transmission providers and satellite operators who provide dedicated networks and international and domestic dedicated satellite channels.

When establishing operations or making investments in Kazakhstan, it is important to understand the complexities of the market. Following is an overview of the various telecommunications services available in Kazakhstan.

Product services

Mobile communications

In early 1999, two new GSM operators launched their services, namely K-Cell and K-Mobile. As of September 1999 each GSM operator has a presence in several cities in Kazakhstan, including Astana and Almaty, and has established roaming in much of Europe and other parts of the Commonwealth of Independent States (CIS).

Since 1994 Altel has been offering analogue mobile service in Kazakhstan. While having greater coverage within Kazakhstan than either of the two GSM operators, Altel is limited in its international roaming abilities.

Local fixed line voice

The incumbent operator, KT, has inherited the existing infrastructure from the former PTT (Public Telephone and Telegraph) and therefore has the broadest market coverage. It is, however, hampered by outdated technology, poorly maintained equipment, and the obligation to provide service to unprofitable, far-flung villages. In Almaty, KT is upgrading its switches to digital technology, and thus is slowly improving its quality of service. To fill the gap, other local access providers such as Arna and Nursat have emerged to provide digital lines in Almaty. In Astana and all other Kazakhstani cities, KT is the dominant provider of local telecommunications access. Since 1991 KT has managed to install digital toll exchanges in all regional centres, and is now busy laying the fibre optic cables needed to create a nationwide digital transmission ring in addition to the TAE fibre optic cable crossing the southern end of the country.

Internet

From the beginning, Internet service providers (ISPs) have had a 'first mover' advantage over KT. The main two ISPs have been Nursat and Astel. Both companies have dial-up and leased line Internet access in cities throughout Kazakhstan. Recently entering the market has been KT through its subsidiary Kazakhstan Online. One new service provided by both Nursat and Kazakhstan Online is 56k dial-up access, and Internet access through ADSL (Asymmetrical Digital Subscriber Line).

The Internet craze has not bypassed Kazakhstan. Internet cafes are popping up all over the country, and it is quite easy to get a web site designed and hosted. It is expected that a robust e-commerce market will soon follow.

Large corporations are also working with leading ISPs to develop Intranets and Virtual Private Networks (VPNs) based upon Internet protocol.

Kazakhstan-based web sites are also proving to be very popular for investors. In particular, www.expat.kz has attracted numerous visitors. The site www.nursat.kz also provides access to other interesting Kazakhstani web sites.

International voice

KT, as a result of its incumbent position, is the largest provider of international voice services in Kazakhstan. However, because of price and quality issues, dedicated network providers, such as Nursat and Ratel, have picked up market share. These companies provide digital satellite lines with discounted tariff plans for the CIS, Europe and the USA.

Furthermore, some providers have received their own area codes for direct international dialling and therefore have the capability of bypassing KT's domestic infrastructure (eg Nursat utilizes the $+7-571-xxx-xxxx$ numbering plan).

Corporate networks

Many multinational corporations with operations in Kazakhstan and top tier local companies have begun to develop their own corporate telecommunications networks in Kazakhstan. These include frame relay and Internet protocol data networks, VPNs, and corporate telephony networks. It is even possible for companies with investments in remote areas of Kazakhstan to receive a full array of quality telecommunications services. Furthermore, many companies with numerous city offices all over Kazakhstan have eagerly developed VPNs with the latest Internet and VSAT (Very Small Aperture Terminal) technologies.

Satellite channels

For companies with high international data and voice costs, it makes sense to look at establishing dedicated satellite channels to locations outside of Kazakhstan. Companies providing these services include MCIWorldCom and Nursat.

The telecommunications market in Kazakhstan is exciting. It poses unique challenges but offers terrific potential. The race between KT and the smaller players has only just begun. Time will tell which strategies work the best.

2.18

Transport Networks

The Kazakhstan Investment Promotion Centre

Introduction

The transport and communication infrastructure of Kazakhstan includes pipelines, railways, aerial routes, water transport routes, highways, mail systems and telecommunications networks. Pipelines and telecommunications networks are covered elsewhere in this publication.

In recent years, the transport and communication complex has accounted for 9–10 per cent of the national gross domestic income (GDI).

The transport and telecommunications sector has a huge impact upon the effectiveness of market transformations in the economy of Kazakhstan. Indeed the growth in economic production as a whole in many respects depends on the level of this sector's development and efficient utilisation. The low population density (5.8 people per 1 sq km) within Kazakhstan, the dispersion of natural resources and centres of economic activity and the remoteness from non-CIS country markets are determining factors in infrastructure development. They make the transport sector a most important sector for the well-being of the national economy.

In view of the priority given to creating an effective transport network with exterior links for exports, great importance is placed on programmes aimed at improving transport routes and creating effective transport corridors to external markets. Creating legal, organisational and technical conditions for setting up international carriage operations is also important in this respect. Some 55 bilateral and multilateral international carriage agreements have already been signed between Kazakhstan and other countries. Lately, Kazakhstan has joined seven conventions in the field of road transport, nine marine and interior water transport conventions and eight related to civil aircraft.

A developed network of basic transit routes as well as highly skilled manpower in the transport sector are currently available in the Republic.

Investment and restructuring requirements

Sector objectives

Despite what has already been said above, the transport and communication complex of Kazakhstan is facing a series of basic strategic challenges on the path to becoming even more efficient. These include the:

- creation of a rational sovereign transport web integrated into the world transport system and providing Kazakhstan with access to the seas;

- modernisation of existing rail and highways, waterways, ports, airports, and aero-navigation complexes;

- creation of the country's own factory and repair stations for rolling stock of all types;

- building of an industry relating to the provision of modern communication facilities;

- creation of a modern system of telecommunications;

- improvement of the control system and the normative and legal basis for the transport and communication complex.

Investment requirements

The discharge of these tasks requires considerable funds. The total required investment, up to 2030, is estimated to be more than US$25 billion, of which about US$3 billion needed to be spent before 2000 and US$6 billion before 2005. Of this total investment about 40 per cent is required for the development of railway transportation, 23 per cent for highways and motor transport, 25 per cent for telecommunications and 12 per cent for the air and water transport system.

In an effort to create favourable conditions for foreign and domestic investors, goal-oriented and consistent investment policies are pursued within the transport and communication complex. Today, as well as in the long term, preference is given to the attraction of direct investment, which has a series of advantages over any other forms of economic aid.

The practice of transferring property under lease or in trust, under specific investment programmes, is applied in order to attract the necessary volume of investments. In the implementation of some new projects, different forms of concession (BOT and BOO patterns) will be utilised.

A competitive environment is being created and monopolies are being restricted to form an open and efficient transport and communication services market. A programme of reform for state-owned property will be implemented involving the privatisation of plants relating to railways, air, water and motor transport.

The licensing of transport and communication services is subject to the terms of Kazakhstan's Law on Licensing.

In the field of tariff policies, measures are being undertaken to bring the existing rate system closer to market rates. Reform and reduction of the rates is planned on a stage-by-stage basis over the next two to three years. There will be a parallel programme of modernisation within the industry based on the attraction of soft loans. This programme includes planned investment projects worth over US$5 billion.

Railway network

The railway system

The railway is the basic transport system of the Republic of Kazakhstan, catering for more than 85 per cent of overall freight traffic and 55 per cent of passenger turnover. It offers cheap cargo transportation services to CIS (Commonwealth of Independent States) and non-CIS countries. The arrangement and structure of the rail network, as a whole, meets both the interior and exterior transport and economic needs of the Republic, though requiring some improvement. Kazakhstan is interested in utilising its transport and transit potential to develop the key sectors of industry and farming.

New railways now link Kazakhstan to China, Iran and Central Asia, and also to many European countries. The length of the main railways is 13,400 km (including detours and platforms). Of this, 3,611 km are electrified, 10,205 km are equipped with automatic block systems and 12,953 km are equipped with railway radio communication. The length of the two-way lines is 5,087 km. They are furnished with a centralised monitoring system and each track is equipped with an automatic block system from two sides.

Normal heat traction predominates on the railway network, accounting for 75 per cent of the overall network length. The basic railway directions are arranged with self-locking and centralised dispatching. There is an automated control system for transportation on the railways. The total number of the stations is 825, including 11 merchandising yards, 60 cargo stations, 58 local stations and 696 way stations and halts. Electric traction accounts for 27 per cent of the total number of carriages. The carriage rolling stock is handled by 22 car sheds and 42 locomotive sheds. The railways have 2,600 locomotives (diesel and electric), 93,000 freight cars and 2,300 passenger coaches. In the future, electrification of up to 50 per cent of the densest spans is planned, leading to an increase in the average travelling speed of cargo and passenger trains. The manufacture of carriage rolling stock in Kazakhstan's own mechanical engineering plants is also envisioned.

Reorganisation of the railway system

The railway is essentially sound, but some problems exist. Major reorganisation has taken place over the last few years despite an acute financial shortage and a drop in the volume of business owing to the recent financial crisis in CIS and Asian countries. In 1999, a decrease was expected of approximately 12.1 per cent in freight traffic, 6.7 per cent in passenger turnover and 29.1 per cent in major repairs.

An enactment of the government, dated 31 January 1997, was aimed at perfecting and optimising the structure of the transportation system to remove any excessive control links and international junctions of secondary importance and to find a comprehensive approach to the issues of financial and economic improvement. It also created the national state-owned enterprise RGP Kazakhstan Temir Zholy, by merging three state-owned companies – the Almaty Railway, the Tselinniy Railway, and the Western Kazakhstan Railway.

In February 1997 the railway branch management system was reorganised. Then the former divisions of the roads were transformed into affiliated state-owned enterprises similar to the structural divisions of RGP Kazakhstan Temir Zholy. Five branches were created:

- Akmola (railway management in Astana City);
- Sary-Arka (Karaganda City);
- Western (Aktyubinsk City);
- Turkestan (Shymkent City);
- Almaty (Almaty).

A network of forwarding companies has also been created and works successfully in Kazakhstan.

In 1997 the Association of National Forwarding Agents of Kazakhstan (ANEK) was founded; it later joined the Forwarding International Agents Transport Association (FIATA), which has more than 140 country members. This, in turn, created more favourable conditions for the movement of Kazakhstan cargoes worldwide.

In the railway transportation sector, 12 mutual relations agreements have been signed between the Kazakhstan government and the governments of the republics of Belarus, Tadjikistan, Turkmenistan, Uzbekistan,

Ukraine, Azerbaijan, Kyrgyztan, Lithuania, Georgia and the Russian Federation.

It was planned to remove the differential rates along national and international railways and, step-by-step, to adopt uniform rates. The effect of this will be to reinforce the trend whereby transport makes up a smaller component of the domestic production cost price.

Main routes

Located at the heart of the Eurasian continent, Kazakhstan is at a natural transport crossroads. The following transcontinental corridors pass via its territory:

- the Trans–Asian main line – the central direction (Druzhba–Aktogai–Arys–Aktau, Druzhba–Aktogai–Arys–Chengeldy) and the northern direction (Druzhba–Aktogai–Syak–Mointy–Astana–Presnogorkovskaya);

- the Eurasian main line;

- the Central Asian Corridor (Chengeldy–Kandagach–Ozinki);

- the Western Corridor (Aksaraiskaya–Makat–Beineu).

Trans-Asian and Eurasian main lines

More than ten transport corridors operate on the Eurasian continent. The policy of openness and the desire to co-operate with a majority of the states of the Asian region have enabled Kazakhstan to construct and improve transport routes for communication, including the revival of the Great Silk Road as the basis for the Trans-Asian main line.

Upon the completion of construction in 1991 of the railway sections between Druzhba–Alashankou and the frontier of Kazakhstan with China and Tejen–Meshhed (Turkmenistan–Iran), two transcontinental main lines were formed: Trans-Asian (Peking–Almaty–Istanbul) and Eurasian (Peking–Almaty–London). Together they make up the Trans-Asian transport route. These main lines in the east ensure an outlet to the seaports of the Pacific and outlets to Iran, the Urals and into Siberia. In the west they provide links to the industrial centres of Europe and the ports of the Persian Gulf. The Kazakhstan section of this route is 3,800 km long. The estimated capacity for bulk carriage along both main lines is about 10–15 million MTA.

The Central Asian Corridor

The Central Asian Corridor links the Asian CIS republics with the European CIS and non-CIS countries. The length of the Kazakhstan section of this route is 2,500 km.

The Western Corridor

The development of the Western Corridor will be helped by the development of facilities for the transport of railway and maritime carriages through the port of Aktau and will provide transport services to the chief oil-producing regions of the Republic. The development of freight routes along this corridor is linked also to the implementation of the north-south project, which provides an intersection for cargoes from or to Europe (Scandinavia) and Iran (Persian Gulf). The Kazakhstan section of the Western Corridor is 2,500 km long.

As a result of reforms, there will be five ring-type railways in Kazakhstan crossing just about all the regions of the Republic and providing new transit routes across borders.

International routes south-westwards are rather promising for the further development of freight. Kazakhstan is especially concerned with transit directions via Uzbekistan and Turkmenistan to Istanbul and Karachi. The southern route via Kyrgyzstan and China to Pakistan and India, with an outlet to the ports of the Indian Ocean, is becoming feasible, and via these ports further to other countries of the world. The transit flows in this direction from the regions of the Urals and Siberia will also gravitate from the Almaty–Bishkek (Kyrgyzstan)–Kashgar (China) route to the Khundzherab saddle–Islamabad–Karachi (Pakistan) highway. The construction of a 90 km straightened section from Uzunagash settlement (Kazakhstan) to Kemin (Kyrgyzstan) should play a prominent part in this. The implementation of strategically vital civil-engineering projects for new railroad lines with an overall length of 2,985 km, at an estimated cost of US$1,907 million, will enable Kazakhstan to construct a self-contained national railway network.

The building of the Bekdash–Yeralievo railway (500 km), costing approximately US$400 million, is planned to create an international corridor from Turkmenia to western Kazakhstan, and on to the European regions of Russia and to other countries of the CIS.

Railway transportation's development outlook

The renovation of track facilities will be ongoing for years to come in Kazakhstan, as will the electrification of the basic freight routes supporting international freight. The first priority concerns the central and northern directions of the Trans-Asian main lines, to allow the reduction in spacing intervals and time of cargo transportation across the Europe–Asia communication network.

The reorganisation programme envisages a substantial reduction in costs, the immediate discarding of excessive carriages and property, a progressive retreat from barter deals, a large purchase of new machinery, a decrease in administrative expenditure and the removal of various inter-mediaries from the 'customer–railway' chain.

Updating the repair facilities for freight cars and carriages, and also of the existing locomotive fleet, is also scheduled. A preferred solution to the current problems would be to privatise the various elements of the railway infrastructure through the attraction of new investments. Shares have already been issued in facilities such as the Almaty and Akmola railway-carriage repair works and the Aktyubinsk and the Vishnevskiy factories of reinforced concrete cross-ties. The production capacities of these factories are capable of fully satisfying the needs of the railways of Kazakhstan and Central Asia, thus ensuring a reliable home market. These factories are auspicious from the point of view of the potential for a quick return of invested funds.

The restructuring of all control links and the commercialisation of railway activities will be carried out in a coordinated way as part of a detailed investment process. An example of mutually advantageous co-operation in this regard, between Kazakhstan and Japan, is provided by the implementation of the project for reconstruction of the Druzhba railway station and the Aktogai–Druzhba section. This was achieved by means of a long-term loan – US$68 million – provided by the Japanese Economic Cooperation Fund (OECF), with co-funding from Kazakhstan. To date, US$36 million has been utilised. The project was expected to be completed by 2000. One of the largest projects being considered is the building of a wide transport corridor along the Astana–western Kazakhstan segment, which comprises a telecommunication trunk, railway and motor lines. It will connect the centre of the country to its dynamically developing western part. There are, however, three alterna-tives also being considered: a railway between Zhezkazgan and Kyzylorda, one between Arkalyk and Chelkar, or one between Kostanai and Aktyubinsk. They will be financed by the OECF. A feasibility report was to be completed in 1999 before building could start.

The investment plan for the sector envisions:

- completion of the first phase of Druzhba station;

- reinforcement of the Druzhba–Aktogai railroad line;

- reconstruction of the Almaty Station passenger car-repair shed for the full-scale repair of coaches;

- rehabilitation of the track between the stations of Beskol and Druzhba;

- building of the Alakol Lake bypass;

- updating of the telecommunication links between the Aktogai and Druzhba stations;

- working with the European Bank for Reconstruction and Development (EBRD) to credit the project of reconstruction of the Almaty-Astana highway, which will be completed in 2000;

- prolongation of works to fortify the Beineu–Mangyshlak railway section;

- solution to the electrification issues relating to the Chu–Almaty and Pavlodar–Ekibastuz sections;

- talks with the OECF about starting to credit the second phase of the Druzhba station in 2000;

- talks with the OECF about crediting the construction of the following new railways: Arkalyk–Chelkar; Ust-Kamenogorsk–Charskaya (145 km); Aksu–Konechnaya (185 km); and the upgrading of the Mointy–Sayak and Druzhba–Aktogai.

Following this planned development, a national network of railways will be formed, and the development of new and existing repair and production facilities will have been accelerated.

Highways

Background

The highways are vital to the development of the national economy and to the creation of trade links with other countries. Their role becomes more important wherever railway communication is underdeveloped.

The length of the highways for general use in Kazakhstan is 87,337 km. The total length of national route roads is 17,670 km (60 per cent of all motor transport routes). Of these, 11,800 km are regarded as being of international standard. The total length of local route roads is 69,667 km. There are more than 3,000 bridges and flyovers along the network of highways.

The highways and man-made structures are maintained using the Road Fund, which is derived from the highway users' deductions; fares for entrance to, exit from, and transit within the territory of the Republic of Kazakhstan; the tax on gasoline and diesel fuel; and charges levied for travel on some state-owned highways.

Kazavtodor, the national state-owned enterprise for maintaining national route roads, was established in December 1998.

Development plans

The economic need to develop international communication means there is a need to attract investment to maintain the roads, to bring them into conformity with international standards in terms of hardness and flatness, to improve the maintenance organisation and to promote safe driving. Services for drivers (hotels, motels, camping sites with shops, cook-shops, medical aid, etc) and new transport services (maintenance, refuelling, help with accidents), will also be created.

Special attention will be paid to village roads, many of which will need to be hardcored and tarmaced. The approximate total investment required in the motorways of Kazakhstan is US$681 million. This will allow Kazakhstan to quickly improve the state of the highways along major transport corridors, where a growth in traffic intensity (particularly large and heavy transport) is expected.

The Republic has developed a programme 'Roads of Kazakhstan for the period 1996–2000 and up to 2010', whereby most attention is to be paid to international routes approved by the United Nations (UN), the (ESCATO) and the Organization for European Economic Cooperation (OEEC).

It is planned to rehabilitate the basic fragments of all five existing international routes (extent 7,000 km) before the end of 2000. This will ensure that freight transit links are provided between the industrially developed regions of the Republic and adjoining states.

A present deficiency in the amount of money in the Road Fund means that exterior loans need to be attracted to prevent deterioration in the network of major highways. The implementation of a series of big investment projects has been initiated amounting to US$0.5 billion. The projects are funded by means of loan agreements with the Asian Development Bank, the World Bank and the International Bank for Reconstruction and Development (IBRD).

The first priority is the upgrading of the Almaty–Astana road. In order to improve the environmental situation of the capital and to liberate transport streams, the construction of a bypass around Astana City is also proposed.

Another important project is the reconstruction of the Almaty-Borovoye motorway using loans from a number of international finance institutions.

A northern road corridor passing through the cities of Atyrau, Oktyabrsk, Aktyubinsk, Karabutak, Atbasar, Astana and Pavlodar with an overall length of 2,120 km will be created as part of the road network. This requires the construction of the missing section between Karrabutak and Torgai and the renovation of the existing roads. The Aktyubinsk–Khromtau–Karabutak–Aralks road is currently being renovated as a matter of priority, and a feasibility report for the civil-engineering project relating to the Karabutak–Torgai highway is almost completed. Currently, there is also a plan to rehabilitate and reconstruct separate sections of the southern, western and central transport corridors, whereas the eastern corridor will be studied and priority sectors will be selected. Development of the southern track to provide access to the ports of the Indian Ocean will be based on a quadrilateral agreement between Kyrgyzstan, China, Pakistan and India.

The motorways along the international route that exits Kazakhstan via Uzbekistan and Turkmenistan to the ports of Iran and Turkey are developing dynamically. Studies have been completed over the choice of priority sections for the rehabilitation of the Shymkent–Uralks–Samara international route. This route ensures a link between the republics of Central Asia and Russia, and the European CIS countries. The rehabilitation of various sections of this route is planned for 2003 with the help of a Japanese loan (OECF). During the period 2001–10, it is planned to restore the rest of the international routes (4,800 km), in order to optimise their use, and to complete the creation of a network of highways of international importance in the region.

The Asian Development Bank's second loan to reinforce the Shymkent–Bishkek–Almaty–Khorgos motorway, which is part of the Trans-Asian China–Iran–Turkey highway, is currently being prepared.

An arrangement for the financing of three projects connected with the revival of the Great Silk Road has been reached with the Asian Bank for Reconstruction and Development. In 1999 work will commence on repairs to the Almaty–Georgievka road, in 2000 the Georgievka–Turkestan will be overhauled, and in 2001 the Khorgos–Almaty routes will be upgraded. The medium-term project list contemplates a start to the Atyrau–Pavlodar and Maikapchagai–Omsk projects, prior to 2003.

The feasibility of forming a Europe–Caucasus–Asia motor transportation corridor (the TRASECA project) is being studied. This corridor would complement existing routes via Russia.

Motor transport

Background

Transport enterprises dealing in commercial freight traffic transported 852.415 million tons of cargo in 1998. Only 19.4 million tons of this freight was transported by motor transportation enterprises, which was 33 per cent less than in 1997. This indicates that the carrying capacity of the motor transport system is underused. Within the motor transport sector 68 per cent of freight journeys are carried out using urban and suburban communication routes, 29 per cent are long-distance and 3 per cent are international. The bulk of transit journeys along Kazakhstan's international roads, which currently account for approximately 1 million tons of various cargoes, is expected to have grown by at least 50 per cent before the end of 2000.

Table 2.18.1 Motor transport development for 1993–98

Indicators	1993	1994	1995	1996	1997	1998
Bulk of carriages (million tons)	1,382.2	979.6	954.2	805.6	620.7	852.4
Traffic (million tons-km)	29,213.0	15,656.0	10,765.0	9,628.0	6,480.6	19,219.0
Number of trucks	375,179	352,668	318,811	295,378	256,779	–
Passengers carried (millions)	2,105.4	1,760.2	1,669.7	1,221.0	1,025.5	–
Passenger turnover (million passengers-km)	24,896.0	18,674.0	17,643.0	12,943.0	11,523.8	71,758.0
Number of buses	56,195	54,808	54,006	47,506	46,244	–
Number of cars	955,353	991,656	1,033,305	997,544	973,323	–

Recent developments

The only state-owned enterprise in the motor transport system is the Republican State Motor Transportation Enterprise (RGAP), which provides emergency services. In general, the departments of passenger transport perform the functions of state regulation and monitoring.

Most of the motor vehicles used by transport and forwarding companies meet international standards. The League of International Motor Carriers of the Republic of Kazakhstan caters for the interests of international hauliers in Kazakhstan while the Forwarding Agents' Association caters for the interests of Kazakhstan forwarding agents.

The Republic of Kazakhstan adheres to 7 basic international agreements and conventions relating to international road transport, and more than 20 bilateral government-to-government agreements concerning international road transport have been signed.

The investment policies conducted in order to secure the normal operation of the transport corridors and the increase of transit freight levels envision attracting government-guaranteed loans from abroad for a period up to 2003 totalling over US$600 million.

The programme of restructuring and privatisation of the road freight industry, begun in 1992 as part of a United States Agency for International Development (USAID) technical help project, is approaching its end, although some motor transportation enterprises are still sold through open auctions. Most motor transport enterprises have been privatised. A post-privatisation programme has been implemented for the motor freight transport sector within the framework of an EBRD project of technical help.

To help the passenger transport sector, a project for updating the operation and the organisation of urban passenger transport in Kazakhstan has been worked out. The European Union (EU) has allocated 450,000 ECU for this project within the framework of the TACIS Programme.

The implementation of the IBRD's 'Urban Passenger Transport' project amounting to US$40 million, should be completed. It aims to keep up the work capacity of urban transport in the cities of Almaty, Karaganda, Shymkent, and Astana. Within the framework of this project 289 MAN buses (170 for Almaty, 56 for Karaganda, 40 for Shymkent and 23 for Astana) were delivered.

A programme to acquire city buses for the Pavlodar oblast has been completed by the KFV line: 33 buses worth 6.5 million DM were purchased.

Water transport

Waterways and ports

The water transport system of Kazakhstan is represented by many enterprises involved in the river transport of freight and passengers, as well as cargo-handling facilities in river ports and seaports. The water transport system comprises six river ports and two seaports; the total length of the river exceeds 4,000 km. The inland waterways include the rivers Irtysh, Ural, Ili, Ishim and Syr-Darya; the water reservoirs of Bukhtarminskoye, Ust-Kamenogorskoye and Shulbinskoye; and the Balkhash and Zaisan lakes. The Aktau and Atyrau commercial seaports are the two major seaports of the Caspian Sea.

Shipping

Almost all water transport joint-stock companies are private. Dry-cargo and tanker steamships with a load capacity of 600 up to 1,400 tons are used to carry cargoes by the river transport system. Steam tugs with a capacity of 150 up to 600 hp and non-navigable barges with a load capacity of 600 up to 1,800 tons are also used. Passenger steamships with a capacity of 50 up to 200 persons are used for passenger journeys.

Four docks and several shipbuilding yards enable the repair and building of a variety of vessels that make up the cargo and tug fleet.

Kazakhstan's own merchant marine fleet for carrying oil and dry-cargoes was established in the early 1990s. The closed joint-stock company National Marine Shipping Company Kazmortransflot (ZAO

NMSK Kazmortransflot) was created in 1998. In 1999 it is planned to begin the transportation of Caspian oil using the oil tankers of this national company.

The state-owned enterprise, Aktau Commercial Seaport (RGP AMTP) was created on business lines and is vital to the promotion of international links. One of its basic purposes is to carry oil and dry-cargoes amounting to more than 6 million tons and 2 million MTA, respectively.

The priority investment projects in the field of water transport are:

- the reconstruction and expansion of Aktau port, the breakwater and the access dam to the mooring line;

- the reconstruction and repair of the Bukhtarminskiy and the Ust-Kamenogorskiy sluices;

- the building of a grain terminal in the Aktau port;

- the reconstruction of the ferry in the Aktau port;

- the reconstruction of bulk-oil docks, nos. 4, 5 and 8.

- a deepening of the water area in the Aktau port;

- the acquisition of a merchant marine fleet.

The acquisition of a merchant marine fleet will be based on private enterprise by creating joint shipping companies. The required investment for the first stage of the merchant marine fleet's creation is US$80 million.

Air transport

The national airline of Kazakhstan is Air Kazakhstan. It is responsible for most international and inland air journeys originating in the Republic. Most of the airline's passenger journeys (70 per cent) are domestic in nature. The paramount objectives of the company are to improve the quality and expand the range of its services, to serve the national market for air travel and to renew its air fleet.

As of 1 January 1999, there were 44 airlines operating in the Republic, including the national carrier Air Kazakhstan CJSC, 11 regional and 32 private airlines. There are 21 airports of national importance. Self-maintained joint-stock companies have been created for each airport. While flights through the main five airports (Almaty, Astana, Aktyubinsk, Atyrau and Karaganda) are intensive, the others provide no more than seven flights per day. Twelve airports are able to service international flights: Astana, Aktau, Aktyubinsk, Almaty, Atyrau, Karaganda, Kostanai, Taraz, Uralsk, Ust-Kamenogorsk, Pavlodar and Shymkent. Only four of the airports are profitable so far – Astana, Kostanai, Karaganda (Sary-Arka) and Atma-Atyrau i Perevozchiki.

Table 2.18.2 Air transport's basic performance for 1993–98

Indicators	1993	1994	1995	1996	1997	1998
Passengers carried (millions)	3.6	2.3	2.0	1.5	1.7	1.0
Cargoes (000 tons)	21.4	20.0	24.5	25.1	24.1	17.0
Passenger turnover (million passengers-km)	6,826	4,641	4,713	3,308	2,064	2,045
Turnover of goods (million tons-km)	69	87	145	137	79	64

Passenger journeys account for most of airport business (95 per cent). The potential value of the air transport market in the Republic of Kazakhstan is currently about US$812 million per year.

The various Kazakhstan airlines regularly carry passengers to both CIS and non-CIS countries. Most air journeys are to Russia, the United Arab Emirates, Turkey and Germany.

Development plans

In terms of attracting investment, the airports in Almaty and Astana are priority. To stabilise its development, the joint-stock company Almaty Airport was transferred to a consortium of three companies: JSD Airport and Ground Services, Air Finance Europe Limited, and Lufthansa Airport & Ground Services Almaty (LATAS). The largest air carriers from Austria, Hungary, Germany, Greece, Israel, Turkey, China, Pakistan, India and the CIS use the airport. There are plans to build passenger terminals up to international requirements at the airports of Almaty, Shymkent, Turkestan and Aktau.

Astana airport is now modern and comfortable. In 1998 a credit agreement was signed between the governments of Kazakhstan and Japan stipulating the allocation through the OECF of a soft loan for the Astana International Airport project. The reconstruction of the runway and the building of a VIP terminal, plus the reconstruction of the air terminal building, are practically completed. The national state-owned enterprise, International Airport Astana, has been created to manage the airport.

In 1999–2000 it is planned to reconstruct the runway in Atyrau and purchase navigational equipment for the airport. The Turkish company, Magdenli Ground Services & Transport, is participating in the contract for the management and updating of Atyrau airport. It has purchased 50 per cent of the shares of ZAO Atma-Atyrau i Perevozchiki.

The acquisition and operation of modern planes such as the Boeing 767 (leased under state guarantees) are among the priorities for development of the air transport system. The implementation of a targeted government programme for the replacement of aircraft in the national air fleet will require 15 to 17 planes. In order to modernise its aircraft fleet Air Kazakhstan JSC is planning to attract a non-state foreign loan amounting to US$10 million guaranteed by the state. The annual attraction of non-state exterior loans amounting to US$100 million was also contemplated in the State Investments Programme for the years 1999–2000, under a state guarantee for aircraft acquisition.

In 1997, regulations governing the charges and rates for the ground–handling and operation of aircraft were applied to the national airports. Fixed rates are now prescribed for these services.

Part 3

Business Development

Progress in the Business Climate

Douglas Townsend, Mia Nybrant and Kathryn Wells, ITIC

Introduction

ITIC was a co-sponsor of and contributor to the 1995 book *Doing Business in Kazakhstan* published by Kogan Page. In assessing progress in Kazakhstan's economic development since then, ITIC has been able to draw on the experience of its close relations with investors and host authorities and on the results of its annual reviews of the investment climate.

In 1996 Prime Minister Akhezan Kazhegeldin, leading a strongly pro-business government, requested ITIC's assistance in the development of Kazakhstan's investment policy. As a consequence, ITIC conducted a survey of investor opinion on doing business in Kazakhstan and the analysis and evaluation of that survey were published at the end of 1996.[1]

The results clarified the attractions and the obstacles presented by Kazakhstan's investment climate at the time, and the directions to be taken for pro-business policy change.

As a result of the interest generated by the 1996 survey, among both the Kazakhstani government and the business community, ITIC has since conducted annual surveys and reports on the investment climate. Summarised below are the views of investors on four critical areas which have influenced their evaluation of business opportunities in Kazakhstan over the last four years. These criteria are also of great importance to legislators and policymakers when considering economic and tax reform.

Political and business environment

In the 1996 survey, foreign investors were very cautious when replying to questions about their dealings with government officials. The integrity of contracts, once undertaken, were not always honoured. With regard to doing business with the government, one respondent remarked that there is 'No feeling of partnership yet,' and business interactions were perceived as being 'very adversarial'. In the 1999 survey,[2] some progress seems to have been achieved, with respondents citing the political environment, including the negotiation of contracts, political stability and corruption, as the least troublesome of the survey indicators. Although now viewed as being the least difficult area, problems still persist, as evidenced by the official war on corruption. Further, as the 1998 report[3] shows, the extent of the unofficial economy was shown to be very high.

Bureaucracy

In all surveys, bureaucracy has been cited as the major barrier to business in Kazakhstan. In the 1997 Survey,[4] overlapping jurisdictions among different ministries, as well as unnecessary laws that encouraged bureaucratic delays and corruption, were highlighted as being of particular difficulty. However, it was also pointed out that foreign investors must make an effort to have a clear understanding about the exact functions and competencies of the various ministerial authorities in order to be able to conduct business effectively. The trappings of bureaucracy remain a burden, particularly in current tough economic times. Thus ITIC now focuses to a larger extent on training programmes encompassing good governance.

Legal system

The need to generate legislative and administrative stability by the government was recognised as being of great importance in 1996. One respondent then cited the 'need for more security to protect investment from bureaucratic development which often favours local partners – perhaps positive protective measures under government administration'. In 1999 the problems still exist, especially with the lack of transparency and an absence of secondary legislation and regulation. The pace of legal change, however, is perceived as having increased, as has the availability of local legal experts. Much store is being set by the new, comprehensive World Bank-funded Legal System Reform Project.

Tax/fiscal regime

The first modern tax code in the CIS (Commonwealth of Independent States) was adopted in Kazakhstan in 1995. ITIC assisted considerably in the development of that legislation, and has since worked very closely with legislators and policy makers on its elaboration. The surveys confirm the criticality of the tax/fiscal regime, and ITIC has focused its efforts on reform of tax policy development of regulations and instructions as well as other aspects of tax administration.

In the survey of 1996, the link between the size of foreign investment and the tax regime was confirmed. Although the Kazakhstani tax code was the most investment-friendly of the CIS countries, its erratic administration acted as a barrier to investment.

In response, ITIC has carried out a number of education and outreach programmes, some funded by the UK Know How Fund (Department for International Development). These have encompassed training in the development of oil and gas taxation, of policy-makers and legislators from the Ministry of Finance and the Ministry of State Revenues, and parliamentarians, through Almaty-based workshops with the UK Inland Revenue, HM Customs & Excise experts and industry consultants. There have also been UK-based programmes for key members of the Majilis to study UK taxation practices, particularly focusing on the natural resources sector, drawing on the expertise accumulated in the UK from the North Sea oil sector. ITIC worked closely with the Kazakhstani Ministry of Finance and the UK Inland Revenue in the development of the UK–Kazakhstan Tax Treaty to clarify questions impeding the implementation of the treaty.

In the 1999 Survey, Kazakhstan compared favourably with certain other CIS countries (namely Azerbaijan, Ukraine and Uzbekistan) and was on a par with Russia with regard to the perception of the tax/fiscal regime as a barrier to investment (see Figures 3.1.1 and 3.1.2).

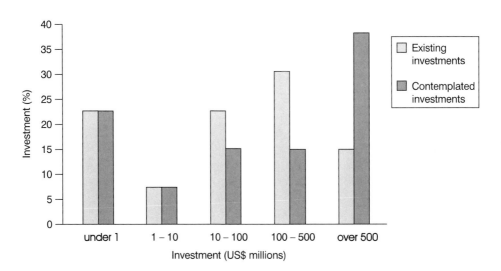

Figure 3.1.1 Dollar size of existing and contemplated investments in Kazakhstan

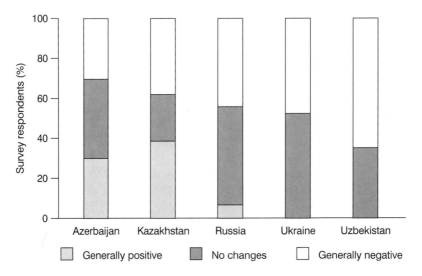

Figure 3.1.2 Characterisation of changes in investment climate in 1999

Conclusion

There have been serious consequences from the Asian contagion and the 1998 Russian financial crisis. Trade with Russia still accounts for 30 per cent of Kazakhstani exports and was badly affected. The tenge devaluation in April 1999 has made Kazakhstani exports competitive *vis-à-vis* other countries in the region and commodities prices have recovered, but the economy was nonetheless forecast to contract slightly in 1999. The Kazakhstani government has been swift to respond with fiscal tightening and an acceleration of privatisation, but it needs to do more to enable investors to realise the many potential opportunities available. Central to this realisation is the continued reform of tax policy and administration.

Notes

1 ITIC *Kazakhstan Survey, The Investment Climate in the Republic of Kazakhstan*, June 1996, International Tax and Investment Centre.
2 ITIC *Special Report: Comparative Tax Study and Investment Climate Survey for Azerbajian, Kazakhstan, Russia, Ukraine and Uzbekistan*, June 1999, International Tax and Investment Centre.
3 ITIC *Special Report: A Comparative Study of Tax and Investment Parameters for Kazakhstan, Russia, Ukraine and Uzbekistan*, February 1998, International Tax and Investment Centre.
4 ITIC *Kazakhstan Survey, The Investment Climate in the Republic of Kazakhstan*, May 1997, International Tax and Investment Centre.

3.2

Investment Strategy

Mark Campbell and Yelena Titova,
KPMG Almaty

Introduction

This chapter is not 'over technical' and focuses on the perhaps less obvious issues that should be addressed in any foreign investor's business strategy in Kazakhstan. A more detailed analysis of the points raised will no doubt appear in further detail in other parts of this publication. Our aim here is to show the breadth and range of issues that should be considered both before taking an investment decision and once an investment is under way.

Getting started

The initial business trips and 'fact-finding' missions have all been completed. As well as having built up a general picture of the investment and business climate in Kazakhstan, you also, after visiting Almaty twice, know several bars, restaurants, nightclubs and other Almaty haunts. You have also been volunteered to open up your employer's business venture in Kazakhstan.

You have a general/vague idea of what is necessary to get things going. First, you have to get the business registered. You decide therefore, to arrange an appointment with your business adviser, and this is what you are told.

Choice of legal entity

It is necessary to determine the type of legal entity through which you will conduct business in Kazakhstan. You are informed that a penalty (100 per cent of turnover) applies if the conduct of non-registered business activities is discovered by the authorities. You establish that there is a choice of three main routes for conducting business operations:

1 registration of a branch and conducting of business through a foreign legal entity; or

2 registration of a representative office principally for observing market conditions and intelligence gathering (this is also a preliminary requirement before a foreign bank may commence commercial activities); or

3 creation of a new Kazakhstani legal entity. A Kazakhstani legal entity as a route for a foreign investor may be wholly owned by the foreign entity or be a joint venture with a local investment partner. This decision may be dependent on the following factors:

  - the advantages and assistance that a local investment partner could provide. This would mean that a Kazakhstani legal entity should be created;

  - assessment of currency risk;

  - taxation.

You determine that for your business, a joint venture with a local partner may be the best way of meeting your business aims. For companies interested in subsurface use (ie, oil exploration, mining etc) a joint venture with a Kazakhstani organisation with experience, and, often more importantly, local knowledge can be invaluable.

The joint venture (JV) company is subsequently registered. One factor that was taken into account while taking this decision was the National Bank of Kazakhstan's currency regulations. These stipulate that half of all hard currency receipts for trade/commercial operations received by Kazakhstani legal entities must be sold and converted into local currency (tenge) within ten working days of receipt. You are aware that between April to June 1999, the tenge has devalued by 60 per cent and this risk has been factored into investment plans. You have estimated in your business plan that as commencement of actual trading is not expected for 18 months to 2 years, you will take the gamble that all significant local currency devaluation movement will have taken place before then.

Taxation issues have also been examined; initial visits to Kazakhstan made you aware of risks and pitfalls. In general, however, the taxation system is at least the same for Kazakhstani and foreign legal entities. Dividend withholding tax is not expected to be a problem in the near future and, as this tax would require substantial profits to have been generated, it is considered to be a nice problem to have. You have by now also ensured that payroll taxes and all other taxes that may have an impact are being adequately complied with.

You are advised to explore what potential tax benefits may be available if a project receives and qualifies for the Agency of the Republic of Kazakhstan's (AKI) support. AKI backing (available only for development of specific economic sectors), tax benefits such as a five-year corporate income tax holiday and import duty concessions may be obtained. If you intend to conduct subsurface use operations, a contract for subsurface-use with Kazakhstan authorities will be required. Such subsurface-use contracts contain tax provisions which, if drafted appropriately, may provide some form of tax benefits. Clarity of the intent and meaning of subsurface-use contracts is extremely useful in the event of future disputes and it is recommended that subsurface contracts be professionally reviewed before they become effective.

Licensing

Depending on the nature of proposed and intended business activities, some form of licence may need to be obtained. If, like many foreign participation JV companies, you intend to conduct subsurface operations (eg mining or oil exploration), a subsurface-use licence should be obtained. Your business adviser informed you of this during the enquiry stage of Kazakhstan operations.

Staffing and recruitment policies

From past experience, you are fully aware that a key factor in business success is that good and appropriate staff be hired and trained. Working in an emerging market such as Kazakhstan, makes it particularly important for the 'right kind' of expatriate employees to be deployed. A range of 'testing' issues will be encountered by expatriate managers, and in many cases, patience and understanding will be required in a country still accustomed to Soviet business practices.

When selecting local employees it is worth bearing in mind the need to ensure appropriate levels of accounting and tax compliance. An experienced chief accountant is invaluable for ensuring that the more 'Soviet style' procedures that still remain in force are adhered to. However, it is not all that likely that such a chief accountant will be able to comply with western/International reporting requirements. As you intend to grow to a substantial size, you therefore decide to involve an expatriate, at least for the development stages of your project, in the accounting function.

Often in the case of JVs with foreign participation, it is only the foreign partner that contributes investment funds. You are therefore keen to ensure that resources are deployed effectively and require, as the foreign investor, appropriate control of the JV. It is important to develop key Kazakhstani staff as this will ensure that future profitability is maximised and that your more mature staff are monitored, understand the eventual requirement for profit and are aware that employment depends more on market-driven business objectives than on pre-1991 objectives. The old adage, 'He who pays the piper calls the tune' is very much worth keeping in mind.

You should also aim to explore effective remuneration policies and ensure that taxation of fringe benefits, payroll taxes and reporting requirements in relation to both local and foreign employees are minimised.

Day-to-Day Operations

Each day, and certainly each week, are likely to bring their challenges. You may desperately need to clear some goods and equipment through customs, and be encountering frustrating delays. Applications for work permits for yourself and your other expatriate staff may be subject to meticulous reviews and hold-ups. Registering vehicles and dealing with your landlord all contribute to the broad experience that you will receive while living in Kazakhstan. These types of issues are important and should be taken account of in your investment strategy – doing so will increase your chances of success. If something is expected, it should not cause shock or surprise. In Kazakhstan, as elsewhere, to be prepared is to be forewarned.

Conclusion

A large range of issues will be encountered (and only a few have been referred to here) when devising and implementing your Kazakhstan Business Strategy. The other chapters in this publication will no doubt address many of the points raised in more detail and serve to answer further questions posed here.

Mark Campbell is a senior tax manager at KPMG Almaty. Prior to arriving in Almaty in February 1999, he had spent more than three years in Baku, Azerbaijan; the experience he gained there has proved to be invaluable in Kazakhstan.

Yelena Titova is a tax consultant at KPMG Almaty. She has been with the company for more than two years during which time she has seen its Almaty office grow from just a few people to over 50 staff.

3.3

The Foreign Investment Regime

James E. Hogan, Aigoul Kenjebayeva, Donald K. Blackwell, Salans Hertzfeld & Heilbronn

The Foreign Investment Law

The Law of the Republic of Kazakhstan, 'On Foreign Investment', dated 27 December 1994, as amended, otherwise known as Foreign Investment Law, is the principal body of legislation governing the rights and obligations of foreign investors in Kazakhstan. It sets forth an important array of guarantees for foreign investors, as well as certain benefits that are available to enterprises with foreign investment. The Law builds upon the benefits provided in the original 1990 Foreign Investment Law, although it also eliminated a number of other benefits, such as tax holidays, that used to apply to foreign investments under certain conditions. Moreover, in conjunction with other Laws, the Foreign Investment Law significantly restricts the ability of government officials to grant special benefits or guarantees to foreign investors.

National treatment

Pursuant to the Foreign Investment Law, foreign investors are accorded rights under the legislation of Kazakhstan on a national treatment basis. With few exceptions, they may be treated no less favourably than their domestic counterparts or other foreign investors. Moreover, the Foreign Investment Law confirms the applicability of prevailing norms of international law, including a guarantee against nationalisation and expropriation, except for important public purposes, in which case the payment of 'prompt, adequate and effective compensation' is mandated. Finally, the Law guarantees to foreign investors the right to freely repatriate profits arising from their activity on the territory of the Republic of Kazakhstan.

The role of the state

In a break with the not-so-recent past, current Kazakhstani legislation has greatly reduced the role of the state as a direct participant in foreign investment projects. The authority of the government to conclude contracts with foreign investors in the name of the Republic of Kazakhstan is expressly limited to certain cases and even then in a manner specifically provided for by legislation. It should be noted that, with respect to the conclusion of subsoil-use contracts, a 'competent body' designated by the government is authorised to conclude such contracts on its behalf.

Similarly, guarantees in the name of the government may be issued only where and in the manner specifically provided for by Kazakhstan legislation. In the absence of a guarantee, where a contract or project has merely been approved or confirmed by the government, the responsibility of the state is limited.

These restrictions were imposed in order to rectify the chaotic situation that existed shortly after independence. A large number of government guarantees were then issued by a multitude of state bodies, without control or co-ordination by the central bank, and contracts that were seriously at variance with legislation were concluded by state bodies as a matter of course.

Stabilisation

The Foreign Investment Law sets out a stabilisation provision offering foreign investors protection against unfavourable changes in legislation and other legal developments. In essence, the Law provides that in the event of a worsening of the position of a foreign investor due to changes in legislation and/or the entry into force or change of conditions in international treaties, those terms which were in force at the moment of the making of the investments shall apply for a period of ten years. With regard to investments carried out under long-term (exceeding ten years) contracts, the original terms will apply for the duration of the contract. With respect to contracts, the Foreign Investment Law sets out a similar provision to ensure that the conditions of contracts shall prevail over changes in legislation.

Although the Law is nearly five years old, no mechanism has yet been established for determining precisely how this concept is to be implemented in practice. In the absence of a mechanism through which the foreign investor's right to stabilisation is confirmed and registered by a central authority, such a foreign investor is potentially left subject to the arbitrary interpretations of individual state and local officials. At least in the area of taxation, the tax authorities so far have taken a narrow view of stabilisation, placing on the foreign investor the burden of demonstrating, to their satisfaction, the unfavourable impact of new legislation.

Most importantly, and especially so for foreign investors in the natural resource sector, there has been considerable debate over the proper interplay between the stabilisation offered by the Foreign Investment Law and the analogous stabilisation provisions offered under a series of other legislative acts. These other legislative acts with special importance to investors in the hydrocarbon sector, include the Petroleum Law, the Subsoil Code, the Tax Code, the Civil Code, and for qualifying investors, the Law on Direct Investments.

Arbitration

The Foreign Investment Law permits the settlement of disputes involving foreign investment by international arbitration before any of several bodies that are expressly listed. These include arbitration bodies formed in accordance with the Arbitration Rules of UNCITRAL (United Nations Commission on International Trade Law), ICSID (International Centre for Settlement of Investment Disputes) and the Stockholm Chamber of Commerce. As a continuation of practice from the Soviet era, the preferred neutral forum for the resolution of contractual disputes between Kazakhstan and foreign entities is usually arbitration in Stockholm under the Rules of the Arbitration Institute of the Stockholm Chamber of Commerce.

The Republic of Kazakhstan is a signatory to a number of international treaties on the subject of the enforcement of international arbitration awards, including the 1958 Convention on the Recognition and Enforcement of Foreign Arbitral Awards (the New York Convention), which was ratified by the Republic of Kazakhstan in 1995. In view of this ratification, arbitral awards made in any country that is a signatory to the Convention must be recognised by Kazakhstani courts, subject to certain exceptions set out in it.

For example, a court may refuse to recognise and enforce an arbitral award if a competent authority in the country finds that the subject matter of the dispute is not capable of settlement by arbitration under its legislation or is contrary to public policy. Under the ICSID Convention, which may apply only to contract disputes between a contracting state and a subject of another contracting state, there exists a separate mechanism for the enforcement of an award, which is set forth within the body of this Convention.

There is, as yet, no reported practice that would indicate the manner in which enforcement issues would be applied by Kazakhstan courts, and Kazakhstan has not adopted a specific law on international arbitration. All the same, the independent ratification of the New York Convention by the

Republic of Kazakhstan has vastly improved the utility and effectiveness of dispute resolution by foreign investors before international arbitral tribunals.

Other provisions

Other noteworthy provisions of the Foreign Investment Law include a right to redress for illegal actions of state agencies, freedom in the use of revenue generated from activities in Kazakhstan, access to information, and protection in the event of a state audit. It should be noted that domestic enterprises with foreign investment are required to make entries into their books of account in accordance with Kazakhstan accounting rules.

The Law on Direct Investments

On 28 February 1997, the President of the Republic of Kazakhstan signed a new Law on State Support of Direct Investments (the Law on Direct Investments). This Law establishes a mechanism by which qualified investors, by agreement with the Agency of the Republic of Kazakhstan on Investments, may receive certain tax and other benefits in relation to investments made in five priority sectors of Kazakhstan's economy. Set out in a Presidential Edict dated 5 April 1997, these are:

- industrial infrastructure;
- the processing industry;
- projects in the new capital city of Astana;
- housing; social services; and tourism;
- agriculture.

Specific benefits that are authorised by the Law on Direct Investments for qualified investors include a reduction in the applicable rates of land tax and property tax by up to 100 per cent of the basic rate for up to five years following the date of the contract. Benefits also include reductions in income tax for up to five years from the date of receipt of taxable income (but not more than eight years after conclusion of the contract) and a reduction in the applicable rates of these taxes by up to 50 per cent of the basic rate for an additional period of up to five years. Finally, benefits also include a total or partial exemption from customs duties with respect to imported equipment, raw materials and other goods necessary for the realisation of the investment project. The Law does not authorise exemptions from value added tax (VAT) or any other taxes.

The precise extent of the tax and other advantages granted to a qualified investor is to be determined on the basis of the amount of the investment in fixed assets, the priority of the specific sector of the economy and other factors.

Qualified investors will also benefit from various general undertakings of the government with respect to the repatriation of profits, freedom to set prices and non-interference by government bodies. The Law is applicable to both foreign and domestic investors, although, for the moment, it is likely to be of most relevance to foreign companies with the capital necessary to make substantial investments in Kazakhstan.

One of the substantial drawbacks of the structure envisaged by the Law on Direct Investments is that the Agency on Investments retains rather wide discretion to terminate a contract concluded with a qualified investor, without court involvement. In the event that a contract is terminated prematurely, the qualified investor is responsible for the reimbursement of losses to the government. The investor is also liable for the payment of all taxes that would have been due if tax benefits had not been granted, together with tax penalties under Kazakhstani laws of general application.

Moreover, all contracts concluded under the Law on Direct Investments would be subject to its very weak stabilisation language. Pursuant to the Law, in the event of amendments and changes to legislation occurring after the conclusion of a contract with the Agency on Investments 'which lead to the impossibility of further performance of the original terms of the contract, or which lead to a material change of its economic conditions', the qualified investor and the Agency on Investments 'shall introduce changes and amendments to the contract by mutual agreement'. The foregoing stabilisation language is largely illusory, as the parties would under any circumstances have the ability to amend their contract by mutual agreement.

On the plus side, the Agency on Investments structure might allow the legal possibility of negotiating a specific tax regime to apply to qualifying investment projects, albeit within the strict limits of those benefits that are authorised by the Law on Direct Investments.

Structuring Transactions

Zaid S Sethi, Director of Tax and Legal Services, PricewaterhouseCoopers

Introduction

It is an accepted fact that commercial transactions, be they local or cross border, require well-thought-out structuring. While careful structuring of a transaction is the key to business success, it is also probably one of the most difficult objectives to achieve in that it requires the efficient use of limited resources to realise commercial opportunities. Such efficient structuring requires an understanding of a wide range of influencing factors that include commercial, cultural and tax issues relevant to doing business in new markets.

It is clearly not possible to address all the issues that need to be taken into account comprehensively, but we do hope to provide a framework that should enable us to identify a number of the most important issues that need to be addressed. In working towards that goal we shall focus on three main areas as follows:

- commerce;
- culture;
- taxation.

Commerce

Broadly speaking, the last five years have seen Kazakhstan attract investments in a number of market sectors. Each market sector has a focus on particular types of transactions both in terms of the seller/buyer relationship and the nature of the goods and services involved in the transaction.

The main areas that we shall be looking at under this heading are:

- flow of goods and services
- location of supplier and customer
- movement of funds
- foreign exchange risk

Flow of goods and services

The flow of goods and services will include not only the logistical issues imposed by the geographical location of the source and destination markets but also barriers imposed by political or wider economic boundaries.

Kazakhstan, while being an independent republic, still retains a number of political and economic ties with other countries of the former Soviet Union. These include:

- visor privileges allowing the flow of personnel;
- value added tax (VAT) agreements with Ukraine, Moldova, Azerbaijan, and Kyrgyzstan on export and import of goods, works and services;
- customs harmonisation agreements with Russia, Belarus, and Kyrgyzstan;
- customs agreements with Russia and Kyrgyzstan.

The change in the manner in which goods and services can be transported means that the location of the supplier and consumer may not always be clear, thus increasing the risk of a misunderstanding in the transactions effected. It is therefore becoming increasingly important to ensure that documentary evidence is available to assist in explanations of both the form and the substance of transactions.

Location of supplier and customer

The location of the supplier and the customer is important not only in view of taking advantage of the co-operation agreements that exist but also in dealing with domestic issues such as:

- inland transportation of goods;
- customs clearance regulations;
- legal and tax status of the supplier and customer in Kazakhstan;
- delivery deadlines which may be subject to climatic conditions (ie Kazakhstan is a country with climatic changes of up to +50°C in summer down to –50°C in winter).

Movement of funds

It is important to note that, except in a few cases, all payments for transactions between 'residents' must be carried out in the local currency, the tenge (KZT). Cross-border transactions between 'non-residents' and 'residents' may be settled in hard currency; however, non-residents should be aware that despite the fact that, unlike some of its neighbours, Kazakhstan does not impose formal foreign currency controls, there are a number of procedural conditions supported by detailed documentary evidence that need to be met before hard currency is allowed to leave the country.

Payments in hard currency, whether the funds are sitting in a hard currency account or whether the hard currency needs to be bought to settle a hard currency debt, will require sufficient documentation to demonstrate that

- a genuine hard currency debt exists;

- the debt is required to be settled in hard currency.

Banks will only allow the transfer of hard currency out of the country if these conditions are met. There is little point in providing a list of documents set out in the banking regulations issued by the National Bank of Kazakhstan as these are subject to frequent change.

Foreign exchange risk

Until the Russian crisis of August 1998, the tenge saw some stability despite complaints over a long period of time that the local currency was overvalued and that overvalue could not be sustained. Even following the Russian crisis, there was some confidence that a devaluation, when it happened, would not be of the kind that Russia experienced. April 1999 saw the devaluation of the tenge; most commentators agreed that it was long overdue and, when it did finally happen, was generally well-managed.

The acceptance of weakness in the tenge, particularly by the government, does mean that the possibility of future correcting measures involving the realignment of the tenge to hard currencies is now present in the psyche of the investment community. Thus, foreign currency exposure has become a more important consideration particularly in terms of export finance and credit facilities.

Culture

Doing business efficiently in any country requires an understanding of local cultural attitudes.

Kazakhstan is a Central Asian country that has a large number of different ethnic groups. Despite the so called exodus of the early years following independence things appear to have settled down to the extent that a Kazakhstani culture has emerged, a product of all the major ethnic groups but dominated by Russian and Kazakh influences. Tradition plays an important part in daily life and those familiar with other countries with nomadic ancestry will recognise certain common characteristics.

Deals are not negotiated in the same way as they are in the West. Differences, for instance, might include:

- decision makers are less visible than one might be used to in the West;

- criticism is not easily accepted and great effort is therefore expended to ensure that the decision taken will not be questioned;

- errors of judgement are rarely condoned;

- experience of cross-border transactions is limited.

There is also the problem of which language you should expect to do business in – Kazakh or Russian. The Kazakh language is increasingly being used in the corridors of power; however, Russian is still the language of business and there is an increasing number of people, among both the local and foreign investor communities, who are bilingual in Russian and German or French or Turkish or Korean or English. Having said that, an issue that is even more contentious than deciding what language governs a transaction is the question of which language is predominant in the event of disputes on interpretation.

Taxation

As noted above, political and economic boundaries play an important part in structuring transactions, particularly in ensuring that the supplier and consumer are not caught between the taxation authorities of two countries that have competing tax collection interests.

Three separate elements can be identified in considering the taxation costs of structuring transactions:

- identification of tax leakage points;

- legal status of parties involved in the transaction;

- double tax treaties.

Identification of tax leakage points

A well-structured transaction will, to a large extent, define the tax collection rights of the countries involved in the transaction and thus ensure that tax costs are adequately taken into account in determining an acceptable contract price.

In addition to the location of the goods, the 'tax' borders that the goods need to cross before they get to the destination country will need to be considered. This is in order to mitigate tax leakage for which no credit may be available in the home country and that will thus result in an additional direct cost of the goods and services.

Legal status of parties involved in the transaction

The taxation costs of the transaction can be very different depending on the legal status of the parties involved.

Perhaps most important in terms of cross-border taxation is the principle of residence, which stems from the concept of identifying a taxpayer in the country of destination. In considering this we are not merely restricting ourselves to the traditional tax issues facing representative offices, branches and legal entities from a tax on profits point of view but also looking from that at other factors which contribute to the identification of taxpayers who need to pay or are exempt from local taxes.

The identification of a taxpayer in another country, as most practitioners will confirm, is not always obvious. For example, different rules may be used to determine the location of taxpayers or the same category of tax may be defined differently.

Further, a branch of a foreign legal entity may be treated as being resident for certain taxes but non-resident for others. This may have a serious impact on whether or not particular country tax privileges may be available. For example, to qualify for benefits within certain economic boundaries it is necessary to register a legal entity in Kazakhstan, whereas for, say, currency regulation purposes, a branch is deemed to be a non-resident.

Double tax treaties

It is usual nowadays for transactions not to be limited to the supply of goods without the added supply of services either from the supplier direct or from the deal broker. This clearly leads to greater reliance on international agreements to assist in the delineation of tax responsibilities and obligations of the parties and on the residence principle in determining the relevant taxation authorities that will share the overall tax take.

It should be noted that as with a number of former Soviet republics, the use of treaties signed between various countries and the former Soviet Union has been discontinued. New treaties have now been signed that are generally based on the OECD (Organisation for Economic Cooperation and Development) Model Convention. These treaties are useful in that, in attempting to encourage trade co-operation and to mitigate the effects of taxation barriers on the cross-border transfer of technical assistance, they allow a limited domestic direct income-tax-free presence in the host country. It should be noted that in Kazakhstan, this could be for as little as six months, depending on the treaty in question. At the time of writing, Kazakhstan has 22 treaties in force with a large number under negotiation.

While treaties are often useful in structuring transactions it should not be forgotten that Kazakhstan is new to this area of trade negotiation; therefore, treaty protection may take considerably longer to obtain than in countries where treaties are commonplace.

Conclusion

In this short chapter it has been possible to touch on only a few of the important issues that need to be considered when determining an efficiently structured transaction. There are of course a number of other considerations that need to be taken into account. Although the list is almost endless we set out the following as indicative of the wide range of issues that need to be addressed:

- dispute resolution;
- recovery/control of goods;
- customer credit status;
- banking facilities available locally;
- related party transactions;
- licensing of activities;
- movement of employees.

As with all commercial activities, it cannot be sufficiently stressed that obtaining timely, relevant and cost-effective advice is key to the successful structuring of a transaction and to dealing with an environment that may be new to many potential investors.

3.5

Financing with the European Bank for Reconstruction and Development (EBRD)*

European Bank for Reconstruction and Development (EBRD)

Introduction

The European Bank for Reconstruction and Development (EBRD) is among the largest foreign investors in Kazakhstan. Through its projects, the Bank aims to assist Kazakhstan in developing a market economy and works alongside other foreign and domestic investors to achieve this. By helping to mitigate project-financing risks, the EBRD can help foreign investors achieve commercial success in Kazakhstan.

The role of the EBRD

The EBRD was established in 1991 in response to major changes in the political and economic climate in central and eastern Europe. Inaugurated less than two years after the fall of the Berlin Wall, the Bank was created to support the transition to market economies of countries in the region following the widespread collapse of communist regimes.

Based in London, the EBRD is an international institution with 60 shareholders (58 countries, the European Union (EU) and the European Investment Bank (EIB)). Each shareholder is represented on the EBRD's Board of Governors and Board of Directors.

---

* Information correct as of October 1999

The Bank finances projects using a variety of debt and equity instruments in both the private and the public sectors, providing direct funding for financial institutions, infrastructure and other key sectors. Its investments also help to develop skills, to improve the efficiency of markets and to strengthen the institutions that support these markets.

A strength of the EBRD is its in-depth knowledge of its region of operations. As the largest foreign investor in the region's private sector, the EBRD is aware of the problems and the potential of each of its 26 countries of operations. Working closely with private investors, the Bank's staff recognises these countries' concerns about investment in the region and the political and economic uncertainty.

The EBRD operates according to sound banking principles in all its activities and promotes good business practices. It is careful to ensure that it is 'additional' to the private sector, complementing rather than competing with other private sources of finance.

The Bank's initial capital base was EUR10 billion, which was doubled to EUR20 billion in 1997, allowing it to continue to meet the growing demand for its services and to maintain its commitment to financial self-sustainability.

EBRD financing

The EBRD is keen to encourage co-financiers to take part in its operations – in fact it usually limits its own involvement in private sector projects to 35 per cent of total project cost or capital structure. Apart from private sector companies, the main co-financing partners for the EBRD are commercial banks and other financial institutions.

The principal forms of direct financing provided by the EBRD are loans, equity and guarantees. Loans are tailored to meet the particular requirements of the project. The credit risk may be taken entirely by the Bank or partly syndicated to the market. An equity investment may be undertaken in a variety of forms. When the EBRD takes an equity stake, it expects an appropriate return on its investment and will only take a minority position. Guarantees are also provided by the Bank to help borrowers gain access to funding.

Mitigating risk for investment partners

One of the Bank's main advantages is its ability to bear risk, allowing it to extend the boundaries of commercial possibilities in its countries of operations. Where possible, it shares the project risk by acting with other private sector bodies, such as commercial banks and investment funds as well as multilateral lenders. With its AAA credit rating, the EBRD is able to raise funds at the best rates from the international capital markets.

By utilising its experience in the region and its advantages as an international financial institution, the EBRD is able to mitigate certain risks, making it an attractive partner. The Bank's participation in a project can help to ensure that the operation is well prepared and implemented. For example, the EBRD will ensure that the project complies with local laws and regulations and that it is financially viable. To help a client to attain the required levels of corporate governance and project preparation, the Bank is often able to provide technical-assistance funding made available by donor governments.

The EBRD's involvement in a project indicates to the market that the project meets rigorous technical, legal, financial and environmental standards. The Bank is able to structure projects in a way that is likely to attract other financing partners and thereby minimise the risks and costs for the parties involved. One of the main ways of achieving this is by co-financing with private banks, allowing participating banks to benefit from the Bank's preferred creditor status.

The sound management and profitability of a project can be enhanced by the EBRD's presence in an operation. When the Bank takes an equity investment in a company, it uses its influence on the board to promote good management and to mediate where necessary between local and foreign partners.

A major concern to potential investors is political risk, which again the EBRD can help to mitigate. Since all the Bank's countries of operations are represented on its Board of Directors, each member country has the opportunity to object to the approval of any EBRD-financed project. This helps to reduce the threat of any subsequent political risk.

Activities in Kazakhstan

As at 31 August 1999 the EBRD had approved 11 investment projects in Kazakhstan with a total operation cost of EUR1,379 million, where the Bank's lending has totalled EUR532 million. Of these investments, over 90 per cent are in the private sector. The EBRD's private sector pipeline has been driven by:

- institutional and regulatory reforms of the financial sector;
- support for small and medium-sized enterprises (SMEs) through local banks;
- restructuring of infrastructure;
- privatisation of the industrial sector.

Case study

The EBRD is providing a US$40 million loan to Karaganda Power Company (KPC), a private power and heat utility in Kazakhstan's second largest city, Karaganda. The loan is the first significant financing in the power sector and is aimed at ensuring a reliable supply of heating and electricity in the city and its surrounding region.

KPC is owned by a joint-venture holding company, owned equally by subsidiaries of National Power Plc of the UK and Ormat Industries of Israel. The two companies will contribute US$22 million to the project.

The financing will enable KPC to modernise and repair the company's electricity and heat generation facilities and distribution system. The modernisation will reduce heat and water losses in the district heating network and improve environmental performance and health safety standards.

The region of Karaganda is the largest industrial area in Kazakhstan. it contributes some 23 per cent of the country's gross domestic product (GDP), although its population is only 7 per cent of the total.

KPC operates two combined heat and power (CHP) plants with a total capacity of 470 mw, 1,400 Gcal/hr, the main heat transmission network of 136 km and the secondary heat distribution network of 450 km. Through a subsidiary, KPC is also responsible for the billing and collection for heat, hot water and electricity services.

The company supplies heat and electricity to the 600,000 residents of Karaganda. It sells electricity directly to large customers, which account for 35 per cent of its current sales; this is projected to rise to almost 50 per cent in 1999.

Key objectives

The Bank's fundamental objective in Kazakhstan continues to be the encouragement and facilitation of a dynamic private sector. As such, the EBRD's activities are primarily focused on five areas:

- finance;
- industry and manufacturing;
- infrastructure;
- energy and natural resources;
- agriculture and agribusiness.

In addition, the Bank initiated and assisted the government in setting up the Foreign Investment Advisory Council (FIAC). The FIAC is chaired by President Nazarbayev and includes representatives of foreign companies investing in Kazakhstan; it will advise the government on improving the investment climate in the country. The Bank is the only international financial institution involved with the FIAC.

Finance
The Bank's emphasis is on the continued implementation of the existing financial vehicles for SMEs: the GIMV Kazakhstan Post-Privatisation Fund, and the Kazakhstan Small Business Programme. It will also continue to focus on equity investments in selected private banks as well as non-banking institutions in order to increase the efficiency of the sector.

Industry and manufacturing
Kazakhstan inherited a very specialised manufacturing base from the Soviet era, with heavy industry geared towards supply for the whole of the former Soviet Union. The EBRD seeks to support the privatisation process of this sector through the financing of restructured and privatised plants, as illustrated by the Ispat-Karmet Steelworks project, and by eliminating existing bottlenecks through participation in commercial greenfield operations.

Infrastructure
Telecommunications. Given recent developments in this sector, the Bank is becoming increasingly involved in a strategically oriented manner and in the long-term development of the sector. Initially, grant funds available will be used to facilitate the privatisation and restructuring of Kazaktelecom. In addition, a major need of the sector is the development of the regulatory environment. The Bank will also focus upon GSM projects and small regional telecommunications projects.

Transport. The transportation system will play a vital role in Kazakhstan's transition towards a market economy, by diversifying its trade corridors away from the heavy reliance on Russia towards alternative channels to reach international markets. The EBRD's priorities for transport include the emphasis on the improvement of foreign exchange, with particular reference to the promotion of commercial and market-driven operations. The aim will be to involve the private sector, either by way of creating new entities or by transforming existing ones that are involved in international and inter-regional trade. Efforts will continue to focus upon the implementation of the Aktau Port Rehabilitation Project (Phase I), along with the preparation of Phase II. The Bank will further develop the principal ideas agreed for the rehabilitation of the railway sector as well as examine potential involvement in other areas of transportation such as aviation.

Municipal and Environmental Infrastructure.   The Bank will continue to follow the development of high priority projects within the municipal services sector closely, and in particular that of private initiatives. The Bank will also work together with the government to identify donors that could provide grant co-financing for any selected project.

Property and Tourism.   Kazakhstan's stable growth rate over the past few years has attracted the attention of property developers and businessmen travelling to the region. In order to accommodate the increased foreign interest in the country, a number of hotels and property developments have been built. The Bank has been following these projects closely, as most of them to date carry sovereign guarantees but have been met with limited success. The government has indicated that it will not continue to provide such support, thereby jeopardising the economic viability of these projects, and this issue has been discussed with the authorities. However, the Bank will continue to review opportunities based upon developments within the market.

Energy and natural resources

Energy.   In line with the government's policy of privatising the sector, the Bank intends to focus on private sector investments. It will continue to seek opportunities to co-operate with the privatised power producers and distributors: specific projects include the Almaty Power Project with Tractebel and Karaganda Power Project with Ormat.

Oil and Gas.   The government has continued to emphasise the development of the oil and gas sector, and the associated transportation issue, as one of its key priorities. The huge potential for hard currency earnings through the oil and gas sector is gaining even more importance due to budgetary pressures. It is therefore through the development of oil and gas transportation routes, including pipelines, as well as through the refining sector that the Bank can provide additional value. The Bank is considering projects in all these areas.

Mining.   Metallurgy plays a special role in the economy, and most of the interest expressed to date by the international mining community has been in the gold and copper areas. The Bank is continuing to support development in the mining industry through joint ventures with foreign sponsors, funding specific project-related activities in the gold, copper, lead and zinc industries.

Agriculture and agribusiness

Kazakhstan continues to be heavily dependent upon agriculture and its related industries but the sector faces acute problems. The Bank will continue to focus on the areas of distribution and processing of agriculture products, and on food and beverages production. The main objective will be to identify and use strategic partners to help introduce new technology and capital, develop a new marketing strategy and introduce modern management know-how and training. Efforts will continue in the identification of small- and medium-scale investment projects through the Post-Privatisation Fund and the Small Business Programme.

Additional information

Further information about the EBRD's activities in Kazakhstan and its projects with investment partners can be found on the Bank's web site at www.ebrd.com. The site contains the full text of the Bank's key publications, such as the *Annual Report* and *Financing with the EBRD*, which details the Bank's lending requirements. More information about the investment climate in Kazakhstan and its latest progress in the transition process can be found in the EBRD's *Transition Report*, published each November.

Contacting the EBRD

Michael Davey
Director, Kazakhstan, Kyrgyzstan
European Bank for Reconstruction and Development
Kazybeh Bi 41
4th Floor
480100 Almaty
Kazakhstan
Tel: +73272 581476
Fax: +73272 581422

Suzanne Gaboury
Principal Banker
Central Asia Team
European Bank for Reconstruction and Development
1 Exchange Square
London
EC2A 2JN
United Kingdom
Tel: +44 20 7338 7144
Fax: +44 20 7338 7590/7681

3.6

Venture Capital

Marat Terterov

Introduction

Several investment funds have operated in Kazakhstan since its independence; this chapter will focus on the main venture capital funds that remain today. The present situation is different from that which existed before the Russian currency crisis of August 1998; at that time more funds were available. Some had already raised capital but withdrew after the crisis; others were in the process of raising funds and were liquidated or substantially cut back on their profile and investment programme in the aftermath of the crisis.

Today there are four funds that both remain active and have a reasonably high profile as foreign investors. Two are sponsored by the European Bank for Reconstruction and Development (EBRD): the Eagle Kazakhstan Fund (formerly GIMV Kazakhstan Post-Privatisation Fund) and the AIG Silk Road Fund (SRF). There is also the Central Asian American Enterprise Fund (CAAEF), which is sponsored by the US government, and finally the Kazakhstan Asset Management's Kazakhstan Investment Fund (KIF), which represents Swiss, American and British investors. These funds typically invest in small and medium-sized enterprises (SMEs) representing many industries in Kazakhstan, and usually exclude companies that produce, for example, strong liquor, tobacco or weapons, or are involved in gambling. The funds seek to make equity or combined debt-equity investments ranging from US$1 to US$10 million. The average length of investment is between four and six years and exit strategies vary.

The Eagle Kazakhstan Fund (formerly GIMV Kazakhstan Post-Privatisation Fund (the KPPF))

The Eagle Kazakhstan Fund (formerly the KPPF) is a venture capital fund created with funding from the European Bank for Reconstruction and

Development (EBRD); it has a total capital of €33m of which €30m is provided by the EBRD to invest in small and medium-sized companies in Kazakhstan. Eagle Venture Partners is the manager of the fund, and it is a consortium of investment companies that include GIMV, Corpeq, Rabobank, Ewic-West and Sigeji. GIMV, a Flemish investment company, quoted on the Brussels Stock Exchange with a market capitalisation of more than US$1.5 billion, has also committed to invest up to €3m in the Fund. The Eagle Kazakhstan Fund is also supported by a technical assistance grant of €20m provided by the European Union's (EU) technical assistance programme. The EU's support enables the Eagle Kazakhstan Fund to deploy legal, financial, environmental and marketing experts to evaluate investment proposals. Additionally, the EU's technical assistance is used to monitor and add value to companies in which the Eagle Kazakhstan Fund has already invested, by providing marketing, accounting and other kinds of support.

It is important to note that the Eagle Kazakhstan Fund is one of a family of similar regional venture funds (RVFs) that have been established across the CIS (Commonwealth of Independent States) and eastern Europe. The EBRD also has its own separate programmes in Kazakhstan that it manages directly and which provide finance for direct investment in large enterprises, projects, on-lending and micro credits.

The Eagle Kazakhstan Fund started operations in Kazakhstan in April 1996 and can invest in both start-up and existing companies. The Eagle Kazakhstan Fund's current portfolio includes joint ventures that are exclusively with Kazakhstani enterprises as well as joint ventures with partners from the United States, Great Britain, France and Belgium. The fund was renamed in early 2000 from the GIMV Kazakhstan Post-Privatisation Fund to the Eagle Kazakhstan Fund after merging with three Russian venture funds that are also funded by the EBRD.

The Eagle Kazakhstan Fund's investment criteria may be summarised as follows:

- It invests in small and medium-sized companies, whose state ownership does not exceed 33 per cent of their equity capital.

- It can invest between US$0.3 million and US$5 million in a single project but is most interested in projects requiring US$2–5 million.

- It cannot own more than 54 per cent of the shares of any company (49 per cent EBRD, 4.9 per cent GIMV).

- It cannot invest in companies that produce weapons, strong liquor or tobacco, or are involved in gambling or financial services.

- At least two-thirds of the money that the Eagle Kazakhstan Fund invests in a company must be to provide new financing and therefore a maximum of one-third may be used to buy out existing shareholders.

- The Eagle Kazakhstan Fund invests primarily with the purpose of ultimately taking an equity position in a company, but may also give loans that either support its equity investment or are convertible. These loans are frequently granted with a grace period. The Eagle Kazakhstan Fund, however, seeks an equity rate of return on its total debt and equity investment in any one company.

- The initial planned life of the Eagle Kazakhstan Fund is ten years. Within a period of five–seven years following its investment, the Fund will seek to sell all of its shares.

The Eagle Kazakhstan Fund provides ongoing support to its investees, is an active investor and seeks to add value through its participation on the Board of Directors and through the use of consultants paid for from the EU-funded technical assistance grant. In fact, the Eagle Kazakhstan Fund's ability to be able to fund large amounts of post-investment support, using its large EU grant is an important distinguishing factor compared with the other venture capital funds in Kazakhstan. Examples of the support the fund has provided for its investee enterprises have included: finance directors, MIS/accounting system implementations, International Accounting standard audits, technical and production experts, marketing directors, market research and trade partner search and introductions.
The Fund's target industry sectors are bottling, brewing and wine production, cable television, confectionery, distribution, food processing, franchises, packaging, pharmaceuticals, telecommunications, information technology, internet, oil service companies and warehousing.

Investment targets must have good management and a good business plan. In addition, the following criteria make a firm more attractive as a potential investment target: significant growth prospects for their product or service; local production/import substitution; good brands; good marketing and distribution. The Fund welcomes opportunities to co-invest with a foreign investor who will add value to an enterprise by committing management expertise and experience.

The Eagle Kazakhstan Fund has now invested over 40 per cent of its €33m capital in six companies. These are:

- **Foodmaster:** US$2.8 million debt and equity investment in a dairy and juice producer, packager and distributor based in Almaty.

- **Rainbow paint:** US$3.9 million debt and equity investment in a start-up paint factory in Almaty.

- **Spectrum:** US$2.2 million debt and equity investment in an Almaty-based mobile trunk radio company.

- **UKPF (Ust-Kamenogorsk poultry factory):** US$3.9 million debt and equity investment in a privatised poultry farm in Ust-Kamenogorsk.

- **Bauta:** US$2.1 million debt and equity investment in a water desalination and packaging facility in Bautino on the Caspian Sea.
- **Rustam:** US$0.7 million debt and equity investment in a cereal processing facility in Ust-Kamenogorsk.

Contacts: Greg Curtis, Alessandro Manghi, Yelena Yunusova, Irena Sokolovskaya,Talgat Kukenov, Indira Nazhmidenova
Tel: International (7-571) 360-3296 In Almaty (7-3272) 33 13 57
Fax: International (7-571) 360-3295 In Almaty (7-3272) 50 39 09
E-mail: gimv@kazfund.almaty.kz

The AIG Silk Road Fund (SRF)

The SRF is a US$70 million long-term direct equity investment fund. Designed to invest in Kazakhstan, Azerbaijan, Kyrgistan, Turkmenistan, Uzbekistan and Tajikistan, the SRF has offices in Almaty, Kazakhstan and Baku, Azerbaijan.

Typically, the Fund invests in equity ranging from US$3–US$10M where it takes a 'significant minority' equity interest, usually ranging from 20 to 49 per cent. In larger transactions, the SRF can access capital in other AIG (American International Group) investment entities to increase the size of its participation to US$50M. The SRF is a temporary investor; within a period of two to five years following its investment, it will seek to sell its shares to the other investors.

The SRF employs an 'active' approach to its investments, usually seeking board representation and opportunities to enhance the long-term value of the companies in which it invests. This may come in the form of helping to raise additional finance, arranging strategic partnerships, or in providing a 'sounding board' for strategic business decisions.

The SRF is one of 11 emerging-market direct equity funds, managed and sponsored by AIG Capital Partners, a wholly owned AIG subsidiary. With total capital of nearly US$6.5 billion and teams totalling over 120 private equity professionals, these funds currently operate in major emerging markets in the CIS, eastern Europe, Asia, and Latin America. In each of these funds, AIG has directly contributed a minimum of 10 per cent of the capital base.

AIG is a major provider of financial services. AIG Capital Partners' investment approach is straightforward. It seeks to combine strong local presence in each market with AIG's global network. Within this framework, it maintains a disciplined investment focus on management, market, and company fundamentals.

Contact: Boris Evseer
Tel: +7 3272 608 273
Fax: +7 3272 608 272

Central Asian American Enterprise Fund (CAAEF)

The CAAEF is a privately managed profit-oriented venture capital institution. Its objective is to facilitate the establishment of market economies in the former central Asian republics of the Soviet Union by investing in small and medium-sized businesses in Kazakhstan, Kyrgyzstan, Tajikistan, Turkmenistan, and Uzbekistan. The CAAEF provides financing to commercially viable enterprises and also has a Micro Loan Programme that provides loans to the smallest businesses. It welcomes the participation of international partners willing to provide risk capital, management expertise and new technology to businesses in central Asia and of companies that wish to develop a long-term presence in central Asia and explore new markets for US exports.

Since commencing operations in 1994, the CAAEF has disbursed more than US$73 million in equity and loans to over 400 businesses and entrepreneurs in the five countries of central Asia. Individual transactions vary from large equity investments in new manufacturing facilities to micro loans for commercial traders plying their wares in the bazaars. The CAAEF currently provides financial support through two mechanisms:

- Equity and debt financing to medium-sized enterprises, with a strong bias towards new projects involved in manufacturing products for export or import substitution, and providing financial support in amounts ranging from US$100,000 to a general ceiling of US$5 million.

- A Micro Loan Programme targeted to assist small entrepreneurs.

While equity investments have represented the largest component of the CAAEF's financial support in the past, problems with the performance of many of the investee enterprises led, in early 1999, to the CAAEF reigning back its direct equity investments, and moving to a more cautious investment approach, using instead mainly convertible loans which allowed it to take collateral and produce some current income. Also due to currency convertibility problems in Uzbekistan, the Fund has effectively withdrawn from the area and is focusing most of its current efforts in Kazakhstan. A greater emphasis is now placed on financing existing businesses to assure their continued growth and development. Start-up enterprises will still be considered for financing, but they will represent a smaller percentage of the CAAEF's total portfolio. Experience has shown that start-ups require extensive management support; while the CAAEF will continue to provide such technical assistance, it will rely on the involvement of strategic partners experienced in the given industry to lead these efforts.

In common with other funds, the CAAEF's portfolio companies' recent difficulties have been the result of inexperienced management, inadequate marketing and extenuating circumstances beyond their control. By restricting the number of new investments in start-ups and relying on partners, the CAAEF expects significantly to improve its portfolio's performance while reducing the need for further reserves.

The CAAEF is a proactive investor, seeking solutions and opportunities to the myriad challenges that face each business. Technical assistance is provided to the management of each company; if the company's efforts are unsuccessful, the CAAEF will recruit professional managers from the region for those companies that lack strategic partners.

As the CAAEF looks for new opportunities in financial services, distribution, healthcare and other sectors experiencing rapid growth, critical investment criteria will include management strength, prospects for the sector and the level of government intervention. Experience has clearly demonstrated that weakness in any one of these areas can fatally flaw the best potential opportunity.

Contact: John Owens
Tel: +7 3272 63 8815
Fax: +7 3272 69 45 89

The Kazakhstan Investment Fund (KIF)

The KIF is managed by Kazakhstan Asset Management and has committed capital of US$105 million. It is a five-year closed-end fund and, after this period, shareholders may vote, by a simple majority, to continue the Fund or to liquidate and distribute the assets within a further two years. The principal subscribers participating in the KIF are long-term investors in London, Switzerland and North America.

The Fund intends to achieve long-term capital appreciation through participation in equity and convertible securities of companies operating in Kazakhstan. It will always identify an exit strategy such as seeking to invest in enterprises capable of achieving a listing on a stock exchange. It will also seek to co-invest with foreign corporate investors who will bring in expertise – management – as well as equity. The KIF will always take a minority stake in such enterprises, and will normally seek to obtain board representation but not management control. It will focus its interest on local companies operating in industries essential to the economic development of Kazakhstan.

Any enterprise in which the KIF invests must:

- be a market leader in the business sector in which it trades;

- have a well-defined business strategy;

- have proven managerial skills; if not the other parties will provide them;

- have made all the administrative arrangements necessary to achieve its business objectives;

- be in compliance with existing laws and regulations.

The KIF's target industry sectors are as follows:

- telecommunications;

- power generation and distribution;

- manufacture of construction materials;

- banking and insurance;

- transport;

- media;

- industries that use local raw materials;

- real estate;

- hotels and tourism;

- mining.

The Fund has made investments in Almaty Power Consolidated, the power utility; Khan Tengri Hotels, which owns a hotel in Atyrau on the Caspian Sea; Golden Eagle Partners, which has fee-based revenue as well as income from a subsidiary operating in the oil distribution business; and Central Asia Cement, based in Karaganda.

Contact: Javier del Sel
Tel: +7 3272 50 37 23
Fax: +7 3272 62 89 03

Conclusion

The venture capital industry in Kazakhstan differs from that in North America and Europe. In North America or Europe, once an investment has been made, the role of the venture capitalist is usually limited to monitoring the progress of the investment. In Kazakhstan there is a lack of experienced management and marketing skills are weak; this means that the venture capitalist frequently has to play a significant active management role in the enterprise in which he has invested. There is often therefore a strong preference among venture capital funds to co-invest with a foreign investor that will be able to take responsibility for the management of the enterprise, thus easing the burden on the venture capitalist.

Future Investor Outlook in 2000

Given increased production competitiveness following the devaluation of the Tenge from 85T/$ to 135T/$ in April 1999, both Presidential (Nursultan Nazarbayev – 7 years) and Parliamentary (Majilis – 5 years) elections in 1999, an increase in the world oil price from less than US$10 to over US$25 a barrel and a very open and supportive policy to direct foreign investment, coupled with new improved shareholder protection legislation, Kazakhstan is now widely viewed as one of the most promising countries for foreign investment in the CIS.

Part 4

Building an Organisation

Incorporating a Company

Russell W. Lambert, Managing Partner,
PricewaterhouseCoopers

Introduction

A foreign company wishing to provide services in Kazakhstan will have to determine whether it needs to be legally registered. Operating without proper legal and tax registration can bring unnecessary exposure to the company and lead to tax issues and penalties. The choice of entity depends on the activities the investor wishes to perform as well as the flexibility the investor wishes to have with regard to repatriating revenues.

The choice of corporate structure is important; different categories have different financial and tax implications. The most common corporate structures for foreign companies having a presence in Kazakhstan are branches, representative offices, limited liability partnerships and joint-stock companies.

Permanent establishment

The definition of a Permanent Establishment under the Kazakhstan Tax Code is broad and includes:

- a permanent place of activity for a taxpayer, through which he carries out entrepreneurial activities;

- a construction, installation, or assembly site, including supervision activities;

- an installation or construction that is used for exploration of natural resources, a drilling installation or vessel that is used for exploration of natural resources, including supervision activities;

- an entity that renders services.

Double taxation treaties with Kazakhstan generally provide for a standard period of 12 months during which a company can provide services in Kazakhstan before it is considered a permanent establishment. In such cases the permanent establishment does not need to be legally registered in Kazakhstan. However, following amendment No 28 of the Tax Code, companies providing services without a registered permanent establishment do have a tax registration obligation. The registration must be made within ten days of starting business activities in Kazakhstan. This requirement must be met irrespective of whether or not these activities are later recognised as subject to taxation in accordance with the tax legislation of the Republic of Kazakhstan and international treaties concluded on behalf of the government of the Republic of Kazakhstan. Registration enables the tax authorities to monitor the level and period of activities in Kazakhstan.

If a company creates a permanent establishment it becomes a taxpayer in Kazakhstan. A foreign taxpayer not only has to be registered with the tax authorities but also must be legally registered with the Ministry of Justice and the Statistical Committee as an entity recognised by the Civil Code. A taxpayer cannot register as a payer of taxes with the tax authorities until it is legally registered.

Corporate form

The Kazakhstan Civil Code defines the concept of a legal entity in Kazakhstan and sets out the types and forms that may be formed. A legal entity is an organisation with the right of business authority or operational management, and is liable for its obligations. It may be an organisation which, as its principal activity, generates income.

A legal entity is subject to state registration with the Department of the Ministry of Justice and with the Statistical Committee. It is worth noting that a legal entity is deemed created from the time of its registration, and that this may not be retrospective to the date the activity commenced. This is particularly important in determining the right to income and expenses of the newly formed company. Registration as a taxpayer with the right to deduction against corporate income, is subject to legal registration. Expenses incurred prior to the registration may be disallowed as deductions, but conversely, income earned prior to the registration may be taxable.

Edict No 2255 Concerning Business Partnerships governs the law on organisations generically categorised as Kazakhstan legal entities. A business partnership is recognised as a commercial organisation. A commercial organisation is a legal entity with a charter fund divided into shares and that is formed with a view to generating profit as the main purpose of its activities. Under this law, the following types of legal entity may be formed:

- general partnership;

- limited partnership;

- limited liability partnership;

- partnership with additional liability;

- joint-stock company.

Both the Civil Code and the Law on Business Partnerships include provisions for the founding and constitution of a legal entity.

It is worth noting that, in addition to the law governing the formation of such entities and their constitution, the activities of organisations are also governed by other legislative acts. Such organisations include banks, insurance companies and investment companies.

A business partnership is a resident of Kazakhstan and is required to operate in local currency only. In addition, it must seek permission from the National Bank to operate an overseas bank account. A Kazakhstan legal entity with foreign participation must undergo an annual audit, and submit the audited financial statements/report along with the final tax declaration by 31 March of the year following the tax year.

Branch

A branch is defined in the Civil Code as a separate division of a legal entity that carries out all or part of its function. As with representative offices, a branch is subject to the by-laws of the legal entity of which it is a subdivision. It is also subject to state registration with the Department of the Ministry of Justice and the Statistical Committee.

A branch must be registered as a taxpayer with the tax authorities and is required to submit a balance sheet with its corporate return. Although a branch is not considered a legal entity for tax purposes under the Civil Code, it is subject to the same tax obligations and rights as a legal entity.

Under current legislation, a branch is considered a non-resident with respect to currency regulations. It is therefore able to operate in hard currency and fewer restrictions apply to the repatriation of revenues and to payments being made outside Kazakhstan.

Representative office

A representative office is defined in the Civil Code as a separate subdivision of a legal entity, which carries out the protection and representation of the interest of the entity. It is permitted to enter into transactions on behalf of the legal entity, but it does not take on the function of the legal entity in its commercial activities. A representative office is not a legal entity. However, it is subject to the by-laws approved by the legal entity of which it is a subdivision. It is also subject to state registration with the Ministry of Justice and Statistical Committee.

Although as a rule a representative office does not carry out the commercial function of its parent with a view to the extraction of income, it must nevertheless be registered with the tax authorities for the purposes of paying taxes for its employees. Over the last two years the burden of reporting for taxes has increased and a representative office is now required to file property tax declarations in respect of the property used in its activity.

In some tax offices, representative offices have been required to file corporate tax declarations.

Registration of a branch or representative office

Following the submission of the required documents to the Department of the Ministry of Justice in the district where the entity conducts its activities, the authorities have 15 working days to review the documentation and register the entity. Upon completion of the registration with the Ministry of Justice, the entity should register with the Statistical Committee, which according to law should not take more than five working days.

The following documents are required (in Russian and Kazakh) for registration with the Ministry of Justice in order to set up a branch or a representative office in the Republic of Kazakhstan:

- a registration application (drafted by the Ministry of Justice) for completion by the foreign company;

- a notarised copy of the parent company's Charter or Articles of Incorporation;

- a notarised copy of the Certificate of Incorporation of the parent company or any other document which certifies that the company is a legal entity in accordance with the legislation of its country;

- two notarised copies of the Corporate Statement of the branch or the representative office;

- a notarised decision of the board of directors of the parent company to establish a branch or representative office in Kazakhstan;

- a notarised power of attorney issued to the representative of the parent company in Kazakhstan;

- the original or notarised copy of the lease agreement of the premises of the branch or representative office in the Republic of Kazakhstan;

- seal of the branch or the representative office.

Registration of a business partnership

When all the required documents in proper form have been submitted to the Department of the Ministry of Justice in the district where the company operates, the authorities have 20 working days to review the documentation and register the company. Upon completion of the registration with the Ministry of Justice, the entity should register with the Statistical Committee, which according to law should not take more than five working days.

The documents that need to be submitted differ per partnership; however, the following documents (in Russian and Kazakh) are always required:

- registration application (drafted by the Ministry of Justice) for completion by the foreign company;

- set of foundation documents (ie the foundation agreement and the charter of the new company);

- the original or notarised copy of the lease agreement of the premises of the branch or representative office in the Republic of Kazakhstan;

- seal of the new company.

Registration with the tax authorities

Within ten days after legally registering a company in the Republic of Kazakhstan, the company needs to register with the tax authorities. In order to register the company should submit the following documents (in Russian and Kazakh):

- application form;

- notarised copy of the Confirmation of Registration with the Ministry of Justice;

- Notarised copy of the statistical card;

- Notarised copy of the Charter document.

Licences

When choosing a corporate form it is important to inquire whether the company will need a licence to perform the planned activities. Edict 2200 lists the activities that do require a licence. This area of law is under continuous development and enquiries should be made to determine whether a licence is required for a particular business. Some licence regulations provide that such licences may only be granted to residents of Kazakhstan, which excludes branches of foreign legal entities. Therefore, the investor does not always make the choice as to the corporate form to provide services in Kazakhstan.

Agency Distribution and Franchise Agreements

Zhaniya B Ussen, Assistance LLC in Almaty and Alastair Moody, Ledingham Chalmers in Edinburgh

Introduction

As an alternative to establishing a formal corporate presence in Kazakhstan, foreign companies may, on a short- or long-term basis, sell and market their products through local agents, distributors and franchisees. This chapter discusses the major features of the law concerning agency, distributorship and franchise agreements that may be of interest to foreign producers or suppliers importing goods into Kazakhstan.

The laws regulating franchise agreements and some aspects of agency and distributorship agreements are found primarily in the Civil Code.[1] Unlike many other emerging markets, the parties are, subject to certain mandatory requirements, free to determine most of the terms of their contractual relationship whether as independent sales representatives, independent commercial agents, employee agents, independent local distributors or local franchisees. There are no legal restrictions regarding the nationality of the local agent, distributor or franchisee so that both Kazakhstani and foreign companies or individuals, subject to certain registration requirements, may be represented.

Agency

Agency is the legal relationship whereby the agent has authority to contract with third parties on behalf of the principal. Thus the agent has power to legally bind the principal. There are two main types of agency relationship: 'employee agent' and 'independent agent'. Agents may be either individuals or corporate entities.

The nature of the agency relationship is important for, under the laws of Kazakhstan, where an individual agent has an employment relationship with a principal, the contract is governed by Kazakhstani labour law. The law provides the employee agent with certain statutory protections in relation to the termination of contract and may make the principal/employer liable for social security, health and pension fund contributions in Kazakhstan. Additionally, withholding of income tax liability may arise to the principal where the employee agent is an individual who is not formally registered as an entrepreneur.

Where the parties' description of the relationship with their agent is that of an independent agent, this may not, in itself, be sufficient to prevent the agent being deemed an employee agent by the tax authorities. One of the principal distinctions between an employee agent and an independent agent is that an employee agent is paid a salary by the employer/principal whereas an independent agent is remunerated by commissions.

Distributorship

The term 'independent distributorship' refers to the legal relationship whereby one person, a local distributor, buys goods from a foreign supplier and resells them to the distributor's customers for its own account. The distributor has no authority to bind the supplier and all risks associated with the resale remain with the distributor. As the distributor is purchasing goods for resale, it must maintain an inventory and may keep such goods in warehousing prior to resale and distribution.

As with agency agreements, the Civil Code does not specifically recognise distributorship agreements although the law does recognise forms of contract not expressly provided for by law.[2]

In practice, distributorship agreements have been widely used in Kazakhstan and specific reference is made in the monetary control regulations concerning import and export transactions,[3] as well as in certain other normative acts.[4]

Franchise agreements

The term 'franchise' is defined by the Civil Code as the legal relationship whereby one person, a franchisee, is authorized by another person, a franchiser, to use in the franchisee's business operations, the trade name, trade marks, patents and other commercial information of the latter.[5] The concept of franchise is relatively new to Kazakhstan, being referred to for the first time under the Special Part of the Civil Code which was adopted in the summer of 1999.

Creation of the agency, distribution and franchise relationship

The creation of an agency, distribution or franchise relationship is consensual and generally requires agreement to be made in writing. No notarisation or registration of the agreement with government agencies is necessary.

Fixing Prices and other restraints

Under an agency contract, the title to goods remains with the foreign supplier until such goods are sold in Kazakhstan. The agent does not generally have the right to determine independently the terms of sale as this falls to the principal.

However, an issue with regard to antitrust/price-fixing laws may arise with distributorship agreements. Although the Civil Code does not expressly prohibit resale price maintenance and the setting of minimum prices with regard to distributorship agreements, the provisions of the Unfair Competition Law[6] must be considered, particularly where the parties to a distribution agreement are different and independent from each other.

Unlike in agency and distributorship agreements, the Civil Code expressly prohibits the setting of minimum or maximum prices for goods or services sold under a franchise agreement. This prohibition is broadly similar to European Union (EU) legislation on franchise agreements[7]. Under the Civil Code the following restrictions are permitted:

- the franchiser may grant an exclusive franchise in the contract territory of the franchisee or retain exclusive rights to the franchise itself on that territory;

- an obligation on the franchisee not to compete with the franchiser within the contract territory with regard to the franchisee's business activity carried out in accordance with the exclusive rights granted by the franchiser;

- an obligation on the franchisee to refrain from obtaining a franchise from a franchiser's competitors or potential competitors;

- an obligation on the franchisee to obtain the consent of the franchiser with regard to the location of premises and their exterior and interior decoration operated under the franchise agreement.

Among the provisions which are specifically prohibited by the Civil Code are:

- the franchiser's right to determine the price at which the goods or services are to be sold by the franchisee or the upper or lower limits of such prices;

- any prohibition on the sale of goods or services to certain categories of customers.

Export payments

In accordance with the monetary laws of Kazakhstan, 50 per cent of any export payments made in foreign currency are subject to mandatory conversion into the national currency, the tenge.[8] The local agent may wish to avoid such limitations by using other arrangements, such as making payment to an overseas bank account of a third country, although such an arrangement may be in breach of local monetary laws with possible administrative and civil sanctions and should be treated with caution.[9]

Termination of independent agency, distributorship or franchise agreements

The Civil Code lays out the termination provisions for agency, distributorship and franchise agreements. Under the Code, terminations may be made by:

- the mutual consent of the parties;

- expiry of the term of the agreement;

- material breach of an agreement by either party;

- impossibility of performance of contractual obligations;

- court order declaring a party to the agreement bankrupt or insolvent;

- termination of a governmental act which is the basis for the said agreement.

In addition an agency agreement may also be terminated unilaterally at will by either the principal's revocation of his authority or by an agent's refusal to continue performance of the agency relationship.

Any franchise agreement which is silent as to expiration, in addition to the grounds for termination stated above, may also be terminated by either party giving to the other at least six months' notice of their intention to terminate.

Individual agents (registered as entrepreneurs), distributors and franchisees may have the right to compensation in the form of damages (calculated on the basis of actual loss and lost profits) as a result of termination of their contract.

Laws affecting imports

The use of an agency or distributorship agreement which involves the import of goods to Kazakhstan may require valid licences and approvals for the importation of certain categories of goods as well as compliance with import control regarding quotas, tariffs, labelling and certification rules. Additionally a distributor or a foreign supplier as principal (or otherwise) may be subject to customs clearance payments including customs tariffs, customs duties, excise tax and value added tax (VAT).

Tax issues for foreign suppliers

A crucial area of concern to a foreign supplier or foreign franchiser is whether they will be subject to taxation in Kazakhstan with respect to the income resulting from the sales of their products. Under the tax laws, a foreign supplier or foreign franchiser is liable for income tax where such supplier or franchiser carries out business through a permanent establishment in Kazakhstan or otherwise derives income from Kazakhstani sources.[10]

The term 'permanent establishment' refers to a more or less permanent place of taxpayer's operation whereby it, fully or partially, carries out its business, including any such business carried out through an authorized person. A foreign supplier's representative office, branch, plant, factory or its rendering of consulting and other services within the territory of the Republic of Kazakhstan constitutes a 'permanent establishment' for these purposes. An agent is generally recognized by the tax authorities as being a 'permanent establishment' of the foreign principal, unless the agent is legally and economically independent from the principal and is registered as an independent taxpayer in Kazakhstan. A distributor or a franchisee is less likely to be deemed a 'permanent establishment' of the foreign supplier or the franchiser as it is acting on its own behalf in marketing and distributing the products.

Any income of the permanent establishment is subject to Kazakhstani income tax at the rate of 30 per cent (subject to the deduction of permitted associated expenses). Relief from such tax treatment may be sought by a foreign supplier on the basis of an applicable double taxation treaty to which Kazakhstan is a party.[11] In addition to income tax, a permanent establishment of a foreign company may also be subject to a tax on net income of a permanent establishment at the rate of 15 per cent and VAT at the rate of 20 per cent. The taxable base for tax on net income of a permanent establishment is calculated as the difference between the adjusted taxable income and the amount of income tax accrued.

Supplier's withholding tax

A Kazakhstani source of income includes income which results from the sale of goods in Kazakhstan when, at the time of contracting, the goods were physically located in Kazakhstan including income in the form of royalty, interest and dividends.

In accordance with 1 July 1998 amendments to the Tax Code, the definition of income from a Kazakhstani source has been expanded to include income received from all types of services, including offshore services, where payment of income is accrued as a tax deduction by a Kazakhstani taxpayer.

Also, where a Kazakhstani source of income is paid to a foreign company that is not registered as a Kazakhstani taxpayer, income tax should be withheld at the source of payment by an entity or an individual without deduction of associated expenses. Such withholding tax is applicable regardless whether payment is actually made in Kazakhstan or outside. In the event that tax is not withheld on the payment then under the Tax Code and Tax Instruction No 43,[12] a penalty equivalent to 100 per cent of the withholding tax payable may be imposed by the tax authorities.

The amount of the withholding tax paid may be reclaimed in full or in part on the basis of an applicable double taxation treaty.

In addition to the above, if a foreign supplier is not registered for VAT in Kazakhstan, a Kazakhstani buyer or distributor may also be found liable for VAT on payments made to a foreign supplier on sale of goods in Kazakhstan qualifying as a Kazakhstani source income, with full credit for inputs.

Notes

[1]   Civil Code of the Republic of Kazakhstan (Special Part) No 409–1 ZRK of 1 July 1999, Chapters 25, 41, 43 and 45.
[2]   Article 380 of the Civil Code of the Republic of Kazakhstan (General Part) No 268-XIII of 27 December 1994, as amended.
[3]   For example, Instruction on Organization of Export and Import Monetary Control at the Republic of Kazakhstan (adopted by the Ministry of State Revenue of the Republic of Kazakhstan and the Resolution of the Board of the National Bank of the Republic of Kazakhstan No 271 of 5 December 1998).

4 For example, the Joint Order of the Ministry of Finance of the Republic of Kazakhstan No 42 of 29 January 1999 and the Ministry of State Revenue of the Republic of Kazakhstan No 29 of 29 January 1999 'On Tax Regime of the Final Production Sharing Agreement for Karachaganak Oil and Gas Field dated 18 November 1997 entered between Adgip Karachaganak B.V., BG Exploration and Production Limited, Texaco International Petroleum Company, Lukoil Public Joint Stock Company, Kazakhoil Closed Joint Stock Company and the Government of the Republic of Kazakhstan' contains examples of various distributorship arrangements.

5 Since trade mark licensing and technology transfer are the core of most international franchise agreements please refer to Chapter 4.6.

6 Law of the Republic of Kazakhstan No 232–1 'On Unfair Competition' of 9 June 1998 is treating price agreements between the competitors as unfair competition with possible criminal, administrative and civil sanctions.

7 Regulation 4087/88, Application of Article 85(3) to Categories of Franchise Agreements, Off. .J. 1988 L539/46, CCH Com. Mkt. Rep.

8 Instruction 'On Mandatory Sale of Income in Foreign Currency from Export of Goods (Works, Services)' adopted by the Decree of the Board of the National Bank of the Republic of Kazakhstan No 54 of 28 March 1999, as amended.

9 Law of the Republic of Kazakhstan No 54–1 'On Monetary Control' of 24 December 1996, as amended; Code of the KazSSR 'On Administrative Misconducts' of 22 March 1984, as amended, Article 167.

10 Law of the Republic of Kazakhstan No 2235 'On Taxes and Other Obligatory Payments to the Budget' of 24 April 1995, as amended (the 'Tax Code'); Instruction of the Ministry of Finance of the Republic of Kazakhstan No 33 'On the Procedure for Calculation and Payment to the Budget of Income Tax for Legal Entities' of 28 June 1995, as amended.

11 Kazakhstan has effective tax treaties with more than 20 countries, including the UK, the USA, Canada, Italy, the Netherlands, Sweden and Turkey.

12 Instruction of the Ministry of Finance of the Republic of Kazakhstan No 43 'On Administrative Provisions on Taxes and Other Obligatory Payments to the Budget' of 1 July 1995, as amended.

4.3

Accounting and Audit

Ernst & Young

Statutory requirements

There have been significant changes in statutory requirements affecting accounting in Kazakhstan since the last edition of this book in 1995. The prescriptive USSR Chart of Accounts and the detailed rules on determining costs of production have been replaced by standards that are much closer to western models. In particular, the cash basis of accounting normally required in the past has been superseded by an accruals basis.

Books and records

Kazakhstan accounting laws require that all legal entities must keep books of account and records of all accounting transactions. Kazakh accounting standards (KAS) require that the books of account be maintained in Kazakhstan and include a general ledger organized by financial statement classifications and a journal of transactions in chronological order. Books and records for all transactions must be retained for at least three years after the last date of entry.

Method of accounting

Financial accounting is based on the accruals method of accounting. Income is recognized when earned, expenses and losses are recognized and recorded when incurred.

Financial statements

The managing director of a legal entity is responsible for issuing financial statements within three months after the end of the entity's financial year. Financial statements must be prepared in Kazakh tenge and should include a balance sheet, an income statement, a cash flow statement and notes to the financial statements with comparative information for the prior year.

Sources of accounting principles

The National Commission for Accounting was formed in May 1996. It establishes the main principles and general rules for accounting as well as the requirements for internal controls and independent audit of Kazakhstan legal entities.

The Commission has developed and approved a set of guidelines for recording the financial and economic activities of legal entities known as the General Chart of Accounts. While the specific forms are not mandatory, a company must record its financial activities in a way that permits them to be classified in accordance with KAS.

The major KAS provisions comprise:

- the standard format to be used in preparing annual financial statements;

- the required books and records of transactions, as well as the period of time for which they must be retained;

- general accounting principles to be followed in preparing the annual financial statements.

The Kazakhstan Tax Law imposes additional tax accounting requirements, including the method of tax depreciation and the rule that certain deductions may be accrued for tax purposes only if they are recorded in the financial statements.

Accounting principles and practices

Fundamental concepts

Under KAS, the fundamental accounting concepts are fair statement of accounts, going concern presumption, consistency of accounting principles, relevance, materiality, reliability, neutrality, completeness, comparability and prudence. These concepts are consistent with those of the international accounting standards on which KAS are based.

Financial reporting

The aim of financial reporting is to provide users with useful, relevant and reliable information concerning the financial position of a legal entity, the results of its business activities and changes to its financial position for the reporting period.

Reporting period

Annual financial statements are prepared on the basis of the calendar year. The initial reporting period for a legal entity begins from the date of legal registration and runs to 31 December of that year.

Legal entities must submit their annual financial statements no later than 30 April of the year following the reporting year to:

- shareholders indicated in foundation documents;
- state statistical bodies in the region of Kazakhstan where the entity is registered;
- state supervisory bodies with jurisdiction over the entity.

Financial statements are not required to be made available to the general public.

General information disclosed in financial statements

All material information should be presented in such a manner that the financial statements are clear and understandable to users. The classification of items and monetary sums indicated in financial statements should be supplemented with explanatory information. Specifically, the notes must provide information about fixed assets, provisions, reserves, short- and long-term liabilities, capital and decreases in capital caused by losses.

Financial statements should indicate the name of the legal entity, location, reporting date and reporting period. They should include a short description of the type of activity conducted by the organization, its legal form and the unit of measurement in which the financial statements are presented.

Accounting policies and supplementary information must be disclosed in the notes to the financial statements. The notes must provide sufficient information to ensure that the financial statements present a true and fair view of the company's operational results and of its financial position. The effects of changes in accounting policies must be quantified and the reasons for the change must be explained.

Audit requirements

A law governing audit activities was passed in November 1998. Under this law, an audit is an independent appraisal of the financial statements and other documents of legal entities. An audit is performed to assess the accuracy of financial statements and whether or not the financial statements comply with Kazakhstan standards.

Audits may be classified as either obligatory or voluntary. Obligatory audits are those stipulated by the legislation of Kazakhstan, ie audits of KAS financial statements of Kazakh legal entities. Voluntary audits are those carried out at the discretion of the legal entity, for example the audit of financial statements prepared by a Kazakh legal entity in accordance with international accounting standards.

Foreign legal entities with branches conducting activities in Kazakhstan are not required to issue financial statements related to their activities in Kazakhstan. As a result, they are not required to undergo audits. Rather, they need only a limited-scope audit confirming the accuracy of information reported on their tax declarations.

Accounting profession

Individuals signing audit reports to be submitted in accordance with Kazakhstan legislation must be members of the Kazakh Chamber of Accountants and Auditors. To qualify as an auditor, an individual must have five years' experience and pass required examinations. Only persons with higher education and work experience in economic, financial, accounting and analytical, control and revision or legal fields are permitted to apply for certification.

4.4

Taxation: An Overview

Ernst & Young

Introduction

In the early days of independence, Kazakhstan's tax system was closely based on the Soviet model. It included 45 separate taxes, many with their own laws and instructions. Accounting procedure also followed the Soviet model, which was the product of a system of state reporting with very specific guidelines for the chart of accounts and requirements regarding where and how expenditure should be recorded. Accounting and tax reporting were on a cash basis.

The combination of these accounting and tax rules resulted in a system very different from international norms and this proved a significant challenge to foreign investors.

By 1999 there had been significant changes, and accounting standards now follow international norms more closely and the tax system has been brought much more in line with those found in G-7 countries. Many taxes have been eliminated and a comprehensive Tax Code has been introduced with supporting explanatory instructions. Kazakhstan now has, for example, a network of double taxation agreements, transfer pricing legislation and a system of foreign tax credits.

The speed of change has been remarkable and it is not surprising that the administration of the tax system is taking time to catch up. In particular, Kazakhstan has not had the time to build up a body of precedence and case law on the interpretation of the tax code such as exists in the UK or USA. This can lead to practical problems of interpretation for more complex transactions and resulting commercial uncertainty for investors. It should also be noted that there have been no less than 29 sets of amendments to the current tax code since it came into force in July 1995. Sometimes taxes have appeared and disappeared in a matter of a few months. This is another factor creating uncertainty for investors, though guarantees of stability in foreign investment legislation and individually negotiated contracts afford some measure of protection.

Overview of the tax system

The tax system in Kazakhstan includes the following principal taxes and levies:

- income tax on individuals and legal entities;
- value added tax (VAT);
- customs duties;
- excise duties;
- social taxes;
- pension fund contributions;
- land tax;
- property tax;
- vehicle tax.

Table 4.4.1 shows the rates applicable at 1 September 1999 for all taxes and levies in Kazakhstan. It should be remembered that tax rules change frequently in Kazakhstan and readers should obtain up-to-date information before engaging in transactions. A comprehensive review of the current tax system was initiated in January 2000. A new tax code is to be introduced with effect from 1 January 2000.

Table 4.4.1 Kazakhstan taxes and levies as at 1 September 1999

Types of taxes	Rate (%)	Tax basis and notes
Corporate income tax	30	Aggregate income less deductions
	10	Applicable to income derived from direct land utilization by companies for whom land is the main production assets
	15	Net income after corporate income tax. Applies to the branches of foreign legal entities (subject to relief under double tax treaties)
VAT	20	Turnover derived from the sale of goods, work performed and services rendered, as well as imported goods and export of goods to CIS except Kyrgystan, Uzbekistan, Azerbaijan, Moldova
	10	Sales and import of foodstuffs including meat, fish, flour, bread, milk and dairy products, eggs, corn, mixed fodder, sugar, among others.
	0	Export of goods to non-CIS member states as well as to Kyrgystan, Uzbekistan, Azerbaijan,

Table 4.4.1 *continued*

Types of taxes	Rate (%)	Tax basis and notes
		Moldova. Sales of gold and platinum by Kazakhstan residents who are producers thereof. Sales by residents of the Republic of Kazakhstan in the territory of the Republic of Kazakhstan by producers in the textile, sewing, leather and footwear industries
	Exempt from VAT	Lease and sale of buildings with the exception of the first sale; financial services including loans and insurance; geological exploration and geological prospecting operations; international conveyance of goods or passengers from Kazakhstan to non-CIS member states, etc
	16.67	Revenue of foreign legal entities, which are not registered in Kazakhstan, derived from a sale of goods (work and services) in Kazakhstan (representing income derived from sources in Kazakhstan). Rate of VAT (16.67%) is withheld from gross invoice values by payers to achieve 20% of the net invoice values

Special payments and taxes on subsurface users:

• Subscription bonus	Rate in contract	One-time payment for the right to conduct subsurface use activities while concluding contract
• Commercial discovery bonus	Rate in contract	Payable when a commercial discovery is made. Not paid under a contract for exploration of minerals resources that does not presume extraction of the minerals
• Extraction bonus*	Rate in contract	Periodic payment due when attaining the extraction output level set out in a contract
• Royalty	Rate in contract	Value of extracted commonly occurring useful minerals and underground water based on average selling price
	Rate in contract	Value of extracted gold, silver and platinum based on average selling price of international non-ferrous metals exchanges as defined by the government
		Basis for other minerals depends on the type of extracted minerals and is based on average selling price
• Excess profit tax	0–30	Payable when IRR is more than 20%, taxable basis is net after tax income
		Not applicable to production sharing contracts and contracts for production of commonly occurring useful minerals

Table 4.4.1 *continued*

Types of taxes	Rate (%)	Tax basis and notes
Excise tax	Various depending on goods	Excisable goods include spirits and alcoholic beverages, caviar, fish delicacies, chocolate, tobacco, jewels, furs and leather, cars, petroleum (except for aviation fuel), diesel fuel, crude oil, etc.
Fee for registration of securities	0.1 0.5	The face value of the initial issue of shares or bonds The face value of subsequent issue of shares or bonds.
Fee for a national identification number	0.1	For emission of shares which is not subject to state registration
Land tax	25–3,000 tenge	Per unit of area of land depending on the quality, location, water supply of the land and annual government coefficients
Property tax	1	Average annual net book value of capital goods and fixed assets (including intangibles) except for vehicles
Vehicle tax	4–117 times MIR	MIR (monthly index rate) – currently 725 tenge. Coefficient depends on age of vehicle, engine size, etc
Social tax	21	Salary and wage payment made to local employees. Different rate for expatriates
Pension fund contributions	10	Salary and wage payment made to local employees
Environmental protection fund contributions	Various	Payments include compensation for polluting the environment within established norm, for polluting the environment in excess of allowed limits and for environmental damage caused by violating environmental legislation
Customs duties	0–100	Imports are subject to customs duties that range from 0 to 100% of the customs value, depending on the nature of the import. A full or partial exemption may be obtained for property imported on a temporary basis

* As of 1 July 1998 extraction bonus abolished for new contracts.

Administration

Filing and payment
The tax year is the calendar year. Kazakhstan's tax system operates on the principle of self-assessment. The Tax Service is responsible solely for verifying the accuracy of the calculation and the timeliness of the payment of taxes. Taxpayers are required to submit tax declarations and to make periodic payments of tax, the frequency of which depends on the level and type of tax concerned.

Tax audits
The Tax Service has the right to carry out audits of legal entities and individuals in connection with payment of taxes and other obligatory payments to the budget.

Tax on legal entities

Income tax (profits tax)

Legal entities created under the laws of Kazakhstan are deemed tax resident and are subject to profits tax on their worldwide income. The general rate applicable to most entities is 30 per cent. The taxable base consists of income (including capital gains) arising from the business activities of the legal entity less any expenses incurred in connection with the generation of that income (other than those of a capital nature).

Non-resident legal entities operating in Kazakhstan through a permanent establishment are taxable only on Kazakh source income. A foreign legal entity is considered to have created a taxable permanent establishment in Kazakhstan if it provides services in Kazakhstan or establishes a permanent base for selling goods. However, 'permanent' does not necessarily mean long term; a period of a few weeks can constitute permanent. The taxable base for permanent establishments is the Kazakh source income and capital gains of a foreign legal entity, less attributable expenses.

Both Kazakh legal entities and permanent establishments of foreign legal entities are required to make monthly advance payments of profit tax. They must submit quarterly preliminary declarations of profits tax during the tax year and an annual tax return by 31 March of the year following the tax year. The balance of any tax liability due must be paid by 10 April of the year following the tax year.

Under the Tax Code a foreign legal entity may have Kazakh source income without creating a permanent establishment, for example if it provides services outside Kazakhstan to a Kazakh legal entity which takes a tax deduction for the cost in Kazakhstan. Such income is subject to Kazakh tax withholding to be applied by the payer. The tax is due on the whole sum paid without any deduction for expenses incurred by the foreign legal entity. Rates vary depending on the type of income (see Table 4.4.2.)

Table 4.4.2 Income tax withholding from payments to non-residents not registered for tax purposes in Kazakhstan

Type of income	Rates (%)
Dividends and interest	15
Income from insurance, international freight and international telecommunications	5
Royalties, management and consulting services, rent income and other income	20

Foreign legal entities whose activities do not create a permanent establishment may be able to eliminate or reduce the withholding of income tax by securing relief under a tax treaty.

Currency

Taxable income must normally be measured in tenge. Any foreign currency income or expenditure must be translated into tenge at the rate prevailing on the date the income arises or the expenditure is incurred. Foreign exchange gains and losses are excluded from the calculation of taxable income.

Interest

Interest on loans in tenge is deductible at a rate of up to one and a half times the refinancing rate of the National Bank of Kazakhstan. Interest on hard currency loans is deductible up to two times the LIBOR rate on the relevant currency.

Tax depreciation

Accounting depreciation is not deductible for tax purposes. Intangible and tangible assets are depreciated/amortised by category on a declining balance basis with maximum rates ranging from 3 to 30 per cent. The applicable rate is applied to the balance sheet value of the asset category at the end of each tax year.

Loss carryovers

Losses from business activities can be carried forward for up to three years (seven years for entities operating under a contract for the extraction of mineral resources). There is no loss carryback provision.

Treatment of groups of companies

The Tax Code does not include any provisions permitting related enterprises to consolidate their tax returns and transfer profits and losses among members of a corporate group.

Partnerships

Income received through a general partnership or a consortium is distributed between its partners and will be taxed as part of the income of each partner. A limited liability partnership (sometimes referred to as a limited liability company) is subject to tax at the entity level, separately from its partners.

Dividends

Dividends are subject to income tax withholding at a rate of 15 per cent, whether paid to individuals, or foreign or Kazakh legal entities.

Tax concessions

Foreign investment law provides for certain limited tax concessions for foreign investment in priority sectors of the economy (see Table 4.4.3). Concessions need to be negotiated on a case-by-case basis. Investment contracts with the government usually provide tax stability so that the main tax rules applying to the project will remain in effect throughout the project's life, regardless of any subsequent changes in general tax rules.

Table 4.4.3 Tax incentives

Types of taxes	Incentives	Applicable
Corporate income tax	Exemption from tax	Applicable to income derived by companies from construction in Astana
Corporate income tax, land tax and property tax	Up to 100% reduction of tax rate for the first 5 years and up to 50% reduction for the subsequent 5 years	Available to investors (both foreign and domestic) involved in the priority sectors of the economy and concluding a contract with the Agency on Investments
Corporate income tax	Reduced rate of 20%	For companies registered and carrying out business activity in Astana Special Economic Zone

Mineral extraction activities

There are special tax rules and separate taxes for mineral extraction activities. These are dealt with in detail elsewhere in this publication.

Personal income tax

Employers in Kazakhstan must withhold income tax from the salaries of employees paid in Kazakhstan. This requirement applies regardless of whether the salaries are paid in foreign currency or in tenge. Foreigners paid abroad are required to make quarterly advance payments of income tax.

Citizens of Kazakhstan who receive income only from their primary place of employment are not required to file tax returns. However, self-employed individuals and foreign nationals in Kazakhstan must file tax returns. The income tax declarations are due by 31 March of the year following the reporting year, and final payments are due no later than 10 April.

Residents and non-residents – territoriality

Residents are taxed on their worldwide income. Non-residents are taxed only on Kazakh-source income, ie income earned for services provided in Kazakhstan, regardless of where the payment for services is made. In addition, Kazakh-source income includes income for any work, regardless of where it is performed, if the payment of the income is claimed by the payer as a tax deduction in Kazakhstan. For tax purposes, an individual is a resident of Kazakhstan if he is present in Kazakhstan for 183 days or more in any period of 12 consecutive months. Generally, all monetary and in-kind benefits provided by an employer to an employee constitute taxable income to the employee.

Personal allowances

A tax-free allowance is given to each taxpayer and each dependent. The rate is changed each year. For 1999 it was approximately US$65.

Rates

Personal income tax is charged at progressively higher rates as income increases. The maximum personal tax rate is 30 per cent, and this rate is reached at a relatively low annual income of approximately US$4,300. Income received in foreign currency is converted into tenge at the exchange rate of the National Bank of Kazakhstan prevailing on the date when the income is received. Married persons are taxed separately, not jointly, on all types of income.

Tax treaties

Kazakhstan has entered into double tax treaties with a number countries, including the UK and the USA, which may provide relief from taxation in Kazakhstan(see Table 4.4.4). Under most of these treaties, an individual will not be taxed on income earned in Kazakhstan if:

1 he is present in Kazakhstan for 183 days or less in any period of 12 consecutive months,
2 his salary is paid by or on behalf of an employer that is not resident (ie incorporated) in Kazakhstan,
3 the salary is not deducted for tax purposes by a taxpayer in Kazakhstan.

Table 4.4.4 Kazakhstan double tax treaties

Country	Dividends (%)	Interest (%)	Royalties (%)
No treaty	15	15	20
United Kingdom	5–15[b]	10	10
United States	5–15[b]	10	10
Netherlands	5–15[b]	10	10
Azerbaijan	10	10	10
Italy	5–15[b]	10	10
Hungary	5–15[b]	10	10
Pakistan	12.5–15[b]	12.5	15
Poland	10–15[b]	10	10
Turkey	10	10	10
Ukraine	5–15[b]	10	10
Uzbekistan	10	10	10
Canada	5–15[b]	10	10
Russia	10	10	10
Germany	5–15[b]	10	10
Kyrgyzstan	10	10	10
Lithuania	5–15	10	10
Belarus	15	10	15
India	10	10	10
Bulgaria	10	10	10
Sweden	5–15	10	10
Korea	5–15	10	10
Iran	5–15	10	10

[a] Income from international telecommunications or transport is subject to tax at the rate of 5%; insurance payments are taxed at a rate of 5%.
[b] Depending on ownership percentage.

Value added tax (VAT)

Kazakhstan has a VAT system based on similar principles to that found in European Union (EU) countries. VAT is charged on the value created in the production of goods or provision of services. The standard rate of VAT is 20 per cent, though certain foodstuffs are subject to VAT at 10 per cent. Legal entities and individuals engaging in commercial activities must charge VAT on supplies of goods and services. VAT also applies to the import of goods.

Taxable base

The taxable base is the turnover from the sale of goods or services in Kazakhstan. The taxable base on imports includes the customs value of the goods, including any import duties.

The amount of VAT payable to the budget is the difference between the amount of VAT charged on goods or services sold (output tax) and the amount of VAT payable on goods or services purchased (input tax).

Zero-rated goods

Certain supplies, including exported goods and services, are taxed at a zero rate. For zero-rated sales the seller is entitled to reclaim from the government all input VAT related to the sale. In practice, it is difficult to obtain repayment, and offsetting repayment against other tax obligations may be pursued as an alternative.

Exemptions

Several types of turnover are exempt from VAT. Input VAT incurred in the course of the supply of exempt goods is not reclaimable by the supplier and must instead be deducted as a cost. Some of the major exemptions include:

- the lease and sale of land or buildings, with the exception of the first sale of such property;

- financial services, including the maintenance of bank accounts, operations with securities, cheques, debentures, deposits and certificates;

- geological exploration and geological prospecting work.

Non-reclaimable items

Input VAT cannot be reclaimed on the following:

- inputs not directly associated with the production process;
- buildings;
- cars.

Although it is not reclaimable, VAT on buildings and cars may be capitalised as part of the asset and recovered in part through tax depreciation.

Customs duties

Imports into Kazakhstan are subject to customs duties, ranging from 0 to 100 per cent of the customs value, depending on the nature of the import. In addition to the customs duties, the importer must pay a customs-processing fee which is currently 0.2 per cent of the total customs value of the goods. There are no customs duties on exports with the exception of various types of wheat.

Certain categories of goods imported on a temporary basis for a period of up to one year are exempt from customs duties. This period may be extended for an additional year, but the importer must pay a partial duty of 3 per cent of the normal duty for each month that the goods remain in Kazakhstan beyond one year.

Equipment and spare parts that are imported as part of a contribution to the equity of a Kazakh legal entity are exempt from customs duties. This exemption does not apply to foreign legal entities.

Excise duties

Excise duties are payable on certain goods produced in or imported into Kazakhstan that are deemed to be luxury items or goods used in gambling businesses. The list of goods subject to excise duty includes, among others, the following:

- alcoholic beverages;
- tobacco products;
- jewellery made from precious metals;
- crystal;
- passenger vehicles;
- petrol and diesel;
- firearms;
- salmon, sturgeon and caviar.

Exported goods are not subject to excise duties if the producer provides proof of their export. Depending on the particular goods, duty rates vary from 5 to 100 per cent of the value of the goods or a flat rate per volume or quantity of the goods.

Social taxes

Employers in Kazakhstan must pay a social tax on behalf of all employees who are citizens of Kazakhstan. The tax is assessed as 21 per cent of gross salaries paid to employees less pension fund contributions that are withheld from the salaries. The social tax also applies to foreign nationals but at dramatically lower flat rates.

Pension fund contributions

A pension fund contribution, of 10 per cent of their gross salary, must be paid by local employees. This is allocated to an individual's personal pension account, which may be the state scheme or one of a number of private schemes.

Land Tax

Land tax is payable on inhabited land and land used for agricultural, industrial, transportation, communication, defence or other purposes. The tax is imposed on legal entities or individuals that either own or have a right to permanent use of the land. The amount of tax levied depends on the quality, location and water supply of the land and not on financial returns from the use of the land. The rate of land tax varies depending on the designated use of the land and the quality score of the land.

Property tax

Property tax is assessed on the financial accounting net book value of fixed assets at the rate of 1.0 per cent, with the exception of vehicles, which are subject to vehicle tax.

Vehicle tax

Owners of vehicles, including legal enterprises, pay a vehicle tax at graduated rates based on the engine capacity.

4.5

Information on the Conventions for the Avoidance of Double Taxation as of 1 September 1999

Russell W. Lambert, Managing Partner,
PricewaterhouseCoopers

Convention valid	*Date of exchange of notes*	*Effective date*	*Ratified by only[2] (RoK)*	*Signed but not ratified[3]*
Great Britain	21 August 1996	1 January 1993	Turkmenistan	Estonia
Italy	26 February 1997	1 January 1994	Romania	Moldova
Poland	13 May 1995	1 January 1996	Georgia	Latvia
the USA	30 December 1996	1 January 1996	Mongolia	
Pakistan	29 January 1997	1 January 1996	France	
the Netherlands	28 April 1997	1 January 1996	Czech Republic	
Ukraine	3 April 1997	1 January 1997	Belgium	
Hungary	3 March 1996	1 January 1997		
Turkey	18 November 1996	1 January 1997		
Uzbekistan	7 April 1997	1 January 1998		
Azerbaijan	7 May 1997	1 January 1998		
Russia	29 July 1997	1 January 1998		
India	28 August 1997	1 January 1998		
Belarus	13 December 1997	1 January 1998		
Canada	30 March 1998	1 January 1996		
Lithuania	11 December 1997	1 January 1998		
Kyrgyzstan	31 March 1998	1 January 1999		
Sweden	2 October 1998	1 January 1999		
Bulgaria	24 July 1998	1 January 1999		
Germany	21 December 1998	1 January 1996		
Korea	9 April 1999	1 January 2000		
Iran	3 April 1999	1 January 2000		

[1] Interstate procedure on ratification has been completed in both countries .

[2] Interstate procedure on ratification has been completed in one country only.

[3] Signed at Governmental level.

4.6

Intellectual Property

Zhaniya B Ussen, Assistance LLC in Almaty and Alastair Moody, Ledingham Chalmers in Edinburgh

Introduction

Intellectual property is defined by the Civil Code of Kazakhstan (General Part, Article 125) as the exclusive right of a person to the results of his intellectual activity and to other similar ways of distinguishing a person, his goods, works or services. Article 961 of the recently enacted Special Part of the Civil Code details the types of intellectual property rights available, being principally patents, trade marks and copyrights. Although there may be some similarities in these kinds of intellectual property rights, they are different, serve different purposes, and are regulated differently.

This chapter is designed to provide a helpful overview and understanding of the recently adopted laws on patents, trade marks and copyrights in Kazakhstan in the light of the country's forthcoming accession to the World Trade Organization (WTO). In the event that specific legal advice is required, this article should not be relied upon and it is recommended that individually tailored legal advice be sought from counsel in Kazakhstan.

In addition to these recent developments in its national legislation, Kazakhstan recognises a number of major international intellectual property treaties. A detailed list of the multilateral international treaties (together with the corresponding implementation acts) to which Kazakhstan is a party is provided in Table 4.6.1.

Table 4.6.1 Multilateral IP international treaties to which Kazakhstan is a party

Treaty	*Date and name of the Republic of Kazakhstan implementing Act*
1883 Paris Convention for the Protection of Industrial Property	5 February 1993 Declaration of the Republic of Kazakhstan on International Treaties in the Area of Protection of Industrial Property. Treaty effective as of 16 February 1993
Madrid Agreement for the International Registration of Marks of 14 April 1891	5 February 1993 Declaration of the Republic of Kazakhstan on International Treaties in the Area of Protection of Industrial Property. Treaty effective as of 16 February 1993
1970 Patent Cooperation Treaty	5 February 1993 Declaration of the Republic of Kazakhstan on International Treaties in the Area of Protection of Industrial Property. Treaty effective as of 16 February 1993.
Convention establishing the WIPO of 14 July 1967	5 February 1993 Declaration of the Republic of Kazakhstan on International Treaties in the Area of Protection of Industrial Property. Treaty effective as of 16 February 1993.
Eurasian Patent Convention, Moscow, 9 September 1994	Decree of the President of the Republic of Kazakhstan No 2364 of 18 July 1995 on ratification. Treaty effective as of 4 November 1995.
1886 Bern Convention on the Protection of Literary and Artistic Works	Law of the Republic of Kazakhstan No 297–1 of 10 November 1998 'On Adherence of the Republic of Kazakhstan to the Bern Convention on the Protection of Literary and Artistic Works.'

Table 4.6.1 *continued*

Treaty	Date and name of the Republic of Kazakhstan implementing Act
Universal Copyright Convention, Geneva, 1952	Declaration of the Government of the Republic of Kazakhstan to the General Director of UNESCO of 6 August 1992; Diplomatic Note of the Ministry of Foreign Affairs of the Republic of Kazakhstan to the General Director of UNESCO No 18/87 of 17 January 1995. Treaty is effective from 27 May 1973.
Agreement on Cooperation in the Area of Protection of Copyright and Allied Rights, Moscow, 24 September 1993	Decree of the Supreme Council of the Republic of Kazakhstan of 16 June 1994 'On Ratification of the Agreement on Cooperation in the Area of Protection of Copyright and Allied Rights.'

Patents

Nature of the patent

Patents are governed by the Patent Law enacted on 16 July 1999,[1] which specifies the type of intellectual property that may be patented and the conditions under which a patent may be obtained. Chapter 52 of the recently enacted Special Part of the Civil Code[2] sets out the regulations for patents for inventions, utility models and industrial designs. In addition, provisions related to patents are also found in the Criminal Code,[3] which imposes criminal sanctions for the infringement of patents and other intellectual property rights.

A Kazakhstani patent is a grant of an exclusive property right to the patentee, or his or her heirs or assigns to use and exploit certain types of industrial property and to exclude others from exploiting such property. The three types of industrial property that may be protected by patent rights are inventions, utility models and industrial designs.

The definition of invention covers the structured and functional characteristics of any device, machine, apparatus, method, substance, manufacturing process, chemical compound and composition, strain of micro-organism, plant or animal cells, as well as the new application of a previously known device, method, substance or variety.

The utility model patent covers *inter alia* the utilitarian features and application of manufacturing articles. The industrial design patent protects only the appearance of a manufactured item, and not its structure or utilitarian features.

It must be noted that the right of exclusive use conferred by the Kazakhstani grant of patent does not merely entitle the patent owner to exclude others from use of the invention, utility model or industrial design,[4] but also requires such owner to make use of the protected subject matter. The use may be achieved by any means, including sale, offer for sale, license, manufacture and importation of a product containing the patented right. Where the patent owner fails to use its invention, utility model or industrial design for any continuous term of four years without a valid excuse, a court, in response to a motion of any interested person, may order the owner to grant such interested person a non-exclusive licence in respect of that use.

Regulatory agency

The patent is issued by the state patent organization, Kazpatent,[5] which administers the patent laws relating to the grant of patents. Kazpatent has the power to examine applications and grant patents, and publishes and disseminates patent information as well as recording the assignment of any patents.[6]

Provisional patent

The Patent Law allows the issue of a provisional patent for an invention and industrial design; however, no provisional patent may be filed in respect of a utility model. The major difference between the provisional patent and the full patent is in the scope of Kazpatent's examination of the patent application. The documents supplied in connection with the application for a provisional patent are examined by Kazpatent solely with respect to compliance with the formal requirements, and, unlike the full patent application, it is not examined on its merits.

Term of the patent

The patent confers an exclusive right to the patentee throughout Kazakhstan for the term of the patent subject to the payment by the patentee of maintenance fees.[7]

The term of the provisional patent in respect of an invention is five years from the date of the first filing of the application with Kazpatent with a possibility of extension for a further three years.[8] The term of the full patent in respect of an invention is 20 years from the date of first filing. The Patent Law also allows extension of a full patent for invention for a maximum term of five years in a case where the patentee is subject to the statutory requirement to obtain a special permit for the use of the patent.

For industrial design the term of the provisional patent is five years from the date of first filing. The term of the full design patent is ten years from the filing date with a possibility of extension for a further five years.

The term of the patent for a utility model is five years with a possibility of extension for a further three years.

Conditions for obtaining a patent

The Patent Law requires that the subject matter of the patent must be new, 'non-obvious' and have industrial application.

The condition of novelty is satisfied if the invention, utility model or industrial design is not known from the prior art (this is a legal term which means that things are already in existence or could be in existence). To qualify as new, an invention, utility model or industrial design must not have been known, published, made, or used publicly anywhere in the world before the invention was made by the applicant. It must not have been described by anyone in a printed publication anywhere in the world. It can have been the subject of public disclosure made by the applicant or a person duly authorised by the applicant as a demonstration or an exhibit in any officially recognised exhibition held on the territory of a country participating in the Paris Convention. This last exception holds provided the application for the patent is filed within six months of such public disclosure.

To be 'non-obvious', an invention, utility model or industrial design must not be obvious to a person having ordinary skills in the area of technology related to such invention, utility model or industrial design, and it must not be apparently anticipated from the prior art.

The term 'industrial application' in this connection refers to the condition that the subject matter has a useful purpose and could be manufactured and practically used in industry, agriculture, medicine and/or other areas of activity.

The patent is granted upon the new machine, device, or other subject matter and cannot be obtained for a mere idea or suggestion. A full description of the actual machine or other subject matter for which a patent is sought is required. Discoveries, scientific theories and mathematical methods, management methods, rules, programs for calculators and algorithms *per se*, projects and construction plans, construction proposals, proposals contrary to public interests and to principles of humanity and morality are not patentable.

Filing an application for patent

The following application documents in the Kazakh or Russian language must be filed with Kazpatent:

- Formal request to issue a patent.

- Description of the invention, industrial design or utility model is to be made in such full and adequate detail to enable any person skilled in the particular technological area to which such invention, industrial design or utility model pertains to make and use the same.

- Formula of invention or utility model indicating its nature and substance (or a set of impressions or make of industrial design).

- Drawings and other materials are generally required for understanding the essence of the invention, industrial design or utility model and must show every feature specified in the description.

- Any summary of the invention or utility model would generally include a statement of the object and purpose of the invention or utility model.

- Power of attorney in favour of a representative or a patent agent.[9]

- Petition for issuance of a patent for invention (in the case of a non-provisional application).

- Filing fee.

The specific requirements for the compilation of an application can be obtained from Kazpatent.

An official printed copy of the patent with specifications, drawings, and claims is provided to the patentee.

Conventional priority

The Patent Law allows an applicant to claim a priority for the patent on the basis of the 1883 Paris Convention for the Protection of Industrial Property (the 'Paris Convention'), or other applicable international or regional treaties. Conventional priority under the Paris Convention means that the application for a patent must be submitted to Kazpatent within a certain period of time from the date of first filing in another member country of the Paris Convention. This period is 12 months in the case of a first application for inventions and utility models and 6 months in the case of industrial designs. Under the Convention such applications to Kazpatent will be regarded as if they had been filed on the same day as the original application in the other member country. In addition to the Paris Convention, priority may be claimed under the 1970 Patent Cooperation Treaty (the 'PCT'). The PCT affords to its members, which include most industrial countries, a 20- or 30-month extension period to file an application in the PCT countries.[10] An applicant may also seek to protect its invention by seeking a Eurasian Patent from the Eurasian Patent Office in Moscow.

Assignment of patent rights

Rights for the grant of a patent or provisional patent, as well as the rights of a patent owner may be assigned fully or partially to a third party. The Civil Code and the Patent Law provide for such assignment by an instrument in writing that is subject to mandatory registration with Kazpatent. Failure by the parties to observe this requirement renders the assignment void and unenforceable.

Protection of patent rights

Kazpatent, through its Appellate Council, has the authority for pre-trial settlement of certain types of disputes, such as Kazpatent's refusal to grant a patent, or a third party's challenge to a patent that has already been granted. However, a decision of the Appellate Council is not final and may be appealed to a court within six months from the date of the decision.

Otherwise, if patent rights are infringed, the patent owner may sue for relief in the appropriate court of Kazakhstan. The following remedies are made available to a patent owner under the Patent Law in the case of an infringement:

- injunctive relief;
- compensation in the form of damages or confiscation of illegally derived income;
- confiscation of counterfeited products;
- mandatory publication of an acknowledgement of the violation of the patent rights.

Trade marks

Trade marks, service marks and appellations of origin

Trade marks are governed by the Law 'On Trade Marks, Service Marks and Appellations of Origin of Goods' (the 'Trade Mark Law'). General trade mark issues are also addressed in the Special Part of the Civil Code, Chapter 56. Sanctions for the infringement of trade marks are provided by the Administrative Code,[11] Article 170–2, as well as the Criminal Code, Article 184.

A trade mark relates to any word, name, symbol, or device that is used in trade with goods. The trade mark indicates the source or origin of the goods or services, it symbolises or guarantees the quality of the goods that bear the mark and distinguishes the goods from the goods of others. In other words, a trade mark is a brand name. Trade mark rights can prevent others from using a confusingly similar mark but do not prevent others from making the same goods or from selling the goods under a non-confusing mark. Similar rights can be acquired in a service mark, which are used in the sale or advertising of services.

In addition to trade marks, the Trade Mark Law provides protection for the use of the name designating the origin of goods. For example, country names, names of other locations – including historical names – as well as names of other geographical points or combinations of the same that are used for distinguishing goods, specific qualities of which are primarily associated with the place of manufacture.

Registration of trade marks

Trade marks used in Kazakhstan must be registered with Kazpatent to trigger the exclusive rights of the trade mark owner to use the mark in Kazakhstan. Registration is made by formal application, in the Kazakh or Russian language, and filed with Kazpatent. The application must be accompanied by the trade mark's imprints, a list of goods and/or services for which registration is sought in accordance with the international classification of goods and services, a filing fee, a power of attorney in favour of a representative or patent agent and a certified copy of the first application under the claimed conventional priority (if any).

Upon receipt of a complete application, Kazpatent will review the application in a two-stage process. The first stage is referred to as 'provisional expertise' and is to be made within two months from the filing date, during which time Kazpatent reviews the content of the application, verifying observance of the formalities with regard to its compilation. The second stage is referred to as 'full examination' and is to be performed within 12 months of the filing date. At this stage Kazpatent will review the application to make sure that no grounds exist that would prevent the trade mark's registration. Registration of a trade mark is confirmed by Kazpatent by the issuing of a trade mark certificate.

Information on the registering of trade marks is published in Kazpatent's official guide.

Conditions for registration

The Trade Mark Law provides that the mark may not be registered if it is any of the following:

- a well-known mark, or a mark with no distinguishing feature;

- public property, or a state symbol, or a generally accepted symbol or term;

- offensive to morality and public policy;

- in conflict with a prior registered mark, or otherwise constitutes information or is related to goods and services for which registration is already requested;

- deceptive or misleading with regard to the quality of the goods, the manufacturer, or appellation of origin;

- considered to constitute information or resemble the name or nickname, portrait, or facsimile of any person in the absence of proper authorisation;

- Seen to contain the words 'like', 'as', 'similar', 'of the type', 'in style', or similar.

Term and extension

The term of a trade mark is ten years from the date of first filing and may be extended for further periods of ten years upon the application of the trade mark owner, such further application to be filed within the last year of each ten-year term.

The conventional priority which may be claimed under the Paris Convention is six months.

Use of trade mark

Trade mark rights ultimately require use of the mark in connection with some goods or services. Such use may be accomplished by displaying the mark in commercial advertisements, publications, letterheads, signs, and exhibits held in Kazakhstan. Failure by the trade mark owner to use the mark for a continuous period of five years following the date of registration may entitle any interested person to challenge the trade mark's registration.

Registration of the trade mark gives its owner the right to use the registration symbol ®, and the words 'trade mark' and 'registered trade mark', which may deter others from using the mark. Additionally, the trade mark owner has the right to sue unauthorised users of the trade mark for damages, or recovery of profits.

Assignment and licensing

A trade mark may be a subject of transactions, and rights thereto may be assigned or licensed fully or in part to any person. An assignment or licensing agreement must be made in writing and registered with Kazpatent. The licensing agreement must contain a clause requiring a licensee to maintain the quality of goods or services at a level not lower than the quality of goods and services of the licensor.

Copyrights

Protected rights

Copyright is governed by the Copyright Law,[12] which resembles the 1886 Bern Convention on the Protection of Literary and Artistic Works, to which Kazakhstan adhered in 1998. The general issues relating to copyrights and allied rights are also addressed in the Civil Code (Special Part), Chapters 50 and 51.

Both the Copyright Law and the Civil Code permit copyright protection for the following types of original works of authorship:

- literary and dramatic works, including any accompanying music;

- stage productions, pantomimes, and choreographic works;

- motion pictures, sound recordings, and other audiovisual works;

- pictorial, graphic and sculptural works;

- musical works, including any accompanying words;

- items of applied art;

- pieces of architecture, urbanisation and gardening;

- photographs, maps, sketches, illustrations, and the like;

- computer software, etc.

Allied rights that are covered by the Copyright Law and the Civil Code, Chapter 51 relate to stage productions, performances, phonograms, broadcastings and cable broadcast organisations.

Copyright protects the form of expression rather than the subject matter of the work and extends to scientific, literal and artistic works regardless of their purpose, content and value of method and form of expression.

Originality

Copyright protection is available only for original works of authorship. They must be published in Kazakhstan or otherwise recorded in a tangible form to qualify for copyright protection, and must be in a form that can be reproduced or otherwise communicated. A work is deemed to be published in Kazakhstan if it is published therein within 30 days from the date of first publication outside Kazakhstan.

Protection mark

Copyright arises automatically when the work is created, and unlike patents and trade marks, no registration is required for copyright to exist. The rights to enforce copyright, however, are maximized if the copyright is registered with the Copyright Agency of the Ministry of Justice.[13] Registration involves filing the appropriate application form along with the required fee and deposit of the work. The owner of the copyright is also entitled to give notice of its rights and to use for that purpose the copyright protection mark, consisting of three elements:

1   roman letter 'c' in a circle – ©;

2   name of the copyright owner;

3   year of first publication of the work.

Protection mark for allied rights is similar but instead of roman letter 'c' it has roman letter 'p' in the circle.

Term of protection

Copyright exists in goods for 50 years after the death of the author or 50 years after the first publication of the work, whichever is longer, provided such publication is made for the first time within 30 years from the death of the author. Protection of the attribution rights of authorship, name and reputation of the author is timeless. For a work made under an employment or other contract, the copyright exists for ten years after the publication of the work.

Allied rights are protected for a term of fifty years from the date of first performance or stage production, or fifty years from the date of first release of the phonogram or its first recording in case of an unrelated phonogram.

Assignment and licensing

Assignment or licensing of a copyright may be exclusive or non-exclusive and must be made in writing. The Copyright Law prescribes that an agreement for assignment or licensing must be specific with regard to the scope of the assigned/licensed rights, term and territory for which such rights are granted, and royalty payments.

The Copyright Law also entitles the owners of copyright and allied rights to form non-profitmaking organisations to manage their propri-etary rights on a collective basis. Such organisations are authorised to license the proprietary rights of the owners. Licensing agreements entered into by such management organisations are subject to registration with the Copyright Agency.

Infringement and remedies

Copyright protects writing and other artistic creations of an author against unauthorised copying.

The Copyright Law provides for civil, administrative and criminal liability for violation of copyright and allied rights. Protection is generally achieved by court judgment providing for:

- recognition of rights of copyright;

- restitution of the situation existing prior to violation of the copyright;

- injunctive relief;

- recovery of the profits received by a violator as a result of infringement;

- damages including lost profit or payment of compensation in an amount up to fifty thousand times the monthly index established under the laws of Kazakhstan;

- confiscation of counterfeited production, materials and equipment used in such production.

Other applicable legislation offering protection of intellectual property rights

Confidentiality and trade secrets

The basis of protection is stated in the Constitution of the Republic of Kazakhstan,[14] which in Article 6 provides for equal protection to both state and private ownership.

Trade and commercial secrets are protected by the Civil Code (General Part),[15] Article 126, the Civil Code (Special Part), Chapter 55; the Law on Private Business,[16] Chapter IV; and the Unfair Competition Law.[17] Practically, any business information which is not publicly known may be recognised as a trade and commercial secret, including by virtue of a written confidentiality agreement. Articles 126 and 638 of the Civil Code extend the duty of maintenance of trade and commercial secrets to contractors and employees of the trade secret owner. Unauthorized disclosure of trade secrets is viewed as unfair competition.[18] An aggrieved party may seek to remedy any breach of confidentiality, divulging trade and commercial secrets and unfair competition by seeking damages, including lost profit, and informing the Antimonopoly Committee, which may impose either administrative penalties or criminal sanctions onto the unfair competitor.[19]

Customs regulations

The Customs Code[20] was amended on 16 July 1999[21] to provide for special border measures to deal with pirated goods and counterfeit trade mark infringements. Articles 218–1 to 218–5 of the Code provide for restrictions on the importation to and exportation from Kazakhstan of goods protected by intellectual property rights. To seek such restriction an owner of intellectual property rights must apply to the customs authorities of Kazakhstan to include the goods in the special customs register. Such a restriction will prevent the customs authorities from giving clearance to the goods. Moreover, the customs authorities are obliged to notify the owner of intellectual property rights of the name and address of any person who attempts to import/export the violating goods. The owner of infringed intellectual property rights must then promptly file a lawsuit to prevent the customs authorities from releasing any of the violating products.

Computer Circuits

Protection of integrated computer circuits are not covered by the above Patent Law and are intended to be governed by separate laws that have yet to be adopted. The relevant provisions are also made as part of the Civil Code (Special Part), Chapters 53 and 54. Exclusive rights to integrated computer circuits are protected for a term of ten years from the date of registration with the authorised agency.

New breeds of animals or varieties of plants

New breeds of animals or varieties of plants are also not covered by the Patent Law but by the Civil Code and have yet to be adopted. Rights are to be protected for 25 years from the date of first filing with an as yet unspecified authorised agency. A special future law is also expected to describe the conditions for obtaining the relevant protections.

Notes

[1] Patent Law of the Republic of Kazakhstan No 427–1 dated 16 July 1999 (replaced the Patent Law No 3400 of 24 July 1992).

[2] Civil Code of the Republic of Kazakhstan (Special Part) No 409–1 ZRK of 1 July 1999.

[3] Criminal Code of the Republic of Kazakhstan No 167–1 of 16 July 1997, as amended as of 23 July 1999, Article 184.

[4] As for example, in the United States. See, Title 35 of the United States Code, and *Rules of Practice in Patent Cases*, Title 37, Code of Federal Regulations, US Government Printing Office.

[5] Formerly examinations of patent applications were conducted by the National Patent Agency established in 1992 which was replaced in 1997 by Kazpatent, pursuant to the Decree of the Government No 1552 of 12 November 1997 'Issues of the Agency for Strategic Planning and Reforms of the Republic of Kazakhstan, Establishment of the Republic's State Enterprises "Kazpatent" and "Information and Calculation Center of the Committee for Statistics and Analysis of the Agency for Strategic Planning and Reforms of the Republic of Kazakhstan"'.

[6] Decree of the Government of the Republic of Kazakhstan No 142 of 25 February 1998 'Issues of the Republic's State Enterprise on Patent and Trademarks, Kazpatent'.

[7] Decree of the Cabinet of Ministers of the Republic of Kazakhstan No 1369 of December 1994, as amended, 'On Patent Fee'; Decree of the Cabinet of Ministers of the Republic of Kazakhstan No 889 of 20 October 1992, as amended, 'On the Procedure for Payment and Amount of Fees for Patenting of Inventions, Industrial Designs and Utility Models, Registration of Trade Marks and Service Marks, Registration and Grant of Rights of Use of the Names of Origin of Goods'.

[8] Under the former legislation, the maximum term of a provisional patent for invention was five years without extension.

[9] Foreign companies and individuals domiciled outside Kazakhstan are required to deal with the Kazpatent through a registered patent agent.

[10] Conventional priority for inventions under the PCT, 20 months; under the PCT Chapter II, 30 months. Kazakhstan is a member of both the PCT and the PCT Chapter II.

[11] Code of the Kazakh SSR 'On Administrative Misconducts' of 22 March 1984, as amended.

[12] Law of the Republic of Kazakhstan No 6–1 of 10 June 1996 'On Copyright and Allied Rights'.

[13] The Copyright Agency has been established by the Decree of the Government of the Republic of Kazakhstan No 846 of 25 June 1999 'Issues of the Committee for Copyrights of the Ministry of Justice'.

[14] Constitution of the Republic of Kazakhstan of 30 August 1995, as amended.

[15] Civil Code of the Republic of Kazakhstan (General Part) of 27 December 1994, as amended.

[16] Law of the Republic of Kazakhstan No 1543-XII of 4 July 1992, as amended, 'On Protection and Support of Private Business'.

[17] Law of the Republic of Kazakhstan No 232–1 of 9 June 1998 'On Unfair Competition'.

[18] Law 'On Protection and Support of Private Business', Article 21(3).

[19] Order of the Agency of the Republic of Kazakhstan for Regulation of Natural Monopolies and Protection of Competition No. 15-OD of 9 April 1999 'On Approval of the Rules for Application of the Measures of Antimonopoly Reaction for Violation of Antimonopoly Legislation'.

[20] Law of the Republic of Kazakhstan 'On Customs Business at the Republic of Kazakhstan' No 2368 of 20 July 1995, as amended.

[21] Law of the Republic of Kazakhstan No 426–1 of 16 July 1999 'On Amendments and Additions to the Decree of the President of the Republic of Kazakhstan with the Effect of Law "On Customs Business at the Republic of Kazakhstan"'.

4.7

Property Holdings

CMS Cameron McKenna

Property Rights

The Constitution (adopted on 30 August 1995) stipulates that all land is (and is to remain) in the ownership of the state subject to specific, given exceptions.

The Land Law (dated 22 December 1995) establishes the following estates in land:

- the right to own;

- the right to permanent use;

- the right to long-term temporary use (from 3 to 99 years);

- the right to short-term temporary use (up to three years).

Foreigners (including individuals, legal entities, multilateral institutions and foreign states) are prohibited from acquiring a permanent right to use land. The permanent right to use land is effectively reserved for the state and for those (local) entities involved in forestry and agriculture. Further, foreigners who wish to acquire rights of ownership to land can only do so where such land is specifically reserved for production or residential use or intended as a site for construction.

The Land Law provides that any owner of land has an unfettered right to deal with such land, subject to any contrary stipulations in the law. It may therefore be possible for a landowner to grant to a foreign investor a long-term temporary right to use such land in excess of 99 years. This has rarely happened in practice and the issue may now be merely a matter of semantics with the expanded legal development in July 1999 of the concept of the lease.

It is also possible for a foreigner to acquire either a right to use land (short or long term) or the right of ownership of the same pursuant to an agreement (in the form stipulated by the legislation) with the Investment Agency of the Republic of Kazakhstan. The grant of such rights in this manner (usually as an incentive to foreign investment) is, in practice, rare.

Ownership of a building (or other structure) carries with it the right of ownership (or right of permanent use where this is possible) to that part of the land on which the building (or structure) is situated and, in addition, all such land necessary for the operation and enjoyment of the same. In principle, these two rights are inseparable from each other. Unfortunately, during the privatisation of certain state enterprises, buildings were very often transferred to the ownership of the newly privatised company but the rights to the appurtenant and underlying land remained with the state. This situation is directly contrary to the provisions of the Land Law and thus when structuring an investment with an immovable property aspect, careful due diligence must be undertaken of the title of the investment target to any immovable property. If the state remains the residual owner of the relevant plot(s) of land, the investment target should be obliged to obtain a transfer of the same into its ownership.

Registration

In accordance with the Civil Code (General Part) (dated 27 December 1994) and the Land Law, rights, which include security interests, to land and buildings are subject to mandatory registration with the Committee of Registration Service of the Ministry of Justice. Unfortunately, in practice, registration is not always carried out. Historically, there seemed to be little reason to register such rights as the land was owned by the state and the buildings were owned by state companies. Today, many Kazakhstani companies, including those that were privatised, do not register their rights because of the costs involved. Unfortunately, without registration, there is no proof of title and, consequently, no transactions (including sale, assignment or mortgage) may be carried out in respect of the property. Again, careful due diligence will be required prior to making an investment where property rights are involved and, when necessary, the investment target/vendor should be required to effect registration.

Leases

General leases

The Civil Code (Special Part) (dated 1 July 1999) developed the concept of the lease in Kazakhstani law. Supplemental to the chapter on the general construction of a lease agreement and the relations of the lessor, lessee and third parties, are specific sections dealing with leases of buildings and installations; leases of enterprises; and financial leasing.

The principle of the lease arrangement (as articulated in the Civil Code (Special Part)) is that an item of property should be transferred into the possession of another person or entity for a temporary period and in consideration for payment. The Civil Code (Special Part) provides that unless it is stipulated elsewhere, the general chapter on leasing will apply to all the sections on specific forms of leasing. In brief, a foreigner may lease: a plot of land (subject to the restrictions above); a building or other structure or the whole of a building or other structure together with the underlying/appurtenant land.

Each lease agreement must state: the identities of the parties; the subject matter; and the amount of the lease payment. Failure to do so will invalidate the agreement. The Civil Code (Special Part) does not provide for a maximum lease term but notes that such a stipulation may be imposed by other legislative acts. If one of the parties to the agreement is a legal entity, or if the term of the lease is for more than one year, it must be in writing. If the lease agreement provides the lessee with a right of subsequent purchase there are certain other requirements as to the form the agreement should take.

It is important to note that the lease of property will not affect the pre-existing rights of any third parties in respect thereof. Prior to granting the lease, the lessor is obliged to inform the lessee of all third party rights to the property. Failure to do so will allow the lessee the right to demand a reduction in the amount of the lease payments or, alternatively, to terminate the lease.

The Civil Code (Special Part) sets out various rights of the lessee and the lessor. In particular, the lessee is entitled to quiet enjoyment and freedom from interference by the lessor while the lessor is not liable for the actions of any third party which infringe the rights of the lessee.

Lease of buildings and structures

Various requirements are stipulated for an agreement on the lease of a building or other structure: it must be in writing and in only one document (ie not duplicated) and must be signed by both parties. The only other specific requirements are that the act on transfer of the building/structure must be attached to the agreement and, where the lease is for a term of more than one year, it must be registered with the appropriate regulation centre.

Lease of an enterprise

An enterprise is, in effect, the whole of the business of a legal entity as a going concern and includes all of its assets, liabilities, rights and obligations. Under the Civil Code (General Part) an enterprise could be sold or mortgaged. Pursuant to the Civil Code (Special Part), the same may now be leased. In respect of any immovable property forming part of the enterprise, the lease will therefore extend to such immovable property. One significant point to be aware of is that before the lease comes into effect, the consent of all of the creditors of the lessor/the enterprise to the lease must be obtained. Failure to do so will not necessarily invalidate the lease, but will entail joint and several liability for the lessor and the lessee in respect of such debts.

Trust management of property

The principal behind trust management is that the transferor transfers the possession and/or the right to manage immovable property to the transferee on payment of a fee. The exact scope of the powers of the transferee should be set out in the management agreement and may include the right to: insure, repair, lease, sell or mortgage the managed property. Although principally a creature of contract, a trust management arrangement may be established by court order particularly, in the event of the bankruptcy of the 'transferor'.

Certain features of the trust management arrangement should be noted. First, once the arrangement has been put in place, there is a moratorium on pre-existing unsecured creditors bringing actions for enforcement against the managed property. Second, if the manager causes loss or damage to be occasioned to the managed property and is unable to show that he/she acted with all due care and skill in the performance of his/her duties, the manager may be ordered by a court to indemnify the owner or beneficiary of the managed property in respect of such loss or damage. Third, the manager will be liable for any losses or damages suffered by a third party through the manager's improper performance of his or her duties. Where such third party brings a claim against the owner or beneficiary of the managed property instead, the manager may be ordered to reimburse or indemnify the owner or beneficiary for any amounts paid to such third party.

Mortgage

It is possible to take a security interest in plots of land as well as in the buildings thereon. Note, however, that the grant of security over a family home will require a waiver of interests by all adult family members who reside there and a mortgage over land held in common ownership will require the consent of all of the common owners. In addition, prohibitions exist against taking security over land dedicated for common use; national defence; special environmental status; or 'service lands' (similar to tied cottages).

The Civil Code (General Part) states that a mortgage of a building or structure is only permissible where the land plot on which the aforementioned is located or which it requires for its use is also mortgaged by the same instrument.

In general, a mortgage over a building or other structure will be documented in a mortgage agreement. Pursuant to the Law on Mortgage of Immovable Property (dated 23 December 1995), certain mandatory provisions must be included in such an agreement. These provisions include: the names and addresses of the parties; details of the secured obligation (value and the required date for fulfilment); and details of the mortgaged property. The mortgage agreement must then be registered with the appropriate Centre for Immovable Property of the Committee of Registration Service of the Ministry of Justice. The mortgage will only be effective from the date of registration of the agreement with the Centre.

Before a foreign investor takes security over buildings and the appurtenant/underlying land, it should first oblige the mortgager to convert any permanent rights to use such land into a right to own. Failure to do so will reduce the value of the security on enforcement at public auction. The secured creditor, as a foreigner, will be barred from acquiring the secured property and must look to the proceeds of the auction instead.

4.8

Employment Law

Russell W. Lambert, Managing Partner,
PricewaterhouseCoopers

Overview

Despite the fact that a new Labour Code has been in the development stage for the last two years without a final draft reaching Parliament, legislation regarding employment of foreign workers has been adopted. Since 1997, at least, Kazakhstan has developed a policy of controlling the influx of foreign employees into Kazakhstan. In March 1999, registered unemployment was 3.6 per cent of the workforce, which is less than the 4 per cent reported for the same month in 1998.[1]

Even though the official unemployment rate is relatively low, the political need for authorities to secure employment for Kazakhstan's population is significant. Some local authorities accept that foreign investors need to secure their investment by employing their (own) core management as well as by bringing in well-trained specialists. However, others do not accept the need for foreign employees when unemployment is still an issue in their region. Current legislation attempts to address two issues: (i) control of foreign workers and (ii) unemployment.

Work permits

Background

On 25 June 1999 Decree 862 concerning 'The Approval of the Rules for Licensing of Hiring of Foreign Manpower and Exporting of Manpower from the Republic of Kazakhstan Abroad' was adopted. Under this Decree foreign citizens may exercise occupational and professional activities in Kazakhstan on a contract basis. The Decree gives guidelines as to the content of the contract and should include provisions concerning return of the worker to his/her home country at the expense of the employer.

This new Decree replaced Decree 924, which was the cause of some concern for foreign investors. The work permit process under Decree 924 was unclear and burdensome on the foreign investor bringing employees into Kazakhstan. It first involved applying for a licence to employ such individuals; the licence then permitted the employer to employ specifically named individuals in Kazakhstan. The licence was granted for one year and 'work permits' could not be granted for a period longer than the licence. This legislation was ambiguous and placed foreign investors in a position of uncertainty. Local officials took advantage of this uncertainty and a number of foreign investors were made to obtain licences in order to employ foreign workers, irrespective of whether they had to by law or not.

Foreign investors have worked closely with government representatives, including the Ministry of Labour and Social Protection, to introduce this new legislation, which removes, at least in part, any ambiguity, and it is now much easier for them to clarify whether or not a work permit is needed. Foreign investors continue to work with government representatives to improve legislation and procedures to the mutual benefit of both, including through the Foreign Investment Counsel founded by the President of the Republic of Kazakhstan.

Who needs a work permit?

A work permit is not required for an individual on a business trip to Kazakhstan, which is not defined in the legislation and therefore has no restriction on the length of the business trip. In practice, it will be necessary to show the authorities that the individual is not providing services in Kazakhstan.

The following are not required to obtain a work permit:

- members of official diplomatic, consular representations and international organisations;

- individuals training at secondary special and higher educational establishments;

- religious activists of associations officially registered in Kazakhstan;

- employees of foreign mass communications media, accredited in Kazakhstan;

- individuals who have resident permits for the Republic of Kazakhstan.

For all others a work permit should be obtained. Kazakhstani legislation does not provide for any short- or long-term period during which foreign citizens can work in Kazakhstan without a permit. Therefore, a permit should be obtained prior to the commencement of employment in Kazakhstan.

Obtaining a work permit

The obligation to obtain a work permit rests with the employer, and it is also the employer who receives the permit for the employee.

A work permit can be obtained from the Ministry of Labour and Social Protection in Astana or from an authorised body elsewhere. In practice, the employer should apply to the authorised body in the region where the employee will be employed. When applying for a work permit, the following documents should be submitted:

- a list of all people the employer wishes to employ in Kazakhstan;

- a copy of each prospective employee's contract;

- an HIV certificate, in accordance with international standards, for each prospective employee.

Some local authorities may ask for additional documents. Although these documents are not requested by law, refusing to submit them could significantly delay the process.

The authorised body has two weeks to issue a decision that is then forwarded to the Ministry of Labour and Social Protection. The Ministry then has another two weeks to consider the application. An exception is made for the City of Almaty, which was granted special status under Law 258–1 of 1 July 1998. Almaty has the authority to issue a work permit without sending the documents to the Ministry.

Under the provisions of the Labour Code, a work permit should be valid for the duration of the contract, but no longer than three years. In practice, authorities may grant work permits for a lesser period than the contract period although, strictly, employers should be able to rely on the length of the contract.

A work permit is granted for a specific person in a specific position and the employer needs to reapply for any replacement of an outgoing employee. Two individuals working on a rotation basis need to obtain separate work permits even though they cover the same position.

Quotas

Work permits are granted, based on quotas established by the Ministry of Labour and Social Protection, for each professional group and as a total of foreign employees. The quotas are primarily for statistical reasons and should not be arbitrarily applied as a reason for refusing an application. Currently, quotas are not published, but foreign-investor working groups are liaising with the Ministry to resolve this issue.

Employing citizens of Kazakhstan

The Labour Code and the Law on the Employment of the Population govern employment of Kazakhstani citizens as well as general labour conditions. The Labour Code dates from 21 July 1972 when Kazakhstan was still part of the USSR. Specialists have been drafting this new Labour Code which has been amended several times since the early 1990s but to date has not been finalised. Therefore, an employer has to deal with essentially Soviet-era regulations, which provide significant protection to an employee.

Contract

Physical admission to work is deemed to constitute a labour agreement, irrespective of whether the acceptance of a work offer was properly documented under Kazakhstani legislation. Generally, employers enter into contracts with employees for an indefinite period, for a specific period (but not more than three years) or for the period of the fulfilment of specified work. The contract should be drafted in Russian but the employer may retain a duplicate version in an alternative language.

Both parties should agree to a probation period that should not exceed three months (and in certain cases six months) and should be stated in the contract. If employment continues after the probation period, the employee is considered to have become a permanent employee of the company.

Termination of a contract

A contract can be terminated under certain conditions:

- mutual consent of the parties;
- expiration of the term of employment;
- drafting of the employee into military service;
- dissolution of the labour agreement by the employee, the administration or the trade union;
- transfer of an employee, with their consent to a different enterprise, institution or organisation;
- refusal of the employee to be transferred to a different locality with the different enterprise, institution or organisation;
- based on a court verdict.

An employee has the right to dissolve an indefinite labour contract by giving two months' advance notice in writing. The administration of an enterprise, institution or organisation can dissolve a contract based on the following:

- liquidation of the enterprise, institution or organisation or reduction in the numbers of personnel;
- non-compliance by the employee with the terms of the position held or non-performance of work;
- systematic failure of the employee, without valid reason, to execute work requested of him/her;
- absence without leave and without a valid reason;
- failure to come to work for a period longer than four months (expect in certain cases such as pregnancy);
- re-instalment at work of an employee who previously filled the same position;
- arriving at work intoxicated;
- committing theft at the place of employment.

Working time

The length of a normal working week for employees over the age of 18 may not exceed 40 hours spread over 5 working days. The working day should include a break for rest and food, for a period no longer than two hours; this is not to be considered working time.

Under the Labour Code, overtime performed by an employee should not exceed 4 hours during a 2-day period or 120 hours in a year; the employer is mandated to keep a precise account of overtime worked by each employee.

Leave and holidays

All employees are entitled to annual leave of at least 15 working days. Additionally, Kazakhstan celebrates the following national holidays:

1–2 January	New Year
8 March	International Womens' Day
22 March	Nauryyz Meiramy
1 May	Day of the Unity of the People of Kazakhstan
9 May	Victory Day
30 August	Day of the Constitution of the Republic of Kazakhstan

25 October   Republic Day

16 December   Independence Day

There are no public holidays for Christmas and Easter in Kazakhstan.

Law on employment of the population

On 1 January 1999, Law No 341 of 30 December 1998 of the Republic of Kazakhstan, Concerning the Employment of the Population, came into effect. The stated purpose of this Law is to reduce unemployment and to protect the unemployed, and an agency has been appointed to implement this policy. As the new Law does not identify the agencies and quota amounts further regulations are expected.

Under this Law, legal entities are required to provide the relevant authorities with employment policy information including population employment statistics; information about prospective structural changes or other changes resulting in dismissal of employees; data about manpower requirements; and data on which individuals have been laid off, employed or dismissed. Employers concealing vacancies will be subject to administrative penalty, the amount of which is not currently defined.

Affirmative action

The law provides that the local authorities will establish an annual quota for the employment of individuals in several categories. In the event that an employer does not fulfil the quota and reports a vacancy, the local authorities will have the right to assign a candidate from these categories to that vacancy. The categories are:

- young people up to the age of 20;
- single parents and parents raising many children, where the children are minors;
- parents who raise disabled children up to the age of 16;
- the disabled;
- persons who have been unemployed for at least one year (without regard to the reason for their most recent termination);
- persons of pre-pension age (two years prior to their pension);
- parolees;
- military servicemen dismissed from the military service without pension rights ;

- refugees and migrants;
- women;
- rural population;
- people who reside in areas of ecological disaster.

Notes

[1] EIU Country Report, 2nd quarter 1999, 23; Statistical Review of Kazakhstan, No 1, 1999.

4.9

Dispute Resolution

CMS Cameron McKenna

Introduction

Unfortunately, foreign investors rarely give sufficient consideration to what may happen in the event of their investment going wrong. Because of this, two important considerations should be borne in mind from the outset when negotiating the terms of investment: the applicable governing law and the forum for the settlement of disputes. The provisions of local legislation will necessarily have an impact upon these considerations therefore an appreciation of the relevant legislative provisions is essential.

As a general rule, commercial disputes that involve a foreign element (a party which is a foreign company or a company with a foreign shareholding) can be considered:

- by international or local arbitration if the parties have an agreement to this effect;

- by the courts of Kazakhstan where the parties do not agree to arbitration.

Litigation in local courts

Organisation of courts

The court system consists of the Supreme Court, the Oblast Courts, the Almaty City Court, the Military Courts and the District Courts. Commercial disputes may be considered at first instance by either a District Court or an Oblast Court with jurisdiction to hear the dispute. In accordance with the Civil Procedure Code, effective from 1 July 1999, a matter may be referred to a court in the Republic of Kazakhstan where:

- it relates to matters of commercial, financial, real estate, natural resource or environmental law; and/or

- there is a causal nexus with the Republic of Kazakhstan (for example, the defendant is a local company or the underlying agreement or arrangements between the parties was to be performed within the Republic of Kazakhstan).

Moreover, certain categories of dispute may only be heard by a Kazakhstani court. These include:

- those concerning immovable property (including land and buildings) located in the Republic of Kazakhstan;

- transport agreements;

- certain other non-commercial cases as defined in the legislation.

If the value of the claim at the date of application for a hearing is less than five thousand monthly calculation indices for the relevant year (approximately US$25,100 in June 2000), the case will be dealt with by the District Courts at first instance. For claims with a value in excess of this amount or where one of the parties is a foreign individual/legal organisation, the case will be dealt with by the Oblast Courts.

Statute of limitations

The rules in relation to limitation periods for litigating a claim were introduced by the Civil Code (General Part) dated 27 December 1994. Generally, claims can be brought before a court only within three years of the date that the cause of action arose. Other limitation periods exist for specific types of claims (for example, in relation to taxation, the limitation period is five years).

Application fees

Court fees of approximately 3 per cent of the value of the claim are payable by a corporate plaintiff and should be made in full at the time of lodging the application for proceedings at the court. They are reduced to 1.5 per cent of the value of the claim in appeal proceedings. These are non-refundable, but a successful plaintiff is entitled to recover them from the defendant.

Appeals

For a period of ten days after the date of judgment in a case at first instance, any party to such case may appeal the judgment to a higher court. Appeals may be made under two different procedures: cassational and full appeal. In the cassational procedure, the higher court will review the proceedings but will not retry the case, while in a full appeal, the claim will be retried. A full appeal may only be made to an Oblast Court against the decision of a District Court or to the Almaty City Court from a District Court situated within Almaty. All other appeals must be made in the cassational procedure.

The passing of the period for making an appeal does not necessarily mean that the prevailing party has definitively and finally won the case. The office of the public prosecutor acting on its own initiative may appeal against any decision in which the public has an interest at any time within one year of a decision. It is not necessary that the public prosecutor must have been involved in the case from which the decision is appealed. Experience shows that 'public interest' can be broadly interpreted.

Recognition and enforcement of foreign judgments

Foreign governing laws

In accordance with the Civil Code (Special Part), foreign investors are entitled to provide in their agreements with Kazakh legal entities/individuals that such agreements be governed by a foreign law. Note, however, that the provisions of a foreign law will only be applicable to the extent that they do not contradict the public policy of Kazakhstan. Moreover, in relation to certain defined transactions, the law of the Republic of Kazakhstan must be the governing law thereof. In particular, this includes transactions involving immovable property (land and buildings).

The Civil Code (Special Part) also provides that the transfer of securities in a Kazakhstani legal entity must be governed by Kazakhstani law. This is a new and worrying development as the legislation of the Republic of Kazakhstan does not provide the remedies that one would normally expect to find in other more well-developed jurisdictions. If this provision is rigidly enforced by local courts, foreign investors may be forced to negotiate agreements for the purchase and sale of corporate securities under two governing laws. Some parts of the agreement would be governed by Kazakhstani law and the rest of the agreement by a foreign law. More importantly for the many large investors in Kazakhstani national resources, the Petroleum Law and the Law on Subsurface Use contain provisions requiring that some contracts must be governed by the laws of Kazakhstan.

Although a Kazakhstani court may give effect to a foreign law, properly selected by the parties to a contract as the governing law for such contract, it may be unable to determine what the foreign law provides for.

In such cases the Kazakhstani court may apply Kazakhstani law, notwithstanding the selection of foreign law in the contract. In addition, it is not clear from practice whether any legal right or remedy would necessarily be enforced by Kazakhstani courts in accordance with its terms, notwithstanding that such right or remedy would be valid and legally binding under Kazakhstani law.

Recognition of foreign awards

The Foreign Investment Law (dated 27 December 1994) provides that in the event of a dispute between a foreign investor and a state body, the parties must first attempt to resolve the dispute by negotiation. If after three months the dispute has still not been resolved, either party may refer the dispute to a Kazakhstani court or, where the agreement between the parties provides, to any one of the following arbitration authorities:

- arbitration authorities established in accordance with the Arbitration Regulations of the Commission of the United Nations Organisation for International Trade Law;

- the Arbitration Institute of the Chamber of Commerce in Stockholm;

- the Arbitration Commission of the Chamber of Commerce and Industry of the Republic of Kazakhstan.

Although this list is not exclusive, experience has shown that the appointment and enforcement of awards of these bodies is most effective in practice. Note that in 1992, Kazakhstan signed the 1965 Washington Convention on the Settlement of Investment Disputes Between States and Nationals of Other States; however, this Convention has never been ratified and so the arbitration mechanism provided thereby (ICSID and the Additional Facility of ICSID) is not currently available.

As a separate right under the Foreign Investment Law, a foreign investor and a Kazakhstani individual or legal entity may agree to refer to international arbitration any dispute other than a dispute concerning matters within the exclusive competence of the courts of Kazakhstan. This is of particular importance because Kazakhstan is not a party to any multilateral or bilateral treaties with England (or indeed with any other western jurisdictions) for the mutual enforcement of court judgments. Consequently, should a judgment be obtained from a court in England, it is highly unlikely to be given direct effect in Kazakhstani courts. Kazakhstan is, however, a party to the 10 June 1958 New York Convention on Recognition and Enforcement of Foreign Arbitral Awards (the Convention). Accordingly, a foreign arbitral award obtained in a state that is party to the Convention should be recognised and enforced by a

Kazakhstani court. This is subject to the qualifications in the Convention and compliance with Kazakhstani civil procedure and the procedures established by the Kazakhstani legislation on commercial arbitration for the enforcement of arbitration awards. The supremacy of the Convention is guaranteed pursuant to the provisions of the Civil Code (General Part).

In practice, however, reliance upon international treaties may require the relevant Kazakhstani officials to be educated as to the effect and procedures under the treaty, which may not be entirely consistent with the legislation relating to local procedure or with court rules. This could cause delays in enforcing decisions in Kazakhstan, particularly if enforcement is sought from courts outside principal commercial centres such as Almaty.

Obligations to be fulfilled or complied with outside Kazakhstan may not be enforceable under Kazakhstani legislation if such fulfilment or compliance is contrary to the public policy or legislation of countries outside Kazakhstan. This also applies to obligations to be fulfilled within Kazakhstan, should such obligations be contrary to Kazakhstani public policy. Such public policy considerations could apply in specific circumstances where, for example, the interests of creditors, employees, the national or local economy, public health and safety or national security are involved.

As a matter of English law, when an arbitral tribunal is determining the proper law of a contract, it has to apply the Rome Convention of 1980. This states that where the parties have chosen a foreign law (whether or not accompanied by the choice of a foreign tribunal) this shall not, where all other elements relevant to the situation at the time of the choice were connected with one country only, prejudice the application of rules of law of that country that cannot be derogated from by the contract (the 'mandatory rules'). In addition, the tribunal may give effect to the mandatory rules of the law of another country with which the contract has a close connection, if, and insofar as under the law of the latter country, those rules must be applied whatever the law applicable to the contract. In making such a decision regard is to be given to the nature of the mandatory rules, their purpose and to the consequences of their application or non-application. There is therefore a risk that in the event of a dispute being taken to arbitration in London pursuant to an arbitration clause in an agreement, the arbitral tribunal would apply the law of Kazakhstan on the basis of the mandatory rules of Kazakhstan regarding, for example, land law. In any event, if an arbitral tribunal made an award that ignored the mandatory rules of Kazakhstan (especially in relation to land) and applied English law, there is a strong risk that a Kazakh court would refuse to enforce such an award on the basis that to do so would be contrary to the public policy of Kazakhstan.

Pursuant to the terms of the Convention, the Civil Procedure Code and the Foreign Investment Law, Kazakhstani law allows for the direct enforcement of arbitral awards obtained abroad without re-examination of the underlying case. Clearly, however, any enforcement proceedings to be commenced in a court in Kazakhstan would need to be commenced in accordance with Kazakhstani civil procedure. Consequently, provisions in an agreement that are contrary to the civil procedural rules of Kazakhstan could be ineffective.

Moreover, if an agreement includes terminology, formulations and approaches based on a legal style other than that common in Kazakhstan, in any proceedings for enforcement, the court officials may need to be educated as to the operation of such provisions. Of course, it is difficult to predict how such provisions would be considered and whether they would in any event be given their proper effect.

Conclusion

In practice, Kazakhstani counterparties usually accept the choice of a foreign governing law and international arbitration as the forum for dispute resolution, particularly where the value of the foreign investment is significant. While this should be of considerable comfort to the foreign investor, regard must be given to the points made above concerning legality and enforceability and also to the practicability of litigating a claim before an international arbitration tribunal. If possible, resolve the dispute informally and consider the use of arbitration or litigation only as a last step.

Part 5

Case Studies

The Almaty Poultry Farm (Bertra)

Marat Terterov

Bert Van Lier, founder of the Almaty Poultry Farm (which he aptly named 'Bertra'), is not someone you would label as 'your typical Dutch farmer'. Back in the late 1980s Van Lier, then the owner of a dairy farm near the city of Maastricht, in Holland, became a little tired of the predictable lifestyle that this part of the Dutch countryside provided. He began to yearn for a new way of life in a society that – according to Van Lier – would be free of regulation. Van Lier saw the collapse of the Berlin Wall and the subsequent emergence of various opportunities east of the River Oder as his moment for escaping the system.

He acted upon the opportunity almost immediately. In 1989, through some Dutch contacts involved in agricultural artificial insemination programmes, he gained the chance to travel to Poland to look at some business prospects. The trip gave him a taste of the environment for which he yearned, but nothing concrete came of it. Soon after, he was made an offer through the same connection to head somewhat further east, several thousand miles further east in fact – to the vast steppes of the Soviet Union's former bread basket, the Republic of Kazakhstan.

Van Lier was invited to travel to Kazakhstan in 1992 to investigate the possibility of buying a dairy farm, since it was suggested to him that the government's new economic reforms, particularly the mass privatisation programme, would allow him to acquire a rural enterprise in the former socialist republic. The Dutch farmer had virtually no previous knowledge of Kazakhstan and formulated little expectation of what it would be like in the country. He spent several weeks looking at farms, found one that he liked (valued at around US$500,000) and signed a letter of intent for the purchase of the enterprise with the Kazakhstani government.

Seemingly content with his decision, Van Lier travelled back to Holland in order to sell his farm near Maastricht and then returned to Kazakhstan to take up his new business endeavour. But upon his return things had changed drastically. It is not certain what happened in Kazakhstan during the few weeks that Van Lier was in Holland, but the result was clear.

Someone in a relatively senior government position in Almaty vetoed the sale, since there was at the time (and to a strong degree still is today) significant local resistance to having foreigners as outright owners of Kazakh land. Van Lier, seeing his dream of owning and managing a dairy farm in the former Soviet Union slip away, was now in a precarious position. He no longer owned a farm in Western Europe and it seemed he could no longer become the owner of such a venture east of the Oder.

So Van Lier began to improvise. Determined not to return to his old life, and having around US$20,000 to work with, he looked for opportunities in other sectors. While today one will find most western consumer goods available in Almaty and other parts of the Republic, in the early 1990s the Kazakh consumer market was highly underdeveloped by western standards. Van Lier exploited the opportunity offered by this deficiency and took to the import–export business, bringing beer, Philips televisions and videos and, later, tulips into the hungry domestic market.

His operation proved very resourceful, adapting quickly to the local ways and methods of doing business. It was simple in many ways back then – few formal rules that governed trading, buying and selling. Many of the goods were appearing in the Republic for the first time and customs officials had little experience in pricing, duties, etc. Trading and import–export business of this nature was essentially based on good relationships and good organisation at the time, and for a novice to the game, Van Lier proved noticeably skilful in networking relationships and forging good local business partnerships. He did not, however, form his own enterprise, concerned that that this would attract excessive interest from officialdom (ie random tax inspectors), and preferred the low profile approach of working through his local partners. Though he was not earning much more than enough to cover his expenses at the time (which were back then very small), on the basis of the relationships he had by now forged in the country, Van Lier was clearly expanding in Kazakhstan.

It was during this time that Van Lier forged good relations with one of Almaty's fastest growing business groups, Raimbek. Also initially a trading enterprise, the politically well-connected Raimbek had formed an impressive capital base during the 'early years' and was interested in investing some of its capital in business-expanding activities. The tulip business, in which Raimbek was also involved, was not faring well for Van Lier, and during one of the meetings between the two, Van Lier's desire to get back into the business which he really knew was discussed. During their meeting, Raimbek explicitly told Van Lier that Kazakhstani land ownership laws would still not allow him to realise his dairy farming ambitions in the immediate future. However, there was an opportunity in the poultry farming business, and it was suggested to the Dutchman that he may want to look at one bankrupt, state-owned *ptitsa-fabrica* (bird [chicken] factory or chicken farm) that might be possible to acquire.

Unable to get into the dairy business, the pragmatic Dutch farmer went to the outskirts of Almaty to view what was one of thousands of state-owned enterprises left in appalling condition after the collapse of the Soviet Union. The site, consisting of 38 chicken houses, each 96 metres long and 18 metres wide, produced millions of tons of chicken meat during the height of Soviet Kazakhstan's rural-meats production industry. In 1996, when Van Lier first looked at the farm, it was left with little more than the naked bird houses, their shabby walls and their bare cement floors – the employees and the local mafia had taken everything, all the machinery, processing equipment and everything else that was not nailed or welded to the floor. But for Van Lier, it was an opportunity to get back into a field of business he was far more committed to than selling tulips. He also had the pledge of Raimbek capital behind him, which was far more reassuring than his first attempt to acquire a farm in Kazakhstan some four years earlier.

Thus 'Bertra' the poultry enterprise was born. At first, it consisted of two chicken houses that Van Lier rented from the government and 23,000 broiler chickens and modern processing equipment brought in from Europe to begin production. Once the Dutch farmer got the business up and running, each chicken house would have a production capacity of 38 tons of poultry meat every 49 days, operating on a 5×49-day cycle rotation per annum. The company's two founders, financing the investment with personal capital, also became its principal shareholders and Bertra's equity was divided 70–30 between the two – with the majority retained by the Kazakh.

Raimbek took care of all of the registration and other bureaucratic procedures that were required to make the company operational. The formalisation of the company's legal status went relatively smoothly, but Van Lier admits that this was essentially due to the fact that he had a well-connected, impressive local partner who could get things done in the country. Without Raimbek it was bound to have been a different story. From this platform, a division of labour developed between the two share-holders where each would work to his comparative advantage in the business and for their symbiotic benefit. Raimbek takes care of all official matters to do with the company's official status as an entity operating in the Republic (ie taxation, legal proceedings, registrations, clearing new equipment through customs, etc) and generally stays out of the opera-tional side of the business. Van Lier, the farmer, is the executive decision-maker on all management and operational issues on the farm. He has little interest in the highly convoluted legal regime that governs the operations of the enterprise. He rather puts his faith in Raimbek, with whom he has been involved in business since his first years in Kazakhstan and who the Dutch farmer believes is one of the few people he can trust in the country's highly unpredictable business environment.

Raimbek thus takes care of the administrative side of the enterprise's business, and also resolves major problems as they arise (such as having to reregister the business under new business regulations or renegotiate some of its debt repayments with its major creditors after the tenge devalued alarmingly in April 1999). Van Lier takes care of the small headaches at the operational level. One such headache is the tax inspector, who seems to have become a more than necessary visitor to the farm during the last year or two. Van Lier, who is now a veteran of Kazakhstan's business environment for the small- to medium-sized enterprise (SME) sector, fully understands that the inspectors come purely for the purpose of making money – and not always for the state budget. But for the Dutch farmer, dealing with this day-to-day menace that has developed a specific reputation for nastiness in the former Soviet Union, is essentially a matter of strength, consistency in taxation paperwork, and most of all, psychology. Having long-term business interests in Kazakhstan's rural sector, Van Lier set the rules of the game with the taxman during the first year of Bertra's existence.

Van Lier responded to the inspectors in such a way that Bertra gradually developed the reputation of being a 'clean' company. He knew that the easy way to rid his farm of these unwanted visitors would be to make a discrete, unofficial contribution towards their salary. However, taking the easy way out would create a domino effect. Word among inspectors would spread that Bertra is a company that is in on the local game, and the rent-seeking activity would simply proliferate to the point where the enterprise would not be able to make any realistic fiscal planning. Power would gradually fall into the domain of the inspector and the company would not be able to function productively. Van Lier, however, had one vital card to play – Raimbek. He knew that if things got too out of hand, he could call on his joint venture partner to resolve the problem and was therefore able to promote his own stance towards the taxman. This was to do everything by the book, so to speak. From the outset, Van Lier took a conscious decision to always pay the formal taxes asked of him by a visiting official by bank transfer and never show any liquid currency. Receipts were gathered for all transactions and an understanding has now developed between the Dutch entrepreneur and the state's exponents of budgetary revenue procurement. 'It may be difficult psychologically,' Van Lier says, 'but you must not let it get on top of you during your first year. In the long term you will definitely win out – otherwise word will quickly spread that this is not a clean business. In my case, I don't even give away a chicken!'

Van Lier also realises that it is in the interest of the district Akim's (municipal mayor) career for Bertra to remain a viable business that pays its taxes and employs local labour. With so few production enterprises doing well in the country in the late 1990s, it is clearly to the benefit of the local politicians to keep Bertra healthy. And Van Lier knows this. He is currently seeking to acquire another ten of the original site's chicken houses. With a total of 12 chicken houses in his enterprise, Van Lier is confident that he could outstrip the volume of production achieved by the Soviets with their original 38 houses. 'You must take full control of management,' the Dutchman says, 'otherwise you cannot run the business in the way you know is best.'

Bertra pays its labour well compared to most domestic enterprises: the enterprise employs around 70 workers and they are all paid an extra 3,000 tenge bonus on slaughter day. Bertra also uses modern technology brought in from Europe, which clears customs without any major problems reported, and where possible, employs local resources as inputs for the farm. This seems to satisfy local officialdom, who now not only exercise a good working relationship with the Dutch farmer, but have also been coming to seek his advice on other business development matters.

As for Bertra's future, the Dutch farmer who left western Europe and its lifestyle almost ten years ago is firmly committed to Kazakhstan. He is the first foreigner in Kazakhstan to have founded a successfully operating agro-enterprise in the country, largely without support from institutional structures available for European businesses, such as some of the programmes from the European Union (EU). There are even plans, that he has initiated, to form a farmers' association in his region that would expand his standing in the farming community notably. He has not only put these years of his life into growing a business in the country but has also invested substantial amounts of his own capital into the Bertra poultry farm. The equipment alone is valued at around US$1 million according to Van Lier. The operational financing of the farm is in a healthy condition, and Bertra has recently secured about US$800,000 credit from KazCommerce Bank, one of the country's leading domestic financial institutions, to further expand the business.

However, the enterprise has inherited significant Soviet-era debt, which accounts for the low profitability Bertra shows officially, and much of the farm's income is channelled into debt repayments. At the moment, this is not something Van Lier sees negatively, as his tax bill is thus kept lower, allowing him to keep a comparatively low profile for the company compared to some of the other established foreign joint ventures in the country. His chickens, which largely supply Almaty and its environs, are a popular commodity on supermarket shelves and Bertra has established a leading name in the market. The Dutch farmer is looking to diversify his production and wishes to open a fast food line that would produce nuggets, fillets and other popular chicken-meat items. He is looking to attract a new partner to his business, largely to work on the marketing side in which Van Lier has comparatively little experience. Yet his dream still remains and the Dutch farmer is adamant that one day we will see him herding his vast head of cattle out in the expanses of the Kazakh steppe.

BG International: Our Experience in Kazakhstan

BG International

BG's (British Gas) main business is in exploration, production, transportation and marketing of oil and gas. BG first came to Kazakhstan at the very beginning of the 1990s to evaluate business options in the country, where it was known that major oil and gas fields had already been discovered and needed resources for development. The Kazakhstan government welcomed BG as a foreign investor interested in the oil and gas sector.

Getting business established was slow and arduous as would be expected in a former centrally planned economy. Registration of legal entities does take time but is fully manageable. Today there are many service organisations (legal and financial) to assist in company set-up and offer advice. For the Karachaganak Field (an already proven field), following an auction for the exclusive right to negotiate, it took BG (together with partner Agip) till 1995 to sign the first major agreement. Then an additional two years were required before a final production sharing agreement (FPSA) could be signed at the end of 1997. For the north Caspian exploration venture, preliminary agreements were signed in 1993 with the final PSA signed at the end of 1997.

The local workforce is very well educated and has a high work ethic. Following some orientation to the international work environment, Kazakhstani nationals can prove to be very effective in their work. It would be impossible to run any business in the country without a significant contribution from local staff and most non-PSA contractual agreements will need a local partner for effective business development. Most oil and gas exploration and development projects are self-financed. The banking sector is currently developing in the country and a combination of local knowledge and international skills in the banking sector is key to efficient business relationships. Since there is no long tradition of a business community in the country, the areas of finance and tax are still in transition. However, it should be noted that Kazakhstan has progressed further to develop a positive investment climate than any other country with significant natural resources in Central Asia and a do-able business environment has been created.

The development of the legal framework in order to create an effective business environment in the country has also advanced further than in any of the other Central Asian countries. Consequently, we can say that an adequate legal framework exists. However, it is noted that differing interpretations of the laws have sometimes occurred, most particularly with respect to more complicated agreements. We feel comfortable with the contracts we have signed and are currently working with. Some, usually small, conflicts of interpretation exist. We have not had the need to test the conflict resolution mechanisms associated with our contracts to date.

We import significant amounts of equipment into the country and have found the efficiency of customs control similar to many other countries around the world. Occasionally there have been importation delays related to interpretation of importation regulations associated with our contracts. Today there are a number of high technology equipment categories that do need to be imported into the country.

Tax legislation has also advanced significantly towards international standards. However, there still remains further progress to be made in a consistent interpretation of certain tax legislation areas as it affects current existing contracts.

Overall, the business environment in Kazakhstan can be summed up as being one of the very best in the former Soviet Union. Business can make progress and be successful. However, it should be noted that the resources required to bring business forward may sometimes be greater that originally planned. The comparison of experience over original expectation reflects the fact, previously mentioned, that business agreements and operations usually take longer to establish and require greater human or financial resources than often budgeted for.

5.3

De Vries Alexander Financial Services

Ben Carter, De Vries Alexander

De Vries Alexander, the sole financial planning company operating in Central Asia, has its main Central Asian representative office in Almaty, Kazakhstan. Started by Ben Carter, who first came to Kazakhstan in December 1998 after several years spent in Dubai and Azerbaijan, De Vries offers an excellent example of the entrepreneurial possibilities that continue to exist in the former Soviet Union despite the Russian collapse and the knock-on effects in other CIS countries.

Ben Carter first arrived in Azerbaijan from Dubai in early 1997 with a colleague to open the Baku office of a large Middle Eastern brokerage. 'After the twenty-first-century standards of Dubai, our first sight of Azerbaijan was the unfinished, Soviet-period airport, complete with mafia-types, guns tucked into waistbands, meeting groups of working girls returning from the Emirates.'

At that time, many businesses from the Gulf State had either opened offices in Baku or were regularly sending people there to take advantage of the influx of western oil company money into the city. Companies offering everything from Japanese four-wheel drive vehicles to Habitat furniture to rat-catching expertise descended on Azerbaijan. 'The feeling in Baku was one of euphoria – it was to be the "new Dubai". Even seasoned oil men excitedly told anyone who would listen that the Caspian's reserves equalled anything from 5 to 14 North Seas.'

A year later, Carter had resigned from the Dubai company to start his own brokerage, having secured a range of agency agreements from a variety of major offshore insurance companies, fund management groups and banks. In the beginning, the Baku market proved lucrative: although one major western oil consortium had begun to downsize its western workforce, many expatriates continued to live and work in the city. Both in Baku and in Tbilisi, the capital of neighbouring Georgia, the company successfully marketed a broad range of personal and corporate financial products, ranging from expatriate medical and other insurances, offshore retirement plans, offshore company formation services and capital investment products.

However, the good times were short-lived: 'During the summer of 1998 my business partner and I became very concerned at the trends in the country, which impacted negatively on our business. Not only was the pace of downsizing within the oil industry accelerating, but the euphoria of 1997 had completely vanished in the face of poor seismic results and the failure of several consortia to find oil in commercial quantities. And of course the 1998 nosedive in the price of oil directly led to the departure of even more expatriates, who were our marketplace.'

After two years, for Carter personally it was also time to move on. 'I found myself unable to easily tolerate the rampant corruption, the collapsed public amenities, or the pervasive lack of belief in anything or anyone. Occasional bouts of sickness did not help, and many of us felt a sense of anger at the indifference of the authorities to the plight of the bulk of the population, who live in poverty.

'Perhaps the turning point was a visit I made to a former collective farm in Imishli, in the south of the country, where I came face to face with hundreds of refugees from the early 1990s' war with Armenia. They were living in the cattle cars of a train. Indeed, they had already been there for four years and were clearly forsaken by the government. For me, it was time to leave.'

Carter began to look for a solution and the former head of Proctor and Gamble in Kazakhstan suggested a visit to Almaty.

Carter immediately felt that the visit would be successful. 'At the airport in Baku there were the normal attempts (at least four in the space of an hour) by policemen and customs officials to rob me, whereas the standards of cleanliness and service offered by the stewards of KazakAir came as a most welcome surprise. I arrived in Almaty with a good impression of the country, and very keen to find out more.'

The three-week visit was a huge success, and Carter decided to move to Almaty on a more permanent basis. He returned in January 1999 and since then developments have been rapid. Within a few months of arriving in Kazakhstan, the company has been transformed, with the addition of four new shareholders and the injection of US$50,000 of working capital. The new shareholders are mostly drawn from the expatriate community but the board includes a Russian whose abilities Carter praises highly.

'I suggested the formation of a new company to several of my clients, who, in addition to being friends, all possess complementary professional and commercial skills, and are in key positions within the business scene in Kazakhstan. I was delighted when they all accepted my offer to join the company. De Vries Alexander aims to be a major force in the offshore financial services market. In addition to our dominance in the marketplace in Central Asia, our Moscow office has been opened and from Moscow we will soon expand into Central and Eastern Europe, and from there into the more traditional financial services markets of the Middle East, the Far East and Africa.'

Given the small size of the company, Carter points especially to the need to structure correctly one's business to take best account of local tax and other issues. 'It is fundamentally important to take advice from the western legal and accounting professionals resident in-country as to how to structure one's business in the best way, and to be prudent in the choice of local partners, if indeed that is necessary. One cannot do business in any country of the former Soviet Union without having one's eyes fully open to the reality of the business culture; the endemic lack of trust found throughout the CIS; the logistical problems of operating over such vast distances; or the social, political and ethnic problems.'

De Vries tackled these issues by opening a representative office, which involves much less tax-reporting paperwork than either a branch or a joint venture structure. By definition, operations in-country involve representing the De Vries parent, a foreign legal entity. The solution adopted is the usual one of a registered offshore corporation. All commercial transactions must be seen to be out-of-country, which has not proved difficult as in De Vries' case, a client's money is transferred from one bank account outside Kazakhstan to the account of the institution with whom the client is investing. Thus the in-country role is limited to the provision of advice and information.

'Finding ourselves without competition in a pleasant town – the mountain scenery is stunning – with a sizeable expatriate population, has proved an unexpected surprise. Most brokers in my industry prefer more exotic locations, but my long-time fascination with all things Russian had brought me here, it seemed, as if drawn by a thread.' All comparisons with previous experiences have proved favourable, even though many problems are common. 'I had the distinct impression that by moving some 2,000 kilometres further east from Azerbaijan, I had actually come much closer to Europe. The Russian and Ukrainian population is much smaller than in the dying days of the Soviet Union, but it still constitutes some 40 per cent of the country's population and the level of education and potential capability is high. The Slavs and urban Kazakhs are Soviet in attitude (that means fundamentally closer to European ways than the Azeris), and whilst there are some basic differences in assumptions and culture, the outlook of the young generation is essentially western.'

Nevertheless, attitudes are still Soviet, and while there have been great changes – the pace of privatisation has been especially fast in Kazakhstan – there are real difficulties. 'One common complaint from western business people is that whilst the Kazakh authorities are keen to attract every investment dollar possible, they do not view the making and exporting of profits as an automatic quid pro quo. Another perception is that the current leadership's nullification of an effective political opposition may lead to a further exodus of Slavs, which will without doubt further dilute the skills base in the country. And of course the CIS culture of the backhander and the bribe thrives as an institutional part of doing business.'

For De Vries' clients, being able to buy the personal insurances that foreigners working abroad must have in such locations (life, medical, critical illness, income replacement) or arrange essential long-term planning such as pensions, or simply take advantage of the company's services to grow capital or invest the extra disposable income they enjoy as expatriates, is a welcome and important addition to the range of services they require.

Fitzpatrick International Ltd

Marat Terterov

In 1996 the Ministry of Health of Kazakhstan expressed its interest in having a contracting company build a 'presidential' hospital for the Republic's, about to be proclaimed, new capital city of Astana. The 240-bed hospital project was valued at around US$40 million and the finance appeared to be in place from a consortium of international creditors, including the British and French governments. The contract was won by the British company Fitzpatrick International and construction began in November 1997. The facility is designed to operate to British standards, and is to include three operating theatres, X-ray laboratories and physiological and gynaecological units. The hospital site is on the outskirts of Astana, just off the Astana–Karaganda highway, and work was ongoing during the summer of 1999. Construction was due for completion in December 1999 and the high-standard facility was expected to be operational in 2000.

Fitzpatrick has employed around 200 workers in developing the hospital site and, while most of the labour is local, has had to import some specific tradesmen and site supervisors from Britain and Turkey. Certain aspects of the project require fairly specific work and Fitzpatrick has hence turned to its expatriate human resources to design, for example, a cladding system and to carry out some of the roofing work. But the British firm has found that obtaining work permits and the necessary visas for the expatriate staff has been time-constraining and it is becoming increasingly evident that Kazakhstan's government wants foreign companies to utilise as much local human resources and raw materials as possible. However, it is evident from a highly specialised construction project of this nature that the local resources base is not capable of supplying all the contractor's needs.

While some materials are procured locally and are cheap (ie cast iron and various pipes), 70 per cent of the goods and services being used to construct the hospital are purchased and supplied from the UK (which was one of the pre-conditions negotiated in the project's financing structure). Some of the project's major inputs are procured from the local raw materials base, including cement and bricks, which has at times been a problem as the locally produced cement has on occasions been too wet and not fit for Fitzpatrick's purposes. It would certainly be of benefit to Fitzpatrick to have another British company such as Blue Circle producing cement locally in Astana, its management suggests. However, management adds that for the most part the locally made bricks have been of an acceptable quality.

As for the rest of the many necessary inputs required for the construction site, these have to make the long journey from Britain to this region of central Kazakhstan. During the summer, the road journey from the UK takes around seven days but is generally considered by companies like Fitzpatrick to be an expensive exercise in getting equipment to the country. Then there is the hurdle of confronting customs, which calls on a vast amount of documentation to be presented in (virtual) perfect order. While customs can delay the entry of equipment into the country, it is generally not viewed by Fitzpatrick management as a major obstacle for doing business. Most of its equipment arrives at the construction site in reasonable time and the whole procedure simply calls for more strategic planning, being so far from the source of many of the project's inputs. Good relations and a flexible approach towards customs officials have also helped the British builder-contractor. Further, Fitzpatrick's management's experience with the government's procurement officials (taxation and other forms of inspectors) appears to have been far from problematic, though again, there seems to be an overly extensive array of documentation which had to be available for presentation in the right order. However the company has not faced any noticeable disputes, and has not had to ask the British Embassy in Almaty nor the Astana based Kazakhstan Foreign Investment Agency to assist in resolving problems with officialdom.

While for many logistical reasons Astana's presidential hospital is a demanding project for its major contractor, Fitzpatrick's experience with Kazakhstan's (business) regulatory environment does not appear to have been an overly burdensome one. The company has utilised local services where possible, such as employing the large state-owned KazCommerce Bank for its banking services. While the bank imposed some very minor restrictions on Fitzpatrick's corporate account (ie limitation of two with-drawals per day), the British contractor receives preferential treatment from the bank and can transfer money to and from the UK with relative ease.

A representative of Fitzpatrick's client, the Ministry of Health, has a presence on the site and inspects the progress of the work on a daily basis. It took the two parties (the Ministry of Health representative and Fitzpatrick's management) some time to establish good working protocol

– to feel each other out, so to speak – but now relations seem to be well developed. However, it still appears that the client wants to have an overseeing hand in literally every detail of the entire project. But this may be as much to do with seeking to learn about new techniques, equipment and project management, as it is with the hangover of a controlling mentality developed during the Soviet era. It certainly does not seem to bother Fitzpatrick management. In fact the only real obstacle that does succeed in bringing Fitzpatrick's project in Kazakhstan to a complete standstill is the weather, which had dropped down to an incredible –37°C at times. But such cold spells are generally brief and by early in the new millennium, the new capital of the Republic of Kazakhstan is likely to have a British hospital.

FoodMaster

Erlan Sagadiev, General Director, FoodMaster

Developed Technology Resource Inc (DTR), a Minnesota-based firm, began its CIS-based activities selling dairy processing and packaging equipment to Commonwealth of Independent States (CIS) countries, including Kazakhstan. While preparing the market research for our clients, DTR found that the industry had potential for a company that could introduce good quality dairy products, western packaging equipment and sound management. DTR therefore decided to invest in a small shop that began making yogurt at Issyk dairy plant. Today, FoodMaster has grown to five plants, including two cultured dairy products plants at Astana and Almaty, two cheese plants at Kordai and Shymkent and one long shelf life juices and milk plant in Almaty. The sales for 1999 were US$13.5 million.

The company's main customers are stores. FoodMaster makes 20 different types of products including kefir, packaged milk, sour cream, ice-cream, hard cheese, soft cheeses and cheese spreads, juices and nectars.

It was not too difficult to register and start the business. Kazakhstan had a quite complex and contradictory Tax Law for a while but it changed its Tax Code in 1998 and the situation has since much improved. Licences and other approvals are getting to be easier to obtain from year to year, but they were not too bad in 1995 when the business was started. Setting up the operations was difficult, however, primarily because the company had to train almost all its staff and change attitudes to work held by many.

In terms of governmental help, the company received tax breaks from the Agency for Investments in 1999. It also received a grant for approximately US$360,000 from the United States Agency for International Development (USAID) in 1996 that was handled through Try Valley Growers and later ACDI/VOCA. This helped to bring quite a few consultants and helped with some equipment. The Kazakhstan government also provided three plants and the following reliefs: no income taxes for three years; no land and property taxes; and it lowered value added tax (VAT) for dairy products in Kazakhstan from 20 per cent to 10 per cent in 1998.

All the company's staff are local. FoodMaster did not and does not employ expatriates. Local employees are more effective and, of course, less costly in the long-run. However, a lot of training needs to be provided initially. The same applies for a local partner. Most partners are not qualified to run operations that will be acceptable for western companies, so the key is to either train your partner or hire local staff and train them. Your partner or your local staff should bring knowledge of the local market and good connections. The government treats companies that are fully or partly owned by foreigners in the same way. The company will be subject to frequent tax inspections if there is a suspicion that it is expatriating profits through price transfers.

The business was initially financed by DTR, a publicly held company that raised money through public offering in 1994. Back then, DTR had set up a joint venture with Agribusiness Partners International (API), which is an OPIC-guaranteed venture fund that was dedicated to invest in CIS agriculture projects. The joint venture was able to receive additional funds from API and invest in FoodMaster's expansion in Kazakhstan. In 1999 the European Bank for Reconstruction and Development (EBRD) had invested US$1.8 million in FoodMaster in exchange for newly issued shares. The company's main bank is Kazkommertsbank (KKB), which provides long- and short-term loans to FoodMaster. Most of the long-term loans are through special government programmes giving an 11 per cent annual rate. Short-term loans vary between 17 and 20 per cent. The company's total credit amount from Kazkommertsbank is US$1.5 million. However, at some time in 1998, KKB lending reached as high as US$3 million. Generally, any financially sound business in Kazakhstan will not have a hard time finding funds.

For the most part, the legal system is effective and the conflict resolution procedures, although slow, are predictable and enforcement is effective. In 1997–98 a number of companies went bankrupt very quickly and the bad debt recovery rate for many creditors was low. From the middle of 1998 the number of businesses going bankrupt decreased dramatically and FoodMaster therefore does not have a high level of debt write-offs. The tax laws and the whole of the business law system stabilised in 1997–99 and became much more simple, predictable and effective. In 1995–96 the tax laws were poor and changed quite often.

FoodMaster depends heavily on foreign-made dairy processing and packaging equipment, spare parts and packaging material. Clearing customs was very difficult, long and costly up to 1999. Many codes were unspecified and the Customs Tax Code was applied too liberally by the authorities. In 1999, after the government had clarified and simplified customs procedures, the situation has become somewhat better. But it is far from being easy to clear customs and still very costly.

Another problem for a potential investor is the quality of their purchasing department. Any small mistake made in customs documentation can be very expensive. FoodMaster spent one year organising and training the company to adopt ISO-9000 standards; the biggest relief and savings from adopting those standards across the whole company was in the purchasing department.

After lowering VAT for the dairy industry from 20 to 10 per cent and excusing some of FoodMaster's plants from paying income tax, the whole tax burden for the company has become sustainable. However, there are still many clauses in tax legislation that hurt companies. For instance, one cannot take currency devaluation losses to offset profits in a current year. In an environment of high inflation, this badly effects all companies that have high dollar-denominated costs and dollar loans. The company can lose money due to currency devaluation and still have to pay income tax.

In general, the health of your business depends strongly on the economic stability of the country. Kazakhstan's economy has not been stable lately and went through heavy devaluation in 1999. The economy's monetisation level kept going up and down, which directly affected sales volumes. Consumer confidence is quite low at this stage. However, in terms of legal and other institutions, Kazakhstan is far better than most other CIS countries for a private company to do business in.

5.6

Gallaher Plc

Marat Terterov

Any visitor to the Illisky district, just on the outskirts of Almaty, will find perhaps the most modern production facility in Kazakhstan. The site is the cigarette factory of Gallaher Plc, a historic Irish tobacco producer established in Londonderry in 1868. Based in Surrey, England, Gallaher is a highly profitable corporation listed on the London Stock Exchange that set a record operating profit of £390 million for 1998. Gallaher had been exporting cigarettes to Kazakhstan through a local agent since 1993 and had subsequently built up a substantial market in the country.

However, there was some concern that Kazakhstan's government would increase tariffs on imported cigarettes, a move that would undermine Gallaher's exports to the country. Consequently, in 1996, Gallaher started looking for a site around Almaty to build a factory to manufacture cigarettes in Kazakhstan to satisfy domestic demand. The company purchased a large block of land just outside the city. (The Illisky district was favoured as the local Akim (mayor) was reportedly quite energetic about developing his municipality into an industrial projects zone.) Godbeer Associates, a British-owned local contracting company, was appointed to develop Gallaher's new site into a state-of-the-art cigarette factory and construction began in July 1997. The cash-rich tobacco company financed the project internally and by early 1999, after an investment of around US$25 million, Gallaher inaugurated its ultra-modern cigarette manufacturing plant, with production beginning in early March.

For a 100 per cent foreign-owned company (now a joint venture between Gallaher Plc and Reemtsma Tobacco of Germany) operating in Kazakhstan without the guiding support of a local partner, Gallaher reports few major obstacles in the way of its business. The company's senior management followed the conventional business ethic of formulating good working relations with the local Akimat (town hall) which, as in the case of Chimkent's Akimat and RJ Reynolds' enterprise in that city, is highly supportive of Gallaher's business.

The company's management meets with the Akimat on a frequent basis, as part of its strategy of maintaining good relations with the local administration. Gallaher tries to help the Akimat's department in such ways as it can and ensures that all taxes due are paid on time. It appears to have few difficulties dealing with government inspectors and tax officials when they come to visit the modern site. These visits come from many departments (local, city and national) covering areas such as health and safety, labour regulations, sanitation and environment. Again following local procedures and maintaining proper records is essential in this area.

Furthermore, while numerous businesses in the Republic view customs procedures with great scepticism, Gallaher has successfully imported the majority of its building materials and production equipment without experiencing major delays. This being said, Gallaher agrees that customs clearances are generally not easy as the paperwork tends to be overly complicated and a contract is required for all imported items (everything has a commercial value according to the operational philosophy of the customs officials). Getting the paperwork as close to perfect as possible is highly recommended to ensure a smooth clearance; but even this does not provide a guarantee that delays will not be encountered.

Gallaher employs the services of ABN AMRO Bank Kazakhstan and all of Gallaher's financial transactions with officialdom take place through bank transfers. The company insists on following all of the government's official regulations and other instructions for the conduct of its business in the country. Given the size of its investment in the country, the company sees it as essential to maintain a law-abiding presence. The legal framework in Kazakhstan is relatively new and continues to develop. At times, this can result in retrospective legislation that can be challenging especially to the first-time businessman. It pays to employ reliable legal advice to ensure that you are prepared to deal with the legal environment. Gallaher is in the privileged financial position to be able to follow this prescription.

While the company is – to a large degree – able to stay on top of the changing legal codes, it has found that obtaining work permits to bring in new employees from abroad can be a timely process. Around 14 different documents are required to be presented to officialdom in a procedurally correct manner or risk further delays. It is quite possible, however, that through such action the government may be sending an indirect signal to foreign companies that it wishes them to use local human resources. It may also displease the government that Gallaher employs few of the area's raw materials, as it is a highly self-sufficient enterprise. While Kazakhstan's lands are a rich source of tobacco, Gallaher, like the RJ Reynolds enterprise in Chimkent, imports its tobacco from subsidiary companies abroad. Unfortunately the locally grown product is semi-oriental and is unsuitable for the company's famous Virginia-Blend. The company even generates its own electrical power from the national grid, and has built a (back-up) power-generator behind the cigarette factory.

However, although it has been operational in Kazakhstan as a production enterprise for a relatively short time, the company's business experience is sending positive signals from an atypical business climate. Gallaher employs around a hundred employees, and on the whole finds the workforce very well-educated, competent, reliable and easy to communicate with in English. Like the RJ Reynolds dual-sector project at Kabisco, Gallaher sees the peculiarities of the local business environment as challenging but hardly a structural barrier. It has major interests vested in the country and at the moment is seeking to expand its production further. There is presently talk of doubling the workforce and extending production to three shifts per (24-hour) day.

Overall it is all about doing business and that in itself is all about where your market is. For Gallaher, the market happens to be this massive Central Asian republic – a place where doing business comes with its own price, complexities and nuances. The country is so distant from 'anywhere', Gallaher's management suggests, and it is generally expensive to get things it. The high logistics costs result in Kazakhstan not being a cheap location for business, but cheaper than Europe nonetheless. As it consolidates further in the country, however, Gallaher is also seeking to attract other foreign business to Kazakhstan. The company suggests that printing companies, who could serve some of Kazakhstan's major tobacco industry players' need for packaging, would be particularly welcome. With this thought in mind, as he looked across the wide empty fields adjacent to the cigarette factory, Gallaher's general manager remarked, 'It would be nice to have a neighbour.'

5.7

Globalink: Our Experience in Kazakhstan

Siddique Khan, Globalink

Globalink arrived in Kazakhstan in 1993, one of the first foreign companies to establish an active presence there. As the Central Asian region's leading freight forwarding company, Globalink has grown substantially in Kazakhstan since the beginning of free-market reforms. With a vital series of links with airlines and other cargo forwarders throughout the world, Globalink provides cargo transportation services to companies that are bringing machinery and equipment, inventory or other commercial goods and even household effects from one point to another. Increasingly over the years, the company's staff have been able to travel throughout the Republic, visiting industrial, commercial and even cultural sites, foreign embassies and national government buildings and see the work 'we've' done. As observers – and contributors – to the development of the business climate in Kazakhstan over the years, Globalink is in a unique position to reflect on the progress that has occurred.

There are several legal forms a business being established in Kazakhstan might take. These include a representative office, a branch or an affiliated company. Each has its advantages and limitations, so it is important to consider this point carefully. It makes sense to seek tax and legal counsel in doing this to ensure the process is properly handled. Globalink have recently been impressed by the ability of some local law firms to register companies in Kazakhstan and no longer believe it is necessary to rely on the better known, and more expensive, names in this regard.

In the eight years since independence, Kazakhstan has become more and more receptive to building quality and durable relationships with foreign investors. Therefore, the government is generally as helpful as any government tends to be when it comes to building businesses. The State Agency for Investments under the Ministry of Foreign Affairs is a good starting point and can be accessed through the website www.kazinvest.kz. Other information about the economic and market situation in Kazakhstan can be accessed through www.kazecon.kz. The

State Agency on Statistics responds to formal inquiries for information, and if a business will depend on imports or any major shipping of goods, it makes sense to contact the Customs Committee and deal through a licensed customs broker.

Because the market economy in Kazakhstan is still relatively new, there is naturally a significant learning curve that any business setting up here must experience. That said, the business infrastructure has improved enormously since the early 1990s. This includes telecommunications possibilities, access to technology, effective administrative support and the proliferation of business associations and professional service firms. Sharing anecdotal experience with other businesspersons in related fields is worthwhile and despite the competitive characteristics of businesses here, like anywhere, there is also a co-operative nature that brings people, and businesses, together. In terms of the availability of human resources, Globalink have on the whole been very impressed. In general, Kazakhstan is fortunate to have a well-educated workforce whose specialists are often very accomplished in their fields. We have specifically felt fortunate to be joined by many honest, hard-working and resourceful local employees who are key to the smooth operation of our business and our ability to offer our customers superlative service.

We are not involved in a joint venture with a local partner, but rather are an independent business. Anecdotally, we can say that experiences with local joint ventures have been mixed and success depends entirely on finding the right partner. Business incentives are offered to 'strategic investors' by the government based on involvement in specified areas of the economy. Because we are a service company, we do not qualify for these. Instead, we have learned that the best way to do business here is by following the rules and not cutting corners. Building trust is essential to any long-term player in this region and being straightforward and fair in all business dealings ultimately earns long-term customers. It may sometimes be slower, or more frustrating to do things 'the right way', but ultimately we've learned there is no serious alternative.

Though our business was privately financed, a myriad of financing sources exists for qualified businesses with realistic and prospective business plans. Kazakhstan's financial infrastructure has also improved enormously over the time since we first started doing business here. In addition to a number of professionally run and well-capitalised local banks (Kazkommertzbank, Halyk Savings Bank of Kazakhstan, Turan Alem Bank and CenterCredit Bank), a number of foreign banks, such as ABN-AMRO, Citibank and Hong Kong Shanghai Bank have commercial affiliates in Almaty, the largest city and 'commercial capital'. Some foreign governments offer financing for companies setting up businesses in Central Asia and it may be worth contacting donor agencies such as the European Union's (EU's) Technical Assistance for the Commonwealth of

Independent States (Tacis), worldwide lending organisations such as the World Bank or European Bank for Reconstruction and Development (EBRD), or commercial services attached to your embassy.

Many companies have been pleasantly surprised to find that Kazakhstan's judicial system can be fair and responsive to complaints brought before it. The basis of Soviet law, which, of course, preceded Kazakhstan's own civil and criminal codes, was reasonably substantial and broad in its scope. The transition to an open market, however, has required numerous changes. A Law on Foreign Investment was one of the first major pieces of legislation to profoundly affect the operations of many foreign businesses. Recently, the Civil Code has been amended to take into account many of the changes and bring Kazakhstan's legal base closer to international standards. Accounting principles have been brought into line with GAAP, based on an accrual system, which – after some initial confusion – is becoming clearer and more user-friendly. One concern many companies have is the fast pace at which some laws may change or be amended, and this creates a need for businesses to be especially vigilant about keeping up to date on legislative developments.

Globalink's professional relations with the customs authorities have allowed the company to help its customers import items necessary to their businesses and lifestyles. The nature of what is being imported, however, is a critical consideration as the application of value added tax (VAT), customs and excise duties and other tariffs apply to specific situations. Dealing with a company that has a Customs Brokerage Licence and a proven track record in effectively clearing shipments can make all the difference, and it is important to research carefully what business partners you chose for freight-forwarding solutions. Also, as above, laws and regulations are constantly being reviewed and changed, so it is important to deal with a company that is on top of these changes.

While there have been a series of complaints about the administration of tax policy, the basis of Kazakhstan's Tax Code is reasonably simple. Tax rates may be higher than they are in some countries, while they are lower than those in others. Many who have done business throughout the Commonwealth of Independent States (CIS) have remarked that Kazakhstan's tax structure is remarkably fair. As mentioned above, there are always two ways to address business problems: the right way and the easy way. If a company takes the extra steps necessary to ensure that its declarations and tax filings are in order, it is making the sensible decision of protecting itself. As the regional economy struggles with challenges in the last two years, tax authorities are becoming increasingly aggressive about collections and audits are not uncommon. For this reason, it pays to take the Tax Code seriously.

Business in Kazakhstan is not necessarily easy, but it can be rewarding. This is a country of tremendous promise – a vast territory with massive mineral reserves and a relatively small population. Among Central Asian nations, Kazakhstan stands out as a pillar of stability and reform. Long-term players in this market can succeed, and there is evidence of successes. To be frank, there are also challenges – culturally and in other respects – that may deter the faint-hearted. A general downturn in the regional economic performance became most pronounced after Russia's crisis of 1998 and has scared away some businesses and, to be sure, has slowed the progress of others. But Globalink view this as a business cycle, and business cycles can change like the weather. What remains true, though, is that the potential for growth in this country is strong and Globalink look forward to continuing to grow with Kazakhstan for many years to come.

Godbeer Construction Group Ltd

Marat Terterov

Godbeer Construction Group, a British contracting company now operational in Kazakhstan for almost seven years, is a good example of a robust medium-sized enterprise that has proved to be a highly capable operator in the rugged Kazakh construction and building industries. GCG started its operation in Kazakhstan in a rather adventurous, modest manner when David Godbeer (founder of the company) was invited by a long-standing client to look at some business opportunities in the country. The UK in the early 1990s was experiencing a recession, with the construction industry being particularly hard hit. Although Kazakhstan seemed a distant place to go to earn a living, it nevertheless seemed worth a visit. This proved to be the case with GCG when shortly after David's first visit they were engaged to design and construct a desalination plant in Bautino, a small village located on the eastern coast of the Caspian Sea.

The time-frame for the project was not easy and there was a considerable learning curve to overcome especially in respect of local approvals and administration procedures. Nevertheless the work was completed and the plant has been operational for some years. Most satisfying from GCG's point of view was the opportunity to employ local labour, most of whom had not been employed for many years. Acceptable standards were difficult to achieve at first but perseverance paid off and it's fair to say the local people displayed an enthusiasm for work and learning often hard to find these days in the West. This has largely dictated GCG's employment policy during the last seven years: namely to use local labour as much as possible, pay reasonable wages and supply the proper tools to do the job. These principles, together with competent supervision, have undoubtedly played a major part in their success in the Kazakhstan construction market.

Since the desalination project, GCG has expanded in Kazakhstan, developing a name for itself as a highly reliable, no-nonsense local contracting company. It has developed quite an extensive CV, carrying out building and renovation contracts, mostly for expatriate businesses. Its

clients include Exxon (for whom it has carried out numerous maintenance and up-keeping jobs), Gallaher Tobacco (for whom it built a
state-of-the-art facility for cigarette production just outside Almaty), the
British Council and the British Embassy (for whom it has renovated
offices and domestic real estate). In fact there was plenty of work and
enough contracts to keep not only David employed in Kazakhstan, but
also James, his son, who he pulled out of the UK just after he finished
university to help out with business locally.

GCG has developed in a manner entirely appropriate for the
Kazakhstan market. A total turnkey service is provided including project
management, design, construction, engineering services and
procurement. The principle is to work with the client as a team from feasibility through to completion applying a combination of western
management 'first track' techniques with local knowledge and experience. In this way a quality cost efficient project can be completed in a
timely fashion. It is true that there needs to be an element of trust, especially for foreign investors with no or little experience in the region, but
GCG's past successes show that this trust is well founded. Costs may at
first appear to be higher than those of other contractors, but this is
usually because GCG refuse to give unrealistic prices and programmes in
the hope of securing additional monies as the work proceeds. GCG does
not work that way – professionalism and integrity may have caused them
to lose some contracts, but these qualities have also rewarded them with
quality contracts from quality clients, which is the only market that they
wish to operate in.

GCG works out of an office in Almaty and employs a team of around 35
local skilled and semi-skilled workers to carry out its various contracts,
which these days are mostly in Almaty. The labour is not expensive to
employ and is of a generally high standard, and like many western
companies in Kazakhstan, GCG pays its workers comparatively high
wages.

GCG is a company owned and managed by expatriates who are registered in Almaty. The company also has a joint venture company called
PRIS – Godbeer. PRIS is a local design company with a staff of about forty
people including architects, engineers and administration personnel
supported by the latest computer design technology (AutoCAD). This
joint venture helps to secure local approvals quickly and efficiently and to
ensure that all work is carried out in strict compliance with Kazakhstan
laws. This is very important, especially for fast track projects.
Organisations that fail to appreciate and comply with Kazakh regulations
and legislations risk delays and many problems.

Finally, you do not see Godbeer putting up their billboards in
prominent locations around Almaty. In fact, their advertising and
marketing efforts are very low profile. Work is mainly achieved by word of

mouth and client recommendations. Certainly in the seven years that they have been in Kazakhstan, they have built a reputation as a contractor you can rely on. Just walk into the crowded Irish pub in Almaty on a Friday night and you will see that – where word of mouth matters – Godbeer receive plenty of advertising.

Scot Holland Estates

Roger Holland, Scot Holland Estates and Marat Terterov

Scot Holland Estates is a real estate services company with most of its business centred in Kazakhstan's three main cities, namely Astana, Almaty and Alyrau. Its major clients are large foreign organisations – essentially from the oil and gas sector, accounting firms, law firms and some fast moving consumer goods companies. The company locates and provides rental accommodation for its clients, and supports any of their other needs during their stay in the country. In 1999, the company staged it's first 'Ideal Home Exhibition' in the five-star Regent Almaty Hotel.

The company launched its operation in Kazakhstan in September 1994, almost under what one may refer to as an 'accidental corporate strategy' during a time when the institutional culture for capitalist business development in the former Soviet Union was only beginning to emerge. The company's founder, Roger Holland, was initially interested in major population centres in the former Soviet Union, and was not specifically focused on any one location. His initial choice for the company was Vladivostok, in the Russian far east. However, it turned out that he missed his flight from Moscow to Vladivostok and, eager to get things started, flew to Almaty the following day. Hence Scot Holland Estates was baptised on Kazakhstani territory.

Receiving little if any assistance to open its operations in the country, it took Mr. Holland four to five months and fees to a US law firm of around US$10,000 to open his business in Kazakhstan. Since it was not possible to open a bank account until all documents were organised and supplied to the Ministry of Justice, the company was forced to operate on a marginal basis – cash transactions – during its first half year in the country.

Business commenced slowly and office space was both expensive and of poor quality. Many essential business inputs taken for granted in the developed market economies were scarcely found in Kazakhstan, reliable market information was hard to come by, and the only really helpful people that the company could find were several local, willing employees.

Mr. Holland has found most of the workforce intelligent and well qualified but often lacking in marketing skills, which they have been forced to learn on the job rather rapidly due to the company's 'fees by results' (commissions-based) remuneration policy.

Early business development was further complicated for Mr. Holland as there was no framework in place for the type of legal entity it wished to register. At the time, most foreign companies in Kazakhstan were either representative or branch offices whereas Mr. Holland was actually starting a foreign company in Kazakhstan, which made it slightly cumbersome for the legal regime to accommodate. Roger Holland initially chose to operate Scot Holland Estates independently, without a local partner, since he thought there was no point in bringing someone into the business whom he did not know and thus immediately double the risk inherent to opening an enterprise. After three years of business, however, Roger Holland decided to take one of his work colleagues into the company as a full partner, apparently one of the best decisions Holland has ever made.

The company never looked for finance externally to begin its original operation, rather relying on some start-up capital provided by Holland himself. The local banking system has since been employed to conduct basic financial transactions, with few reported problems (though the banking system is known to be somewhat bureaucratic).

Further, the company does not come into much direct (physical) contact with the legal environment. Holland has recently registered some patent trade marks and hopes that it can maintain its rights in this area. Another company recently attempted to use one of Holland's trade marks, 'Ideal Home' for an exhibition, but after some negotiations between Holland and this enterprise, the latter seems to have ceased employing Holland's trade mark. In theory, the lease agreements that the company's clients sign are watertight, as these have usually been reviewed by Baker and Mckenzie, a law firm that operates in Kazakhstan. However, if a landlord refuses to honour the agreement (as may happen), the local culture would usually preclude the case from going to court. Even if it were to, it is unlikely that Holland's client would get any financial compensation from the landlord.

Scot Holland Estates rarely deals with the customs authorities, since one of the attractions of the marketing and real estate business in the country is that imported goods and services are rarely required.

As far as the taxation environment, Holland claims that Kazakhstan's taxes are high for businesses such as his. There are numerous and changing smaller taxes that companies have to pay over and above the 30 per cent corporate profit tax and it all adds up. The company pays all that it is asked, however, and observes the country's regulatory norms in this area. Holland recently employed a local Kazakhstani auditor who has further guided the company in working correctly within the parameters set by the taxation environment.

Overall, Scot Holland comments that you can do 'good business' in Kazakhstan, but you have to be flexible, patient and resourceful. The larger you are, Holland adds, the more attention you receive, since everyone takes notice of, and is attracted to, 'the big boys'. The bureaucracy tends to pay lesser attention to the smaller players. Further, it is vital to establish good relationships with key people (in government and business alike) and employ the talent that is to be found locally. However, there still seems to be a lack of trust between locals and foreigners – the latter are still too often seen to be overly interested in taking Kazakhstan's immense natural wealth and running. Only time and positive experiences will change this viewpoint. The final note for those would-be newcomers eyeing the Kazakhstani market is that business in Kazakhstan will not be easy during the next five years or so, with some successes and notable failures bound to occur. The country is likely to prosper in the end, according to Holland, though this will take considerable time, and probably coincide with President Nazarbayer's vision for the year 2030.

5.10

The Tsessna Corporation

Marat Terterov

During the late 1980s, economic liberalisation measures instituted by reformist Soviet Communist Party Secretary-General Mikhayil Gorbachev allowed for a degree of mixed ownership enterprises to start emerging in the Soviet Union. Liberalisation of the traditionally socialist-oriented Soviet economy led to the emergence of a new trend in Soviet business management techniques – the partially private, profit-oriented 'cooperative' enterprise. This early version of what one may refer to as 'people's capitalism' resulted in numerous cooperative enterprises proliferating throughout the Soviet Union. Entrepreneurial Soviet citizens began to experiment with production of goods and services for a profit that they would now be able to legally retain in a private capacity.

One such enterprise, Tsessna, was founded by the (then) mayor of Tselinograd (present-day Astana), Kazakhstan, about two years prior to the Soviet collapse in 1991. Initially operating in the grain processing and bread production market (at the time Soviet Kazakhstan's economic *raison d'être*), during its ten-year existence Tsessna has grown into one of newly independent Kazakhstan's largest quasi-private corporations and holding company controlling multiple productive and service entities.

Based in the new Kazakh capital of Astana and strongly supported by the highest political authority in the Republic, Kazakhstan's state-led transition towards a market economy has worked in favour of Tsessna's corporate expansion and development. The corporation has consolidated its position in the grain and wheat business, as well as diversified its commercial activities to include construction, wood processing, processed meats and sausage manufacturing, beer brewing, sowing and textiles, banking, advertising, media, telecommunications and security services. The company is one of the largest investors in the country, particularly in Astana, investing KZT1.5 billion in projects in the capital during 1997 alone.

Tsessna has developed a number of strong commercial relationships with foreign corporations and financial institutions (including Citibank, Deutsche Bank, the Central Asia America Enterprise Fund, Koch Supplies

Inc of the USA, Weinig of Germany and Okrim of Italy). It also operates representative offices through affiliated companies in Russia, Italy, Germany, New York, Hungary and the Czech Republic. Some of Tsessna's more prominent corporate holdings are briefly introduced below.

One of Tsessna's leading holdings is Akmola Astyk LLC, a technologically closed circuit grain-processing facility and agro-industrial complex. The enterprise is capable of taking the grain from the spike and processing it right through to the finished bread or cereal product. It consists of three grain elevators (350,000 ton capacity), five flour mills (350,000 ton capacity), a cereal production plant (305,000 ton capacity), two bakeries, ten farming enterprises and one animal feed production plant. Tsessna's senior executives claim that through Akmola Astyk they are seeking to revive Kazakhstan's reputation as a major international grain and wheat producer. Akmola Astyk has benefited from its commercial relationship with the Italian company Okrim, which has supplied the Kazakh firm with a mill capable of processing 40 tons of grain per day.

Tsessna's meat processing enterprise Yrys (pronounced *eereez*) is one of Kazakhstan's several joint ventures founded with the assistance of capital channelled through the Central Asia America Enterprise Fund (CAEEF). Commencing operations as of September 1997, Yrys' shareholders are presently Tsessna, CAEEF and Koch Supplies Inc of the USA. The enterprise is supplied with modern American equipment that enables it to produce up to 2,500 kg of high quality processed meats per production shift. Yrys employs a combination of local and imported raw materials and produces a range of over 40 different kinds of sausage, salami, and national delicacies that are currently found in around 55 stores, cafes and restaurants in Astana under the brand name Batyr.

The company's products have developed a strong reputation in Astana and have retained their marketability through sophisticated packaging techniques (including vacuum and thermo-packaging, employment of selective casing and marking, as well as the addition of selective spices for extra freshness). However, the Russian banking crisis of 17 August 1998 and the subsequent devaluation of the Kazakh tenge had a negative impact on Yrys' debt repayments (debt to the CAAEF was denominated in dollars and has increased in dollar terms after the devaluation) and production suffered. The company's general director was replaced in early 1999 and while the new man in charge has brought production levels back towards optimal levels, Yrys' sales are being further undermined by large volumes of low quality Russian sausage entering Kazakhstan illegally.

Tsessna has also prioritised the construction sector as a central component to its business development. Within this context, Tsessna's Concern Naiza LLC has become effectively engaged in building and renovations projects in the country's new capital city. Concern Naiza LLC commenced its activities with the manufacture of construction materials produced to European standards, but more recently has become involved in earthwork and buildings overhaul. The company has entered into a number of 'turnkey' projects with the government (ie infrastructure projects including housing development, public works, railways and highways), the most significant of which include the VIP-terminal of Astana airport, the Agip petroleum services station, and a building for a secondary school in the ninth micro-rayon in the capital.

Further, Tsessna's Adite LLC, has become an active wood-processing enterprise, providing clients with the latest environmentally friendly wooden door and window sashes with three panes of glass according to European standards. Adite LLC has been equipped with high technology equipment by the German company Weinig and also has sawing mills capable of converting forest wood into lumber. Adite's wood-processing activities have been employed in the majority of Astana's significant infrastructural development projects.

5.11

The Usk Kamenogorsk Poultry Farm

Marat Terterov

During the Soviet period, the city of Usk Kamenogorsk in north-east Kazakhstan was neighbour to one of the country's largest poultry farms, the Usk Kamenogorsk Ptitsa Fabrica (UKPF), which was located in the village of Molodyezhny some 20 km outside the city. Producing poultry meat since 1975, UKPF was a vertically integrated enterprise where all phases of the production and business cycles – breeding, growth, hatching, processing and distribution – were combined within the company. UKPF's 20 hectare site had a daily slaughter capacity of 32,000 broilers (chickens), and with a production cycle of 250 slaughter days per year, the enterprise was capable of slaughtering 8 million broilers per annum. UKPF was an impressive avatar of Socialist preconceptions about the way to control a society's means of production and was by far the largest producer of poultry meat in Kazakhstan, as well as the third largest among all producers of the Soviet socialist republics.

The fortunes of UKPF began to change in an alarming manner during the early 1990s as the enterprise joined thousands of others in the former Soviet Union to see the state, the economy and the political system collapse around them. As equipment would no longer arrive from the newly proclaimed Russian Federation, and as the incipient government in Almaty became increasingly bankrupt, most of UKPF's 700–strong workforce were failing to receive their wages. Workers and management turned to the discrete looting of the many assets of the enterprise and by 1994 production stopped completely. UKPF ceased to operate. Those employees who continued to turn up to work as they had done on a daily basis for the last 20 years, had to be reminded by UKPF's director that there was no longer any work for them. Only a group of around 20 armed men were employed by the local municipality to guard the now hollow alleyways of UKPF's slaughterhouses from further banditry.

The director now turned to measures that sought to revitalise the paralysed enterprise and began to construct a business plan to attract possible investors. His plan called for finance of around US$3.7 million, which would be deployed to replace breeding stock and feedmill equipment, purchase nutritional additives and ingredients, and procure poultry meat packaging and other complimentary equipment. UKPF's output would hence include whole (chicken) carcasses packed ready for distribution, eggs, and other supplementary products such as sausages and smoked chickens.

UKPF approached several institutions for finance, including the Central Asia American Enterprise Fund (CAAEF), Exim Bank and several others, but failed to secure an agreement. It was in this context that the Kazakhstan Post Privatisation Fund (KPPF) was also approached to consider investing in UKPF in 1996. From an initial perspective, this poultry industry project presented an attractive investment opportunity as the absence of UKPF's production since 1994 left a major shortage of domestically produced poultry meat in the Republic.

Following a feasibility study, the KPPF committed finance of US$3.7 million in a mix of debt and equity. Thus in March 1998, as a result of KPPF managed injection of capital, UKPF commenced the 'second' phase of production in the enterprise's history. Word spread quickly in Molodyezhny and the nearby *deryevni* (villages) that the paralysed centre of gravity of their economic subsistence since the mid-1970s was soon to be resurrected. There was even gossip among the 90 per cent unemployed workforce of the area that ex-employees would soon be invited back to work.

UKPF was registered rather quickly (within two months) as a joint-stock company and the British international legal firm, CMS Cameron McKenna, undertook all of the legal documentation necessary for registration. Cameron McKenna's fee was paid by the European Commission's (EC's) Technical Assistance for the Commonwealth of Independent States (Tacis) programme. Though there may have been some 'rent-seeking' or other 'political' interests that could have delayed registration and incorporation of the company, given the overall dire state of production in the country, it was clearly in the interest of the Kazakhstani government to get the enterprise operational once again. It should be mentioned further that Kazakhstan's parliament approved a new joint stock company law later in the year, which required the reregistration of numerous enterprises around the country, including UKPF, a significant administrative disruption to enterprise management.

Also in 1998 the government found a new way of implementing value added tax (VAT), which was particularly disruptive for newly established companies who were facing enough difficulties finding their feet in a business environment of increasing uncertainty. The new VAT law was abolished in the early summer of 1999, which, although seen as a positive step by the UKPF executive, did little to decrease the overall unpredictability of the business climate. Barring the capricious nature of the government's legislative policies, UKPF does not report any major problems with the taxation authorities when they come to inspect the enterprise.

Taxes payable by the enterprise are many: income tax, VAT, social tax, land tax, fixed assets tax, transport and environmental taxes, royalties and customs duties. Their collection is for the most part consistent with what UKPF's accounts department expects to pay. A number of auditing companies (including KPMG, PricewaterhouseCoopers, the Kazakhstan Central Audit Company and the NPV Audit Company) have been employed by the enterprise to assist with advice on taxation as well as training staff in internationally recognised accounting practices. Hence, unlike that of other enterprises in the country, UKPF's experience suggests that the problem with taxation is not so much with how it is enforced, but rather changes in the legal regime that create confusion and uncertainty for enterprise management. For example, transport taxes were increased three times in May 1999.

On the operations side, UKPF's production has now grown to around 90 per cent of its originally designed capacity. It is functioning once again as a vertically integrated enterprise since it now markets and distributes its frozen chicken meat (to Almaty, Astana and throughout the Republic) and has facilities for breeding, an eggs hatchery, broiler houses, feed milling and broiler processing. Operations recommenced at UKPF when KPPF, the enterprise's main shareholder, employed the Tacis programme to contract out European specialists to bring the latest processing technology and feed meal techniques to establish feed meal requirements necessary for production.

At first it was envisaged that a parent stock of chickens to begin the breeding process would be brought in from Britain. But at 3.5 kg, the British birds were somewhat large for local parenting conditions and several fleets of Dutch broilers were flown out to Kazakhstan to commence the production cycle. Six shipments of parent stock have since been delivered. UKPF continues to rely on foreign equipment, such as British feed meal, premix and medicine products from a number of western countries, and various types of imported packaging.

Good relations with customs officials are mandatory to get shipments into the country according to company management and all of its import contracts require compatibility with – locally and internationally – required standards, certificates approved by the authorities, etc. But even then, customs procedures can still be unpredictable and subject to varying moods and whims of the head officials responsible for shipment clearances. Nevertheless, the resurrection of UKPF from its four-year-long paralysis has clearly reinvigorated the Usk Kamenogorsk area and the company's new British/Dutch management team, installed by the KPPF in January 2000, has now raised production to 9,000 tons of meat per year, making it far and away the number one chicken producer in Kazakhstan. The UKPF is, without a doubt, a major Kazakhstan investment success story.

Appendices

Appendix 1

Investor Opportunities

Encouraging investment

Introduction

The Law 'On the State Support of Direct Investments' stipulated the establishment of a special body – the State Investment Committee (SIC) – authorised to act in order to attract investments to the priority economic sectors by granting incentives and preferences to investors. The SIC was re-designated as the Agency of the Republic of Kazakhstan on Investments ('Agency on Investments') on 1 June 1999.

The sectors of highest priority include the important industries, which have been designated as those needing to attract intensive investment and identified as crucial to the economic development of Kazakhstan.

In accordance with the Decree of the President of Kazakhstan, the State Investment Committee adopted 'The List of Priority Economic Sectors to Attract Direct Domestic and Foreign Investments for the Period Until 2000', dated 7 August 1998.

The priority economic sectors for attraction of foreign investment are:

1. **Industrial infrastructure** – rail, motor roads with bus terminals, airports and terminal facilities, air navigation facilities, sea and river terminals, bridges and over-under-passes, gas pipelines, thermo-electric power plants, power transformation facilities and power transmission grids, telecommunication networks.
2. **Manufacturing industry** – production of apparel, yarn, textiles, footwear, fur and leather products; production of furniture and accessories; manufacture of new types of cardboard-paper products; industrial processing of agricultural products; processing of sea food and fish-breeding products; provision and storage of agricultural products; manufacture of children's food and nutritional products; manufacture of confectionery, non-alcoholic beverages and wines; output of new high technology machinery, equipment and tools; manufacture of vehicles and transport equipment etc.
3. **Establishments in Astana City** – establishments associated with the relocation of senior and central government bodies to Astana.
4. **Housing, social and tourist centres** – commercial housing; health care and educational establishments; mass fitness, recreation, culture and tourist establishments.

5. **Agriculture** – cultivation of high-yield cereal and oil-producing crops on the basis of advanced technologies; production of the high yield seeds of plant-growing products; production and breeding of highly productive cattle and poultry as well as of pedigree cattle; production of highly effective, environmentally-friendly forage and forage additives.

Incentives and preferences

The major criteria that determine the granting of incentives and preferences when concluding contracts with the SIC and the Agency on Investments (since June 1999) are the following:

- involvement in priority sectors of the economy;
- the total amount of direct investment planned;
- the number of new job opportunities;
- the environmental impact of the project.

Incentives and Preferences

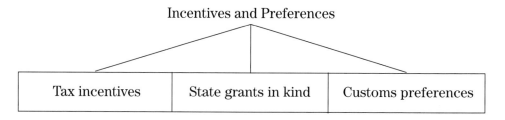

| Tax incentives | State grants in kind | Customs preferences |

Tax incentives

According to the tax regulations of Kazakhstan, foreign investors are eligible for the following tax incentives and preferences:

1. Income tax:
   (i)   Reduction of income tax rates, by up to 100 per cent of the base rate, is granted to an investor within the period stipulated by the tax law;
   (ii) Reduction of the income tax rate is granted to an investor on projects that are important to the state but that do not provide the required rate of return on the investment;
   (iii) Reduction of the income tax rate, by up to 100 per cent of the base rate, is provided to attract foreign investments for the development of projects creating new job opportunities, increasing the country's production output, increasing exports and decreasing imports. The amount and period of validity of such incentives are determined according to the priority level of the investments and depending on which economic sector the project is intended to benefit.

2. Land Tax:

Temporary exemption from land tax and the reduction of the tax rate is granted to investors involved in the construction of new industrial and agricultural facilities;

3. Property Tax:

Temporary exemption from property tax, or a reduction of the tax rate, is granted to investors when constructing new industrial facilities of a capital-intensive nature or when investment in equipment and industrial capitalisation leads to a considerable surplus of expenses over earnings in the first years of implementation. The exemption is granted only from the tax on the property used in the activities, as defined within the contract terms.

The reduction of income, land and property tax by up to 100 per cent is normally valid for a five year period from the contract's conclusion. A reduction (by up to 50 per cent) of the base rate of income tax, land tax and property tax may also be granted for a subsequent five year period.

State grants in kind

State grants in kind are fixed assets, non-tangible assets, production resources, land and land-tenure rights. In cases of agricultural investment, the utilised land is granted to foreign investors with the free rights of land-tenure for an agreed temporary period.

Customs preferences

An investor shall be granted exemption from customs duties on imported goods required for the project's realisation. This exemption is granted to investors on a specified volume of imported goods and for a period defined within the contract agreed with the SIC or the Agency on Investments.

There are two kinds of legal regime that the country offers to foreign investors: the *national* and *the most favoured* regime.

Kazakhstan allows foreign investors to use either of these regimes and they are therefore free to choose the one that offers them the most favorable conditions.

The Kazakhstan Post Privatisation Fund

Who we are

The GIMV Kazakhstan Post-Privatisation Fund (GIMV KPPF) is:

- a venture capital fund managed by GIMV, a Belgian investment company

- created with funding from the European Bank for Reconstruction and Development (EBRD)

Our investment funds

- A capital of 30 million ECU provided by the EBRD.
- A further 3 million ECU co-invested by GIMV.

Our history

- The Fund started operations in Kazakhstan in April 1996.
- The Fund has invested in both start-up and existing companies.
- The Fund's current portfolio includes ventures exclusively with Kazakh enterprises as well as with joint venture partners from the USA, Great Britain, France and Belgium.

Our team

Based in Almaty, the team consists of two expatriate professional staff, four local professional staff, and an administrative support team. In addition, GIMV provides support from Belgium.

Investment targets

Small and medium sized companies in Kazakhstan, whose state ownership does not exceed 33 per cent.

Technical support

GIMV KPPF is supported by a technical assistance grant of 20 million ECU provided by the European Union's technical assistance programme.

Investment criteria

- Strong management team.
- Significant growth prospects for products/services.
- Local production/import substitution.
- Well recognised brands with strong lead market position.
- Good marketing and distribution.
- A foreign, strategic partner.

Investment policy

- The Fund invests in small and medium sized companies whose state ownership does not exceed 33 per cent of their equity capital.
- The Fund can invest between 300,000 ECU and 5 million ECU in a single project.
- The Fund will not own more than 55 per cent of the shares of any company (49.9 per cent EBRD, 5 per cent GIMV).
- The Fund cannot invest in the following sectors: military, strong liquor, tobacco production, gambling and financial services.
- At least two thirds of the money that the Fund invests in a company must be to provide new financing (ie a maximum of one third may be used to buy out existing shareholders).
- The Fund invests primarily in equity capital, but may also give supporting loans.
- The Fund can provide long-term debt financing for its investees with a one to two year grace period.
- The Fund seeks a good overall rate of return on its total equity and debt investment in any one company.

Our role as investor

- The Fund is a medium term investor: the planned life of the Fund is ten years.
- The Fund is an active partner, and seeks to add value post-investment through:
  - its participation on the board of directors (strong on corporate governance);
  - the use of EU-funded technical assistance by co-financing:
    - finance director
    - marketing consultant(s)
    - technical/production consultant(s)
    - market research
    - MIS/accounting system implementation
    - international accounting standards audit
    - environmental audit
    - environmental action plan

Within a period of five to seven years following its investment, the Fund will seek to sell all of its shares.

Our investee companies

The Fund has now invested over 40 per cent of its 33 million ECU capital in six companies:

FoodMaster: US$2.8 million debt and equity investment in a dairy and juice producer, packager and distributor based in Almaty;

Rainbow Paint: US$3.3 million debt and equity investment in a start-up paint factory in Almaty;

Spectrum: US$2.2 million debt and equity investment in an Almaty-based mobile trunk radio company;

UKPF (Usk Kamenogorsk poultry company): US$3.9 million debt and equity investment in a privatised poultry farm, in Usk Kamenogorsk;

Bauta: US$2.1 million debt and equity investment in a water desalination and packaging facility in Bautino, on the Caspian Sea;

Rustam: US$0.7 million debt and equity investment in a cereal processing facility in Usk Kamenogorsk.

Some target sectors

- Bottling
- Brewing and wine production
- Cable television
- Confectionery
- Distribution
- Food processing
- Franchises
- Packaging
- Pharmaceuticals
- Telecommunication/Information Technology/Internet
- Upstream/Downstream Oil Service Companies
- Warehousing
- Construction materials

Probable rejection sectors:

- Primary Agriculture
- Textiles

Our investment procedure

Preliminary contact and submission of a business plan to the Fund

Preliminary analysis

Rejection or in-principle agreement ⎫ up to 1 month

Detailed analysis and negotiations, legal, financial and environmental due diligence

Business plan accepted

Investment proposal

Final EBRD/GIMV Investment Committee decision ⎫ 1–4 months

Contract preparation and signing

Our future

- Merger with three Russian venture funds, also funded by the EBRD.
- The Fund to be re-named 'Eagle Venture Partners'.
- The Fund has US$18 million left to invest with local companies.

Appendix 2

Visitors' Information

General information

Geographic position

The Republic of Kazakhstan is situated in Central Asia between the Ural River and the lower courses of the Volga River to the west, the Alatau Mountains to the east, the West Siberian plateau to the north, and the Tien Shan mountain chain to the south. The territory of the Republic stretches 1,600 km north to south, and more than 2,800 km west to east, occupying an area of 2,717 thousand sq km. In terms of area, the Republic is the ninth largest country in the world.

Most of the area of Kazakhstan is flat and low-lying. In Central Kazakhstan, vast plains give way to the isolated low mountainous range of Saryarka; to the south and southeast they melt into the mountainous systems of Altai, Sauyr-Tarbagatai, Dzhungarski Alatau, and Tien Shan. The highest point is the Hahn Tengri Peak (6,995 m).

Nearly all the rivers of Kazakhstan disgorge into the Caspian and the Aral seas or the Balkhash, Alakol, and Tengriz lakes, except for the rivers of Irtysh, Ishim, and Tobol, which flow into the Kara Sea. The biggest river is the Irtysh, which stretches for 1,700 km within the area of the Republic.

Kazakhstan is bordered to the north, northwest, and west by Russia, to the southeast by China and to the south and southwest by Kyrgyzstan, Uzbekistan, and Turkmenistan.

Climate

The climate of the Republic is deeply continental, and extremely dry. It is severely influenced by the Arctic region and Eastern Siberia. The absence of any natural barriers in the north of the Republic leaves the country vulnerable to cold arctic winds and arctic air masses. Conversely, the high mountains rimming the east and the southeast of Kazakhstan act as a barrier to air masses from the south. This accounts for the rather unsparing winters over the greater part of the area of the Republic. In Kazakhstan summers are hot and dry, with hot winds.

Population

The Republic has a population of 15.6 million people. Citizens of more than 100 ethnic groups live in the country, the greater part of which are the Kazakhs (more than 50 per cent) and Russians (more than 30 per cent). Amongst the other large ethnic groups are Ukrainians, Germans, and Uzbeks.

According to the Constitution of the Republic of Kazakhstan, Kazakh is the official language. However, Russian is the language of business and of interethnic intercourse.

Regions and cities

Kazakhstan is politically divided into 5 economic regions and 14 oblasts: Western Kazakhstan (Aktyubinsk, Western-Kazakhstan, Atyrau, and Mangistau oblasts), Northern Kazakhstan (Kostanai, Northern-Kazakhstan oblasts), Central Kazakhstan (Akmola, Karaganda oblasts), Southern Kazakhstan (Almaty, Zhambyl, Kyzylorda, and Southern-Kazakhstan oblasts), and Eastern Kazakhstan (Eastern-Kazakhstan, Pavlodar oblasts).

Table A.2.1   The Brief Characteristics of Kazakhstan's Oblasts

Oblast	Area, 1,000 sq km	Capital	Population, million people	Density, per sq km
Western Kazakhstan:				
Aktyubinsk	298.7	Aktyubinsk	0.7	2.3
Atyrau	112.0	Atyrau	0.5	4.4
Western-Kazakhstan	151.2	Uralsk	0.7	4.6
Mangistau	166.6	Aktau	0.3	1.8
Northern Kazakhstan:				
Kostanay	170.4	Kostanay	1.15	6.7
Northern-Kazakhstan	122.4	Petropavlovsk	0.6	4.9
Central Kazakhstan:				
Akmola	180.5	Kokshetau	0.95	5.2
Karaganda	398.8	Karaganda	1.8	4.5
Southern Kazakhstan:				
Almaty	223.2	Almaty	1.7	7.6
Zhambyl	144.6	Taraz	1	6.9
Kzylorda	228.1	Kzylorda	0.7	3.0
Southern-Kazakhstan	116.3	Shymkent	2	17.1
Eastern Kazakhstan:				
Eastern-Kazakhstan	276.9	Usk Kamenogorsk	1.7	6.1
Pavlodar	127.5	Pavlodar	0.9	7.0

There are 82 cities and towns in the Republic. The biggest are Almaty, Shymkent, Karaganda, Zhambyl, Semipalatinsk, Pavlodar, Usk Kamenogorsk, Astana, Uralsk, and Aktyubinsk. On 10 December 1997 the city of Astana was proclaimed the new capital of Kazakhstan.

Travel information

Visas

Kazakhstan requires a visa for travel to the Republic. Russian visas are only valid for Kazakhstan if you are in transit (ie when you are travelling to another country through Kazakhstan). A transit can last no longer than three days. For all other purposes, a Kazakhstan visa is mandatory. A visa can cost between US$80 and US$500, depending on its status and term. A visa usually takes about two weeks to obtain. For more details on visas, contact the nearest Kazakhstan embassy.

A visa cannot be obtained at airports upon arrival in Kazakhstan, with the exception of diplomatic visas. Therefore, when checking in for a flight to Kazakhstan, the airline will check all documents, including visas, and will not allow a person to board the airline if all documents are not in order.

Since there are few Kazakhstan embassies in the world, procuring a visa may require some organisation and forethought. In some countries, it may be possible to request that a Kazakhstan visa be arranged by a Russian embassy if a Kazakhstan embassy does not have a presence there. However, it is worthwhile confirming this with the Russian embassy first and inquiring about any additional documents that may be required.

When obtaining a visa through a Kazakhstani embassy or consulate, an invitation from a host organisation in Kazakhstan, a negative HIV test, three passport photos and the completed application form (which should be available from the embassy) are usually required. Upon receipt of the visa, confirm that the dates in the visa are correct and cover the period of stay. Should travel to other countries be included in the itinerary during the visit to Kazakhstan, ensure that the Kazakhstan visa is not limited to a single entry.

Customs

When arriving in Kazakhstan, two forms are required. They are normally distributed on the aircraft when flying to Kazakhstan. The first form is rather short and is for entry into and exit from Kazakhstan. This form should be completed for both entry and exit, and submitted during passport control. After passport control, half of the form will be returned and may be requested upon departure from Kazakhstan.

The other form should be filled out in duplicate for customs procedures. It lists the amount of money, and in which denomination, is being imported as well as valuables and other items. During customs clearance both forms will be stamped and one will be returned. The one that is returned must be submitted upon departure from Kazakhstan together with a new form. The new form again requests information concerning money and valuables being exported from the country. The authorities will confirm that valuables were not sold and that more money is not being taken out of the country than was brought in. Individuals are not permitted to take more than US$3,000 cash out of the country. It is worth mentioning that tenge may not be exported.

Registering with the department of foreign affairs (OVIR)

Within three days of arrival in Kazakhstan, an individual has to register at the Department of Foreign Affairs. As proof of registration, the passport will be stamped with dates corresponding to the visa. If an individual does not obtain the required OVIR stamp, a penalty fee may be assessed if stopped by the police or upon passport inspection at the airport during departure.

Carrying your identification documents

According to Kazakhstan legislation, foreigners must carry their passport with the visa and the OVIR stamp or, recently, a copy of all three, provided it is notarised by the foreigner's embassy, at all times. The police can stop anyone at any time and ask to see their documents. Failure to produce the requested document can result in detainment until the original passport is produced, complete with a visa, an OVIR stamp and, often, a penalty.

Travel

Five of the well-known European airlines fly to Almaty and, together, offer flights to and from Kazakhstan on every day of the week. Except for British Airways, all flights arrive in Almaty between midnight and 4.00am, under the current schedules. British Airways' current schedules offer arrivals between 10.00am and noon. All flights depart again within three hours of arrival. During winter, travellers should plan for delays, since the airport in Almaty frequently has problems with fog and snow and often closes.

To fly to Astana, the only way is to fly into Almaty and then take Air Kazakhstan to Astana. There are several flights in the morning and evening to and from Astana.

The national air carrier, Air Kazakhstan, also operates most of the internal flights between cities in Kazakhstan. It currently also offers flights to some international destinations such as Budapest, Hanover, Beijing and Urumqi (China). Trains frequently provide an alternative for journeys within Kazakhstan and to certain neighbouring countries.

Table A.2.2   Schedule of international flights to and from Almaty

Airline	From	To	Arrival in and departure from Almaty
Austrian Airlines	Vienna	Almaty	Wednesday, Friday
British Airways	London Heathrow	Almaty	Tuesday, Saturday
KLM Royal Dutch Airlines	Amsterdam	Almaty	Sunday, Tuesday, Thursday
Lufthansa	Frankfurt	Almaty	Monday (twice), Thursday (twice), Friday
Turkish Airlines	Istanbul	Almaty	Monday, Wednesday, Friday, Saturday

Accommodation

In Almaty, travellers have several options for hotel accommodation, including the Hyatt Regency Almaty and The Regent Ankara (both international five star hotels), as well as the Hotel Astana and Hotel Ambassador (both international four star hotels) and Hotel Dostyk and the Otrar Hotel (both well know national hotels).

Hyatt Regency Almaty *****
Rates vary from US$289 to US$1489 (prices exclude 20 per cent VAT).
All major credit cards are accepted. Breakfast is not included.
Tel: 7–3272–501–234
Fax: 7–3272–508–888

The Regent Almaty – Ankara Hotel *****
Rates vary from US$295 to US$2,050 (prices exclude 20 per cent VAT).
All major credit cards are accepted. Breakfast is not included.
Tel: 7–3272–503–710
Fax: 7–3272–582–100

Hotel Ambassador ****
Rates vary from US$130 to US$230, VAT excluded but breakfast is included.
Tel: 7–3272–696–583
Fax: 7–3272–696–441

Astana Hotel ****
Rates: double US$150, deluxe US$198. Prices include VAT, breakfast not included.
All major credit cards are accepted.
Tel: 7–3272–50–70–50
Fax: 7–3272–50–10–60

Hotel Dostyk (former Communist Party hotel)
Rates vary from US$110 to US$350, VAT and breakfast are included.
Mastercard, Visa, Diners Club are accepted.
Tel: 7–3272–63–65–55
Fax: 7–3272–63–09–94

Hotel Otrar (former Intourist hotel)
Rates vary from US$90 to US$250, VAT and breakfast included.
American Express and Visa are accepted.
Tel: 7–3272–33–00–76
Fax: 7–3272–33–20–56
When travelling to Astana, one has fewer options, but the following hotels are recommend by business travellers that have stayed in Astana.

Intercontinental Hotel *****
Rates start at US$260. (Prices exclude 20 per cent VAT).
All major credit cards are accepted. Breakfast is included.
Tel: 7–3172–39–10–05
Fax: 7–3172–39–10–10

Komfort Hotel
Rates start at US$144, including VAT.
All major credit cards are accepted. Breakfast is included.
Tel: 7–3172–37–10–30
Fax: 7–3172–37–10–21

For more information on hotels and restaurants, please contact PricewaterhouseCoopers in Almaty and ask for a copy of the PricewaterhouseCoopers Telephone Directory.

Business tips

Drivers
Drivers are a necessity for foreign business people in Almaty as business hours in Kazakhstan can be long and sometimes irregular. Drivers are most easily and reliably hired through the inviting organisation. Current rates are about US$10 to US$12 per hour or US$35 a day on a temporary

basis. Very few drivers speak English or any other western European language, although more and more do understand directions and one should be able to communicate without a translator.

It is possible to hire a car from AVIS (Tel: +7–3272–503–555; Fax: +7–3272–503–555). Payment can be made by major credit cards such as American Express, Visa, Diners Club, Master Card/Eurocard. Both the Hyatt Regency Almaty and the Regent Hotel have hotel cars available for personal hire. It is best to check the hourly and daily rates charged by each hotel.

Translators/Interpreters

Even moderately fluent Russian speakers sometimes find an interpreter useful in business negotiations. It is also becoming more and more important to have an interpreter who speaks both Kazak and Russian and can interpret actions as well as words. Interpreters could be best arranged through the inviting organisation, and cost between US$50 and US$100 per day.

Appointments

Appointments are generally kept in Kazakhstan unless there is a good reason for breaking them. However, in the business climate in Kazakhstan it happens frequently that a meeting is cancelled because other issues became even more urgent. Therefore, one should try not to schedule appointments more than two days in advance and confirm the appointment an hour before arrival.

Working hours

Standard working hours are nine to six, five days a week, with most people working a 41 hour week. Shops tend to be open late on weekdays and on Saturday, while a few are also open on Sunday. Most shops, offices and banks close for an hour or so during the day between 1.00pm and 4.00pm for lunch. Bazaars (baraholkas) are open every day from 9.00am until 5.00pm except Mondays.

Currency

Kazakhstan has a cash economy, and, except for some hotels and a few restaurants, there are few opportunities to pay with credit cards or travellers cheques. Most payments should be made in cash and *only in tenge*.

There are many foreign exchange points around, but it may be more reliable to use the banks or the hotels, where possible, since rates and security measures vary across the country. When changing money, worn or damaged bills must be avoided as most places accept only bills in good condition. US dollar bills, as well as the German mark bills, must be post-1990, ensuring that they have a metal strip encoded in them.

Automated teller machines (ATMs) can now be found in many places in Kazakhstan and especially in Almaty. ATMs dispense local currency and usually offer a reasonable rate of exchange.

Public Holidays
Before spending a lot of money for a round-trip ticket to Almaty, you should be aware of the following official Kazakhstani public holidays:

1 and 2 January	New Year
8 March	International Women's Day
22 March	Nauryz (Kazak New Year)
1 May	Labour Day, Day of Unity of the People of Kazakhstan
9 May	Victory Day
30 August	Constitution Day
25 October	Day of the Republic
16 December	Independence Day

Christmas and Easter are not public holidays in Kazakhstan.

Health

More often than not, a change in diet and partaking of the national custom, vodka, is the cause of stomach complaints in Kazakhstan. Visitors usually require a few days for acclimatisation. Although Kazakhstan citizens may believe that water out of the tap is safe, it is not recommended. Bottled water and soft drinks are readily available at stores and kiosks.

While Kazakhstan is presently not known to have any particular diseases, travellers planning to spend extended periods of time in the Republic should make sure that they are up to date with tetanus, rabies, hepatitis, polio, cholera, typhoid and encephalitis inoculations. Even for short visits, it is strongly advised to be appropriately vaccinated. Consult a doctor or a travel clinic before travelling to Kazakhstan, allowing time for vaccinations.

Foreigners are advised to bring ample supplies of required medications and their own syringes for use in an emergency, as these tend to be in short supply in Kazakhstan.

Safety

In any city where disparities in income levels are large, crime tends to be targeted at the (comparatively) wealthy and Kazakhstan is no exception. Recently, Kazakhstan has been experiencing an increase in cases of violent crime.

Foreign visitors are advised not to dress in a flamboyant fashion and to be discreet in their conduct. Hotel safes should be used, where possible, to avoid carrying excess sums of cash.

A couple of tips on modest behaviour and on avoiding difficult situations are provided below. These tips are only designed to alert the traveller, not to frighten him or her. Most Kazakhs are friendly and willing to help.

- *Walking in Almaty: Never* walk alone, especially at night. If someone walks toward you, stops in front of you and/or starts talking to you, *do not stop*. If somebody in front of you drops a wallet or anything valuable, *do not pick it up* or you may find yourself the target of a scam.

- *Staying in:* When staying in an hotel room or apartment, *never* open the door *to anyone* who is unfamiliar.

- *Driving:* While in a car, *always lock the doors* as soon as you get in and keep windows closed even if temperatures are high. Avoid driving late at night, especially in deserted areas.

- *Public places:* Always be alert when you are in public places and if you think the situation is suspicious, do not hesitate to alter your plans or route.

Almaty is no different from other big cities. If you are being attacked, just do what your assailants want. It is not worthwhile acting bravely, and you risk injuries trying to protect replaceable goods.

Customs and traditions

When invited by a Russian or Kazakh as a guest to their home, consider it an honour. Thus, it is impolite to decline an invitation. It is customary to bring something for the house and, if dinner is to be served (which is usually the case), something for the table. Shoes should be removed when entering the house. Greeting traditions, such as kissing each other or shaking hands, depend on the relationship with the host(s). If shaking hands, never do so over the doorstep.

Once seated at the dinner table, the host will likely offer a glass with vodka and will give a toast in the guest's honour. The host will likely toast the health of everyone present, as well. All guests are expected to give a speech. The guest should stand, hold the glass of vodka (or alternative) high and speak to the host of the table. Something should be said in honour of the host and/or hostess, wishing long and happy lives with family and friendship, complementing Kazakhstan, then followed by 'nazdarovje' and a sip, after which the speaker may sit down. 'Nazdarovje' means, in English: 'to your health'.

Stories abound about eating sheep heads and other pieces of meat to which many visitors are not accustomed. These menus may not be offered in the larger cities, like Almaty, because the hosts are usually aware that visitors are not familiar with these dishes. In rural areas, though, anticipate a menu including the native Kazakh dishes.

Language

The language spoken in business and daily life is Russian, although Kazakh is heard outside of the major cities. However, the Government has decreed that the legal language is Kazakh. Increasingly, Kazakh is taught in schools and children's nurseries.

It may be helpful to learn some Russian or Kazakh words. The Kazakhstani people seem to appreciate it when visitors show interest in their way of life and in communicating in the National (Kazakh) or common (Russian) language.

English:	*Russian*:	*Kazakh*:
Hello!	Zdrastwuytshe!	Assalam Alaikum!
How do you do?	Kak dyee la?	Kal Kalay?
Good bye!	Dosvedanya!	Saubol!
Thank you!	Spasiba!	Rakhmet!

Tips for a free afternoon

Even though business in Kazakhstan can be time consuming, your schedule may allow you to see something of the city. Here are some ideas:

Zilyony Bazaar: Zilyony Bazaar means Green Market, called this since it is largely a food market with quality caviar from the Caspian region. Some traditional Kazakhstan souvenirs may be found. Bargaining is common in this region. Always be aware of potential pickpockets.

Panfilov Park: Panfilov Park is downtown Almaty, near the Zelyony Bazaar. A memorial demonstrating a common Soviet design bears an eternal flame in commemoration of those who died during the civil war of 1917 and both World Wars.

In the centre of the park is the spectacular Panfilov Cathedral. Built out of wood, without nails, this cathedral survived a major earthquake at the beginning of the century. The Russian Orthodox Church restored the church in the early 1990s.

Medeo: This is the world's most famous open air skating rink on which 200 records have been broken. Situated within thirty minutes of Almaty, one can enjoy the breathtaking views all year.

Kok-Tu-Be Needle: Closer than Medeo, this television tower sits atop the hills to the east of Almaty. It has nice views and shashlyk (similar to kabobs) restaurants.

Appendix 3

Regions of Kazakhstan

Atyrau

Over the past few years most foreign companies have started their Kazakh activities in the old capital Almaty. Now expansion into, or moving into, the different regions is becoming a visible trend.

Being an oil-rich area, Atyrau is developing as a major hub for companies active in the oil and gas sector in Kazakhstan. The oil and gas sector is responsible for approximately 30 per cent of Kazakhstan's GDP and this percentage is expected to grow significantly over the years to come.

The economic activity in Atyrau and the Caspian region ranges from actual oil exploration and production to the supply of on- and off-shore services and materials including construction. Atyrau is together with Aktau one of the major ports on the Caspian sea. The main advantage of Atyrau over Aktau is the presence of an airport with (limited) international connections.

Formerly called Guriev, the region was established in January 1938 and renamed Atyrau in 1991. It covers 118,600 sq km with seven agricultural and two urban districts. The population encompasses 464,000 people, 58.9 per cent of which live in urban areas. The population density is low and averages 3.9 people per square kilometre.

The Atyrau region is the country's richest region in natural resources, especially in hydrocarbons. Development of the resource base in the area is closely related to high level deposits of oil and gas that may be classified into two groups.

The first group (Embinsk area) encompasses oil deposits at Dossor, Makat, Iskine, Baichunas, Munaily, etc. that have been developed since the beginning of this century. The economic significance of these onshore resources has been declining over the last decades.

The main attention of the business community attracted by the oil and gas development and production potential in the region, is focused on the second group comprising Tengiz, Korolevskoye, Ogaiskoye, and others. The Tengiz area, being the largest and richest area, represents the main layer of the country's newly born oil sector base. The aggregate volume of Tengiz and Korolevskoye is estimated at 25–50 billion barrels. Inderskoye, an area rich in ore such as anhydrides, lignite, brimstone and salt layers etc, is just one example of deposits of other natural resources in the region.

There is a meagre water supply in the region that is mainly provided by the Ural river and three other rivers – these are the Uil, Emba and Sagiz – running unused into the desert. Approximately 53 per cent of the local population are reportedly available in the labour market.

The railway is the main means of transportation and stretches out for 750 km in the region. The most important lines connect Atyrau–Oktyabrks, Atyrau–Ganyushkino–Astrakhan (Russia), Makat–Kulsary–Beneu.

Atyrau is also a seaport with connections to Astrakhan, Fort Shevchenko and Makhachkala (Russia), and Uralsk. There is a water pipeline supplying water to Makat and two oil pipelines connected to Russia, one running to Orsk and the other one to Alexandrov-Guy.

There is also the Uzen–Atyrau pipeline providing transportation of oil from all the oilfields of the Atyrau region to the Atyrau Refinery for blending and then export or swapping. The Atyrau–Samara (Russia) pipeline provides delivery of Western Kazakhstan blend to Samara. The Zhanazhol–Kenkiak–Orsk pipeline provides delivery of oil to the Orsk refinery (Russia). The Shymkent refinery (South Kazakhstan) is connected by railroad. There is also an airport operating in the city and a highway network.

Oblast administrations

Akmola oblast, Astana Sergei Vitalyevich Kulagin	Tel: 7-3172-32-04-32 Fax: 7-3172-32-35-31
Almaty oblast, Almaty Zamanbek Kalabayevich Nurkadilov	Tel: 7-3272-62-85-07 Fax: 7-3272-62-30-32
Aktyubinsk oblast, Aktyubinsk Aslan Yespulayevich Musin	Tel: 7-3132-54-47-58 Fax: 7-3132-57-41-05
Atyrau oblast, Atyrau Imangali Nurgalievich Tasbagambetov	Tel: 7-3122-22-21-36 Fax: 7-3122-22-45-97
Northern-Kazakhstan oblast, Oskemen Vitaliy Leonidovich Mette	Tel: 7-3132-66-33-10 Fax: 7-3232-66-13-63
Zhambyl oblast, Taraz Serik Abikenovich Umbetov	Tel: 7-3262-23-18-22 Fax: 7-3262-24-32-89
Eastern-Kazakhstan oblast, Uralsk Kabibulla Kabenovich Dzhakupov	Tel: 7-3122-22-40-13 Fax: 7-3112-22-06-26

Karaganda oblast, Karaganda
Mazhit Tuleubekovich Yesenbayev

Tel: 7-3212-42-10-60
Fax: 7-3212-42-10-52

Kostanay oblast, Kostanay
Umirzak Yestayevich Shukeyev

Tel: 7-3142-39-46-90
Fax: 7-3142-53-34-91

Kzylorda oblast, Kzylorda
Berdibek Mashbekovich Saparbayev

Tel: 7-3242-27-21-46
Fax: 7-3242-26-12-25

Mangistau oblast, Aktau
Lyazzat Ketebayevich Kiinov

Tel: 7-3292-33-45-12
Fax: 7-3292-43-45-52

Pavlodar oblast, Pavlodar
Galymzhan Badylzhanovich Zhakiyanov

Tel: 7-3182-32-33-35
Fax: 7-3182-32-32-06

Northern-Kazakhstan oblast, Petropavlovsk
Daniyal Kenzhetayevich Akhmetov

Tel: 7-3152-46-46-84
Fax: 7-3152-46-42-70

Southern-Kazakhstan oblast, Shymkent
Kalyk Abdullayevivh Abdullayev

Tel: 7-3252-44-45-44
Fax: 7-3252-44-68-77

Principal commodities produced in the oblasts

Akmola oblast

Motor vehicles
Concrete
Sodium bichromatum
Air or vacuum pumps
Ploughs and disc
  harrows
Clays and Kaolinum
Grit, road metal
Granite, sandstone
Animal and vegetable
  oils
Auric ore
Auric concentrate
Black coal
Calcium carbide
Ceramic tiles and
  flagstones
Bricks and products
  from clay
Sulphuric acid in

monohydrate
Confectionery and
  cakes
Tinned meat
Forage for animals
Groats
Timber, wooden
  railway sleepers
Spirits
Linoleum
Macaroni and flours
Molybdenic
  concentrate
Milk, cream, ice-cream,
  etc.
Flour
Sodium nitritums,
  Natrii phosphates
  and carbonates
Oxide of chrome

Windows, frames,
  doors
Plastic household
  articles
Bed-clothes
Natural sand
Sulphur
Sulphides, sulphates
Crackers and biscuits
Cheese and cottage
  cheese
Textiles
Knitwear
Ferrochrome silicon
Ferrochrome
Chromic anhydrate
Chromic hardener
Wool, raw hides and
  hides
Ethanol

Almaty oblast

Wines
Shingle, grit, road
   metal
Granite, sandstone
Games and toys
Insulated cables and
   cables, fibre optic
   cables
Clerk's and school
   accessories from
   plastics
Ceramic household
   products and
   decorations,
Porcelain, faience, and

majolica ware
Bricks and products
   from clay
Tinned meat
Animal feed
Timber, railway
   sleepers
Spirits
Macaroni and flours
Milk and cream
Flour
Cleared rice
Tinned fruit and nuts
Sugar
Lead in lead

concentrate
Zinc-lead ore
Cheese and cottage
   cheese
Wool cloths
Fruit and vegetable
   juices
Zinc in zinc
   concentrate
Shampoos, hair
   lacquers
Bay yarn
Accumulators
Ethanol

Aktyubinsk oblast

Instrumentation for
   disconnection of
   electric networks

Natural gas
Granite, sandstone
Wood furniture

Oil
Natural sand
Chromite ore

Atyrau oblast

Soft drinks
Petroleum
Natural gas
Gas-oils
Shingle, grit, road metal
Paraffin
Bricks and products
   from clay
Tinned fish

Tinned meat
Timber, railway
   sleepers
Furnace boiler oil
Ice-cream
Flour
Oil
Petroleum coke; oil
   asphalt

Detergents
Modular building
   constructions from
   concrete
Kitchen salt
Crude or non-refined
   sulphur
Hydrocarbon
   condensed gas

Northern-Kazakhstan oblast

Bicycles
Outer knitwear
Water meters
Shingle, grit, road
  metal
Gold
Auric ore
Games and toys
Household ceramic
  ware from porcelain,
  faience, and
  majolica
Bricks, tiles and
  products from clay
Sausages
Confectionery and

cakes
Tinned meat
Forage for animal
Central heating boilers
Timber, railway
  sleepers
Spirits
Tape recorders and
  other sound-track
  recorders
Macaroni and flours
Vegetable oil
Chalk and dolomite
Milk and cream
Flour
Footwear

Wooden windows,
  frames, doors
Elevators for liquids
Clothes from furs
Natural sand
Radio receivers
Silver
Butter
Cheese and cottage
  cheese
Centrifugal pumps for
  pumping liquids
Wool, raw hides and
  hides
Ethanol

Zhambyl oblast

Barytic ore
Gold
Auric ore
Auric concentrate
Chalk-stone and
  gypsum
Bricks and products
  from clay
Acid phosphoric
  thermal
Leather from hides
Forage for animal
Spirits

Linen-squash machines
Milk and cream
Flour
Meat and food by-
  products
Footwear
Bed-clothes
Clothes from furs
Sugar
Silver
Cheese and cottage
  cheese
Phosphatic raw

Yellow phosphorous
Phosphoric fertilisers,
  mineral or chemical
Cleaning pastes and
  powders
Shampoos, hair
  lacquers
Wool, raw hides and
  hides
Sausages
Ethanol

Eastern-Kazakhstan oblast

Instrumentation for the disconnection of electric networks (over 1000 V)
Soft drinks
Fibre optic cables
Shingle, grit, road metal
Clays and Kaolinum
Wood furniture
Auric ore
Auric concentrate
Insulated cables and cables
Black coal
Sausages
Confectionery and cakes
Tinned fish
Tinned meat
Forage for animal
Groats
Spirits
Macaroni and flours
Vegetable oil
Copper ore
Copper concentrate
Milk, cream, ice-cream
Flour
Natural sand
Zinc-lead ore
Lead concentrate
Butter
Crackers and biscuits
Cheese and cottage cheese
Zinc concentrate
Wool, raw hides and hides
Wool yarn
Electromotors (up to 37.5 Watts); DC generators
Ethanol

Karaganda oblast

Nitrogenous fertilisers, mineral or chemical
Barytic concentrate
Shingle, grit, road metal
Granite, sandstone
Iron oxide
Gold, refined gold
Auric ore
Chalk-stone and gypsum
Lime
Black coal
Calcium carbide
Bricks and products from clay
Sulphuric acid in monohydrate
Coke and half-coke from black coal, lignite or peat
Sausages
Confectionery from
chocolate and sugar, cakes
Tinned fish
Tinned meat
Forage for animal
Timber, railway sleepers
Mayonnaise
Macaroni and flours
Manganese ore
Manganese concentrate
Margaric commodity
Machines for mining industry
Medicines
Copper ore
Copper concentrate
Refined copper
Mineral soda waters
Milk, cream, ice-cream
Detergents
Flour
Windows, frames,
doors from wood
Flat section from iron or steel
Bed-clothes
Instruments for measurement of physical values
Instruments and instrumentation for auto-control or guidance
Zinc-lead ore
Lead concentrate
Silver
Steel
Crackers and biscuits
Ferrous metal tubes
Cement
Zinc concentrate
Cast iron
Hosiery

Kostanay oblast

Aluminium, alum earth
Instrumentation for
  disconnection of
  electric grids (up to
  1000 V)
Asbestos
Bauxite
Wines and vodkas
Shingle, grit, road
  metal
Clays and Kaolinum
Doors, windows,
  frames, jalousies
Wood furniture
Wood containers
Iron oxide
Chalk-stone and
  gypsum
Bricks, tiles, flagstones
Sausages
Confectionery and
  cakes

Tinned meat
Forages for animal
Timber, railway
  sleepers
Macaroni and flours
Vegetable oil
Machines for mining
  industry
Mineral soda waters
Milk, cream, ice-cream
Flour
Footwear
Iron-ore pellet
Beer
Elevators for liquids
Bed-clothes
Home appliances from
  plastics
Natural sand
Instruments and
  instrumentation for
  auto-control or

guidance
Trailers and semi-
  trailers, canisters
Modular metal
  construction
Crackers and biscuits
Cheese and cottage
  cheese
Textiles
School copybooks
Wool cloths
Knit tissues and
  knitwear
Fruit and vegetable
  juices
Centrifugal pumps for
  the pumping of
  liquids
Wool
Ethanol

Kzylorda oblast

Natural gas
Shingle, grit, road
  metal
Bricks, hardware
  products from clay
Sausages
Confectionery and
  cakes
Tinned meat
Boxes, crates and bags

from non-corrugated
  paper or cardboard
Spirits
Macaroni and flours
Milk and cream
Flour
Bonded fabrics and
  products from
  bonded fabrics
Petroleum

Footwear
Elevators for fluids
Tinned fish
Modular building
  constructions from
  concrete and metal
  constructions
Crackers and biscuits
Centrifugal pumps for
  pumping of liquids

Mangistau oblast

Nitrogenous fertilisers
Natural gas
Gas condensate
Granite, sandstone
Rock for building
Sausages
Tinned fish
Tinned meat
Paints and lacquers
    based on polymetric
    compounds

Mayonnaise
Milk, cream, yogurt
Marble
Petroleum
Footwear
Wooden windows,
    frames, doors
Beer
Styrene polymers
Bed-clothes
Natural sand

Modular building
    constructions from
    concrete and metal
    constructions
Cheese and cottage
    cheese
Textiles
Hydrocarbon
    condensed gases
Phosphoric fertilisers

Pavlodar oblast

Unmachined aluminium
Antifreeze compounds
Petroleum
Bulldozers
Vodka
Fibre optic cables
Gas-oils
Shingle, grit, road metal
Alum earth
Corrugated paper and
    cardboard
Fluid chlorine in vials
Chalk-stone and
    gypsum
Products from cement,
    concrete or artificial
    rock
Insulated cables and

cables
Inhibitors of
    precipitation of
    mineral salts
Black coal
Paraffin
Bricks and products
    from clay
Sausages
Tinned fish
Tinned meat
Forage for animal
Timber, railway
    sleepers
Lignite
Furnace boiler oil
Macaroni and flours
Furniture

Milk and cream
Flour
Semifinished meats
Wooden windows,
    frames, doors
Beer
Natural sand
Agricultural tractors
Lubricants
Kitchen salt
Cheese and cottage
    cheese
Ferromanganese
Ferromanganese silicon
Ferrochrome silicon
Ferrosilicon
Ferrochrome

Western-Kazakhstan oblast

Finished fur hides
Natural gas
Gas condensate
Tinned vegetables
Tinned meat
Groats
Timber, railway
  sleepers
Cast iron casting
Macaroni and flours
Vegetable oil

Medicines
Grinding balls,
  hardware for
  grinding mills, from
  cast steel and
  ferrous metals
Milk, cream, ice-cream
Flour
Semi-finished meat
Windows, frames,
  doors

Cleared rice
Tiles, flagstones,
  bricks, goods from
  cement, concrete or
  artificial rock
Clothes from furs
Cheese and cottage
  cheese
Tubes, hose pipes from
  plastics
Wool

Southern-Kazakhstan oblast

Petroleum
Household gas meters
Wines
Cotton filament
Paraffin
Bricks, tiles, and
  products from clay
Confectionery and
  cakes
Tinned meat
Tinned fruit and nuts
Forage for animal
Timber, railway
  sleepers
Asbestos-cement sheets

(slate)
Furnace boiler oil
Macaroni and flours
Vegetable oil (refined)
Medicines
Mineral soda waters
Milk and cream
Flour
Soap
Wooden windows,
  frames, doors
Beer
Bed-clothes
Clothes from furs
Lead, including

secondary
Silver
Cigars and cigarettes
Crackers and biscuits
Textiles
Cotton tissues
Transformers
Knitwear
Asbestos-cement tubes
  and clutches
Cement
Hosiery
Tyres for passenger
  cars and farming
  machines

Astana city

Motor vehicles for cargo
transportation
  Harrows, threshing
    machines,
    cultivators
  Outer knitwear
  Shingle, grit, road
    metal
  Doors, windows,
    frames, jalousies
  Wood furniture
  Artificial and natural
    porous fillers
  Bricks, tiles, and
    product from clay
  Sausages
  Confectionery and
    cakes

Tinned fish
Tinned meat
Forage for animal
Mowing-machines
Timber, railway
  sleepers
Mayonnaise
Macaroni and flours
Washing machines
Medicines
Mineral soda waters
Milk, cream, ice-cream
Flour
Semi-finished meats
Wooden windows,
  frames, doors
Beer
Elevators for liquids

Bed-clothes
Natural sand
Modular building
  constructions from
  concrete
Lighting and lighting
  facilities
Butter
Crackers and biscuits
Cheese and cottage
  cheese
Textiles
School copybooks
Centrifugal pumps for
  pumping liquids
Ethanol

Almaty city

Motor vehicles
Instrumentation for
  video recording or
  video play
Soft drinks
Concrete
Wines and vodkas
Shingle, grit, road metal
Wood furniture
Baking yeast
Games and toys
Bricks, tiles, and
  products from clay
Carpets and tapestry
Sausages
Confectionery, cakes
Tinned fruit and nuts
Forage for animal
Coffee and tea
Cryogen tanks

Mayonnaise
Macaroni and flours
Margarine
Washing machines
Medicines
Bags and bags from
  polymetric
  compounds of
  ethylene
Milk, cream, ice-cream
Soap
Canned meat
Meat and by-products
Wall paper
Footwear
Wooden windows,
  frames, doors
Bed-clothes
Postcards
Clothes from furs

Trailers and semi-
  trailers, canisters
Modular building
  constructions from
  concrete
Cigars and cigarettes
Crackers and biscuits
Electric meters
Cheese and cottage
  cheese
Television receivers
Commonplace-books
School copybooks
Cotton tissues
Knitwear products
Cotton yarn
Digital machines
Hats and headdress

Appendix 4

Business Organisations and Associations

Investment promotion organisations

Foreign Investors' Council

To emphasise the priority placed on improving the investment climate in Kazakhstan and the importance of developing the country's economic policies to encourage foreign direct investment, the President of the Republic of Kazakhstan signed a Decree on 30 June 1998, to establish a Foreign Investors' Council reporting directly to him.

The Councils's primary goals are:

- to place before the President proposals relating to the improvement of legislation governing investment matters and proposals relating to the implementation of large investment programmes and projects within Kazakhstan that are internationally significant;

- to make recommendations concerning the general improvement of the investment climate and the country's strategy for attracting foreign investments;

- to develop proposals for integrating the national economy into the world economic system.

The President guides the Council's activity, approves the agenda, and presides over the Council meetings.

The Council's current members are: the Prime Minister, the chairman of the Agency for Investments and senior government ministers. The Council also includes senior executives from foreign companies including ABN AMRO Bank, British Gas International, Chevron, Deutsche Bank AG, LNM, KPMG, Mitsubishi Corporation, Samsung, Tractebel International and from international finance organisations, including the first vice-president of the European Bank for Reconstruction and Development (EBRD).

Council meetings take place annually or biannually and proxies of companies and organisations not included in the Council's current composition can be invited to the meetings.

The Investment Agency of the Republic of Kazakhstan (ARKI) acts as the working body of the Council.

Investment Agency of the Republic of Kazakhstan (ARKI)

The ARKI is the only state body authorised to implement the State's direct investment stimulation policy. The ARKI took over this responsibility from the former State Committee of the Republic of Kazakhstan on Investments in January 1999 and continues to discharge the same basic functions. These are:

- organisation of operations to attract direct investments into the Republic;

- co-ordination of the activity of State bodies of the Republic of Kazakhstan pertaining to investment projects implemented by authorised investors;

- provision of all conciliatory and permissive documents, licences, visas, and other documents granting the necessary rights and powers for the implementation of each investment project;

- assistance to authorised investors in searching for qualified employees, goods and services in the Republic of Kazakhstan;

- monitoring the implementation of investment projects, including the supervision of investors to ensure that they meet their commitments.

In 1998, 75 contracts were entered into between the State Investments Committee and authorised investors, in priority sectors of the economy. As per the terms of the contracts, the investors undertook to make direct investments in projects within the Republic of Kazakhstan amounting to US$275.3 million (involving US$236.3 million of fixed capital investment), to create 4,394 new jobs and to preserve 6,101 jobs.

In 1998, the State Committee for Investments, as the working body of the government charged with licensing and subsoil management, issued 188 licences for exploration and mining of minerals, including 19 licences for raw hydrocarbons, 73 licences for solid minerals, and 96 licences for underground waters.

The ARKI now has sole responsibility for granting privileges to investors according to Table A.4.1.

Table A.4.1 Granting privileges to investors

No. Name of the Priority Sector of Economy	Total Volume of Investments, US$m	Exemption From		
		Income Tax (years)	Property Tax (years)	Land Tax (years)
1. Industrial infrastructure	Up to 2 inclusive	3	3	3
	From 2 to 4 inclusive	4	4	4
	From 4 to 6 inclusive	5	5	5
	From 6 to 8 inclusive	5+3 (at the rate up to 50%)	5+3 (at the rate up to 50%)	5+3 (at the rate up to 50%)
	From 8 to 10 inclusive	5+5 (at the rate up to 50%)	5+5 (at the rate up to 50%)	5+5 (at the rate up to 50%)
2. Processing industry	Up to 2 inclusive	3	3	3
	From 2 to 4 inclusive	4	3	4
	From 4 to 6 inclusive	5	5+1 (at the rate up to 50%)	4
	From 6 to 8 inclusive	5+3 (at the rate up to 50%)	5+4 (at the rate up to 50%)	5+2 (at the rate up to 50%)
	From 8 to 10 inclusive	5+5 (at the rate up to 50%)	5+5 (at the rate up to 50%)	5+5 (at the rate up to 50%)
3. Establishments in Astana City	Up to 2 inclusive	2	2	2
	From 2 to 4 inclusive	4	5	3
	From 4 to 6 inclusive	5+1 (at the rate up to 50%)	5+2 (at the rate up to 50%)	5
	From 6 to 8 inclusive	5+3 (at the rate up to 50%)	5+3 (at the rate up to 50%)	5+1 (at the rate up to 50%)
	From 8 to 10 inclusive	5+5 (at the rate up to 50%)	5+5 (at the rate up to 50%)	5+5 (at the rate up to 50%)

Table A.4.1 *continued*

No. Name of the Priority Sector of Economy	Total Volume of Investments, US$m	Income Tax (years)	Property Tax (years)	Land Tax (years)
			Exemption From	
4. Housing, establishments in the social sphere and tourism	Up to 2 inclusive	2	3	2
	From 2 to 4 inclusive	4	5	3
	From 4 to 6 inclusive	5+1 (at the rate up to 50%)	5+2 (at the rate up to 50%)	5
	From 6 to 8 inclusive	5+3 (at the rate up to 50%)	5+3 (at the rate up to 50%)	5+1 (at the rate up to 50%)
	From 8 to 10 inclusive	5+5 (at the rate up to 50%)	5+5 (at the rate up to 50%)	5+5 (at the rate up to 50%)
5. Agriculture	Up to 2 inclusive	4	4	5+5 (at the rate up to 50%)
	From 2 to 4 inclusive	5	5+2 (at the rate up to 50%)	5+5 (at the rate up to 50%)
	From 4 to 6 inclusive	5+1 (at the rate up to 50%)	5+3 (at the rate up to 50%)	5+5 (at the rate up to 50%)
	From 6 to 8 inclusive	5+3 (at the rate up to 50%)	5+4 (at the rate up to 50%)	5+5 (at the rate up to 50%)
	From 8 to 10 inclusive	5+5 (at the rate up to 50%)	5+5 (at the rate up to 50%)	5+5 (at the rate up to 50%)

Kazakhstan Investment Promotion Centre (Kazinvest)

In May 1998, the State Committee on Investments created the Kazakhstan Investment Promotion Centre (Kazinvest). Its activities are entirely associated with attracting investments into the economy of the Republic of Kazakhstan.

The main areas of Kazinvest responsibility are:

- elaboration and research of the domestic market and certain economic sectors in order to create a favourable investment climate;
- creation and maintenance of an informational database for investment projects;
- assistance to domestic producers in the search for investment partners, attracting investment resources (project financing) and assisting foreign and home investors to identify and select investment projects;
- creation of an investors assistance system to provide legal and registration assistance;
- participation in the implementation of joint investment projects;
- publicity and presentation measures, including communications via the mass media;
- organisation, collection, exchange and dissemination of information and the creation of relevant databases;
- provision of consulting, innovative, organisational and intermediary services for Kazakhstan and foreign legal advisers;
- establishment and development of economic, scientific and cultural relations between the state and international organisations and companies.

Kazinvest has already formed a database of investment projects, which includes over 400 projects that provide opportunities for investment.

Tacis (Technical Assistance for the Commonwealth of Independent States)

European Union Tacis programme for Kazakhstan

Since 1991, the European Union (EU) has been supporting the transition in the New Independent States and Mongolia. The EU's Tacis programme provides grant finance for the transfer of know-how to twelve countries of the former Soviet Union and Mongolia. In doing so, it fosters the development of market economies and democratic societies. It is the largest programme of its kind operating in the region and has launched more than 3,000 projects worth over 3 billion ECU since its inception in 1991.

Since 1991, Kazakhstan has received technical assistance worth more than 95 million ECU in areas such as private sector development, public administration reform, agriculture, energy and transport. The overall objective of the Tacis programme is to support the transformation of the political, social and economic situation in Kazakhstan in order to raise the standard of living and the quality of life of the local population. The guiding principle underlying the Tacis programme's funded actions is to support the macroeconomic and sectoral policies of the Kazakhstan authorities. Through negotiations with the Kazakhstan authorities, it was agreed that the priority areas within the Indicative Programme 1996–1999 were to support the main axes of the reform programme of the Kazakh government through giving assistance in Structural and Institutional Reform, Agriculture and Agro-industry and Development of Infrastructure. This did not rule out support for other projects if a particularly pressing need was identified and if such activity could be seen as complementary to the general thrust of political and economic reforms.

Currently, a new Indicative Programme is being prepared for the years 2000 to 2004. The new priorities proposed by the European Commission are a concentration of the assistance, support of the objectives of the Partnership and Co-operation Agreement (see below), to move from a demand driven to a dialogue driven programme, to increase promotion of investment and to increase the number of assistance instruments.

One of the priority sectors of the Tacis programme in Kazakhstan has been, and will most probably continue to be, private sector development. In Kazakhstan, private sector development has been supported through assistance to the restructuring of enterprises, assistance to the banking sector, assistance to the Agency for Investment, and support of the small- to medium-sized enterprise (SME) sector. Although assistance to the restructuring of enterprises, the banking sector and the investment agency are essential to private sector development, the following section concentrates on the SME sector. Problems of investors are often similar to problems of SMEs, though SMEs have more trouble fighting the constraints due to their size, their lack of possibilities accessing the Government, and their fragile position.

The SME sector in Kazakhstan

In the address of the President of the Republic of Kazakhstan to the people regarding the development strategy of the country until the year 2030, several priority directions for further development of the economy were stated, in particular in the sphere of small- and medium-sized enterprises. The SME sector is seen as a major area in helping to improve the unemployment situation and provide the Kazakhstan market with low-cost local food products and other consumer goods, as long as tax incentives and regular planning measures are implemented. The Government sees the development of the SME sector as a potential provider of growth for the economy and employment, and as a political target with regard to the formation of a middle class economy, as well as a guarantee to the continuation of the reform process.

According to the Ministry of State Revenue, small businesses make up a considerable portion of the economy of the Republic of Kazakhstan. The number of employees in small businesses constitutes more than 735,000 persons or over 3 per cent of the total number of the employed population. Currently more than 200,000 small business entities are registered, including 53,000 legal entities and 155,000 physical entities. The tax revenue is in excess of KZT22 million for the first half of 1999, amounting to 17.6 per cent of the total tax revenue for the budget.

Constraints in the development of the SME sector

There is no doubt that the government has understood the vital importance of the growth of the SME sector, and signs of willingness to improve the business environment have appeared, backed by a number of legal acts and regulations concerning SMEs. However, major constraints to the development of the SME sector remain, some of which are summarised below:

- Lack of a clear and stable legal environment, which is more a problem of implementation and communication, than of legislation. Laws and regulations are sometimes not published or not physically available, which makes it difficult for SMEs to know how to act. The other concern is that the local officials are unaware of the laws and/or are not instructed on how to implement them. Therefore there are inconsistencies in the implementation of these laws.

- Licensing, taxation and inspections are some of the major areas of concerns for SMEs who have problems with harassment in these areas. They do not know who to turn to and do not have the funds needed to defend themselves. Lack of confidence in the judicial system prevents the SMEs turning to it.

- Access to finance is also an essential issue, since the law concerning lending to SMEs (10 per cent) is not applied.

Tacis programme support to SME development

The Tacis programme has been supporting the SME sector since 1991, with the establishment of SME development facilities in Almaty and Aktyubinsk. The current on-going project concentrates on three main areas:

1. The Project Implementation Unit (PIU), based in Almaty and carrying out a regional programme through local tenders on business training, which give local SME/associations/organisations/consultancies the

opportunity to participate in open tender procedures, be trained by European experts and then forward the knowledge on to other local entrepreneurs;

2. Support to SMEDA (SME Development Agency) Aktyubinsk, which is providing support to SMEs in the regions, not only by helping to get access to finance, but also by giving support in improving their management capabilities and giving integrated assistance;

3. Policy advice to the Agency for Support for the Development of SMEs, which has now become the Agency for Regulation of Monopolies, Protection of Competition and Support for SMEs. The policy advice includes work by a European adviser on reviewing the government SME development strategy and the legal implementation, reviewing government regulations, suggesting improvements for taxation, licensing, franchising, leasing, registration, etc.

Technical assistance in these areas has not been easy, often due to institutional changes, which makes progress slow. However, it now seems that patience and work are beginning to pay off. On 6 July 1999, a new government inter-ministerial committee was established under the head of Deputy Prime Minister Pavlov, with the aim of co-ordinating SME policy between the different ministries and agencies. The Committee is set to meet once a month and each ministry or agency must provide an update to the Committee on how they have improved the environment for SME development. A Tacis adviser was invited to participate as a full member of the Committee. This gives the opportunity to receive first hand information, which is forwarded to the SME donor group (EBRD, USAID, UNDP, GTZ, IFC, Tacis). The SME donor group, who currently works on recommendations for improvement of the SME environment, will also channel common recommendations to the Committee. The results of the work of the government Committee remain to be seen, however coordination is seen as a first step in the right direction.

Signs and hopes for the future

Problems of SMEs can be compared with the problems of foreign investors. A Foreign Investors Council (FIC) was set up in July 1998 by presidential decree. Two high level meetings between members of the FIC, (12 main foreign investors) chaired by President Nazarbayev were held and a third meeting was scheduled for 3 December 1999. The objective of the FIC is to improve the business environment through recommendations on the legal and regulatory framework, taxation and image enhancement. Again, there seems to be strong political commitment to improve the environment for investors. As issues raised at these meetings also concern the SMEs, this would hopefully also have an impact on the SME environment.

On the EU side, a new approach will now be applied with the enforcement of the Partnership and Co-operation Agreement (PCA) with Kazakhstan. The PCA contains important provisions that entail the promotion of trade and investments in general with special regard to improvement of labour conditions, cross border supply of services, development of appropriate commercial rules and development of a transparent regulatory framework.

With these positive signs in mind, there seems to be hope for an improvement of the environment for the development of SMEs as well as for foreign investment. However, as with a transition to democracy, transition to a market economy is a very lengthy process.

The Union of Industrialists and Entrepreneurs

The Union of Industrialists and Entrepreneurs of Kazakhstan (UIEK) was established in September 1992 as a public, non-governmental agency, drawing together the majority of the country's large industrial enterprises and a number of associations.

The UIEK's main areas of activity are:

- active participation in the realisation of industrial policy and in the development of business;

- participation in legislative activity in close interaction with the state;

- relations with other bodies and public organisations;

- assistance with economic, trade, scientific and technical co-operation to foreign countries;

- management development and support of their business activity;

- protection of the rights and legal interests of members of the UIEK;

- development of a system of social partnership.

In pursuit of its working objectives, the UIEK directs it efforts towards:

1. Helping with the preparation and concluding of agreements (documents) with representatives of the government and trade unions.
2. Participating in the development of an optimal legislative and normative basis for business.
3. Assisting with the creation of effective mechanisms guaranteeing the observance of legitimacy in the field of business.
4. Assisting with the promotion of economic, trade, scientific and technical co-operation to foreign countries and establishing direct links between the management and business circles of Kazakhstan and of foreign states.

5. Promoting scientific research on business problems.
6. Promoting education among business circles.
7. Maintaining projects that can further Kazakhstan's science, engineering and technology strengths in internal and world markets and assisting members of the UIEK in mutually advantageous exchanges of patents, technologies and other items of intellectual property.
8. Organising independent public examinations for major administration regulations and other legal issues relating to business.
9. Providing members of the UIEK with legal, advisory and other help and with information on products and services.

Members of the UIEK can be citizens of the Republic of Kazakhstan or foreign citizens and must abide by the Charter of this organisation. The UIEK has the representations of all regional centres and industrial cities of Kazakhstan. Members of the UIEK take an active part in the work of state organisations, representing the interests of the UIEK in customs and tax committees, and at Ministry level for issues of social protection, power, industry and trade. The UIEK also works with the ARKI on the regulation of natural monopolies and the protection of competition, and with the Fund for the development of small business.

The authority of the UIEK is the Congress of the members of the UIEK, which selects the President and the Board. The executive management fulfils the everyday activities of the UIEK, and includes the following departments: legal, investment design, payments and UIEK and Business Centre functions.

Legal services

The legal department provides:

- consultations on legal aspects of industrial and enterprise activity;

- protection of rights of the industrialists and entrepreneurs that are members of the UIEK;

- independent expert appraisal of the administration's legal bills, acts and documents that regulate industrial and enterprise activity;

- participation in the preparation of agreements and contracts;

- assistance in the resolution of disputes between members of the UIEK and third parties.

Design investment

The design investment department renders services in the field of:

- investment policy;

- administrative and industrial consultancy;
- assistance in the determination of methods of economic development and their realisation.

The purpose of this service is to facilitate investment and financial support of business.

The design investment department carries out the:

- selection and analysis of investment projects;
- development of financing schemes for the projects;
- search for potential investors;
- development of business plans and feasibility reports for the projects;
- market research and marketing strategy.

The UIEK has an extensive data bank of investment projects in the priority areas of the economy that require financing, and which could be of interest to foreign investors. As the state's support of priority areas of the economy reduces investment risk, projects in these areas become more attractive for investment.

Payments (clearing) centre

The payment union (or clearing centre) provides the following services:
- holds accounts between firms that operate inside and outside Kazakhstan;
- monitors the circulation and holding of bills;
- acts as a guarantor;
- acts as the arbitration judge for parties.

Business centre

The business centre of the Union can organise business meetings and international conferences and can give support to businesses for their participation in exhibitions and fairs. It will also help firms find appropriate local and international business partners through the use of its extensive data bank.

The business centre carries out:

- consultations on problems of industrial and enterprise activity and development of recommendations to take into account conditions in the economy, in science and engineering, and of business activity in the market of production and services;

- promotion of direct ties between the members of the UIEK and business leaders of the Republic and of foreign states;

- the exchange of know-how to assist members of the UIEK in mutually advantageous sharing of patents and technologies;

- meetings, seminars, conferences;

- staff training;

- analysis of information about achievements in the spheres of science, engineering and technology;

- publicising information about the UIEK's activities in the media.

Thus, the UIEK represents the interests of the industrialists and business people working in Kazakhstan. With the intent of helping members of the UIEK develop mutually advantageous ties of co-operation with partners in CIS countries, the UIEK has signed agreements with similar organisations in Russia, Ukraine, Belorussia, Uzbekistan and Kyrgyzstan. It also has similar agreements with organisations in Moldova and Romania.

The UIEK is one of the founders of the International Congress of Industrialists and Entrepreneurs, on the Advisory Council of International Public Association 'EurAsia' and a member of the International Union of Commodity Producers.

The UIEK can help the industrialists and entrepreneurs of Great Britain with investments in priority areas, and in areas such as leasing, clearing, venture financing, and franchising amongst others.

Kazakhstan Petroleum Organisation
Suite 701, 38 Dostyk Avenue, Almaty, 480100, Kazakhstan. Contact: Aizhan Khamitova, KPA Administrative Coordinator. Tel: 7-3272-91-03-67. Fax: 7-3272-91-76-53. E-mail: kpa1@nursat.kz

Fitzgerald
Ablai Han Avenue, Astana, Kazakhstan. Contact: Richard Fitzgerald.
Tel: 7-3172-35-36-60. Fax: 7-3172-35-15-06

Gallaher
Contact: Roy Bolan. Tel: 7-3272-58-82-31/35. Fax: 7-3272-58-82-30

Globalink
Multimodal Transportation Systems. 90 Adi Sharipov Street, 480059 Almaty, Kazakhstan.
Direct Tel: 7-3272-58-88-81. Mobile: 7-3279-00-50-82. Tel: 7-3272- 58-88-80/67-27-97/67-27-47. Fax: 7-3272-58-88-85/67-27-58
Web Site: www.globalink.kz
Branches: Tashkent, Bishkek, Baku, Ashgabad, Dushanbe, Tibilisi and Yerevan

Godbeer
32 Nusupbekova Street, Almaty, Kazakhstan. Contact: James Godbeer.
Tel: 7-3272-30-43-92. Fax: 7-3272-30-25-38

Kabisco
60 Jibek Joloy St, Shymkent, Kazakhstan. Contact: Andrew Lister,
Tel/Fax: 7-3252-57-28-00

Scot Holland Estates
Suite 510, 81 Ablai Khan Street, Almaty, Kazakhstan. Contact: Roger
Holland. Tel: 7-3272-62-21-16. Fax: 7-3272-62-13-61

Tsessna
43 Mira Street, Astana, Kazakhstan. Contact: S. Dzhaksybekov (Chairman
of the Board). Tel: 7-3172-33-83-77. Fax: 7-3172-33-82-90

Bertra Poultry Farm
Pervomaiskyi, Kazakhstan. Contact: Bert Van Lier.
Tel: 7-3272-35-66-63. Fax: 7-3272-69-57-56

UKPF
Contact via the Kazakhstan Post Privatisation Fund, 64 Zhibek Zholy
Street, Kazakhstan.
Tel: 7-3272-33-13-57. Fax: 7-3272-50-39-09

Table A.4.2 Production infrastructure projects

No	Project	Object name	Project objective	Region	Investment volume ($US)	Payback period (years)
1	The Construction of lignite-fired power plant on the Mamytsky deposit basis	Kempirsaiskoe Mine JV	New power capacity establishment.	Aktubinsk	150 thousand	3
2	Almaty-Bystrovka motorway construction (Kemin)	State Company Road Department under the Ministry of Transportation	Uzun-Agash Bystrovka motorway construction to reduce the distance of the Silk Road by 200 km.	Almaty	230 million	6
3	400 kW low capacity power plant construction on the Tekes river	Kuat LTD LLP	Neighbouring production facility power supply and processed wool production cost reduction.	Almaty	14.8 million	10
4	Atyrau Airport JSC runway reconstruction	Atyrau Airport JSC	Airport capacity improvement to serve large-sized aircraft and helicopter services for the Caspian Sea Shelf exploration.	Atyrau	61.56 million	4.5
5	Atyrau River Terminal JSC reconstruction, cargo processing capacity 1 million tons	Atyrauozenport JSC	Port infrastructure and mooring system modernisation, sea trade-port terminal construction for oil products loading-unloading and sea trade status.	Atyrau	100.3 million	4–5
6	Charskaya – Usk-Kamenogorsk new rail line construction	Express OJSC	New railway construction to reduce distance by 320 km and freight tariff by 20%.	Eastern-Kazakhstan	139.6 million	8.5

Table A.4.2 continued

No	Project	Object name	Project objective	Region	Investment volume ($US)	Payback period (years)
7	Kzyl-Orda – Zhezkazgan new railway construction	State Enterprise Kzyl-Orda Railway Branch	Rail connection between Kzyl-Orda and Zhezkazgan.	Kzyl-Orda	60 million	6
8	Kzyl-Orda – southern frontier Bukhara motorway construction	Kzyl-Orda Zholdary OJSC	Construction of the Kzyl-Orda – frontier railway to reduce the international rail route Russia – Kazakhstan–Uzbekistan by 445 km.	Kzyl-Orda	245 million	6
9	TEZ-2 second stage construction completion	Akmola TEZ-2 AOOT	Power plant capacity upgrade by 185MW and heating by 280 Gcal.	Akmola	47.7 million	—
10	Woollen fabrics production establishment	Kargaly JSC	Product quality and range improvement.	Almaty	13.5 million	7
11	Bathroom appliance manufacturing	Temir-Khamet JV	Production modernisation to improve the product quality.	Almaty	5.2 million	3
12	Lithography tin manufacturing	Arman JSC	Tin production equipment purchasing and installation.	Almaty	0.55 million	1
13	Manufacturing of heavy-wall pipes, portable irrigation units, metal items	Ushtobinsk Research Mechanical Plant JSC	Modernisation in order to improve the pipe product and other steel product range.	Almaty	2.0 million	4
14	Air conditioner manufacturing	Shelf JSC	Satisfy demands of the consumers.	Atyrau	1.5 million	2
15	Brewery workshop reconstruction	Atyraupivo JSC	Brewery facility modernisation in order to improve the output quality and range.	Atyrau	1.4 million	1

Table A.4.2 continued

No	Project	Object name	Project objective	Region	Investment volume ($US)	Payback period (years)
16	Garbage processing complex construction	Parasat JSC	Development of a short-term and highly profitable production, based on waste material recycling, to produce consumer goods, having no analogue in Almaty and Kazakhstan.	Almaty	17.8 thousand	6
17	Diesel engine manufacturing development	Kostanaidisel AOOT	Meeting the local market demand for diesel engines and spare parts for agriculture.	Kostanay	8.5 thousand	4
18	Non-alcoholic beverage and beer production	Rosa OJSC	State investment attraction to purchase the bottling line and plastic bottle production equipment.	Pavlodar	1.3 million	2.7
19	Scrap metal recycling, welding rod manufacturing and marketing	Vtorchermet CJSC	Welding rod output growth.	Pavlodar	1 million	10
20	DT-75 and T-95 tractor transmission manufacturing establishment	Kazakhstantractor OJSC	Supply of Kazakhstantractor OJSC with transmissions to manufacture DT-75 and T-95 tractors, currently imported from Russia; Additional job opportunity creation; Domestic currency circulation improvement.	Pavlodar	2.5 thousand	3.1

Table A.4.2 continued

No	Project	Object name	Project objective	Region	Investment volume ($US)	Payback period (years)
21	High capacity vehicle-based crane manufacturing using existing 16-ton crane manufacturing facilities	Pavlodar Machinery Building Plant JSC	Product range and quality improvement.	Pavlodar	235.5 thousand	1
22	Universal wheel plough tractor manufacturing 1.4-2. (MTZ-80.1, MTZ-82.1 type)	Kazakhstantractor OJSC	Providing the national agricultural sector with universal tractors with the capacity of 1.4-2 T.S., currently imported; New job opportunities creation; Domestic currency circulation improvement.	Pavlodar	50.1 thousand	5.4
23	T-95 universal cat tractor manufacturing	Kazakhstantractor OJSC	Kazakhstan-made product international market competitive efficiency improvement; Tractor market expansion to Cemtral Asia; Local market supply with universal cat tractors with the capacity of 4 T.S.	Pavlodar	102.2 thousand	2.5
24	Garbage processing plant construction	State Enterprise, Gorkomunkhoz	City environment situation improvement through dump elimination.	Akmola	51.3 million	—

Table A.4.2   continued

No	Project	Object name	Project objective	Region	Investment volume ($US)	Payback period (years)
ASTANA SITES						
25	Third water pipeline from the Vyacheslav water facility to pumping station	Akmola-Realty UKS	Meeting of the growing municipal water supply demand using the Vyacheslav water storage facility capacities.	Akmola	64 million	—
26	Decoration brick production facility	Akmola Fund CJSC	Decorative brick manufacturing for the Astana construction industry.	Akmola	10 million	10
27	Technology pool establishment	Akmola Fund CJSC	Establishment of the technical pool facilities with incentive taxation. Low capacity plants construction and imported equipment purchasing.	Akmola	200.3 thousand	—
28	Power transmission facility 110/10 kVA	Gorelectroseti AOOT	Housing and social sphere facility power supply.	Akmola	14 million	—
29	Second water pipeline construction from Nura-Ishum channel pumping station to municipal filter station with overflow duck and sanitary zone establishment	Akmola Realty UKS	Municipal water-supply improvement, reliable and effective water distribution to meet the growing consumption.	Akmola	13 million	—

Table A.4.2 continued

No	Project	Object name	Project objective	Region	Investment volume ($US)	Payback period (years)
30	Glass container and glass sheet production facility	Akmola Fund CJSC	Due to the construction industry activation of the capital status there is a high glass product demand. The import-substituting production development.	Akmola	10 million	—
	Housing, Social sphere and Tourism objects					
31	Turgen Ski Base with 250 customer capacity	Silk Road Kazakhstan National Company	Development of a tourist complex and infrastructure construction. The Silk Road revitalisation programme.	Almaty	4.5 million	4–5
32	Alakol Fitness Centre with 100-customer capacity	Silk Road Kazakhstan National Company	Creation of a tourist base, road and engineering facility construction.	Almaty	650 thousand	4–5
33	Nazugum Sanatorium construction	Zhibek Zholy LLP	Sanatorium inclusion into organised tour programmes to attract tourists. The Silk Road revitalisation programme.	Almaty	625 thousand	5
34	100-customer hotel construction	Zhibek Zholy LLP	Hotel inclusion into organised tour programmes to attract tourists. The Silk Road revitalisation programme.	Almaty	5 million	3
35	Talkhis Tourist Ethnography Complex construction	Zhibek Zholy LLP	Tourist ethnography complex inclusion into organised tour programmes to attract tourists.	Almaty	1.25 million	5
36	Individual cottage construction in VIP village	Akmola Fund CJSC	Providing the international standard lifestyle and security conditions for Astana-based diplomatic missions.	Akmola		—

Table A.4.2   continued

No	Project	Object name	Project objective	Region	Investment volume ($US)	Payback period (years)
37	Municipal housing facility construction in Astana	Asainov and K Industrial Cooperative	Available housing construction (only $US300/sq m) for Astana residents whose housing facilities are due for demolition in accordance with the capital reconstruction plan.	Pavlodar	400 thousand	1.5
AGRICULTURE						
38	Deep grain processing facility construction in Lisakovsk	Arai CJSC	Additional tax incomes and job opportunities establishment.	Kostanay	400 million	4
39	Granulated grain base manufacturing	Arai CJSC	10 additional job opportunities creation.	Kostanay	133 million	2.5
40	Preservation of Auliekosky livestock breed	Moskalevsky Breeding Plant JSC	Preservation and improvement of the Auliekol meat producing livestock. Establishment of the reliable forage base.	Kostanay	200 thousand	3.3
41	Grain processing	Torgai un LLP	Flour product supplies.	Kostanay	40 thousand	2
42	Grain production	Uaisov's farm	Bakery product supplies.	Kostanay	25 thousand	2

Kazakhstan Petroleum Association

The Kazakhstan Petroleum Association (KPA) is an industry forum created for the sharing of non-proprietary information with the goal of facilitating the exploration and production activities of the petroleum industry in Kazakhstan. The organisation initially started out as the informal monthly lunch meeting of interested companies and gradually grew enough to warrant a formal organisation.

We became a registered legal entity in Kazakhstan in March 1998 and established our office at the following address: Suite 701, 38 Dostyk Avenue, Almaty, 480100, Kazakhstan. Our contact is Aizhan Khamitova, KPA Administrative Coordinator, phone number is 7-3272-91-03-67, fax number: 7-3272-91-76-53. E-mail address: kpa1@nursat.kz.

We have several subcommittees that cover areas such as Finance and Tax, Human Resources, HSE, Aviation and External Affairs that are formed on an as-needed basis to focus on specific areas of interest or issues. The members of these subcommittees work on a voluntary basis. Two of the more active subcommittees are the Human Resources subcommittee and the Tax and Finance subcommittee.

The Association elects the Chairman, Secretary and Treasurer of the organisation, who are representatives of the KPA and that form the Board of the Association. Our current officers are: Chairman, David D. Skeels of BG International; Secretary, Gonzague Desforges of Totalfina; and Treasurer, Charles Cram of Mobil.

Members must be petroleum companies with exploration and production activities and must either have an upstream (exploration and production) asset in Kazakhstan and/or have a registered legal entity with a full time representative in Kazakhstan. Members include both Kazakhstani and foreign companies.

We continue to focus on being a forum for information exchange and are also currently addressing several issues of broad interest such as: aviation safety, issues of work permits, visas and OVIR registration, and human resources issues.

Among the major problems that KPA faces is access to up-to-date information in a rapidly changing business environment. KPA can, and does, help in informing the membership on changes in government, legislation and regulations taking place. Other problems faced by the companies have operational or business aspects and, therefore, must be addressed by individual companies.

KPA constantly looks to the future. We have already started a guest speaker programme, and plan more. Also it is likely that we will serve as a common point for translations of various documents, and perhaps assemble a database of oil and gas industry support services and other items. We also plan to co-ordinate with other similar organisations related to mining, etc, as well as continue our contacts with International Tax and Investment Center (ITIC), Kazakhstan Mineral Taxation Committee (KMTC) and other such organisations. The 32 members are looking forward to working closely for the further development of relationships with the Governmental Agencies and Committees, other oil and gas and service companies.

Current KPA members

Agip, Amerada Hess (Kazakhstan) Ltd., Anglo-Caspian Oil, BP-Amoco, BG International, Central Asia Oil, Chevron Munaigas, CNPC International, Exxon Ventures (CIS), First International Oil Corporation, Hurricane Kumkol, JNOC, Karachaganak Petroleum Operating, Kazakhoil, KazakTurkMunai, KCS JSC, Mobil Oil Kazakhstan, Nimir Petroleum Bars B.V., Almaty, OKIOC, ONGC/ISPAT, KerrMcGee Corporation (merged with Oryx Energy Co), Phillips Petroleum Company Kazakhstan, Preussag Energie, Repsol Exploracion Kazakhstan SA, Shell Business Development Central Asia B.V., Tengizchevroil, Tepco, Texaco Petroleum, Total Kazakhstan, Nations Energy, Union Texas Central Asia Ltd., Veba ™el Kasachstan Gmbh.

For more detailed information, please call Aizhan Khamitova, Administrative Coordinator on phone 7-3272-91-03-67, fax 7-3272-91-76-53, or e-mail: kpa1@nursat.kz.

Appendix 5

Sources of Further Information

United Kingdom contacts

Association of British Chambers of Commerce (ABCC)
4 Westwood House
Westwood Business Park
Coventry CV4 8HS
United Kingdom
Tel: + 44 24 7669 4484
Fax: + 44 24 7669 5844

British Council
10 Spring Gardens
London SW1A 2BN
United Kingdom
Tel: + 44 20 7930 8466
Fax: + 44 20 7839 6347

British Invisibles
Windsor House
39 King Street
London EC2 8DQ
United Kingdom
Tel: + 44 20 7600 1198
Fax: + 44 20 7606 4248

City Network for East-West Trade (CeeNet)
Warnford Court
Throgmorton Street
London EC2N 2AT
United Kingdom
Tel: + 44 20 7638 9299
Fax: + 44 20 7588 8555

Confederation of British Industry (CBI)
Centre Point
103 New Oxford Street
London WC1A 1DU
United Kingdom
Tel: + 44 20 7379 7400
Fax: + 44 20 7240 1578

Customs and Excise
Dorset House
Stamford Street
London SE1 9PY
United Kingdom
Tel: + 44 20 7202 4687
Fax: + 44 20 7202 4131

Department for International Development
The Know How Fund
Central and South Eastern Europe Department
Room J1/6A
24 Whitehall
London SW1A 2ED
United Kingdom
Tel: + 44 20 7210 0029/65
Fax: + 44 20 7210 0030

British Trade International Export Publications
Admail 528
London SW1W 8YT
United Kingdom
Tel: + 44 20 7510 0171
Fax: + 44 20 7510 0197

East European Trade Council (EETC)
Suite 10
Westminster Palace Gardens
Artillery Row
London SW1P 1RL
United Kingdom
Tel: + 44 20 7222 7622
Fax: + 44 20 7222 5359

Export Market Information Centre (EMIC)
British Trade International
1st Floor
Kingsgate House
66–74 Victoria Street
London SW1E 6SW
United Kingdom
Tel: + 44 20 7215 5444/5
Fax: + 44 20 7215 4231

World Aid Section
British Trade International
Kingsgate House
66–74 Victoria Street
London SW1E 6SW
United Kingdom
Tel: + 44 20 7215 6157
Fax: + 44 20 7215 4231

European Bank for Reconstruction and Development (EBRD)
One Exchange Square
London EC2A 2EH
United Kingdom
Tel: + 44 20 7338 6000
Fax: + 44 20 7338 7892

European Investment Bank
London Office
68 Pall Mall
London SW1Y 5ES
United Kingdom
Tel: + 44 20 7343 1200
Fax: + 44 20 7930 9929

The International Finance Corporation
European Office
4 Millbank
London SW1P 3JA
United Kingdom
Tel: + 44 20 7222 7711
Fax: + 44 20 7976 8323

London Chamber of Commerce and Industry
69 Cannon Street
London EC4N 5AB
United Kingdom
Tel: + 44 20 7248 4444
Fax: + 44 20 7489 0391

Technical Help to Exporters
British Standards Institute
389 Chiswick High Road
London W4 4AL
United Kingdom
Tel: + 44 20 8996 9000
Fax: + 44 20 8996 7400

Kazakhstan contacts

Ministries

Ministry of Agriculture
49 Abay Street
Astana 473000
Tel: (3172) 321 882, 323 763
Fax: (3172) 323 239

Ministry of Defence
49 Auezov Street
Astana 473000
Tel: (3172) 328 079, 328 085
Fax: (3172) 328 073

Ministry of Ecology and Natural Resources
81 Karl Marx Street
Kokshetau 475000
Tel: (31622) 54 265
Fax: (31622) 52389

Ministry of Education, Culture and Health
57a 9th May Street
Astana 473011
Tel: (3172) 753 149, 241 801
Fax: (3172) 751 929

Ministry of Energy, Industry and Trade
37 Beybytshilik Street
Astana 473022
Tel: (3172) 337 133, 337 134
Fax: (3172) 337 164

Ministry of Finance
60 Republic Avenue
Astana 473000
Tel: (3172) 280 065, 280 985
Fax: (3172) 280 321

Ministry of Foreign Affairs
10 Beybytshilik Street
Astana 473000
Tel: (3172) 327 567, 391 239, 321 452
Fax: (3172) 327 667

Ministry of Information and Public Consent
22 Beybytshilik Street
Astana 473000
Tel: (3172) 322 495
Fax: (3172) 323 291

Ministry of Internal Affairs
4 Manas Street
Astana 473000
Tel: (3172) 341 242, 343 601
Fax: (3172) 341 738

Ministry of Justice
45 Pobeda Avenue
Astana 473000
Tel: (3172) 391 213, 261 434
Fax: (3172) 321 554

Ministry of Labour and Social Protection
36a Jeltoksan Street
Astana 473000
Tel: (3172) 263 327, 326 683
Fax: (3172) 322 691

Ministry of Science
28 Shevchenko street
Almaty 480021
Tel: (3272) 623 896, 695 066
Fax: (3272) 696 116

Ministry of Transport and Communication
49 Abylai Khan Avenue
Astana 473000
Tel: (3172) 326 277
Fax: (3172) 326 288

Government bodies

Committee of the Republic of Kazakhstan on Emergency Cases
300 Baizakov Street
Almaty 480090
Tel: (3272) 695 511, 673 811
Fax: (3272) 470 918

Export-Import Bank of Kazakhstan
118 Pushkin Street
Almaty 480021
Tel: (3272) 622 815, 509 602,633 767, 634 300
Fax: (3272) 507 549
E-mail: eximbalm@sovam.com
KAZAKTELECOM
86 Abylai Khan Avenue
Almaty 480091
Tel: (3272) 695 546, 620 541, 620 888
Fax: (3272) 532 397

KazatomProm
168 Bigenbay Batyr Street
Almaty 480012
Tel: (3272) 675 306, 625 425
Fax: (3272) 503 541

Kazakhgas (Republic Company)
46 Baytursynov Street
Almaty 480012
Tel: (3272) 679 717, 679 714
Fax: (3272) 679 700

Kazakhoil
142 Bogenbay Batyr Street
Almaty 480091
Tel: (3272) 696 903, 626 080
Fax: (3272) 695 405

KaztransOil
Room 301, 84a Gogol Street
Almaty 480091
Tel: (3272) 503 316, 626 080, 611 248
Fax: (3272) 503 939

KEGOC
162 'zh', Shevchenko Street
Almaty 480008
Tel: (3272) 680 329
Fax: (3272) 684 308

National Bank of Kazakhstan (Central Bank)
21 Koktem–3, Satpaev Street
Almaty 480090
Tel: (3272) 479 280, 473 797
Fax: (3272) 479 132

National Statistics Agency
125 Abay Avenue
Almaty 480008
Tel: (3272) 621 323,421 461
Fax: (3272) 420 824

Republic Corporation 'TV and Radio of Kazakhstan'
55a Moskovskaya Street
Astana 473000
Tel: (3172) 327 205
Fax: (3272) 327 205

State Customs Committee
166 Pushkin Street
Astana 473000
Tel: (3172) 750 447
Fax: (3172) 753 109

State Investment Committee
10 Beybytshilik Street
Astana 473000
Tel: (3172) 391 270
Fax: (3172) 391 270

Strategic Planning and Reforms Agency
2 Beybytshilik Street
Astana 473000
Tel: (3172) 326 388, 324 259
Fax: (3172) 326 358

Business organisations

KASE (Kazakhstan Stock Exchange)
67 Aiteke bi Street
Almaty 480091
Tel: (3272) 639 898
Fax: (3272) 638 980
Website www.kase.kazecon.org

AFINEX (Almaty Financial Instruments Exchange)
21 Koktem–3
Almaty 480090
Tel: (3272) 476 083, 509 308
Fax: (3272) 478 482
E-mail: nwave@kise.almaty.kz

American Chamber of Commerce in Kazakhstan
531 Seyfullin Avenue
Almaty 480091
Tel: (3272) 636 818
Fax: (3272) 633 805

Chamber of Commerce and Industry of the Republic of Kazakhstan
26 Masanchi Street
Almaty 480091
Tel: (3272) 670 052, 677 832
Fax: (3272) 507 029
E-mail: tpprkaz@online.ru

Kazakhstan Business Service Foundation
58a Ablay Khan Avenue
Almaty 480090
Tel: (3272) 336 933, 334 955
Fax: (3272) 339 482

Kazakhstan Investment Promotion Centre (Kazinvest)
State Investment Committee
77, Ablay Khan Avenue
Almaty 480007
Tel: (3272) 69 22 97, 62 37 50, 62 52 97, 50 12 77
Fax: (3272) 69 22 37
E-mail: kazinvest@kazinvest.kz

Agency of the Republic of Kazakhstan on Investments
10 Beibitshilik Street,
Astana 473000
Tel: (3172) 39 12 61
Fax: (3172) 39 12 70

Venture capital firms in Kazakhstan

Kazakhstan Post Privatisation Fund (Eagle Venture Partners)
Contacts: Greg Curtis, Alessandro Manghi, Yelena Yunusova, Irina
Sokolovskaya, Talgat Kukenov, Indira Nazhmidenova
Tel: 7 (3272) 33 13 57; 33 57 46; 33 55 82
Fax: 7 (3272) 50 39 09
E-mail: gimv@kazfund.almaty.kz

AIG Silk Road Fund
Contacts: Scott Foushee
Tel: 7 (3272) 608 273
Fax: 7 (3272) 608 272

Central Asian American Enterprise Fund
Contact: John Owens
Tel: 7 (3272) 63 88 15
Fax: 7(3272) 69 45 89

Kazakhstan Investment Fund
Contact: Javier del Ser
Tel: 7 (3272) 50 37 23
Fax: 7(3272) 62 89 03

(www.kazecon.kz) The state Agency for Investments under the Ministry of Foreign Affairs is a good starting point and can be accessed through the following website (www.kazinvest.kz). Other information about the economic and market situation in Kazakhstan can be accessed through (www.kazecon.kz). The state Agency on Statistics responds to formal inquiries for information, and if a business depends on imports or any major shipping of goods, it makes sense to contact the Customs Committee and deal through a licensed customs broker.

The Umit has its own website: http: //www.umit.kz.

Overseas embassies and consulates of the Republic of Kazakhstan

Europe

1. AUSTRIA (Vienna)
Saginbek Tokabayevich Tursunov
Code: 8 10 431 Tel: 367 68 93; 367 61 74 Fax: 367 68 95

2. THE KINGDOM OF BELGIUM (Brussels)
Ahmetzhan Yesimovitch Smagulov
Code: 8 10 322 Tel: 374 95 62; 374 15 90; 374 08 95 Fax: 374 50 91

3. THE UNITED KINGDOM OF GREAT BRITAIN AND NORTHERN IRELAND (London)
Kanat Bekmurzayevich Saudabayev
Code: 8 10 44 171 Tel: 581 46 46 Fax: 584 84 81

4. THE REPUBLIC OF HUNGARY (Budapest)
Tuleutai Skakovich Suleimenov
Code: 8 10 361 Tel: 275 13 00; 275 13 01 Fax: 275 20 92

5. THE FEDERAL REPUBLIC OF GERMANY (Bonn)
Yerik Magzumovich Asanbayev
Code: 8 10 49228 Tel: 923 80 11; 923 80 13 Fax: 923 80 25

6. THE REPUBLIC OF ITALY (Rome)
Olzhas Omarovich Suleimenov
Code: 8 10 396 Tel: 308 891 07 Fax: 308 891 03; 688 913 60

7. THE REPUBLIC OF LITHUANIA (Vilnius)
Ikram Adyrbekovich Adyrbekov
Code: 8 0122 Tel: 22 21 23 Fax: 23 37 01

8. THE REPUBLIC OF FRANCE (Paris)
Nurlan Zhumagalievich Danenov
Code: 8 10 331 Tel: 456 152 06; 456 152 00 Fax: 456 152 01

The United States of America

9. THE UNITED STATES OF AMERICA (Washington)
Bolat Kabdylkhamitovich Nurgaliev
Code: 8 10 1202 Tel: 232 54 88 Fax: 232 58 45

10. THE UNITED NATIONS ORGANISATION (New York)
Akmaral Khaidarovna Arystanbekova
Code: 8 10 1212 Tel: 230 19 00; 230 13 97; 230 11 92 Fax: 230 11 72

The States of the Middle East and Asia

11. THE ARABIAN REPUBLIC OF EGYPT (Cairo)
Bolatkhan Kulzhanovich Taizhan
Code: 8 10 202 Tel: 519 45 22 Fax: 519 45 22

12. THE ISLAMIC REPUBLIC OF IRAN (Tehran)
Vyacheslav Hamenovich Gizzatov
Code: 8 10 9821 Tel: 256 53 71; 256 59 33; 256 59 34 Fax: 254 64 00

13. THE STATE OF ISRAEL (Tel Aviv)
Barganym Sarievna Aitimova
Code: 8 10 9723 Tel: 523 67 76; 523 67 58 Fax: 523 90 45

14. THE KINGDOM OF SAUDI ARABIA (Riyadh)
Bagdad Kultayevich Amreyev
Code: 8 10 9661 Tel: 454 86 60 Fax: 454 77 81

15. THE REPUBLIC OF TURKEY (Ankara)
Baltash Modabayevich Tursumbayev
Code: 8 10 1202 Tel: 441 23 02 Fax: 441 23 03; 679 34 26

Asia

16. THE REPUBLIC OF INDIA (Delhi)
Askar Orazalievich Shakimov
Code: 8 10 9111 Tel: 688 14 61; 611 60 65 Fax: 688 84 64

17. THE PEOPLE'S REPUBLIC OF CHINA (Beijing)
Kuanysh Sultanovich Sultanov
Code: 8 10 8610 Tel: 653 264 29; 653 261 82 Fax: 653 261 83

18. THE REPUBLIC OF SOUTH KOREA (Seoul)
Tulegen Tlekovich Zhukeyev
Code: 8 10 822 Tel: 548 14 15; 516 14 40 Fax: 548 14 16

19. THE FEDERATION OF MALAYSIA (Kuala Lumpur)
Amangeldy Zhumabayevich Zhumabayev
Code: 8 10 603 Tel: 248 41 44; 248 73 76; 248 78 74 Fax: 248 85 53

20. THE ISLAMIC REPUBLIC OF PAKISTAN (Islamabad)
Tamas Kalmukhambetovich Aitmukhambetov
Code: 8 10 9251 Tel: 26 29 26; 26 17 97 Fax: 26 28 06

21. JAPAN (Tokyo)
Tleukhan Tlekovich Kabrakhmanov
Code: 8 10 813 Tel: 379 152 75; 379 152 73/74 Fax: 379 152 79

The CIS

22. THE AZERBAIJAN REPUBLIC (Baku)
Rashid Tururovich Ibrayev
Code: 8 8922 Tel: 90 62 48/49; 90 65 21 Fax: 275 200 92

23. THE REPUBLIC OF BELARUS (Minsk)
Vladimir Ivanovich Alesin
Code: 8 0172 Tel: 33 48 10; 39 12 80; 34 99 37 Fax: 34 96 50

24. THE KYRGYZ REPUBLIC (Bishkek)
Mukhtar Shakhanovich Shakhanov
Code: 8 3312 Tel: 22 55 71; 66 02 72; 66 04 15 Fax: 22 54 63

25. THE RUSSIAN FEDERATION (Moscow)
Tair Aimukhametovich Mansurov
Code: 8 095 Tel: 208 98 52; 927 18 20 Fax: 208 26 50

26. TURKMENISTAN (Ashgabat)
Valeriy Batayevich Temirbayev
Code: 8 363 Tel: 39 55 48; 39 58 24 Fax: 39 59 32
27. THE REPUBLIC OF UZBEKISTAN (Tashkent)
Umirzak Uzbekovich Uzbekov
Code: 8 371 Tel: 133 58 06; 133 59 44 Fax: 133 60 22

28. THE UKRAINE (Kiev)
Nazhmeden Iksanovich Iskaliev
Code: 8 044 Tel: 213 11 98; 247 11 33 Fax: 213 11 98

Consulates

1. AUSTRALIA (Sydney)
Ye.K. Saudabayev
Code: 8 10 612 Tel: 937 175 18; 937 192 40

2. THE FEDERAL REPUBLIC OF GERMANY (Berlin)
A.A. Goropko
Code: 8 10 4930 Fax: 301 95 18

3. THE FEDERAL REPUBLIC of GERMANY (Hanover)
S.I. Derzhiev
Code: 8 10 49511 Tel: 882 05 11 Fax: 882 05 28

4. THE FEDERAL REPUBLIC of GERMANY (Dusseldorf)
Zh.K. Iskakov
Code: 8 10 492132 Tel: 93 16 40; 93 16 41 Fax: 93 16 42

5. THE FEDERAL REPUBLIC OF GERMANY (Frankfurt-am-Main)
B. Isingaliev.
Code: 8 10 4969 Tel: 971 46 70 Fax: 971 468 18

6. CANADA (Toronto)
R.Zh. Kasenova
Code: 8 10 1416 Tel: 593 4 43 Fax: 593 40 37

7. THE GENERAL CONSULATE OF MESHHED
A.I. Ahmetov
Code: 8 10 9851 Tel: 83 05 47 Fax: 83 46 55

8. THE UAE
A.Sh. Abdrakhmanov
Code: 8 10 971 Tel: 506 545 176 Fax: 424 24 82

9. TURKEY (Istanbul)
M.S. Aliev
Code: 8 10 90212 Tel: 514 15 24 Fax: 514 15 25

10. THE PASSPORT AND VISA SERVICE OF URUMCHI
B.Zh. Seitbattalov
Code: 8 10 86991 Tel: 382 12 07; 382 12 03

11. THE SWISS CONFEDERATION (Bern)
Bolat Dzhamitovich Utemuratov
Code: 8 10 4131 Tel: 351 79 69 Fax: 351 79 75

Embassies and international organisations in Kazakhstan

Embassies and international organisations accredited in Almaty (code for Almaty – 3272)

Embassies

AUSTRALIA
Mr. Peter Tesh, Ambassador Extraordinary and Plenipotentiary
480004, 20 Kazybek bi Street
Tel: 63 94 18; 63 95 14; 6396 01 Fax: 8 2 581 1601 (international)

AUSTRIA
Mr. Peter Sulzenbacher, Honorary Consul
Hayat Regency Palace, 480004, 29/6 Satpayev Street,
Tel: 47 32 91

THE REPUBLIC OF ARMENIA
Mr. Arman Vartanovich Melikyan, Provisional Charge d'Affaires
480075, 579 Seifulllin Street, 7th floor
Tel: 69 29 08, 69 29 32 Fax: 69 29 08

THE ISLAMIC STATE Of AFGHANISTAN
Mr. Azulillo Ruzi, Provisional Charge d'Affaires
5 Zeltoksan Street, 4th floor
Tel: 39 59 93; 39 69 55; 32 55 66

THE REPUBLIC OF BELARUS
Mrs. Larisa Vladimirovna Pakush, Ambassador Extraordinary and
Plenipotentiary
ALMALY Hotel complex, 97 48 Gornaya Street
Tel: 50 26 15; 50 28 46 Fax: 50 28 99

THE KINGDOM OF BELGIUM
Daniel Pariss, Honorary Consul
207 Gogol Street, the corner of Dzumaliev Street
Tel: 50 63 24; 50 64 23; 50 64 08 Fax: 50 90 81; 50 95 62; 39 48 39

THE REPUBLIC OF BULGARIA
Mr. Petr Ivanov, Provisional Charge d'Affaires
13 Makatayev Street
Tel: 30 27 54; 30 27 55 Fax: 30 27 49

THE VATICAN (Sacred Throne)
Fr. Marian Oles, Papal Nuncio
480091, 77 Kabanbai Batyr Street, apt. 16, and the corner of Tulebayev
Street
Tel: 63 64 15, 63 67 76 Fax: 63 62 40

THE UNITED KINGDOM OF GREAT BRITAIN AND NORTHERN IRELAND
Mr. Douglas Baxter McAdam, Ambassador Extraordinary and
Plenipotentiary
173 Furmanov Street
Tel: 50 61 91/92 Fax: 50 62 60

THE REPUBLIC OF HUNGARY
Mr. Sandor Simicz, Ambassador Extraordinary and Plenipotentiary
4 Musabayev Street
Tel: 20 09 72; 20 15 38; 20 84 87 Fax: 58 18 37

THE REPUBLIC OF GEORGIA
Mr. Teimuraz Shalvovich Gogoladze, Ambassador Extraordinary and Plenipotentiary
Apt. 3 Mikroraion Druzba 2
Tel: 21 49 30 Fax: 21 38 81

THE FEDERAL REPUBLIC OF GERMANY
Mr. Mikhael Libal, Ambassador Extraordinary and Plenipotentiary
173 Furmanov Street
Tel: 50 61 55/56/57/60 Fax: 50 62 76

THE REPUBLIC OF GREECE
Mr. Konstantinos Tritaris, Ambassador Extraordinary and Plenipotentiary
216/1 Dostyk Avenue, and the corner of Zavodskaya Street
Tel: 50 39 61/62 Fax: 50 39 38

THE ARABIC REPUBLIC OF EGYPT
Mr. Aiman Hamdi al Koni, Ambassador Extraordinary and Plenipotentiary
59 Zenkov Street
Tel: 60 16 22; 61 63 58; 61 77 11

THE STATE OF ISRAEL
Mr. Israel Mei Ami, Ambassador Extraordinary and Plenipotentiary
87 Zheltoksan Street, and the corner of Kazybek bi Street
Tel: 62 48 17; 50 72 15/16/17/18 Fax: 50 62 83

THE REPUBLIC OF INDIA
Mr. Radzhiv Sikri, Ambassador Extraordinary and Plenipotentiary
71 Internatsionalnaya Street
Tel: 67 14 11; 69 46 42; 67 13 25

THE ISLAMIC REPUBLIC OF IRAN
Mr. Hasah Kashkavi, Ambassador Extraordinary and Plenipotentiary
119 Kabanbai Batyr Street
Tel: 67 78 46; 67 50 55; 67 39 33 Fax: 54 27 54

THE KINGDOM OF SPAIN
Mr. Daniel Mota Martinez, Honorary Consul
Apt. 401, 90 Mechnikov Street
Tel: 34 74 44 Fax: 67 19 87

THE REPUBLIC OF ITALY
Mr. Fabrizio Piaggezi, Ambassador Extraordinary and Plenipotentiary
20 Kazybek bi Street, 3rd floor
Tel: 63 98 14; 63 98 04; 63 38 93 Fax: 63 96 36

CANADA
Mr. Charles Richard Mann, Ambassador Extraordinary and Plenipotentiary
34 Vinogradov Street, and the corner of Pushkin Street
Tel: 50 11 51/52/53 Fax: 8 2 581 14 93

THE PEOPLE'S REPUBLIC OF CHINA
Mr. Lee Huey, Ambassador Extraordinary and Plenipotentiary
137 Furmanov Street
Tel: 63 92 91; 63 49 66; 63 92 25 Fax: 63 82 09

THE REPUBLIC OF KOREA
Mr. Lee yen Min, Ambassador Extraordinary and Plenipotentiary
2/77 Dzharkentskaya Street, Gorny Gigant Settlement
Tel: 53 26 91; 53 26 60; 53 29 89 Fax: 50 70 59

THE REPUBLIC OF CUBA
Mr. Marcelo Cabaliero Torres, Provisional Charge d'Affaires
Apt. 23, 70 Zenkov Street
Tel: 61 59 25 Fax: 61 87 90

THE KYRGYZ REPUBLIC
Mr. Akbar Ryskulov, Ambassador Extraordinary and Plenipotentiary
68 Amangeldy Street
Tel: 63 33 05; 63 33 09; 63 25 65 Fax: 63 33 62

THE LEBANESE REPUBLIC
Mr. Assef Nasser, Ambassador Extraordinary and Plenipotentiary
20 Naberezhnaya Street, Alatau State Farm
Tel: 48 71 51; 48 73 14

THE LITHUANIAN REPUBLIC
Mr. Virgilius Vladislovas Bulovas, Ambassador Extraordinary and Plenipotentiary
15 Iskanderov Street, Gorniy Gigant
Tel: 65 14 60: 53 41 03/04; 53 41 02 Fax: 65 14 60

THE PEOPLE'S SOCIALIST LIBYAN ARABIAN JAMAHIRIA
Mr. Ramazan al Mabruk Muhammad al Zhadi, Ambassador Extraordinary and Plenipotentiary
10 Melnichnaya Street, and the corner of Kabanbai Batyr Street
Tel: 54 27 47; 54 27 45; 54 35 19 Fax: 60 85 36

MALAYSIA
Mr. Hashim Ismail, Provisional Charge d'Affaires
87 B Dostyk Avenue
Tel: 65 14 29; 65 17 33

MONGOLIA
Mr. Yumbuugiin Sandag, Ambassador Extraordinary and Plenipotentiary
Aubakirova 1, Sain Street,
Tel: 29 37 90; 29 32 59; 20 08 65 Fax: 60 17 23

THE KINGDOM OF THE NETHERLANDS
Mr. Antonius Hendrikus, Jacobus Maria Spikeenbrink, Ambassador
Extraordinary and Plenipotentiary
480072 103 Nauryzbai Batyr Street, and the corner of Kurmangazy Street
Tel: 63 86 54; 50 37 73 Fax: 50 37 72

THE ISLAMIC REPUBLIC OF PAKISTAN
Mr. Sultan Hait Han, Ambassador Extraordinary and Plenipotentiary
25 Tulebayev Street
Tel: 33 35 48; 33 15 02; 33 38 31; Fax: 33 13 00

THE STATE OF PALESTINE
Mr. Mohammad Abdullah Tarshahani, Ambassador Extraordinary and
Plenipotentiary
38 Kateyev Street
Tel: 60 15 45 Fax: 60 15 45

THE REPUBLIC OF POLAND
Mr. Marek Gavenski, Ambassador Extraordinary and Plenipotentiary
9 Valikhanov Street
Tel: 33 84 67; 33 85 17; 58 15 51 Fax: 58 15 52, 33 74 86

THE RUSSIAN FEDERATION
Mr. Valeriy Dmitrievich Gavenko, Ambassador Extraordinary and
Plenipotentiary
4 Dzhandosov Street
Tel: 44 82 22; 44 64 91; 44 66 44 Fax: 42 83 23

ROMANIA
Mr. Marin Stanesco, Provisional Charge d'Affaires
97 Pushkin Street
Tel: 62 51 72; 62 21 32

THE KINGDOM OF SAUDI ARABIA
Mr. Ibrahim Mohammed Muselli, Ambassador Extraordinary and
Plenipotentiary
137 Gornaya Street
Tel: 50 28 71; 65 77 91 Fax: 61 45 70; 50 28 71

THE UNITED STATES OF AMERICA
Mr. Richard Henry Johnes, Ambassador Extraordinary and
Plenipotentiary
99/97 A Furmanov Street
Tel: 63 39 21; 63 13 75; 63 92 67; 50 76 23; Fax: 63 38 83

THE REPUBLIC OF TAJIKISTAN
Mr. Sadullodzhon Ergashevich Negmatov, Ambassador Extraordinary and Plenipotentiary
58 Dzhandosov Street, and the corner of Gagarin Street, Rissovkhozstroi building, 5th floor
Tel: 45 56 56 Fax: 44 20 89; 45 54 56

THE REPUBLIC OF TURKEY
Mr. Kurultush Tashkent, Ambassador Extraordinary and Plenipotentiary
29 Tole bi Street
Tel: 61 39 32; 61 81 53 Fax: 50 62 08; 54 36 11

THE REPUBLIC OF UZBEKISTAN
Mr. Nasirdzhan Norovich Yakubov, Ambassador Extraordinary and Plenipotentiary
36 Baribayev Street
Tel: 61 83 16; 61 02 35; 61 06 44 Fax: 61 10 55

THE UKRAINE
Mr. Viktor Vasilyevich Bogatyr, Ambassador Extraordinary and Plenipotentiary
208 Chaikovskii Street and the corner of Kyrmangazy Street
Tel: 62 70 73; 62 71 23; 69 18 03; 62 89 25 Fax: 33 05 15

THE REPUBLIC OF FRANCE
Mr. Serge Smessov, Ambassador Extraordinary and Plenipotentiary
173 Furmanov Street
Tel: 50 62 36/73; 50 71 10; 62 74 12 Fax: 50 61 59

THE CZECH REPUBLIC
Mr. Alexander Langer, Provisional Charge d'Affaires
64 Zhibek Zholy Street, and the corner of Ualikhanov Street, 8th floor
Tel: 33 47 13; 33 45 69 Fax: 33 50 88

THE GENERAL CONSULATE OF THE SWISS FEDERATION
Mr. Francois Shmidt, Consul
480091, 146 Zheltoksan Street, Altyn Alma Complex, 5th floor
Tel: 50 35 59; 50 35 69 Fax: 50 13 88

JAPAN
Mr. Hidekata Mitsuhashi, Ambassador Extraordinary and Plenipotentiary
41 A Kazybek bi Street, 3rd floor
Tel: 53 32 04; 53 32 05; 60 86 00 Fax: 60 86 01

Organisations

THE UNITED STATES INFORMATION AGENCY (UCIS)
Mrs. Vivian Walker, Agent
531 Seifullin Street, and the corner of Kazybek bi Street, 6th floor
Tel: 63 30 94/70/33/61 Fax: 63 30 45

THE UNITED STATES AGENCY FOR INTERNATIONAL DEVELOPMENT (USAID)
Mrs. Glen Anders, Agent
97 Furmanov Street
Tel: 50 76 12/15/34/77 Fax: 50 76 33

THE PEACE CORPS
Mr. Willie Williams, Agent
100 Shevchenko Street, and the corner of Seifullin Street, 5th floor
Tel: 69 29 84/85 Fax: 62 43 30

THE EUROPEAN COMMISSION MISSION
Mr. Michael Hamfriz, Head of the European Union Mission, Ambassador
Extraordinary and Plenipotentiary
20 Kazybek bi Street
Tel: 63 99 39; 63 88 51; 63 88 58 Fax: 63 77 52; 63 75 06

THE UNITED NATIONS
Mr. Herbert Berstock, Plenipotentiary
4 Abai Street, Hotel No. 2, KIMEP Institute
Tel: 64 09 70; 64 24 80; 64 22 71 Fax: 64 26 08

UNESCO
Mr. Jorje Sequeira, Representative for Communications in Central Asia
4 Abai Street, Hotel No. 2, KIMEP Institute
Tel: 64 09 70; 64 07 71; 64 26 18

UNICEF (Children's Fund)
Mr. Ekrem Birerdinc, Representative in Central Asia and Kazakhstan
480096, 55 Zhumaliev Street, and the corner of Aiteke bi Street
Tel: 68 28 42; 68 47 57 Fax: 68 45 25

THE OFFICE OF HIGH COMMISSIONER FOR REFUGEES (UN)
Mr. Druquet, Representative
135 Zhibek Zholy Street
Tel: 39 44 82 Fax: 39 44 82

THE WORLD HEALTH ORGANISATION (AIDS PROGRAMME)
Mr. Rudik Addamyan, Regional Councillor
4 Abai Street, Hotel No. 2, KIMEP Institute
Tel: 64 09 70; 64 07 71; 64 22 71; 64 26 18

THE INTERNATIONAL ORGANISATION FOR MIGRATION
Mr. Ruben Levy, Head of the Mission in Kazakhstan
480013, 168 A Zheltoksan Street
Tel: 69 53 11 Fax: 62 70 33

THE INTERNATIONAL FEDERATION OF SOCIETIES OF THE RED CROSS AND THE RED CRESCENT
Mr. Robert McKerrow, Head of Mission
86 Kunayev Street
Tel: 61 88 38; 61 80 63; 54 27 43; 54 27 42 Fax: 54 15 35

THE ASIAN BANK OF DEVELOPMENT
Mr. Peter Hainovski, Permanent Representative
126/128 Panfilov Street
Tel: 63 19 12, 63 93 29

THE EUROPEAN BANK FOR RECONSTRUCTION AND DEVELOPMENT
Mr. Martin Nicholls, Representative
10/A Abai Avenue
Tel: 63 22 47; 63 79 00; 63 85 82; 63 72 67 Fax: 8 2 581 1424

THE INTERNATIONAL MONETARY FUND
Mr. David Hallsher, Permanent Representative
93/95 Abylai Khan Avenue, room 502
Tel: 62 43 04 Fax: 62 38 56

THE WORLD BANK FOR RECONSTRUCTION AND DEVELOPMENT
Mr. Kadyr Tancu Yurukoglu, Permanent Representative
41 A Kazybek bi Street, 4th floor
Tel: 60 85 80 Fax: 60 85 81

THE ISLAMIC BANK OF DEVELOPMENT
Mr. Abdu Hak Kaid, Permanent Representative
65/69 Nauryzbai Batyr Street, rooms 102 104, 106
Tel: 62 35 55; 62 21 33 Fax: 62 34 11

THE INTEGRATION COMMITTEE OF THE STATES MEMBERS OF CUSTOMS UNION
Mr. Nigmatzhan Kabatayevich Isingarin, Integration Committee Chairman
4 Respubliki Avenue
Tel: 62 57 54 Fax: 62 48 97

THE EXECUTIVE COMMITTEE OF INTERGOVERNMENTAL COUNCIL OF CENTRAL ASIAN ECONOMIC COMMUNITY (CAEC)
Mr. Serik Dostanovich Primbetov, Deputy Chairman of the Executive Committee
93/95 Ablai Khan Street, rooms 216, 230
Tel: 62 44 64; 62 44 22 Fax: 62 94 57

THE INTERNATIONAL FUND OF THE ARAL RESCUE
Mr. Almabek Nurushevich Nurushev, Permanent Representative
124 Bogenbai Batyr Street
Tel: 62 51 96 Fax: 50 77 17

THE INTERNATIONAL SCIENTIFIC AND TECHNICAL CENTER (ISTC)
Mrs. Natalya Petrovna Tamarovskaya, Head of Regional Department
28 Shevchenko Street, Academy of Sciences, 4th floor, room 414
Tel: 62 02 72 Fax: 69 62 10

Embassies and international organisations accredited in Astana

THE EMBASSY OF KYRGYZ REPUBLIC
Mr. Akbar Ryskulovich Ryskulov, Ambassador Extraordinary and
Plenipotentiary
2/2 Karaotkel
Tel: 37 11 16; 37 11 19 Fax: 37 11 13

THE MISSION OF UKRAINIAN EMBASSY
Mr. Grigoriy Grigoryevich Osaulenko, Principal of Trade and Business
Mission
17 Respubliki Avenue, and the corner of Kenesary Street
Tel: 33 41 77; 33 05 13 Fax: 33 05 15

THE UNITED NATIONS
Mr. Sergei Mikhailovich Sologub, Principal of the Office for
Communications in Astana of the UNITED NATIONS/UNDP
38 Bokei Khan Street
Tel: 32 63 60

THE REPUBLIC OF GEORGIA
Mr. Teimuraz Shalvovich Gogoladze, Ambassador Extraordinary and
Plenipotentiary
A3 Karaotkel
Tel: 37 14 04; 37 13 31 Fax: 37 11 17

THE MISSION OF THE CONSULATE OF THE UNITED STATES OF AMERICA
Mrs. Aliya Miftakhovna Zhantikina, Administrative Coordinator
66 Sary Arka Street, apt. 44 45
Tel: 32 44 02 Fax: 32 44 02

Appendix 6

Contributor Contact Details

ABN AMRO Bank Kazakhstan
45 Khadzhy Mukana Street
Almaty 480099
Republic of Kazakhstan
Tel: +7 3272 507300/581505
Fax: +7 3272 507303/507298

Arthur Andersen
8a Kurmangaliyev Street
Almaty
Republic of Kazakhstan
Tel: +7 3272 608520
Fax: +7 3272 608521/5811538

BG International
95 Rozybakieva Street
Almaty 480046
Republic of Kazakhstan
Tel: +7 3272 460755/460640/460597
Fax: +7 3272 581835/465968
E-mail: office@bgalmaty.kz
Website: www.bg-international.com

BT British Telecom/A & M
Room 1135
207 Old Street
London EC1V 9NR
United Kingdom
Tel: +44 20 7250 7574

CMS Cameron McKenna
57 Amangeldi Street
Almaty 480012
Republic of Kazakhstan
Tel: +7 3272 507257/695646
Fax: +7 3272 581752
E-mail: cmck@online.ru

De Vries Alexander Ltd
Millennium House
12 Trubnaya Street
Moscow 103045
Russia
Tel: +7 095 787 2778
Fax: +7 095 787 2768
E-mail: dva@sovintel.ru
Website: www.dvainfo.com

DB Securities (Kazakhstan)
11th Floor
10a Abai Avenue
Almaty 480013
Republic of Kazakhstan
Tel: +7 3272 636539
Fax: +7 3272 635617

Eagle Kazakhstan Fund
Room 501
64 Zhibek Zholy
Almaty 480002
Republic of Kazakhstan
Tel (local): +7 3272 331357/335746/335582
Tel (int'l): +7 571 360 3296
Fax (local): +7 3272 503909
Fax (int'l): +7 571 360 3295
E-mail: eagle@kazfund.almaty.kz

Ernst & Young
153a Pr Abaya
Almaty 480009
Republic of Kazakhstan
Tel: +7 3272 608299/509423/509425/509424
Fax: +7 3272 509427

European Bank for Reconstruction and Development (EBRD)
1 Exchange Square
London EC2A 2JN
United Kingdom
Tel: +44 20 7338 6000
Fax: +44 20 7338 6100

Globalink Multimodal Transportation Systems
90 Adi Sharipov Street
Almaty 480059
Republic of Kazakhstan
Tel: +7 3272 588880/672797/672747
Direct Tel: +7 3272 588881
Mobile: +7 3279 005082
Fax: +7 3272 588885/672758
E-mail: globalink@asdc.kz
Website: www.globalink.kz

Alica Henson
Information Manager
Community Partnerships Project
US—Ukraine Foundation
Suite 1026
733 15th Street (NW)
Washington DC 20005
USA
Tel: +1 202 347 4264
Fax: +1 202 347 4267
E-mail: ahenson@usukraine.org
Website: www.usukraine.org

HSBC Bank Kazakhstan
43 Dostyk Avenue
Almaty.480021
Republic of Kazakhstan
Tel: +7 3272 581333
Fax: +7 3272 501501
E-mail: hbkz@hbkz.com

Kazakhstan Investment Promotion Centre
77 Abylai Khan Avenue
Almaty 480091
Republic of Kazakhstan
Tel: +7 3272 692237/625297
Fax: +7 3272 501277
E-mail: kazinvest@kazinvest.kz

KPMG Almaty
105 Abylai Khan Avenue
Almaty 480091
Republic of Kazakhstan
Tel: +7 3272 508855
Fax: +7 3272 508877

Ledingham Chalmers
5 Melville Crescent
Edinburgh EH3 7JA
Scotland
United Kingdom
Tel: +44 131 200 1030
Fax: +44 131 200 1080

Marsh
2nd Floor
84a Kurmangazy Street
Almaty 480072
Republic of Kazakhstan
Tel: +7 3272 636950/631048
Fax: +7 3272 507760
E-mail: sedgwick@asdc.kz

MCIWorldCom
11th Floor, Office 43
157 Abai Avenue
Almaty
Republic of Kazakhstan
Tel: +7 3272 509397
E-mail: jefwcom@kaznet.kz

The National Bank of Kazakhstan
21 Koktem-3
Satpaev Street
Almaty 480090
Republic of Kazakhstan
Tel: +7 3272 504619
Fax: +7 3272 504840

Nursat
242 Furmanov
Almaty 480099
Republic of Kazakhstan
Tel: +7 571 360 5000
Fax: +7 571 360 5120
E-mail: info@nursat.net
Website: www.nursat.net

PricewaterhouseCoopers
3rd Floor
29/6 Satpaev Avenue
Almaty 490070
Republic of Kazakhstan
Tel: +7 3272 608448/608536
Fax: +7 3272 608252

Salans Hertzfeld & Heilbronn
86 Ulitsa Gogolya
Almaty 480091
Republic of Kazakhstan
Tel: +7 3272 582380
Fax: +7 3272 582381

Scot Holland Estates
Suite 510
81 Ablai Khan Avenue
Almaty 480091
Republic of Kazakhstan
Tel: +7 3272 622116
Tel/Fax: +7 3272 581768
E-mail: holland@kaznet.kz

Marat Terterov
St Antony's College
Oxford University
Oxford OX2 6JF
United Kingdom
Tel: +44 7931 383336
Fax: +44 1865 554465
E-mail: maratinodessa@hotmail.com

US Embassy in Kazakhstan
3rd Floor
531 Seyfullin Pr
Almaty 480083
Republic of Kazakhstan
Tel: +7 3272 587917
Fax: +7 3272 587922

Index of Advertisers

ABN AMRO Bank Kazakhstan	ifc
Aon Group Limited	166
Bertling	188
BG International	obc
British Airways	ii
Ernst & Young	vi
GlaxoWellcome	v
HSBC Bank Kazakhstan	xiii
Marsh	viii
Nursat	xiv
Salans Hertzfeld & Heilbronn	94, 103
Scot Holland Estates	viii